BOLLYWOOD
A HISTORY

Books by Mihir Bose

History and Biography:

The Lost Hero
Michael Grade: Screening the Image
False Messiah: The Life and Times of Terry Venables
Memons
The Aga Khans

Business:

The Crash: The 1987–88 World Market Slump
A New Money Crisis: A Children's Guide to Money
Are You Covered? An Insurance Guide
Fraud—the Growth Industry of the 1980s
How to Invest in a Bear Market

Cricket:

Keith Miller: A Cricketing Biography
All in a Day: Great Moments in Cup Cricket
A Maidan View: The Magic of Indian Cricket
Cricket Voices (interviews with players, officials, spectators etc.)
A History of Indian Cricket (Winner of the 1990 Cricket Society Literary Award)

Football:

Behind Closed Doors: Dreams and Nightmares at Spurs.
Manchester Unlimited: The Rise and Rise of Manchester United.

General Sport:

Sporting Colours: Sport and Politics in South Africa (runner-up in William *Hill Sports Book of the Year, 1994)*
Sporting Babylon

Race and Sport:

The Sporting Alien

BOLLYWOOD
A HISTORY

MIHIR BOSE

TEMPUS

To Caroline,
without whose love, dedication, heroic support
and encouragement this book would never have been possible.
She has played the sort of role a Bollywood actress
would love to play but never be able to emulate.

Thurrock
Council Libraries

This edition first published 2007

Tempus Publishing Limited
Cirencester Road, Chalford,
Stroud, Gloucestershire, GL6 8PE
www.tempus-publishing.com

British Library Cataloguing in Publication Data.
A catalogue record for this book is available from the British Library.

ISBN 978 07524 4382 9

Typesetting and origination by Tempus Publishing Limited
Printed in Great Britain

Contents

Mihir Bose Biography

Mihir Bose was born in 1947, just before Indian independence, and grew up in Bombay. He went to England in 1969 to study and qualified as a chartered accountant. Almost immediately, he took to his first love of journalism and writing. He has written for all the major papers in Britain, having worked for *The Sunday Times* for twenty years before moving to *The Daily Telegraph* in 1995. Having concentrated on business journalism in his early years, he now specialises in investigative sports reporting, particularly the growing field of sports business and politics. He has won several awards for his newspaper writing, including Business Columnist of the Year, Sports Reporter of the Year and Sports Story of the Year. His books have been controversial and have also won awards. His *History of Indian Cricket* was the first book by an Indian writer to win the prestigious Cricket Society Literary Award in 1990. His study of sports and apartheid, *Sporting Colours,* was runner-up in the 1994 William Hill Sports Book of the Year Award. He has so far written twenty-one books, ranging from histories and biographies, to books on business, cricket and football. He lives with his wife in West London.

Acknowledgements

A journey of a thousand miles begins, say the Chinese, with a single step.

Back in 1992 when Nick Gordon, quite the most marvellous editor I have worked for, suggested I write about Bollywood, with Pamela Bordes as my photographer, I did not know I had taken the first step. But so it has proved.

This book has come a long way since then and I am grateful to so many people across so many lands and countries that, while I would like to thank them all, I just cannot.

I must thank David Davidar, then of Penguin India, for suggesting my name to Tempus in the first place.

Having grown up in Bombay, when it was called Bombay, and Bollywood was just Hindi cinema, I have always followed it, and the people in this book, whose lives I chronicle, were people who were part of my daily life as a child. My childhood was dominated by the making of *Mughal-e Azam,* and Hindi film-songs were part of the surrounding sounds of our life in Bombay, blaring forth from transistors, as we called them, and from every paan-shop.

Even then, writing this book has been a voyage of discovery and my journey has been made easier by various helping hands.

They include my researchers in various countries, not merely England, but in Russia, parts of Europe, the United States and, of course, India.

I am grateful to Ayaz Memon for introducing me to Subuhi Saiyad who did such a marvellous job both researching material and arranging interviews with key people. I am also grateful to Boria Majumdar for introducing me to Gargee and for her help with research in Calcutta.

I cannot thank Rachel Dwyer enough for putting me in touch with Somnath Batabyal, whose research was exemplary and particularly useful.

Many people generously gave their time and advice.

Old friends like Noel Rands, who acted in *Lagaan,* opened doors for me to English actors now getting acquainted with Bollywood, in particular Howard Lee, the wicket-keeper of *Lagaan.* Noel also did some extremely useful research for me.

My niece, Anjali Mazumder, very kindly introduced me to Stella Thomas, who did a marvellous job of helping me come to terms with Bollywood research, summarising material in a very expert way. Anjali's mother in Canada, my sister Panna, and father, Tapan, not only sought out rare books and DVDs of films but also commented on parts of the manuscript.

My old Bombay friend, Papu Sanjgiri, was, as ever, marvellous in both answering all my many queries and also obtaining information. I am indebted to him for introducing me to Bhau Marathe, whose knowledge of Bollywood music is awesome.

Susanna Majendie, looking for all the world like a schoolgirl again, and with sharpened pencil to boot, went and obtained some very valuable material from the British Library's India office section.

I cannot thank Melinda Scott-Manderson enough. At a most critical time, when it seemed the project might sink, she took charge of the entire production of the manuscript, marshalling forces in a manner that would defeat a Bollywood director and making sure it was done in time. Without her it would not have been. Given that the subject matter is completely alien to her, this was a tremendous feat.

My Godson Daniel Mokades, as ever, proved a most resourceful young man.

Amit Khanna very kindly gave me some of his valuable time, as did Rakesh Roshan, Karan Johar, Kareena Kapoor and too many others to name individually.

My old friend, Hubert Nazareth was, as ever, full of good advice.

And Tarun Tejpal was generous, not only with his time and hospitality, but also with his wisdom.

My oldest school friend, Munir Vishram, shared his memories of Bollywood and put me in touch with Joy and Yashodhara, children of Bimal Roy, whose memories of Bollywood were very insightful.

I would also like to thank my brother-in-law, Amal Chakrabortti, and my sister Tripti, for all their generous hospitality and help.

Peter Foster, who long ago helped me win a cricket match in Udaipur by running for me has, from his perch as *The Daily Telegraph* India correspondent, been marvellously helpful.

Above all I would like to thank Shyam Benegal, a man I had always distantly admired but whom I have come to know in the course of this long odyssey, and whose wisdom I cherish.

I have learnt much from the books and material already available on Bollywood. I have relied on them and a full list is in the bibliography.

All the people I have mentioned, and many I have not, helped me to write this book. They are not responsible for the errors of commission and omission that remain. Those are my responsibility.

London, June 2006

Prologue

Long before Bollywood, there was a flourishing Indian cinema; indeed, even before Hollywood.

If, as Will Hays, the President of the original Motion Pictures Producers and Distributors of America, has said, Hollywood movies define "the quintessence of what we mean by America", then for over a century the Indian cinema has carried an even heavier burden; it has tried to recreate an old nation emerging after centuries of bondage, help it rediscover its roots, while linking it to the present, very different, world.

But, perhaps, because the nation was so long in slavery, because foreigners so often pillaged it, not only its physical wealth, but also its mind, making its intellectuals feel its own culture was so inferior that they were consumed by self-hatred and required outsiders to help to understand it and salvage something from the wreckage of this wounded civilisation, the story of Bollywood is not an easy one to tell.

To be fair, Hollywood, too, is a paradox. As the historian, Neal Gabler, has pointed out in *The Empire of Their Own*, this quintessential American dream "was founded and for more than thirty years operated by Eastern European Jews who themselves seemed to be anything but the quintessence of America. The much-vaunted 'studio system', which provided a prodigious supply of films during the movies heyday was supervised by a second generation of Jews, many of whom also regarded themselves as marginal men trying to punch into the American mainstream." It prompted F. Scott Fitzgerald to characterise Hollywood as "a Jewish holiday, a gentiles [sic] tragedy".

But Bollywood is not only full of paradoxes but also fragile; you try and tell its story and it splinters into many other stories, none of them seemingly related to the original one.

Let me begin with an early attempt by me to tell the story of Bollywood to an English audience. It dates from the time when the West had just begun to be aware of Bollywood, and in particular that the Hindi cinema based in Mumbai could lay claim to be the centre of world cinema, producing many times the number of films that came out of Hollywood. In January 1992, the then editor of *You*, the magazine of *The Mail on Sunday*, asked me to write about Bollywood. A passionate and very creative Welshman, Nick Gordon, had recently heard about Bollywood, was very intrigued by it and pictured it as an Indian version of the Hollywood of the 30s. What he wanted was a piece about these opulent Indian film stars living in their magnificent mansions and recreating a world along the Arabian Sea that had all but vanished along the Pacific.

To introduce a small, but irritating complication, the Mumbai that Nick sent me was not called Mumbai. It still bore the name it had from its birth four hundred years earlier: Bombay, the Portuguese for good bay, the name these foreign founders of the city felt was most suitable for this city that nature had created by joining seven islands. Bombay was also what I had always called the city, having grown up there in the 50s and 60s.

Nor was the term Bollywood, that had so captivated Nick, much liked in Bombay. Many refused to use it; others dismissed it as a bad joke, invented quite recently in a Bombay newspaper by a columnist looking for a bit of colour to write about the movies. That it had caught on seemed to them yet another evidence of a damaged, insecure culture, always needing a foreign crutch to lean on. Even today, the man who coined the term to denote the Hindi film industry, has to defend it against charges that calling the Indian film industry Bollywood demeans something truly Indian, and proves that Indians can only define even their most precious products by borrowing Western terms.

My story begins on a January day on the lawns of one of Bombay's most famous film studios. It is the sort of day Indians take for granted and foreigners, used as they are to images of heat, dust and flies, do not expect.

Mid-afternoon. The sun is shining from a clear, cloudless, blue sky. There is a breeze blowing which would define a perfect spring day in the West, but the locals have begun to sport the first sweaters of the year. They are talking longingly of the cold weather that will come, giving them a chance to wear the suits and other warm clothes they have recently acquired, including some carrying labels from fashionable shops in London and New York. This, of course, is a city where, should the mercury dip below 70 Fahrenheit, the front page of the local paper, *The Times of India*, will inevitably have a story headlined: Cold Snap Hits City.

Gathered along the long table, set in the middle of the well-manicured lawn, are various Bollywood stars, past and present. At one end is the young actor, son of the former Indian cricket captain, Tiger Pataudi. Tiger, having learnt his cricket in England—Winchester and Oxford—came back to rescue Indian cricket and to become its most loved cricket captain. His son, Saif, who also went to Winchester, has now come back to claim a similar status in the movies. At the other end is a rising star who has just made a film which many in Bollywood predict will be a "silver jubilee hit", by which they mean it will be continuously screened in cinema halls for twenty-five weeks, the first step to becoming an India wide hit. However, both these current stars pale into insignificance when compared to the man at the centre of the table who is, in effect, presiding over this impromptu lunch. He is no longer in films but such is his legendary status in Bollywood that everyone refers to him as Sahib, the word once used to denote the all-powerful white man in these parts but now any man, white or brown, who wields power. Whenever Sahib speaks, the hubbub of noise that is constant ceases, and everyone listens with rapt attention.

The food is spicy and delicious, the talk is light and full of banter and thei much gentle teasing of a strikingly beautiful young girl who, I am told by sev people round the table, will be the next big screen goddess of Bollywood, heart throb of millions of Indian males who will stick her photograph on th walls and construct their sexual dreams around her. I turn to her and ask wh I know is a cliché question but one I feel has to be asked, "So how do you fe about being the new sex symbol of Bollywood?"

But I barely finish the question when I realise my clichéd question will no get the sort of clichéd answer I expected. Instead it has detonated like a Moloto cocktail, all the more lethal because I did not know my tongue held such a verba bomb. No sooner has the word sex escaped my lips than all conversation round the table ceases, as if a central switch has been turned off. I can hear sharp intakes of breath all round me. Then the Sahib, who has paid no attention to me, turns to look at me and says, with the sort of venom that he reserved for his many portrayals of screen heroes vanquishing screen villains, "Where do you come from? You look Indian, but you are obviously not Indian. Maybe you have been away from this country for too long. We don't use words like that in India. This is disgraceful. You have insulted this young woman and her honour. You must apologise to her. Right now."

My first reaction is confusion. What am I supposed to apologise for? This is the country of the Kama Sutra, the land where the ancient sculptures at Khajuraho depict sexual scenes in such detail that they leave the imagination reeling, a country where in private, swear words like benchodh, sister-fucker, and maderchodh, mother-fucker, are very common. I have arrived in Bombay to find that the current best-seller is a novel set in Bollywood, which describes the life of one such sex goddess and is liberally spiced not only with words like sex, but tits, stud, maderchodh, salla, bastard, and has very vivid descriptions of sexual scenes.

Then I realise that, while everyone may have been telling me the budding starlet will be the next sex symbol, my sin has been to use the word to her face. What has made it worse is that I have uttered the word in front of the man regarded as the elder statesman of the industry. The starlet is in tears and obviously distressed and the Sahib seems ready to strike me. He is staring at me as if he hopes to pierce me with his eyes. The only way out is for my lips to mouth an instant, grovelling, apology.

But even as I mumble my apologies I cannot help but think of the paradox of this particular Bollywood Sahib asking me to humble myself.

For the Sahib in question has for nearly four decades been one of the great rebels of Bollywood, a man who has always defied convention and who in his time was the ultimate sex symbol of the industry. He is Sunil Dutt, a true, living, Bollywood god.

His real life story reads like a ready-made script for a Bollywood movie. In 1947, as the British leave India, and the sub-continent is partitioned, young Sunil and his family, Hindus in now Muslim Pakistan, escape to Bombay. Life is difficult; he sometimes sleeps on the streets of Bombay but, then, he gets a break in films and becomes a great star when he plays Birju in the film *Mother India*.

Birju is the son of poor peasants who suffer untold hardship at the hands of rapacious landlords It is an old Indian story: downtrodden peasants, heartless, rich landlords, both fighting for a living in a pitiless land. But Birju refuses to accept the age-old feudal oppression that has made the life of peasants like him, and millions of others in India, such a misery. Life is so hard that his father, who has lost his arms in an accident, abandons the family home, leaving Birju to be brought up by his mother. This makes Birju all the more rebellious. Birju seeks social justice, is always ready to lead a rebellion against the landlords and the established order, and the film ends with his tragic death, shot by his own mother after he has killed the evil landlord who has been trying to lure his mother into becoming his mistress. But, as his blood flows and his mother weeps copiously, the blood-red screen dissolves to show clear water gushing from a new dam that will irrigate the fields of these poor peasants, so long starved of water by cruel landlords. Through her tear-filled eyes, the mother consoles herself that her son's blood is turning into life-giving water, recognising the sacrifice of her beloved son as a necessary price to be paid if India is to progress and Indian peasantry get out of its historic poverty. This is the better world that Jawaharlal Nehru, India's first Prime Minister, had promised and which the movie's director Mehboob Khan, like Nehru, a socialist, believed in. The film is one of the iconic movies of Bollywood; many consider it as the greatest Hindi movie ever made, India's equivalent of *Citizen Kane*, a celluloid demonstration of the eternal Indian mother who can also be the agent of change that will help its people's long suppressed desire for a decent life.

But it was what happened during the filming that made Sunil Dutt a legend. While one of the shots was being filmed, a fire broke out; Nargis, the actress who played Birju's screen mother, was trapped on the lit haystacks and as the flame rose higher and higher it seemed she was doomed. Then, when all seemed lost, Sunil ran in to rescue her. Whether this led to the start of their romance is not clear but, soon after the release of the movie, Sunil Dutt married her and Nargis, one of the great stars of Bollywood, quit to become a wife and a mother.

For Indians this was both shocking and amazing. It was hard enough that this was a Hindu-Muslim marriage, Nargis being a Muslim. In a country where integration between different religious groups always stops short of the bedroom, Sunil and Nargis were breaking a long-held taboo. Even more shocking, and very difficult for Indian film audiences to accept, was that this pair, having played mother and son in the movies, had ended up in real life as husband and wife. But, for Sunil Dutt such conventions meant nothing. He was an iconoclast and, like his fictional portrayal of Birju, in real life he loved to defy the established order. By the time the scene on the Bombay lawn was played out that January afternoon, interestingly in a studio created by Mehboob, Nargis was dead, having died of cancer more than a decade earlier, their son Sanjay was now in films and Sunil Dutt had long given up films for politics, representing the Bombay North West seat in the Indian Parliament. But he continued to be the man who did not hesitate to stand apart from the crowd. So, in the 1980s, when terrorists brought violence to Punjab in their demand for a Sikh state, he walked from Bombay to Amritsar, a distance of over 1200 miles, to try and promote peace; he travelled to Hiroshima to campaign against nuclear weapons and he would later go on a peace trip through the entire sub-continent. He counted among his friends President Jimmy Carter and, when on a trip to India, the Indian Government did not set up a meeting between them, Carter insisted on coming to see him and spent some time with his special Indian friend, who was so different to other Indians he had met.

But none of Dutt's celebrated iconoclasm could extend to him accepting the use of the word sex in public company. Bollywood films may be based on the sexual chemistry between stars (Sunil's marriage to Nargis was proof of that), but the one Bollywood convention Sunil Dutt would not break was the one that required that the word sex should not be uttered in public, just as, for all the suggestions of sexuality on the screen, kissing was never shown on the screen; lips could come close but never meet. I had violated this iron convention and Sunil Dutt, the great rebel, found this a rebellion too far.

I knew India sufficiently well to know this was part of the essential hypocrisy of the country. In the Bombay of my youth, when a restaurant owner decided to decorate the walls of his new restaurant with explicit motifs from Khajuraho, some citizens outraged by it got a Bombay High Court order to remove it. The judge saw nothing incongruous in letting Khajuraho be promoted as a must-see site for tourists but deciding that reproductions of scenes from Khajuraho, on the walls of a Bombay restaurant, were injurious to public morality.

But at least the judge could argue Khajuraho was many hundreds of miles from Bombay and not many Indians had ever seen those explicit sexual sculptures. Sunil Dutt, however, made me apologise while the person, standing a few feet away from him, and busy taking photographs of him and the other stars, was Pamela Bordes, who just under three years earlier had been at the centre of the biggest sex scandal in Britain since the Christine Keeler affair. On March 12, 1989, the front page of *The News of the World,* under the headline "Call Girl Works in Commons," wrote:

A top call girl is working in the House of Commons as a Tory MP's aide, we can disclose today. Pamella Bardes [the newspaper and others initially got the spelling wrong. Pamela later made it clear there was only one l in her first name and an o, not an a, in her surname] who charges at least £500 for sex, is research assistant to backbencher David Shaw. And she has escorted Sports Minister, Colin Moynihan, to a glittering Conservative party ball. There the high-class hooker—reputed to be the best paid in London—mingled with other Government ministers and Premier Margaret Thatcher.

The scandal will shock the Commons.

In the House of Commons, a Labour MP tabled a series of questions about the affair. The story not only dominated the media but provoked an embarrassing media war between two prominent editors. Pamela had been the girl-friend of Andrew Neil, then editor of *The Sunday Times* but had been pictured holding hands with Donald Trelford, then editor of *The Observer*. Trelford complained that the way the Murdoch press, in particular *The Sun*, had reported what he called his brief connection with Pamela, insisting there was nothing improper in it, while ignoring her much longer involvement with Neil, was a "crude abuse of media power." It was deeply hurtful to his wife and children and he called on the Office of Fair Trading to widen its inquiry into cross-ownership to extend to nationality of media owners and the scale of foreign interests.

Pamela, herself, claimed her revelations could be more damaging than the Keeler affair. *The Sun,* under the headline: "Pam: I Could Bring Down Govt." reported:

She made her astonishing claim in a phone call to soft-porn publishing magnate, David Sullivan. He said 27-year old Pamela, a close friend, told him 'The City would grind to a standstill if I spoke out. What I could reveal would make the film 'Scandal' look like a teddy bears' picnic.

But, although the intense media intensity forced Pamela to flee to Bali, and then Hong Kong, the story never had the political legs that made the Keeler affair an historic moment in British political and social life, inflicting much damage on Macmillan's Tory Government from which it never recovered. This was more of a story about an exotic, beautiful young girl from a faraway land whose activities titillated the nation for a time. By January 1992, the name Pamela Bordes produced a knowing grin in Britain but not much else, and she herself was keen to forget her past and reinvent herself as a professional photographer. She had been to Africa and photographed refugees and the plight of many other victims of the wretchedly-run, black African states. At the height of her notoriety, *The Daily Mail* had bought her story. Now *You* magazine was sufficiently impressed by these photographs to decide she would be the ideal person to photograph Bollywood. She had accompanied me to take the pictures that were meant to illustrate my article and just before I had posed my question to the starlet, causing Sunil Dutt to explode, the great Sahib had been telling Pamela how much he had admired her ever since she won Miss India and how brave she was to try and make it as a photographer.

If I found Sunil Dutt's attitude depressing, but not surprising, I was quite stunned when Pamela, who had turned to me for support, shunned me. She was almost as horrified as Dutt had been by my question, rebuked me for using the word sex and feared I may have jeopardised our entire assignment. Indeed she tried to distance herself from me and told anyone who would listen, "He has forgotten how to speak like an Indian."

My encounter with Sunil Dutt, revealing though it was, was essentially minor. However, over the next few days I was to learn a lot more about Bollywood, as it came to terms with Pamela. Having grown up in Bombay, I thought I knew this world; now I had to quickly revise my opinions as Pamela took over from the stars and the stars themselves, electrified by this very different star from another world, could not get enough of her. Their reaction completely turned on its head the story I had come to tell.

I had come to write about the Bombay film industry as the modem version of the medieval alchemist's dream: you touch it and it turns to gold. Every day hundreds of young men and women came from all parts of India, hoping to touch this film gold Bombay produced: they knew if they acquired a bit of the star dust they were sure to join the pantheon of gods, their portraits on huge bill-boards that litter the city, their words and deeds—some real, others imagined—reported in the dozen or so film magazines produced there, their fortunes made for ever. Just weeks before I arrived in India, a novel based on the Bombay film industry had become the biggest best-seller in the country's history.

Now Pamela took over the story, becoming for a short time the biggest star in Bollywood. Even at Mehboob studios, it was evident the script was changing. That very morning, a Bombay paper had splashed on her presence in the city and, as we arrived at the studios, Pamela created such a stir that little knots of spectators and some photographers followed her, rather than the stars. And while I grovelled to Sunil Dutt, careful to keep to the conventions of India, Pamela strutted the lawns of the Mehboob studios, almost as sought-after as the stars themselves. Over the next few days, Bombay newspapers carried more front page stories of her photographing the film stars and soon there were more photographers following Pamela, the photographer, than the stars she was trying to photograph. Long before we finished our assignment, producers were queuing up to offer her film roles. In the final reel of this real life film, with a touch which even Bollywood might not have dared script, her own mother, who had shunned her for 12 years, rang to suggest that she should come back to live in India, contest a seat in parliament and fight 'injustice'. The young people of India were, her mother told her, all ready to support her.

By this time I was no longer a man writing a magazine article about Bollywood but a chaperon for Pamela. To borrow John Kennedy's description of his visit to Paris with his wife Jackie, I was the man who had accompanied Pamela to Bollywood. It made me realise how by just being with someone famous you became famous yourself or at least in demand. Stars who did not know I existed, literary and artistic Bombay, which had never cared for me, and friends I did not know I had, beat a path to my hotel door, hoping to gain access to Pamela. A journalistic assignment that had started with a search for Bollywood gold, found me suddenly holding a pot of gold I did not even know existed but which, for a few days, everyone in Bombay hunted—and all because the only way to Pamela was through me. It was a revealing insight into Bollywood and how it both creates and copes with fame.

I had had no inkling that going to Bollywood with Pamela would so dramatically rewrite my script when, a few weeks earlier, I had accepted *You* magazine's assignment. Perhaps I should have been warned by a rather curious request just before I left London. I was invited to a lunch by the editors of the magazine to meet Pamela. This was unusual enough since in previous assignments no such lunches between writer and photographer had been organised. I arrived at the small, discreet, Italian restaurant, tucked away in a side street in Paddington, to find an intensely frightened girl, who was fearful that the moment she stepped on Indian soil her identity would be discovered and the trauma she had suffered, when *The News of the World* revealed her, would be repeated. Pamela had not been back to India since her notoriety, although she had often flown over it to escape from the Fleet Street rat pack. The commissioning editor told me "Pamela is very worried about going back to India. She wants you to escort her." This was a new, totally unexpected, demand.

As a writer I was used to photographers' complaints; usually they felt they were not given sufficient importance or enough time with the subject of the article for their cameras to do justice to them. But I had never met a photographer who could not look after himself or herself. Nor did I know what being a minder to Pamela involved. In any case, I was flying to India via another country so, for a start, we would arrive separately, with Pamela getting to Bombay before I did. It was decided that she would remain at the Oberoi, the grand hotel along the seafront in Bombay where we were booked to stay, until I arrived and, after that, while we tried to discover the secrets of the stars of Bombay, I would try and make sure Pamela's deadly secret was preserved.

My first problem when I got to the Oberoi was actually finding Pamela. She had arrived just before me and was so nervous that she had initially thought of registering as Mrs Bose, which may have raised sniggers among my friends, but could have proved devastating when, as happened a few days later, Pamela was on the front page of every newspaper in Bombay.

Finally, she chose to register under her maiden name, Pamela Singh. But the hotel was told her presence must not be disclosed. I later discovered that in the Oberoi's computer Pamela was listed as "Singh (Incognito), P." I eventually located her, but the Oberoi instituted such an elaborate screening system that, although they knew I was her colleague and staying just a few floors away, even my calls were routed through the operator and via the lobby manager, who would check my name, consult Pamela and only then let me speak to her. When I asked the lobby manager about this, he said, "Sir, this is standard procedure for all celebrities who want privacy."

She had even refused to allow *You* magazine to wire her money to the local Thomas Cook office. She felt having to go to the Thomas Cook office might lead to her identity being discovered. Instead, they wired the money to me and I paid her. However, as she waited for me in Bombay, slowly running out of money, she made anxious calls to *You* magazine and to my home in London, causing no little confusion at home, and some annoyance at the magazine. By the time I arrived, and collected her money from Thomas Cook, she had very nearly run out of cash.

Once in Bombay, she insisted we travel not in ordinary taxis but in hotel cars with tinted glass, a new experience for me but something she was very used to as a sure way of avoiding the prying eyes of the paparazzi. On one of our trips to meet the film stars, she told me the story of why her previous experience had made this necessary. At the height of her notoriety in London, she had fled to Bali, hoping to avoid the Fleet Street pack. But, as she left a Balinese restaurant on a motorcycle, some journalists in a jeep caught up with her. Her motorcycle, in trying to avoid this jeep, crashed, injuring her. For a time she feared she may need plastic surgery. I looked at her face as she spoke; there was not a mark on it, but there was no hiding the terror in her voice.

Of course, a few people in Bombay had to be told who Pamela was. Rita Mehta, the editor of *Cine Blitz*, who exercised a silky control over the stars and was helping us get some interviews, knew the real identity of P. Singh (incognito), but was under strict instructions not to tell the stars, unless she felt it was absolutely necessary to get an interview.

Our initial problem in Bollywood though was not in stopping Bombay journalists discovering Pamela, but finding stars willing to talk to us. Rita had supplied us with a number of contacts and even the home numbers of some stars but, try as I might, I could not get past their secretaries. The secretaries required a little convincing that *You* magazine and *Mail on Sunday* existed and that this was not a hoax. Like most Indians, they thought respectable British media must mean the BBC or *The Times*. But once past this hurdle the secretaries, who were always male, even for the female stars, were helpful and made many promises of interviews with the stars. But, alas, none of them were kept. Suketu Mehta has written that India is the great land of no; ask for anything and the answer is no; it is India's version of the great wall that keeps out foreigners. I was discovering a variation on this theme. Bollywood was the land of the male secretaries who, without actually using the word no, produced the same result.

Appointments were made and broken. On one occasion we arrived at the home of Sanjay Dutt, the son of Sunil, at the appointed time of 1.30 pm, to find a car going in the opposite direction. We were told Dutt Sahib had to go to a shoot at the studio and nobody knew when he would be back.

But we had an appointment, I wailed. The secretary looked at me with pitying eyes, offered sugary tea made with condensed milk and counselled me to wait. As the sun set we were still waiting and the secretary offered me another appointment, a few days later. So it went on; phone calls to stars, encouraging talk with their secretaries, arrival at stars' homes, then endless hours kicking our heels in the anteroom of the stars, drinking sugary tea and being told by the secretary that the star would be back any time; very, very soon; have some more tea.

After a week of disappointments, I was almost ready to give up when, largely thanks to Rita, who had taken a shine to Pamela and enjoyed the cloak and dagger operations she insisted on, we did manage to fix some appointments and even met stars who seemed to wear watches. Quite amazingly, Amitabh Bachchan, India's greatest film star, was our first and very prize catch. I am not quite sure why he agreed to see her. A decade earlier, while making a film, he had badly injured himself. There were fears he might not live and the nation had held its breath, women offering prayers for his recovery, with queues a mile long forming outside the Bombay hospital, offering to donate blood and the media issuing hourly bulletins of his health. Now, after a short break from films, he was about to make a comeback and was, probably, intrigued by the prospect of being photographed by Pamela.

Amitabh had said to come at 6.30 in the evening. As we drove up, the police guards, who stood outside his high-walled house, opened the gate and we were shown into his secretary's office.

I had come prepared for yet more cups of sugary tea and condensed milk but, promptly at 6.30 pm, Amitabh emerged from the house: a tall man, in white Indian pyjamas and *kurta,* topped with a black shawl. I told him we wanted to take pictures and he nodded his head as if this was routine. If he recognised Pamela his eyes gave no hint as he led us across the lawn to his own office. This had some nice sofas and Pamela decided to appropriate a couple to create the right setting on the lawn where she wanted to take his pictures. For the next half-hour, as Pamela set up her lights, Amitabh played verbal chess with me but gave me the impression he had half an eye on what Pamela was doing to his lawn.

In the garden, under the bare gulmohar tree—a favourite of the Mughals— from which lights had been suspended, the servants laid out trays of cheese and tomato sandwiches, chocolates and samosas for us. Pamela, who had been complaining that she had no assistant to work with, recruited the servants and got them to pose for her to check the lights and focus. Amitabh emerged from his office to find his lawn littered with discarded Polaroid shots but dutifully sat in the chair and posed for pictures, responding to Pamela's every command with alacrity.

By the end Pamela was in love with him: "I don't care about his looks—he has such character." Amitabh bade goodbye without acknowledging Pamela in any way but the next day rang Rita Mehta, and told her that he had instantly recognised her. When Pamela heard this, it only increased her love for him.

It did seem that female stars might have a different reaction to Pamela. Dimple Kapadia, who saw herself as a cross between Bette Midler and Barbra Streisand, initially reacted to Pamela with horror. We were talking in the front room of her father's sea-front house in Juhu, while she got ready for the day's shooting: a scene in a Hindi remake of *Lace*. I mentioned to her that Pamela would come and take pictures. "Pamela who?" she asked.

"You know," I replied, "Pamela; Pamela Bordes."

"Oh, please, I don't want to be pictured with her." I hastened to assure her that Pamela would take the pictures and Dimple turned to her make-up man and put some more pancake on her face.

It took three days for Pamela to finally photograph Dimple: appointments were made and cancelled with such regularity that I began to suspect Dimple did not want to be photographed by her. Then she finally had time and was so charmed that Pamela stayed for lunch with the family. Later, Dimple rang Rita Mehta to say, "She is such a sweet girl. I wish you had told me right at the beginning that Pamela would be taking my pictures."

Pamela's identity came perilously close to being revealed at a *mahurat* ceremony. This is perhaps Bollywood's most unique contribution to the making of motion pictures and shows how India shapes and moulds imported ideas. No film in India begins shooting unless a semi-religious ceremony is held to mark the first shoot. The stars and the production team gather together, usually in a hotel where, before a single scene of the film is shot, a coconut is split open, flowers are offered, *arati* is performed with a lit lamp circled round the camera, which is treated as if it was a god in a temple. Then, what Indians call a VVIP, a Very, Very Important Person, gives the clap for the first shot and the shooting of the film can begin. Although the roots of this ceremony lie in the beliefs of the Hindus, similar rites are performed when new machinery is installed. What makes Bollywood unique is that *mahurat* is performed by all film directors, whatever their religion, emphasising the cultural unity in India, despite religious differences.

We had been invited to the *mahurat* of a film called *Bechain (Disturbed)*. The ceremony was at 8.30 pm by the pool of the Hotel Sea Rock, a popular haunt of Bollywood. The invitation itself was a good indication of the *mahurat* ceremony. The front page of the invitation had a photograph of the male and female leads both wearing hats whose brims bore the labels Pink Panther. The film promised to introduce what it called, "New Loving Star Sidhant Salaria" and the back cover had the word Om (the word Hindus use for prayers and meditation, and which is the Hindu equivalent of Amen) painted in very large red colours.

The invitation splendidly illustrated the mix of modernity and tradition that Bollywood so specialises in.

As the ceremony was due to start, I noticed the director's wife had begun to take an interest in Pamela and, just before it commenced, she looked at Pamela and said: "You must have heard this before, but you look exactly like Pamela Bordes, the woman who did all those things in England."

Pamela said: "Really? I don't know anything about her." The director's wife turned to me and said, "Don't *you* think she looks like Pamela?" I mumbled, "I don't know; which Pamela?" Then, fortunately, the director cracked open the coconut and the cameras started rolling.

But perhaps because she had survived the *mahurat* ceremony, or perhaps because we had spent almost a week in Bombay without anyone in the media becoming aware of her, Pamela began to feel confident that she could survive Bombay without being discovered and started tapping into her old network. She arranged to meet Sonu Walia, who could have been her alter ego. Walia saw herself as the Michelle Pfeiffer or Julia Roberts of Hollywood but regretted she didn't get roles that "stretched her". Like Pamela, Sonu had been a Miss India and done modelling. She said that her New Year resolution was to be a "bad girl."

However, this desire to be bad did not extend to condoning kissing on the screen. This was then just being allowed in Hindi films, having been banned for years, but remained a sensitive subject. Sonu did kiss in one film but felt "a simple peck on the cheek would be acceptable, but a long drawn-out kiss would be totally unacceptable." "How long is a long drawn-out kiss?" I asked her. "Oh, one that lasts for ten seconds."

We had to wait slightly longer than that for the Pamela drama to come to its climax. It began to unravel as we decided to "do" a starlet, Kunika.

She was advertised as one of a new breed of Bollywood film stars: her father was in the Air Force; she was brought up in a convent and, unlike many of the other stars, was not afraid to discuss her personal life. She lived with an older man, the son of a famous film star—indeed for some in Bollywood that was her sole claim to fame—and she was quite clear about what she wanted to be: "I am trying to become a vamp."

She could not believe that she was being photographed by Pamela and kept asking me, "Is this the Pamela?" Pamela had decided that the best way to project Kunika, the vamp, would be to shoot her in a swimsuit by the Oberoi pool. As she did so, we were joined by the PR lady from the Oberoi, Joanne Perera. It seemed word was getting out that Pamela was in town and she wasn't sure how long she could hold the dyke. "I am getting calls from all the papers. "Please, Joanne, we know Pamela is there: just tell us where; where are you hiding her?"

The pool overlooked the tower that housed *The Indian Express*, one of the city's leading papers, and I began to wonder how efficient the Bombay press really was. Surely by now, if Fleet Street had been interested, the reporters would have been camping round the pool?

Then suddenly the dam burst and all of Bombay discovered Pamela.

The next morning my phone rang. It was Behram Contractor, editor of *The Afternoon Courier and Despatch*, one of Bombay's liveliest evening papers. He was an old friend and a man famous in Bombay for writing a daily column under the pen-name Busybee that was both humorous and incisive, a must-read in the city. He asked me if Pamela was my photographer. I did not like hiding the truth from Behram but, given the strict conditions Pamela had imposed, I had to deny any knowledge. However, I was fond of Behram and felt I should check with Pamela if she wanted to talk to him. I called her, told her Behram was Bombay's best loved journalist, and she agreed to talk to him but insisted she would ring him. I rang Behram and told him to await a call from Pamela. I felt I had done the right thing with both Pamela and Behram

What followed was extraordinary. That afternoon his paper led with a story headlined "Pamela Bordes in city, but staying behind cameras." Behram felt this was so important it deserved more prominence than the story of the crash of a French airbus where eighty-six of the ninety-six people on board had died.

I had told Behram my conversation was off the record; that I was merely acting as a link between him and Pamela; that we were talking as two old friends. But he reported it as if I was as much the subject of the story as Pamela. He wrote:

> In town, and more elusive than the Scarlet Pimpernel, is the former Miss India, Pamela Bordes… This morning, this reporter finally managed to catch up with her, though only over the telephone, and through the kind courtesy of Mihir Bose. At first, Mr Bose denied any knowledge of Miss Bordes being with him. He was here on his own, doing a story on the Indian film industry, he said. Then, probably feeling bad at letting down an old colleague, as well as most senior journalists in the city, most of whom are his old colleagues, he called again and admitted that Miss Bordes was here. 'Keep your telephone free. I have given her your number and she will call you, but only to chat with you, and not for an interview.' he said. She did call, talking in a crisp British accent, not at all put on. 'I simply can't give you an interview; I'll lose my job' she said. 'The press agency for which I am working has sent me on this reportage with clear and definite instructions that I am not to give interviews, allow pictures to be taken or get myself into the media. My brief is to get on with the job without any distractions.'

I was furious at the way Behram had made me the subject of his story but Pamela treated it as if this was what you expect from the media. That afternoon at Mehboob Studios, as little knots of spectators pointed to her, Pamela strode on to the set as if it belonged to her. Then, while I suffered my humiliation at the hands of Sunil Dutt, she reminisced with him as if they were old friends, photographed Saif Pataudi and then got Anupham Kher, the rising star, to be pictured in garish boots against a lavish set meant to represent a palace.

The next day finally saw the arrival of the Bombay paparazzi as Joanna Perrera was forced to admit that Pamela was in the hotel. It was a curious sight. I was walking across the lobby when suddenly Pamela appeared on the floor above, shouting my name. For a moment I thought she was being excessively friendly, then realised she wanted me to stop someone. He was a photographer and, even as she shouted and gesticulated, he ran past me and the gathering hotel staff. "Get his film, get his film," Pamela kept shouting.

The hotel staff locked the entrances, the film was seized and Pamela pacified. It seemed that as she went to the Oberoi gymnasium to do some exercises the photographer, who had been concealed in the loo, emerged and began taking pictures. If only he had asked, said Pamela, she might have agreed. "He would have had to wait while I got dressed, but I didn't want to be photographed with my hair like this."

The extraordinary interest in Pamela made me realise that she had been right to be fearful in London about returning to India. Ever since her notoriety in England, the Indians had been in a frenzy about Pamela and everyone in India had wanted to claim her. Pamela, who went to school in Delhi, and took up modelling in Mumbai, was claimed by both cities. Tavleen Singh had written in *The Indian Express*, "Wherever you go in Delhi these days—drawing-rooms, restaurants, office, bazaars—you are likely to be asked one question: did you know Pamela Bordes?" *The Sunday Observer*, a Bombay paper not associated with the UK version, had seen it as India's great revenge. In an editorial, it called it, "A case of the former colony getting its own back against the Raj." Under a headline "Atta girl," it wrote, "Sock it to them. Show these fuddy duddies that whatever Christine Keeler could do, an Indian girl can do even better. Eat your heart out Keeler."

And now, with Pamela in their midst, everyone in Bombay wanted to interview her. And, since she was still incognito, all the calls were being directed to me. I had grown up in this city and although by that stage I had been living in London for twenty years, I had kept coming back to write about India. But in the past, apart from the customs and immigration officials, nobody had taken any notice of my comings and goings. Now everyone wanted to talk to me. So many hotel messages would pile up in my room that when I returned from interviews with Bollywood stars it was often difficult to open the door. The editor of *The Times of India* , the city's most powerful newspaper, rang five times—once at midnight—to arrange an interview with Pamela. Dom Moraes, the poet, took a very novel approach in order to get to Pamela. When he rang me he said he did not want to follow the herd and talk to Pamela. "I am more interested in talking to you, the writer who comes with a photographer and finds the photographer the story." But when we met, he spent all the time talking to her; the article he wrote was all about her and, on a later visit, when we accidentally bumped into each other, he acted as if he had never met me. Pritish Nandy, editor of *The Sunday Observer,* who had in the past taken great pleasure in knocking my books in print and describing me as a worthless writer, now rang me repeatedly to get to Pamela. Having been incognito as a writer for twenty years, I had suddenly discovered fame as an agent for a photographer who wanted to remain incognito.

Pamela, herself, was getting the more personal messages. One journalist sent a lovely handwritten note to request an interview: "I am only doing this because my editor has asked me; you know what editors are like. But I don't want to talk about your past, just about your rhinoceros. I shall be waiting in the lobby until 11 pm wearing a suit and looking very despondent."

Pamela asked, "What does despondent mean?" Then said, "They are so sweet over here. Not like the Fleet Street mob."

After all her efforts to remain anonymous, I had expected her to crumble in the face of publicity but she seemed to revel in it, as if a great weight had been lifted off her shoulders. The previous day, at Kamalistan Studios, when we had interviewed Raj Bhabbar, whose principal claims to fame are that he was still a socialist and was once married to two women at the same time, Pamela had played the shrinking violet: she would not let a photographer who had recognised her take pictures of her.

However, by the time we came to Kher, Pamela had acquired half a dozen helpers and it was difficult to know who was the star, Kher or Pamela. "He is so camp," said Pamela as she directed her helpers to pack up her equipment.

The publicity seemed to make even established stars eager to make way for Pamela. Shammi Kapoor was then one of the great established, if aging, stars of Bollywood. Once famous for his dancing movies, Kapoor had, by this time, rationed his work and had a guru on whose instruction he wore an amber necklace and a solitary ruby earring in his left ear. He lived in Malabar Hill, overlooking the lovely bay that frames the city and provides a breathtaking vision of the shimmering Arabian Sea. We were shown into his marble living-room, decorated with the skins of three tigers he had killed. But for Shammi Kapoor it was Pamela, splashed all over the papers, who was the star. When his wife offered me some sandwiches, he said, "Why are you offering all this to Mr Bose? It is Pamela who is the star; she needs the food."

All this was a prelude to the moment when Pamela, the photographer, became Pamela, the star, outshining even the greatest of Bollywood stars. This came when we went back to Mehboob studios to interview Madhuri Dixit. At twenty-two, she was then the great new female star. She was in such demand that a producer who wanted a successful film had to cast her as the leading lady. She saw herself as the Meryl Streep of Bollywood and zealously guarded her privacy. It had taken me days to set up the interview and it was finally agreed the day after Behram broke the Pamela story.

We were shown into her dressing-room on the first floor of Mehboob Studios where Madhuri was getting ready to film a song-and-dance sequence. The dressing-room had a dirty, bare floor, a row of seats around the walls and a toilet that was a hole in the ground.

Pamela took one look at Madhuri's skin and said contemptuously, "It is so bad." She then hurried downstairs to the studios to try to find the right background against which to photograph her and one that would help mask her dreadful skin.

I was left alone in the studio, except for Madhuri's father, who sat in a corner. Madhuri was the female star every Indian fantasised about, having the sort of voluptuous looks that Indians like in their females. But she was also an unmarried woman, presumably a virgin, and she could never come to a shoot without being chaperoned, generally by her mother. But that day her mother could not come so her father had taken over. His job was to make sure nothing happened off the set, even as on the set Madhuri continued to project her sexuality in such a way that most Indian males wanted to take her to their bed. As Madhuri got ready, he buried himself in a Jeffrey Archer novel and every time I said anything he pointed to the book and said, "Very good." It took me some time to figure out that he was virtually stone deaf and had interpreted all my questions as an attempt to determine Archer's literary merit. Madhuri's taste in novels, I later discovered, extended far beyond Archer to science fiction and Asimov.

By now Pamela was in the middle of the Bombay photographic scrum. As she spoke to an old star, who was a follower of Rajneesh, a photographer emerged from the surrounding bush to take a picture. Pamela imperiously demanded the roll and tore it up with some relish.

On the set where she had arranged to photograph Madhuri, some forty photographers had gathered to take a picture of Pamela at work. As she tried to set up her lights, they kept clicking away. "Your flash is interfering with my work," shouted Pamela, but that was hardly likely to clear the throng.

Eventually, Pamela agreed to have her photograph taken; she stepped outside the studios and posed for half an hour. This gesture not only charmed the photographers, it created an immediate fan club. One photographic assistant said, "Madam, I shall give up my work and come and work for you." He appointed himself Pamela's secretary and tried to regulate who could photograph her.

I slipped away to talk to Shobhaa De, the columnist whose caustic tongue is feared by all Bombay. Her novel, *Starry Nights,* based on Bollywood, had become the biggest seller in the history of the country but, for now, Pamela overshadowed everything.

Every few minutes the phone rang, providing virtually a running commentary on Pamela's movements. Every now and again the front doorbell rang and the servant would announce the arrival of another photographer hoping to catch a glimpse of Pamela in the mistaken belief that she had accompanied me to Shobhaa's house.

By this time Pamela had decided that if Bombay's journalists wanted to interview her she would do it in style. So, by the side of the same Oberoi swimming pool where she had photographed Kunika, she spoke to Pritish Nandy.

When he had gone, Pamela said, "You know, he is just like Andrew Neil." Since Nandy is short, dark and balding, I was not sure Andrew Neil would have been flattered.

There being no ready Donald Trelford figure in Bombay, Pamela spoke to a man from *The Times of India* and as she did so I had a call from Shobhaa De. "Mihir, I have fallen in love with Pamela. She is wonderful, such an innocent girl. Ask her to talk to me and I will give her the most favourable publicity."

At midnight came the most important call, from her mother. They had not spoken for twelve years; now she wanted to welcome Pamela back. "Come to Delhi and stand for parliament; the youth of the north are all for you." But, surely, Pamela, I said, you could not stand for Indian elections with a French passport? "Oh," said Pamela, "I could have dual nationality. [India does not allow it.] These things can be arranged."

It was after this call that Pamela finally decided to jettison her incognito image. Oberoi was told she would now be registered under her own name, calls no longer had to be routed through my room and, instead of us ringing stars and finding their secretaries, stars now rang to talk to Pamela.

Even actors, who had ignored her, or treated her with indifference, rang to invite her back to their homes. The day before Behram had run his story, Pamela had photographed the actor known as Jeetendra. Both Pamela and I knew this was very far from the star we were looking for but, at the time, with so few real stars available, we had little choice. Jeetendra's great period had come a decade earlier when he played the all-action fighting, singing, dancing Hindi film hero with such conviction that he was given the nickname Jumping Jack. As if to make sure his screen image matched his real life, he had wooed his wife by pelting her with peanuts. But his last great film had been in 1980 and, although he was still making films, he was very much the aging star who just refused to accept his time had gone.

Jeetendra had agreed to see us after many phone calls. When we arrived, he kept us waiting for hours and, far from wanting to jump, let alone throw peanuts at us, was so disinterested that we were left to search for crumbs while he took more interest in the Test match India were then playing in Australia, where a young Sachin Tendulkar was creating waves. His indifference to the questions I was putting to him or the pictures Pamela was taking was such that, as we drove back, both Pamela and I agreed we could do little with the interview; also, the photographs had not come out at all well.

Now, with Pamela no longer incognito, Jeetendra rang personally to speak to Pamela and invited her back to his house. Pamela felt so secure that she did not need me to accompany her. Later, she returned to describe to me how he not only knew exactly who she was and what she had done but even took her to his special bar room, with its amazing collection of bottles. The incognito photographer, a star of another world, had conquered a Bollywood star, albeit ageing.

Two weeks earlier, Pamela had been fearful of flying in alone to Bombay; now, as I flew back to London, she came to see me off at the airport, quite happy to be seen in public. Just before I boarded my flight she told me she was on her way to the Holiday Inn not far from the airport. There, by the swimming pool, Subhash Ghai, one of Bollywood's great directors and the man portrayed in the Bombay film media as the Oliver Stone of Bollywood, was having his birthday party. Ghai had personally rung to invite Pamela, and Pamela could not wait to get there.

As it happens, Pamela never made it in Bollywood; probably she did not want to and, back in London, Nick Gordon decided that the story of Pamela in Bollywood, and how the stars reacted to her, was much more interesting than the stars whose lifestyles I had been sent to chronicle.

I ended up writing the most extraordinary story I have ever written, not about the Bollywood stars but about the photographer who was supposed to merely take the pictures to illustrate my piece. The stars of Bollywood had at most a walk-on part, completely overshadowed by Pamela. And while the magazine used some of Pamela's pictures, the most arresting were the ones that the Bombay photographers had taken of Pamela at work.

You magazine put it on its cover. It was dominated by a picture of Pamela holding a camera, the Taj Mahal in the background, and an unknown starlet dressed in a sari exposing her thighs. The cover lines read: Pamela's Latest Exposures—Heat and Lust in Bombay.

It is a measure of how far Bollywood has come in the last decade and a half that it no longer needs to be introduced to a Western audience through such curious means. There are Bollywood movies in many a video shop across Britain and the United States; walk into a High street music or DVD store and along with sections on various Hollywood movies there is a small, but distinctly marked, section for Bollywood films; the very term Bollywood is, if not universally known, certainly known to many, and the idea that India is the movie capital of the world strikes nobody as ridiculous or one requiring much explanation. Not long ago one of Bollywood's biggest stars, Aishwarya Rai, was interviewed by CBS for sixty minutes without the channel feeling any need to explain the reasons or dress it up with another story. She was a story in her own right.

The sheer might of Bollywood is now impossible to ignore. Every year the Indian film industry produces more than 1,000 feature films, every day fourteen million see a movie in the country, a billion more people a year buy tickets to Indian movies than they do to Hollywood ones. What is more, while Hollywood is no longer growing, the Indian numbers are likely to grow. India's population, already more than a billion will, in the next decade, surpass China's, making it the most populous country in the world. But India is far behind in the number of theatres needed for such a film- hungry people. The country's 13,000 theatres means thirteen screens per million of the population, the lowest screen average in the world. And unlike the West, most of these screens are single screen theatres.

In the years to come, as India takes to multi-screens, this will change, bringing more people to the cinema.

It is not merely in numbers that Bollywood has trounced Hollywood. Bollywood is the first and only instance of a non-Western society taking a Western product and so changing it that it can now claim to have created a new genre, one that reaches audiences that the original cannot. Suketu Mehta in *Maximum City*, his brilliant biography of Bombay, writes:

> India is one of the few territories in which Hollywood has been unable to make more than a dent: Hollywood films make up barely 5% of the country's market. Resourceful saboteurs, the Hindi movie-makers. When every other country's cinema had fallen before Hollywood, India met Hollywood the Hindu way. It welcomed it, swallowed it whole and regurgitated it. What went in, blended with everything that had existed before, and came back out with ten new heads.

I had a glimpse of one of these heads when, in the summer of 2004, I found myself in Marrakech. Morocco was bidding for the soccer World Cup. The Moroccan bid was led by foreigners—American, French, and English—so much so that it did not feel Moroccan at all. It was as if, in its desire to get this prestigious event, the country had leased its name to foreigners. I knew that something like this had happened many years earlier when the world had been captivated by Humphrey Bogart and Ingrid Bergman in the classic film, *Casablanca*. Bogart portrayed Rick, who ran a café called Rick's Café in Casablanca, but the film had nothing to do with Casablanca, the city, as it was shot on a parking lot at MGM studios in Los Angeles, and the actors never went anywhere near Morocco. When I visited Casablanca, the hotel I stayed in did have a bar called Rick's Café but that was an attempt by Casablanca, the city, to import something Hollywood had invented and the only connection with the movie was the television in the corner of the bar, endlessly showing the original film. Morocco, I sensed, could lend its name to other cultures but never really accept something foreign.

It was as I was pondering this question, sitting on a terrace overlooking the main square in Marrakech, that something happened to make me realise the power of Bollywood and how much more potent it could be in many cultures compared to Hollywood.

The sun had just begun to set; in the distance we could see the sand dunes that surround the city bathed in the golden light of the dying sun then, magically, as the lamps were lit, the hitherto empty square began to fill up with food stalls converting what had been fairly pedestrian, into something from the Arabian Nights. In the midst of all this, a man trundled into the square, carrying a cinema poster on a trolley As he did so, unveiled young girls, reflecting the relaxed Islam of Morocco, rushed to gather round it. My first thought was that, in this very Moroccan setting, it was a film poster of a local movie or perhaps a Hollywood movie. But when I got close, I discovered it was a Bollywood movie starring Shah Rukh Khan, one of the biggest stars of Bollywood. These unveiled young girls were drooling over an Indian actor in the way they would never have done over a Hollywood one.

When I returned to London, this remarkable ability of Bollywood to reach parts Hollywood never did, was emphasised when our new cleaning lady, a woman from Estonia, on seeing me said, "Indian? Ah, Raj Kapoor?"

Raj Kapoor is one of the greatest names of Bollywood, the man who dominated the Hindi cinema for four decades between the 1940s and the 1970s. This Estonian girl could remember how, growing up as part of the old Soviet empire, hoping one day to be free, the family would go to see Indian films, their mixture of songs, dances, a story-line of families splitting, then finally coming together, and the boy always getting the girl, appealing in a way Hollywood could not. It also helped Bollywood that the cold war meant the Soviet Union did not want Hollywood movies, while Bollywood was the sort of safe entertainment that the Estonians and others could be exposed to.

Shyam Benegal, one of India's most original film directors, argues this spread of Indian films reflects a cultural divide in the world between the Anglo-Saxon and the non-Anglo-Saxons' perceptions of films:

> The non-Anglo-Saxon finds it very easy to accept this kind of entertainment. It gets to them more easily. For instance, Latin-Americans: popular Indian cinema is becoming quite popular in countries like Columbia, Bolivia, Peru, or Central American countries, such as Honduras, Ecuador, Guatemala, and Venezuela. In the West Indies, of course, it has always been so, but also in places like North Africa, where the biggest heroes are from Bollywood. In Egypt, the greatest hero continues to be Amitabh Bachchan. Raj Kapoor was in the 50s and 60s but he was replaced by Amitabh. When Amitabh went there as a juror for the Cairo Film Festival a few years ago, they didn't know what had hit them. The women and girls would just descend upon the Hilton Hotel in Cairo. He needed to have armed protection from all these ladies who would write love-letters with their blood and send them to him. And yet the fact is they had seen his films not in the cinema but on video cassettes. Such is the popularity of Indian films that Egypt does not allow Indian films to go there because it would destroy their industry. The Government is very aware that Egyptians would much prefer to see Indian films than their own films. The same thing applies to all of North Africa. In the fifties, Indian films went to Russia, and also to the Middle East, the Mediterranean and to Latin America, replacing films from other countries. In West Africa, French films were replaced by American films, and now Indian films are replacing American films.

So why have Anglo-Saxon countries until recently found Bollywood a strange product?

That may have to do with the attitude that is deeply embedded there. The problem has always been with the Anglo-Saxons.

Benegal's view is that this is due to racism. Perhaps he over simplifies but many Indians would agree:

> I think so. They don't easily identify with people who are coloured. They can't empathise. Sympathy, yes. Sympathy, pity, yes, but they find it difficult to empathise. It's one of those things. European history has been like that. Anglo-Saxon history has been like that over a period of time, so it is a bit difficult for them immediately to take on something like this. People always ask me why it is that Indian films don't win Oscars? You see, because so far Indian films have always been seen as a somewhat deprived, poor cousin of Hollywood. Yet our markets are equally large, as large as those of Hollywood. We are the only two national cinemas that are comparable to one another. No other country in the world produces such a large number of films or caters to such a large audience. But the Indian audience, because we have such a huge population, in the past did not necessarily have to rely on an audience outside of its own nation. Now we do, because we also have a large South Asian population in different parts of world who like the kind of entertainment that India produces. It is a preferred form of entertainment for them because they feel with it. So it doesn't matter. I might be living in South America and I should be seeing Chile and Argentinean cinema, but I might prefer to see an Indian film, which is happening everywhere in the world, and also local people are attracted to it.

Bollywood not only entertains diverse cultures but, just as Hollywood has done, it inspires people from different backgrounds to dream of becoming film-makers. Benegal recalls meeting an Ethiopian film-maker, who now teaches in America and makes films, telling him how *Mother India* made him want to became a film director:

> Gerima Haile told me that if there was one film that influenced him to the extent that he wanted to become a film-maker it was the film *Mother India.* In Ethiopia, he said, they would view films every month; his grandmother would gather her whole clan, children and grandchildren, and they would all go to see *Mother India.* The story of the mother, and then the mother killing the son, and then the dam coming up, which somehow expressed the deepest needs and aspirations of Indian people, had a message not only for Indian people but for people from outside India like Haile and his fellow Ethiopians.

Yet this worldwide spread of Bollywood has come despite the fact that India has, historically, never had a world empire. A country's culture spreads largely through the success of its arms. Americans may proudly boast that they have never had imperial ambitions like the Europeans, although they did acquire the old Spanish empire. But India is that rare country whose troops have never left the country to seek Indian dominions abroad. For two hundred years its troops fought under the Union Jack to acquire and preserve the British Empire but not to seek an Indian empire. Even more crucially for all the economic progress being made by India, it remains outside the cultural system the rest of the world accepts.

Consider the two basic things that visitors to any country have to take into account the moment they arrive: local time and local money.

For a visitor, working out how much his money can buy locally, it is fairly simple arithmetic: you either multiply the currency you are carrying or you divide it by a number.

But in India you have to learn a whole new number system.

Indians do not count in millions and billions. Instead they have their own unique system called lakhs and crores. So, Indians talk of a business making profits of tens of crores of rupees or of a car costing four lakhs of rupees. To understand what they mean you must know that a lakh is 100,000, a crore is ten million.

Even when Indians take to Western things, which they love to do, they make them sound very Indian and wholly unintelligible to the rest of the world. So India has taken to the popular television game, How to be a Millionaire, presented by Amitabh Bachchan. Except, in India, it is called How to be a Crorepati. Call an Indian a millionaire and it will make no impression on him; call him a crorepati, a man with ten million rupees, and he will puff up with pride.

Time presents the visitor with another very Indian situation.

It is fascinating to examine the time at any given moment in the various cities of the world. As you would expect, the hour hand in each city shows a different time, but the minute hand always shows the same time, round the world.

So, 12.33 am in London is 7.33 am in New York, 4.33 am in Los Angeles and 8.33 pm in Tokyo. Only the clock in Delhi stands apart from the world. 12.33 am in London is 6.03 pm in Delhi. India is the only country in the world which measures the time difference with the rest of the world in half hours. Indian standard time is 5½ hours ahead of Greenwich Mean Time, 10½ hours ahead of US East Coast time, and 13½ hours ahead of Pacific Standard Time

When I was a child in India, I was told by an uncle how easy it was to know the time in London. Just take your wrist watch and turn it round, reversing the minute and hour hands: that will give you the time in London. I know of no other country which has such an upside-down relation with world time.

Let us now see how Bollywood has successfully inverted Hollywood. The basic elements of a Hollywood movie are well-known and well-established. There is generally a book or a play which a director is keen to make into a film, a script is commissioned, funding is found, then actors and actresses are cast and the whole film is shot according to a strict timetable.

Bollywood completely reverses the procedure. The script is almost the last thing that is written; often the script is being written as the actors and actresses are on the set getting ready to shoot and the words can often be given to them just before the scene is shot. In Bollywood, the starting point is the telling of the story to the male star whose agreement will make or break the film.

The director who wants to make the movie comes to a star and verbally enacts the story in front of him. If he gets the star, he knows he can on the basis of his name secure funding, usually from privately-held, family-controlled production companies, to make the movie.

Even in *Lagaan*, the Bollywood movie based on a nineteenth century cricket match between Indians and the English, a parable of the story of empire, race and love, which was seen as the first cross-over movie, one that could appeal to Anglo-Saxon audiences and was nominated for Hollywood's Foreign Movie Oscar, this pattern did not change. One Sunday afternoon in Bombay, the director came to the Bombay home of the actor Aamir Khan, performed the story in front of him, convinced him, and then used his name to finance and make the movie.

The mechanics of making a movie in Bollywood is also very different. Unlike Hollywood, Bollywood does not believe in sync sound. In a Hollywood movie, both the action and the words are shot together. But in Bollywood, as a scene is shot the actors and actresses mouth the words they have been given, but it does not matter what they say or that there is terrific noise all around. Later on, in a studio, they will record the words and this will be superimposed on the film. Just as the various songs sung in the film are never sung by the stars, but by what are called playback singers, with the on-screen stars merely mouthing the words.

There was a time, in the 1930s, when Bollywood movies were like Hollywood movies. But just as the coming of sound totally transformed Hollywood, it also made Bollywood take a road very different to Hollywood. Benegal has no doubts the coming of sound produced the divorce between these movie cultures:

> During the silent era of Indian cinema our films used to look like every other film made everywhere else in the world. But the moment sound came we suddenly went back to our theatrical traditional form. That was the moment, 1931, when our first sound film was made, *Alam Ara*, which had something like thirty songs, and after that movies started having sixteen or seventeen songs, and most films from then on used to have a huge number of songs, because music was an essential part of Indian cinema.

This change also reflected something very deep in Indian thinking, the very different way Indians see drama, comedy and the musical. Indians say the West follows a fascist system of thought, which divides various artistic expressions into separate, watertight compartments. India mixes them all together, rather like the Indian dish *kicheree* where everything from rice through pulses to eggs, vegetables and spices, are all thrown into a pot to make a delicious meal So it was with films.

Here is Benegal again:

The West broke up everything: they said, this is drama; they said, this is comedy; they said, this is tragedy. Our films mix everything in one. The same film has everything in it, much like our food, because otherwise we don't feel satisfied. It must have everything. That's traditional. Popular cinema follows that tradition. For Indian films, for their very sustenance, songs were very important. But that is because for any kind of Indian entertainment, particularly community entertainment, songs are important. In any Indian performance before a large number of people, theatrical performance or film or whatever, music and song are essential components. But songs in an Indian film does not make it a musical. A Western musical actually takes a story forward. In Indian films, songs may sometimes interrupt, sometimes they are part of the story. It's a variable, but the whole thing is that they are interludes. They are not musicals in the Western sense. Not at all. This is why it is a different tradition of cinema compared to the Western tradition. They make the audience cry, they make the audience laugh, they make the audience enjoy the song, make their feet tap to the dances; all those kinds of things and all in one movie.

Twenty years after the coming of sound there was another big change in Bollywood. Until the 1940s and even 1950s, Bollywood movies had scripts in the style that Hollywood would have recognised. Some of India's great film directors worked to scripts, tightly-written scripts, often from plays or novels. Benegal says:

There was a time in India—it was an interim period—when films were made to a script. Films in the early 40s and 50s were made to a script. No Bimal Roy films, no Mehboob film, no Guru Dutt films were made on the spur of the moment. They all had written scripts. Some time, from the 60s onwards, what happened was that everybody starting to make films asked what was a valuable property? Now, this sort of thing is done in cinemas all over the world. But here it was a star who was treated as the valuable property. If you have a big star, it means that your risk level has come down. Similarly, securing a music director reduces the risk factor; you can pre-sell your film for a much higher price. You created a package with star appeal—actors, music director, stunt director, dance director and so on even before you thought of the subject for your film. This started in the mid- to late sixties. And it remained that way for a long period.

The divide between Hollywood and Bollywood is further deepened by the very different ways these two movie cultures finance their films. Hollywood studios are owned by some of the great corporations of the world: Sony, TimeWarner, News Corp, Viacom. Even when independent film producers emerge, such as Steven Spielberg, they end up selling out to huge corporations, as Spielberg did with DreamWorks.

There is no similar studio system in Bollywood and big Indian corporations have historically shied away from the film industry. That is slowly changing but it is still light years removed from the ownership of Hollywood studios. Investment in Bollywood movies is still done by small family firms, as if this huge movie industry was in reality a cottage industry.

There are Bollywood directors who buck this trend. Benegal himself is one of them. His most recent film was a biographical study of the Indian nationalist, Subhas Bose, a highly controversial subject in India, working to a script which was massively researched and financed by Sahara, a major Indian company. But while Benegal is part of modern Bollywood, he represents a distinct minority: a movie-maker who does not make art-house movies that appeal only to a very small intellectual group. His films have a much wider clientele, but yet are very different from the Bollywood blockbusters, with a very firm narrative tradition of telling a story, and telling it well and entertainingly.

The emergence of Benegal and other film directors in the 70s also helped Bollywood bridge a gap that was both curious and quite amazing. This was that through much of the immediate independent years, while Bollywood was colonising many parts of the world, creating huge fan bases in the Soviet Union and the Middle East, it could not colonise its own Indian intellectuals, not even the Western-educated Indian élite. They shunned Bollywood movies and, indeed, the best cinema houses in the major Indian cities never screened Bollywood movies. These cinemas were reserved for Western movies which were considered the real thing, Bollywood movies were despised as the movies necessary to keep the illiterate masses amused and hopefully out of trouble. So, in the Bombay of my youth, the major cinemas of south Bombay, which is the commercial centre of the city, where the courts, banks, business houses, art galleries, museums and newspaper offices are located, and whose cinemas, such as Regal, Eros, Metro, New Empire, and Excelsior, are considered the most prestigious in the city, never showed Hindi films. To see a Hindi film you generally had to travel far away from south Bombay to places like Grant Road and other less fashionable places.

Our contempt for Bollywood was matched by our contempt for those who could not speak English. In the Bombay school I went to in the 50s and 60s, the Jesuit-run St. Xavier's, whose most high profile pupil was the great Indian cricketer Sunil Gavaskar, we grew up with utter disdain for the Hindi film industry and all it represented. We considered ourselves part of the élite that spoke English; we used to cruelly mock those who could not speak English properly. They spoke what we called the vernacular and it was not meant as a compliment. Many of them were Gujeratis (people from Gujarat who were then part of the state of Bombay) and we would mock them as Gujubhais, brother Gujeratis, but with no brotherly feeling for them. Hindi movies were for them as they could not speak English very well, while we went to Hollywood movies and, in particular, loved to go to Sunday morning shows, which showed some of the older Hollywood classics.

Benegal says:

> Well, in those days it was not considered to be entertainment worthy of Western-educated people. For this little section of Metropolitan Indian society, it was not considered a kind of entertainment that they would like to be associated with. But that started to change in the 1980s and 1990s. The change was for two reasons. There was greater technical competence in popular cinema than before. Secondly, scholars and intellectuals began to study popular Indian cinema and the reasons for its incredible appeal to the Indian population. They started to examine why popular cinema holds our population in such thrall. This is what made the educated and westernised elite reconsider their own low regard for popular cinema.

It also helped that other factors worked against Hollywood movies in India and deprived the Indian Western educated élite of their traditional cinematic sustenance. In the late 70s, Mrs Gandhi's regime tried to limit Hollywood movies and there were also foreign exchange restrictions, with the result that cinema houses in the major metropolitan cities, which had traditionally shown Western movies, had to fill their blank screens with Bollywood movies. Benegal and directors like him, part of what was called parallel cinema, benefited, and their movies filled screens and introduced Bollywood to audiences that in the past had only seen Western films. The result was the generation that came after us no longer felt any shame in going to a Hindi film in the way that we had.

Benegal dates this change from the 80s and says:

> The clientele that missed seeing Western films, now started to see these films. So that became a market for what today we call parallel cinema, alternate cinema, whatever. But while popular cinema itself continued in its own merry way, there was I think a major impact on it with technological advances—sound getting better, cinemascope visuals and the whole business of blockbusters and television coming in. So the popular cinema had to suddenly compete with all these things and improve their product, their presentation. They could no longer make the kind of films they were making. They had to approach it differently, but they didn't make a different approach in their content. Content remained the same. But the look, the character, all these kind of things changed. There are other reasons as well. It helped that our cinema houses physically got better; our cinemas used to be like dumps—for years. Now they were no longer quite that bad.

But despite all this, one thing remains constant for Bollywood. The writer and novelist Faroukh Dhondy has written:

Bollywood is formula. In the beginning was the formula and the formula was with nationalism and just nationalism. Film inherited the magnificent task of becoming the discernible conscience of the nation. It was the defining medium of what it meant to be Indian. Film, trading in images and icons, was the perfect medium for India. There were subtleties and layers, but the final distillate of good and evil, the boiled-down manifestation of how to pursue being the Indian male or the Indian female became the pursuit and message of Indian cinema. More concretely, the Indian father, mother, daughter, son, husband or wife, became the media's constructs. They evolved, but not even at the speed, say, at which man came from monkey. The social tenets of nationalism went hand in hand with the cultural ones. Ours was the greatest spiritual nation in the world. We could teach the world moral lessons which lesser breeds and shallower cultures were incapable of. Our myths and epics, pervasive in our population, would be embodied in film and become matters of national pride. All these elements were at first, I believe, a conscious and concerted revival aimed at proving to the world and perhaps necessarily, and most importantly, to ourselves that the British must go and that their exit would enable the flowering of our own pride. It was perhaps an ignorant way of national self-evaluation, but it served the purpose of de-colonisation. The dominant liberal tendencies of the time, led by Gandhi and Nehru, prescribed or perhaps just suggested the mores of our cultural output. Could anyone then, or now, imagine a film in which the conquests of Ala-ud-din Khilji or Emperor Akbar's campaign against the Rajputs were truthfully portrayed? It would be deemed unhelpful. It would go against the tenor of 'the project'. It may even arouse antagonistic sentiments between Hindus and Muslims and result in the mindless slaughter of innocents—the result of off-message films. Throughout its history, the liberal industry of film has subscribed to the message. There have been instances of direct political censorship, but no single incident of suppression as in a fatwa against a film. There are in existence guidelines that ban invective against religion and caste, but these are almost unnecessary strictures. The tellers of film tales contrive them in ways that make such censorship unnecessary. The rules are used to filter out allusions that may be construed as wounding to religious sentiment or insults to castes.

If this emphasises how very differently Hollywood treats controversial subjects then, as Dhondy says, the all-important difference between the two movie cultures lies in their very contrasting inspirational sources:

The tradition of Indian films, unlike those of the West, descends directly from the Indian epics, the *Ramayana* and the *Mahabharata*. To say this is to say much more than the facile and oft-repeated nonsense that there are only so many plots in the world and all stories are variants of these. Sometimes the paradigm is eight plots, sometimes a hundred and something. Nevertheless, Indian film heroes, heroines and villains are defined by the dramatic rasas, the energies that, according to the *Natyasastra,* are the constituents of all character and the origins of all drama. There is a sense in which all film is the assertion of myth. The construction of the myth of cattle-farm workers as 'cowboys', is perhaps the most startling. American culture has created other equally powerful myths—the irrepressible underdog, the unhappy but kind hooker, the cats and mice in perpetual antagonistic motion, a play in which each is flattened and annihilated and still lives to fight on.....America created the Invisible men, the Spidermen, the Supermen, the Batmen, the men who flew like birds, had X-ray vision, spun webs of rope and policed the precincts of their crime-ridden cities. These new myths had one characteristic: there was always an explanation for the new-myth hero's abilities. Superman, for instance, derived his powers from the low gravity of the planet Krypton from whence he came. Batman was in fact a millionaire with a dramatic history. Batman and Superman are explained; Hanuman (the monkey god) accepted (in India) as an article of faith. Different eras, different degrees of development, a different approach. The Americans don't make 'mythologicals ', their entire cinema is their mythological, just as they don't imitate the Classics and Romantics. Jazz is their classical music. America, having generated the culture of rapid capitalistic advance and consumer-oriented technology, naturally gave the world the myth of technological advance. It found and finds its expression in the science fiction films, which use these very advances in technology to create the film's special effects. Computers become characters, robots threaten humanity, new dimensions are envisaged and new worlds literally pictured and put into conflict.

Let us now see how Bollywood began.

Part I

In Step with the World

1

The Creators

Modern India has always been haunted by the thought that it gets Western inventions late, long after the West has moved on to better and more advanced things. E.M. Forster's novel, *A Passage to India,* ends with the main English character, Henry Fielding, taunting the main Indian one, Aziz, about India's desire to be an independent country. Fielding snorts, "India a nation. What an apotheosis. Last comer to the drab nineteenth-century sisterhood. Waddling in at this hour of the world to take her seat. She, whose only peer was the Holy Roman Empire, she shall rank with Guatemala and Belgium perhaps."

Yet, cinema has been different. It came to India less than seven months after the first film was shown in Paris. Cinema was born on 28 December 1895 and, as luck would have it, India's name was associated with the birth of film. The venue the Lumière brothers, Auguste and Louis, chose to show their short programme was the Salon Indien, located in the basement of the Grand Café at 14, Boulevard des Capucines in Paris. The organisers had gone to great lengths to make the venue look Indian, with the lavish basement hall decorated with sumptuous Oriental rugs. But there was so little confidence that this new invention would catch on that the owner of Salon Indien, Mr Volpini, refused an offer of 20% of the takings, preferring instead to charge the Lumière brothers thirty francs a day. Despite a man standing outside the building, handing out posters all day, and the cost of the show pegged to a franc, only thirty-three paid customers were attracted. It was a cold day in Paris and that may have put people off, but the fact is, the majority of the hundred who filled the basement seats did not pay for the privilege.

Nor was the beginning particularly encouraging. As the lights dimmed and a photographic projection depicted the doors of the Lumières' photographic factory at Lyon, a murmur of disappointment went round the room: "Why, it is only the old Magic Lantern." But then they saw a new magic on the white backdrop: moving pictures. The gates opened, workers rushed out, followed by dogs and, suddenly, a whole new world began to emerge. One scene called 'Condeliers' Square', which showed a moving hansom cab, was so realistic that a woman in the audience jumped to her feet as the picture of the hansom cab moved nearer and she had the impression it would rush at her through the screen. 'Baby's Dinner', showing Auguste and his wife feeding their infant daughter, also made an impression, in particular with the swaying trees in the background, which made the audience feel they could hear the rustling of the leaves. In all, ten different scenes, with each reel seventeen metres in length, were shown. As the show ended, and the lights came on, the audience broke into cheers. Slow as the first day's taking had been, the shows quickly caught on and soon the brothers were making 2,000 francs a day. Salon Indien had got a hit.

The brothers were keen to advertise their products and quickly sent films and projections far and wide to every continent. The result was that on 7 July, 1896, the same day the new invention was being shown to the Tsar of Russia in St Petersburg, Bombay enjoyed the experiences that had first alarmed, and then so thrilled, the Paris audience.

India had to thank geography for this. Maurice Sestier, the Lumières's man, was on his way to Australia and had to stop over in Bombay. Nevertheless, it meant that when it came to the cinema, India was part of a global phenomenon right from the beginning and did not come waddling in late, long after it was old news in the West. Contrast this with other nineteenth century inventions: the typewriter and the automobile. Both came to India for the first time the same year as the cinema, but the patent for the typewriter had been granted thirty years earlier, and the car had been in existence for more than a decade in the West before the first one was seen in Bombay.

On that June morning in 1896, *The Times of India* , then a British-owned paper in Bombay, had carried an advertisement asking Bombay residents to witness "the marvel of the century, the wonder of the world" at Watson's Hotel. There would, said the paper, be four showings of "*cinematographe," living photographic pictures in lifestyle reproductions at* 6,7, 9 and 10 pm.

Watson's was the ideal place to display this new invention representing, as it did, all that was chic and exclusive in British Bombay. The building itself had been the first iron-framed building in the city, made of cast-iron pillars and tiers of wrought-iron galleries, which had moved Mark Twain, who had stayed there during his visit to the city, to describe it as "something like a huge birdcage… risen like an exhalation from the earth." The hotel was then the best hotel in Bombay and, like many of the best British clubs and hotels in the Raj, not open to Indians. The story in Bombay was that the hotel had a sign saying Indians and dogs not allowed and Jamshedji Nusserwanji Tata, the founder of the great Tata industrial empire of India, had been turned away from Watson's because of the colour of his skin. He reacted by building the Taj and putting up a sign saying British and cats not allowed. The story of racial discrimination may have been embellished in the endless retelling, perhaps even apocryphal, although it illustrated how the Indians responded to the undoubted racism and belief in white supremacy that formed such an essential part of the British Raj.

The British in India operated, as the Indian writer Nirad Chaudhuri has said, an apartheid system. Watson's was located on the Esplanade, that part of Bombay which was European in conception, and where the British had their homes and their businesses, and where Indians were allowed on sufferance. Within walking distance was the Bombay Gymkhana, an English club where the British went to relax and play sports and which did not allow Indians as members. But thirty-eight years after Watson's showed the first film in India, the Bombay Gymkhana would be the venue for the first ever cricket Test match between India and England, seating Indian spectators in special tents and marquees. It would take the Gymkhana another thirty years, long after Indian independence, to open its club-house to the Indians. The apartheid the British practised in India could never be as total and as monolithic as that imposed by whites in South Africa or in the southern states of America. If it made Indians feel inferior in their own land, it also had cracks through which Western ideas and recreations could seep through. In the 1930s, it meant cricket Tests between India and England, at a time when the blacks in America could not play baseball with their fellow whites. It was fourteen years later, in 1947, the year of Indian independence, that Jackie Robinson became the first black man to play major league baseball and the so-called invisible Negro leagues, which had catered for blacks, slowly disappeared. In 1896, the cracks in British apartheid brought film to India.

That evening at Watson's, the audience saw six short films, including the one that had so astounded the Paris audience—a train coming into the station: *L'Arrivée d'un gare de la Ciotat* (The Arrival of a Train at La Ciotat Station). With a camera held near the track, this showed a train gradually increase in size as it pulled into the station until the audience thought it would crash through the screen. It was so realistic that some in that Paris saloon had ducked, while others had vacated their seats in a hurry. The reaction of the Bombay audience matched that of the Paris one.

The Bombay Gazette of July 9 described the evening and the effect the films had on that first night Bombay audience:

> The view included the arrival of a crowded train at a railway station with all the animation and bustle that such an event presents, and the demolition of a wall—a work so realistic that the dust is seen to ascend in volumes when the wall finally totters and falls. The *Sea Bath* is another very good scene: the dashing of waves upon the beach, and the antics of the boy bathers, both being very realistic. But this is beaten by *Leaving the Factory,* which brings a whole crowd of moving humanity onto the canvas and is, without doubt, the most realistic scene of all. *Ladies and Solders on Wheels* is a very vivid representation of the cycling craze, as can be seen any day in Hyde Park. No one who takes an interest in the march of science should allow the opportunity to pass that now presents itself to see the cinematograph, an invention which is attracting a great deal of attention at home.

Cinema, as the critic Amita Malik has written, could not have arrived at a better time for India. It was the turn of the century, there were urban masses eager for mass entertainment and the cinema with its direct visual impact, easy accessibility and its relatively straightforward themes seemed "the natural answer."

The screenings at Watson's generated enough excitement for more showings and these began a week later, on 14 July, at Novelty Theatre, which had a larger seating capacity. It was meant to be for three days but growing public interest meant the screenings continued for several weeks, with the shows regularly advertised in *The Times of India* and receiving good reviews. The programme was also increased from twelve to twenty-four films. The façade of the theatre was floodlit and, under the direction of the organist at St John's Church in Colaba, a certain F. Seymour Dove, a "selection of suitable music" was provided.

Novelty sought to attract Indians by catering to both the prevailing social customs, a feature of which was lack of emancipation for women, and their capacity to pay. By the end of July, the cinema advertised "Reserved boxes for the Purdah ladies and their families" and they even had zenna shows where the cinema was open only to women. They also offered a broad scale of prices. The first screening had a single admission price but, by the end of the month, prices ranged from a low of four annas (25 paise, about .02 of a penny) to a high of two rupees (about 15p).

The Indians the British exhibitors hoped to attract in the main were the Parsis. They had fled to India around the eighth century AD, after the fall of the pre-Islamic Sassanian Empire to the conquering Muslims, arriving by ship to the Western coast of the Indian sub-continent (now Gujarat) to maintain their Zoroastrian religious tradition. The Parsis tell a charming story of how they got asylum in India, one that has lessons for immigration controllers the world over. According to this old Parsi legend, the Raja of Sanjan, the local Hindu king, had given them a cup full to the rim of milk, symbolically stating that the kingdom was already full of people and could not take any refugees. The asylum seekers sweetened the milk with sugar and gave it back to the king, symbolically stating that they would be of immeasurable service to the kingdom and become exemplary subjects of the Raja. The Raja allowed them to keep their customs and traditions, provided they did not try to proselytise, and this Hindu tolerance proved so successful that, although they had lived in India for centuries, they never really lost their identity, or became submerged into the majority Hindu community. Their custom of fire worship was even adopted by Akbar, the greatest of India's Mughal Emperors. When the European traders started arriving in the sixteenth century, they found the Parsis willing collaborators; by the time the British became masters of India in the eighteenth century, the Parsis were the ideal middle men, both in commerce and the social field. Despite having lived in India for 1200 years they portrayed themselves as interlopers and sought common cause with the latest interlopers, the British. Even today, the Indians talk about the Parsi love for the British and a popular joke is about the Parsi matron referring to "our Queen" but "your President".

It was the Parsis who were to pioneer both industrial development and cricket in India, but a month into the showing of the Lumière films, on 5 August 1896, *The Times of India* felt sufficiently concerned about lack of Parsi zeal for film shows to write an editorial rebuking "our Parsi friends" for not taking greater interest in this new medium. It appears that despite the four anna tickets and the attention to purdah ladies, it was mainly the British in Bombay who turned up for the screenings.

The Times of India was being hasty in its judgment. The Parsis would take to films and were some of the early pioneers of the industry but, initially, it was a member of the majority Hindu community who showed the greatest enthusiasm for this new medium. He was a Maharashtrian called Harischandra Sakharam Bhatavdekar, also known as Save Dada. Dada means older brother and is a term of respect. Photographs of him, taken when he was well into his old age, show a man sporting a circular turban denoting his high Brahmanical caste, a large tilak mark on his forehead and his gaunt, skinny, hollow-cheeked face lit up with wonderful luminous eyes which shone through his horn-rimmed glasses. These eyes had been dazzled by the screenings of the Lumière brothers at Novelty and the shrewd businessman in him quickly saw the potential. He was already a professional still-photographer and was so taken by this new invention that he ordered a motion picture camera from London at a price of twenty-one guineas. This was, probably, the first such imported equipment to arrive in the country.

His first use of this camera was to photograph a fight between two famous wrestlers, Pundalik Dada and Krishna Nahvi, at Bombay's Hanging Gardens, which he then sent to London for processing. Meanwhile, he had also brought a projector and become an open air exhibitor of imported films, showing them in a tent cinema he owned. From the beginning, Bhatavdekar realised that only Indian films would not attract audiences, so he exhibited his wrestler's film, along with some imported ones. He kept to this formula for many shows, mixing imported shorts with a film that focused on the training of circus monkeys and another on the fire temples of the Parsis.

In 1901, he filmed the arrival back in India of Sir Mancherjee Bhownaggree, the second Indian to be elected to the House of Commons, and the first from the Conservative party. Bhownaggree had just been re-elected to the House, having first won election in the 1895 election. That election had also seen the defeat of the first Indian ever to be elected to the House—Dadabhai Naoroji. Both men were Parsis but, although they were members of different British political parties, Naoroji being a Liberal, Bhownaggree a Conservative, both were racially targeted in a similar fashion from opposite ends of the British political spectrum. When Naoroji, a Liberal, became the first Indian to stand for the British Parliament, the Marquis of Salisbury, the then Conservative Prime Minister, had said he did not think "a British constituency will take a black man." He was proved wrong.

After the 1895 election, Bhownaggree's defeated Liberal rival, a trade unionist, complained he had been "kicked out by a black man, a stranger." Unlike Naoroji, who in common with many Indian radicals felt more at home with the British Liberals as the party with more sympathy for Indian aspirations, Bhownaggree, who was also known as Bow-the Knee, was an ardent collaborator with the Raj, or as the British put it, "an imperial loyalist". In 1901, Bhownaggree's return to India, soon after his election triumph, was advertised as proof of how well the British connection worked for the Indians who collaborated with the Raj.

Bhatavdekar's most important film came the following year when he filmed the return to India of another famous Indian. Raghunath Paranjpye, an Indian student in Cambridge, had became a Senior Wrangler, a very special distinction in mathematics. This was the ideal subject for Bhatavdekar. It filled the Indians with nationalistic pride for here was proof that, contrary to what their British conquerors told them, not all Indians were inferior human beings and some of them, given the opportunity, could compete with the best of the British. But for the British, Paranjye's success was also satisfying; it proved that given time, and the right education, some of the Indians might become as good as the Europeans, or at least aspire to be.

Bhatavdekar titled his films simply. His first had been called *Wrestler*, the monkey film was called *Man and Monkeys,* the return to India of the Conservative MP, *Landing of Sir M.M. Bhowmuggre* (the difference in spelling indicates how Indian names are transliterated into English) and the Paranjype film, *Sir Wrangler Mr R.P. Pranjype*. His 1903 film, entitled *Delhi Durbar of Lord Curzon*—Curzon being the Viceroy—showed the Delhi Durbar held to celebrate the coronation of Edward VII. It was an exercise in imperial extravaganza, mixing oriental and occidental splendour, and designed to impress Indians with the power and majesty of the monarch, whose subjects they were privileged to be.

The subjects Bhatavdekar chose show the temper of the times. This was the height of the Empire. Cinema came to India the same year that Winston Churchill arrived in India and just months before Victoria celebrated her Diamond Jubilee. Indians vied with each other to pay homage to "her Gracious Majesty". The British were talking of an Empire that would last a thousand years and promoting it as the most beneficial form of rule ever devised by man. The British could point to the peace they had brought to India after many decades of bloodshed and the benefits they had introduced by outlawing such awful practices as thugee and sutee. Yet for all the advertised virtues of British rule, the Raj's policies could not prevent famines; indeed, historians now say the Raj's policies created some of the worst famines in Indian history. In 1896, just as the cinema came to India, famine in the Central Provinces killed 150,000. In Sholapur, in western India, a mob of 5,000, hungry for food, raided bags of grain. The police opened fire, killing many. The 1896 famine was the first of six long years of famine that proved so devastating that historians now call it the great holocaust. *The Lancet* estimated that between 1896 and 1902, nineteen million Indians died. 1896 also saw bubonic plague brought to the country by a ship from China. It swept through Bombay, killing 20,000 people. Fourteen thousand died of cyclone in Chittagong and thrice that number from the diseases that followed.

But none of these awful events featured in any of the films that Bhatavdekar, or others who followed him, made. For, despite the famines, most Indians accepted British rule and went along with the British projection of their rule as a benign administration that benefited Indians. Churchill, whose ship docked at Bombay six months after the first film show at Watson's Hotel, lived in style in India, voraciously read European history, in particular Gibbon, and while his many letters home spoke of his need for money, none of them mentioned the famines and disease that racked the land. He, like many of the British rulers, just did not see such distress and formed an impression—one that remained with him all his life and which he would articulate often—that British rule meant that Indians for the first time could travel in peace and tranquillity from one end of this vast country to another. Not even the educated Indians, for whom Churchill would soon develop such hatred, and who were increasingly clamouring for more say in running their own affairs, wanted to cut the ties with the Empire. The British Empire, they agreed, was the best thing that could have happened to India. Today, Naoroji is classified as a nationalist, as against Bhownaggree, the imperialist, but not even Naoroji demanded freedom for India. That cry was first heard only some thirty years later. In the closing years of the nineteenth century, all that even the most radical Indians wanted was that Britain treat her Indian subjects with fairness and justice and on the same scale as she was treating her white colonial subjects in Australia and Canada.

Bhatavdekar's work as a pioneer exhibitor led to him becoming manager of Bombay's Gaiety Theatre—later renamed Capitol Cinema. But his career as film-maker did not last long. He retired from film-making in 1907, to concentrate on exhibitions, living to a ripe old age and by the time he died, with quite a fortune, in the 1950s, Indian cinema had come a long way.

Not that Bhatavdekar was alone in pioneering film shows in India. He had a rival in Bombay: F.B. Thananwala, who was both an engineer and an equipment dealer. He showed a film about the Muslim Taboot procession and another claiming "splendid views of Bombay".

A more serious rival for Bhatavdekar emerged in Calcutta, then the capital of British India and the second city of the Empire after London. This was Hiralal Sen, who along with his brother, Motilal (their names mean jewels), did enough to be considered as much of a pioneer of the Indian cinema as Bhatavdekar. However, so little is known about Hiralal's work that Indian film historians cannot even agree on a filmography of films or even on the length of his best feature film. As so often with Indian history, there is anecdote and conjecture but little hard evidence.

The two brothers were sons of a lawyer and born in Bakjuri village in Manikganj (now Bangladesh). Hiralal, who, like Bhatavdekar, started as a photographer, saw his first film in Calcutta's Star Theatre, some time in October 1898. This was a show presented by Professor Stevenson which included various items such as *Railway Train in Full Motion, Death of Nelson, The Diamond Jubilee Procession* and *Mr Gladstone's Funeral*. The film that proved inspirational for Hiralal was Stevenson's *The Flower of Persia*. Hiralal's first film, with help and equipment from Stevenson, was based on scenes from *The Flower of Persia* and was shown along with Stevenson's film at the Star. Hiralal, a quick, eager learner, had also joined the film crew that Pathé of France had sent to India and, borrowing a camera, went round Calcutta shooting scenes which included bathers in the river Hoogly, and cockfights. In 1899, he set up the Royal Bioscope in partnership with Motilal, having got a camera from London and a projector from Warwick Trading, a British firm in Calcutta.

The Sen brothers' best work was put on at the Classic Theatre run by Amar Dutta, where they initially showed imported films during intervals between the stage shows. The theatrical tradition was already strong in Calcutta. Star, where the first film had been shown, was also the home theatre for Girish Chandra Ghosh, then one of Bengal's leading actor-playwrights. Hiralal had the interesting idea of filming some of the stage shows and such films were shown as added attractions after the stage performances or during the interval. He advertised them as "superfine pictures from our world renowned plays".

Hiralal made only one feature-length film called, *Alibaba and the Forty Thieves* but film historians cannot even agree how long the film was. He also, probably, filmed the first advertisements, one for C.K. Sen's Jabakusum hair oil, a product targeted at women and advertised as one that would keep their long, dark hair, shiny. Hiralal's advertisement has been lost but the product has continued to sell in India. He also made an advertisement for Edward's Tonic, produced by the well-known north Calcutta drug manufacturers, Batto Kesto Paul.

Hiralal's films show an interesting mix of homage to the Raj and the first stirrings of nationalism. So, there was a film about the 1911 visit to India of King George V and Queen Mary, the title of which tells us how the subject was covered. The title was: *Grand Delhi Coronation Durbar and Royal Visit to Calcutta Including Their Majesties Arrival at Amphitheatre, Arrival at Howrah, Princep's Ghat, Visit to Bombay and Exhibition.* The film showed Indian kings and princes paying tribute to their British Lord, the Viceroy's Cup Race in Calcutta, and the fireworks and celebration to mark the royal visit. This was made in 1912. But, some years before that, Hiralal had also made *The Bengal Partition Film,* which chronicled how Curzon's decision to partition the province sparked the first nationalist agitation in India. A rival company, which dominated the silent era of the Indian film industry, and of which we shall hear more, also made a film on this subject indicating the increasing competition the Royal Bioscope faced. Hiralal, clearly could not cope and, to add to his problems, just before the Royal collapsed, a fire in its studio destroyed all the films. Four years after Hiralal made his last film, at the 1913 Hindu Bathing Festival at Allahabad, he died at the age of fifty-one.

Bombay and Calcutta were not the only places exposed to the new medium: Madras saw film for the first time in 1900, courtesy of Major Warwick, an Englishman. It was almost another decade, 1909, before an Indian, Swamikannu Vincent, a railway draughtsman, obtaining a projector from a visiting Frenchman, held the first show in the Esplanade grounds.

By this time, many people including quite a few foreign firms, were seeking to exploit the Indian market. This had started soon after the first showing at Watson's. In January 1897, Stewart's *Vitograph* came to Bombay's Gaiety Theatre and ran for about a week. In September, "The Hughes Moto-Photoscope, the latest marvel in cinematographs" began showing at various locations, including fairgrounds.

The travelling missions from Europe and America were quickly followed by import of films, projectors and other equipment. Some of the missions also functioned as sales agents. The equipment purchased was used to make films such as *Poona Races 98* and *Train Arriving at Bombay Station*. Along with stage dramas, another genre was the emergence of comics. One week in September 1912 found the Imperial cinema in Bombay showing the *God of the Sun,* along with "two screaming comics". The Alexandra Theatre had a two-hour show, including "five ripping comics." The America-India, apparently the first theatre to install electric fans, offered the *Mystery of Edwin Drood, The Dance of Shiva* and "three real good bits of fun".

As was only to be expected, many of these early film shows were at theatres, sometimes as supplements to plays, concerts or performances by magicians. In Bombay, in 1898, Carl Hertz, "absolutely the world's greatest conjuror," offered film items in colour, along with his magic show. But these events were overshadowed, at least for the time being, by the eruption of outdoor cinema shows, in tents or in the open air. The typical film showman from this era was the photographer-exhibitor. These open air exhibitors would generally equip themselves with films for two or three programmes. Having exhausted the possibilities in one location, he moved elsewhere. Showing in parks and empty lots of big cities soon led to showings in smaller cities and towns and, eventually, to rural travelling cinemas, which still exist in India.

The greatest of these film exhibitors was undoubtedly Abdulally Esoofally (1884-1957). Born in Surat, Gujarat, he started out as a tent showman and travelled throughout south-east Asia, bringing films to large parts of the Far East including Burma, Singapore and Indonesia. In 1908, he returned to India and until 1914, and the outbreak of the First World War, covered most parts of the country. He travelled light. He had a projector, a screen, that he could fold, a tent, and a few cans of films—the films were generally between 100 and 200 feet which Esoofally bought at around six pence a foot. Realising he needed music for his film shows, at every stop he hired a local band. Generally, an Abdulally programme consisted of forty or fifty pictures including gags, comedy, operas, travel films and sports events. The tent could accommodate around 1,000 and customers paid according to how near they were to the screen. In 1914, he decided to stop his wandering and settle down. Along with a partner, he took over the Alexandra Theatre in Bombay, and four years later built the Majestic Theatre, which was to show the first Indian talkie, *Alam Ara*, in 1931.

India, then a colony of Britain, was open house for British and Western film-makers and, just as the British Government did not impose duties on the Lancashire cotton goods, made from Indian cotton, that was imported into India, so foreign film-makers were encouraged to make money from the Indian market.

This meant that from the beginning the Indian film scene was extremely international. France, headed by Pathé, was the leading source but America, Italy, England, Denmark, and Germany were competing for a share of the Indian market.

One of the most interesting foreigners to make a fortune from films in India was the American, Charles Urban, who had taken up residence in London. In 1911, he got special permission from the British Government to film *The Delhi Durbar* through a process he had invented called Kinemacolor. He was so paranoid that people might steal his negatives that he hid them in a pit, dug under the tent he had pitched to stay in while filming *The Durbar*. His efforts paid off splendidly and in fifteen months the film grossed three quarters of a million dollars. In contrast, a film on the visit of George V and Queen Mary, shot by an Indian film producer, K.P. Karandikar, made no money.

The year after *The Durbar* saw an Indian film-maker for the first time use film to tell a story. The film was called *Pundalik*, a popular Hindu drama relating the story of a Maharashtrian saint and based on a play of the same name. It had Indian actors, a British cameraman, and was set in a Bombay garden. Nanabhai Govind Chitre and Ramchandra Gopal Torney got hold of a Williamson camera, a photographer called Mr Johnson, who worked for Bourne and Shepherd, and a well-known photographic studio in Bombay, and assembled the actors in a Bombay garden to film the play from several angles. About forty-five minutes long, it was shown at a cinema owned by Chitre called the Coronation Cinema, along with an imported film called *A Dead Man's Child,* and another film described as "new screaming comics".

The *Pundalik* film has not survived but the advertisement for the film shows the methods used to lure audiences. This began by saying, "Our Pictures have the power of arresting attention. Crowded houses nightly." Then it went on to say about the film, "Almost half the Bombay Hindu population saw it last week and we want the other half to do so before a change of programme takes place." The advertisement ended with the exhortation, "Don't fail to come tonight and bring your friends." But, let alone half of Bombay coming, so few came that

Chitre and Torney did not get their money back, and Torney returned to his day job with an electrical goods manufacturing company. Years later, he did return as an importer of film equipment and producer of silent and sound films, but the first film venture had not been a success. But, even as Chitre and Torney admitted defeat, the man who would make the first feature length film in India, and who is rightly described as the father of Indian cinema, had already been bitten by the film bug and was hard at work.

Dhundiraj Govind Phalke, generally known as Dadasaheb Phalke, was born in a priestly family at Trymbakeshwar, in the district of Nasik, in 1870. He was trained for a career as a Sanskrit scholar, his father, Daji Shastri, being a well-known Sanskrit scholar. But from an early age he showed an enthusiasm for the arts, particularly painting, play acting and magic. His family moved to Bombay when his father got a teaching job at Elphinstone College and this made it possible for Phalke to join the Sir J. J. School of Arts. Here he received his grounding in the arts, especially in photography. He had also by now become a skilled magician, a talent he was to use quite a bit in his films.

After further training at Kala Bhavan in Baroda, and a period as photographer for the Governmental Archaeological Dept, Phalke was offered financial help to start an Art Printing Press. He then settled down, married, and seemed to be consigned to a life of fine printing.

His backers, keen to acquaint him with the latest printing processes, especially in colour work, arranged for him to take a trip to Germany. The arrangement was on condition that Phalke must remain with the company for a stipulated time after the journey, which he did. But when he returned, he knew that a life in printing would not satisfy him. In about 1910, he fell ill and, for a time, lost his eyesight. When Phalke got back his vision, an incident changed the course of his life, and that of Indian cinema.

At a Christmas cinema show in Bombay, he saw *The Life of Christ*. As the images of Christ flashed before his eyes, he mentally visualised the Hindu gods Krishna and Ram and spent a restless night imagining bringing them to the screen. Before Phalke got home, he had decided on a career change. He asked his wife to accompany him for the next screening. It is said that he had no money, and travelling expenses, and the cost of the cinema tickets, was borne by neighbours.

Seven decades later, in the Phalke Centenary Souvenir, published in 1970, Saraswatibhai Phalke would recount the evening that changed her life and launched the career of India's first film director.

We both went to see the 'cinema' in an illuminated tent on Sandhurst Road, where a band was playing. It was called the America-India Cinematograph. The first-class tickets were priced at eight annas. It was Christmas 1911 and the hall was crowded with Christians and Europeans. The lights were then switched off and there appeared the picture of a cock moving on the screen. This was the trade mark of the Pathé Company. Then, a comic picture started, featuring an actor called Foolshead. After every part of the film the lights were switched on and stage items of magic, or physical feats, were performed. The main picture that day was *The Life of Christ*. People were weeping on seeing the sufferings of Christ and the crucifixion. The film was coloured in the Kinemacolour process. On the way back, Dadasaheb said, 'Like the life of Christ, we shall make pictures about Rama and Krishna.' I was not at all happy to hear that and kept quiet.

But like the good wife she was, Saraswatibhai became Phalke's most important collaborator.

Funds were raised by mortgaging his life insurance, and help from friends and relatives. Before he sailed for England Phalke also bought, at a Bombay bookstall, an ABC of cinematography, apparently the work of the British film pioneer, Cecil Hepworth. In England, Phalke met Hepworth, whose Walton-on-Thames studio, near London, was then one of the best equipped in the world. Phalke spent a week there which gave him a chance to examine Hepworth's famous trick photography. He also went to the offices of *The Weekly Bioscope*, where the editor, Mr Cabourne, tried to convince him he could not make money from films. There were, Cabourne pointed out, several failed producers in England. But Phalke was convinced he could succeed and, before he left England, he had impressed Cabourne with his dedication, helped by the fact that like Cabourne, Phalke did not smoke, did not drink and was also a vegetarian.

Early in 1912, Phalke returned to India with a Williamson camera, a Williamson perforator, developing and printing equipment, raw film for several months of work, and a collection of the latest film publications.

However, with money not available for major work, Phalke started with an intermediate project. He decided on a short film in time-lapse photography. The project was a capsule history of the growth of a pea in a pea-laden plant called *Birth of a Pea Plant*. He shot one frame a day to show how the plant was growing. The audience, which included friends, relatives and a prospective financier, were astounded, and Phalke began to gather the money he needed. Even then, at one stage, his wife had to pledge her jewellery, as security for Phalke to secure the loan.

Finance was not the only problem. There were also the problems of getting actors, and in particular, getting females, to perform in front of the camera. India has had a long theatrical tradition, theatre and performance being a part of Hindu mythology. Theatre and dance were supposed to have originated with the Gods, Brahma, the creator, himself, having ordered the first dramatic performance. *Shakuntala*, the most famous play of Kalidas, the great Sanskrit playwright, who had flourished in the golden age of Hinduism, the Gupta period in the fifth century, was centred round a female character. But, by the time Phalke sought female actresses, the golden age of Indian theatre had long passed. At the beginning of the twentieth century, respectable society saw theatre as something to be shunned, and no Indian woman was ready to act in Phalke's films. Even the prostitutes he approached, refused.

The breakthrough came when Phalke discovered a young man working in a restaurant, an effeminate cook with slender features and hands, called Salunke. He was given a raise of Rs. 5, and for the princely sum of Rs. 15 a month, joined Phalke. Phalke was to make Salunke India's first great superstar and, some years later, in another Phalke film, he was to achieve the extraordinary feat of playing both the male and female leads, both Rama, the great God of the Hindus, and his wife Sita, the ideal Hindu woman.

For his first major film, Phalke had chosen the story of Raja Harischandra, a story from the *Mahabharata,* which demonstrates that as long as men remain good and true, they will ultimately triumph. Like many such Hindu mythological tales, the "great sin" of the good king Harischandra, committed quite accidentally, was to interrupt the sage, Vishwamitra, as he was in the midst of yagna, offering sacrifice to the gods. The sage cursed him and the penalty was for the king, his queen, and his young son to be exiled to the forest. This was considered guru dakshina, paying the guru for his misdeeds. The king was then subjected to endless ordeals which included being estranged from his queen. But nothing could make him deviate from the path of virtue. The climactic scene was at a cremation ground where they had brought their young son, now dead, to be cremated. The son's death brought the king and queen, who had become separated as they made their journey through a living hell, back together again. But the travails of the king were not over. The sage framed the queen for murder and ordered the king to behead his own queen. However, as the king gets ready to follow the sage's command, all is revealed. In the sort of happy ending Indian movie-goers love, the sage was revealed not to be a vengeful fire-eating prophet, but an examiner of men's virtues; the ordeals Harishchandra had been put through had been meant to test him. The gods were now satisfied Harischandra had passed all the tests. This so pleased the gods that the Lord Shiva himself emerged on earth and Harishchandra was restored to all his full glory, with the young prince brought back to life.

Right from the first scene, which showed the actor D.D. Dhabka playing Harischandra, teaching his young son archery, Phalke showed a mastery of the new medium. Phalke had chosen his subject wisely. India is not alone in having great mythical stories, but Indian myths are still seen as part of Indian life, preserved down the generations through oral story telling. These are stories that every Indian, certainly every Hindu child, knows, and in a land which has always been more a continent than a nation, with many languages, customs and creeds, they provide a shared narrative, a very real cultural unity.

Phalke, who shot the film in a bungalow in a Bombay suburb, which he had converted into a studio, took his time to tell the story and in the end produced a film that for the period was very long: 3,700 feet. The film was completed some time in 1912. It was first screened on 21 April 1913 at the Olympia Theatre, with regular shows starting ten days later at the Coronation Cinema. Phalke was aware that he would have to do something to attract audiences since feature films of this length were a novelty. So, for the first showings, the programme included Miss Irene Del Mar performing a duet and dance movement, a comical sketch by the McClements, a juggler called Alexander the Wonderful Foot Juggler and some comic shorts advertised as Tip-Top Comics.

Phalke was not only a good film-maker but a shrewd publicist and was quick to devise strategies to attract the paying customers. When he took the film to small towns, known as moffusil towns, he was warned that audiences there expected to go to a show and sit through a stage play for six hours, for which they paid just 2 annas. Yet Phalke's film would last a mere hour and a half for which they would be charged three annas. Phalke's response was to advertise his film thus: "*Raja Harischandra*. A Performance with 57,000 photographs. A picture two miles long. All for only three annas."

The intrinsic merit of the film, plus such publicity gimmicks, worked like a treat, and the film was a great success. The film had critics drooling and gave cinematic flesh to the audience's instinctive feel for Hindu myths. The reviewer in *The Bombay Chronicle* wrote about "the striking effect of the scene of the burning forest, and the cleverness of the apparition of the God Shiva and his restoration of the dead boy to life". This scene would do much to reinforce the religious feelings of the audience. The film was an overwhelming success and it changed Phalke's life.

After the first film, Phalke moved his enterprise to Nasik, not far from where he was born, and his subsequent films were produced there. Phalke set up the studio model, which later Indian producers were to follow. The plot of land, which contained woods, hills, fields and caves, provided a diversity of scenic backgrounds. The estate provided for body-building, fencing, fighting, riding, a library, a reading-room and even a miniature zoo.

His family, which included his wife, Kaki Phalke, five sons, three daughters and other relatives, were all involved in his films, with Kaki Phalke supervising all the laboratory work. A fountain in the backyard was used as a developing tank and actors and actresses helped Mrs Phalke in the technical work.

Over time, Phalke built up his own film family, with the company growing to a hundred employees, all of them living together on the Nasik estate. Except for occasional crowd scenes, no outsiders were involved in his films.

Phalke was a stern disciplinarian, maintaining strict schedules. Infraction of rules brought instant dismissal. He would pose problems before his children encouraging them to participate in the art of film-making.

During the next ten years, Phalke made over a hundred or more films, ranging from short films to ambitious features.

His most ambitious and successful one came four years after *Raja Harischandra*, and showed how well he could exploit mythology to reach out to Indian audiences. If his first film had taken an episode of Mahabharata then, for this one, called *Lanka Dahan,* he described the climactic moment of the other great Hindu classic, *Ramayana*. It showed how Rama rescued Sita from the clutches of the demon, Ravana, burning down Lanka in the process. Salunke played both Sita and Ram and audiences could clearly see his biceps when he played Sita. The tail of the monkey god, Hanuman, whose help was crucial for Ram's crossing of the straits that divides India from Lanka, was also very clearly a rope. But despite this, audiences were enthralled. In Bombay, the first ten days box office collection amounted to Rs. 32,000, a huge sum in those days. J. B. H. Wadia recalls the effect the film had on ordinary Indians:

> *Lanka Dahan* was a minor masterpiece of its time. The spectacle of Hanuman's figure becoming progressively diminutive as he flew higher and higher into the clouds, and the burning of the city of Lanka, in table-top photography, were simply awe-inspiring. I remember that devout villagers from nearby Bombay had come in large numbers in their bullock carts to have their darshan of their beloved God, lord Rama. Many stayed overnight on their improvised dwellings to see the film again the next day.

But if Phalke could reach out to the masses, the Anglicised élite, the much derided 2% who knew English, ignored him. They preferred Western films, as did the English language papers. This was the divide in the Indian film world that Phalke had opened up, a sort of very Indian film apartheid which continued for many generations, until well into the 1980s. The best cinema houses in the big cities, such as Bombay and Calcutta, only showed Western movies, generally American or British. Indian movies were reserved for seedier cinemas in the more run-down inner city areas.

Satyajit Ray, India's greatest film-maker, has told us how, a few years after Phalke's heyday, growing up in Calcutta, he was encouraged to shun Indian films. He describes cinemas showing the latest foreign films:

> ....all stood clustered in the heart of Calcutta Filmland, exuded swank and boasted an élite clientele. On the other hand, the cinemas showing Indian films, such as the Albion, were dank and seedy. One pinched one's nose as one hurried past the toilet in the lobby into the auditorium and sat on hard, creaky, wooden seats. The films they showed, we were told by our elders, were not suitable for us. Since the elders always decided what we should see, the choice fell, inevitably, on foreign films, usually American. We thus grew up on a wholesome diet of Chaplin, Keaton Lloyd, Fairbanks, Tom Mix and Tarzan, with an occasional drama-with-a moral like *Uncle Tom's Cabin*, thrown in.

The apartheid did not cease until the 1980s, when with import of foreign films restricted, the swanky cinema houses of Bombay, Calcutta and other cities, started showing Hindi films. The apartheid was completely eliminated only in the 1990s when Hindi films were relabelled Bollywood and started becoming acceptable in the West. But that was many years after Phalke had been forgotten.

Phalke had little reason to care about this growing film apartheid. He did not advertise in the English papers and was more than content that he was attracting an audience that, in any case, could not read English. This audience also could not identify with French heroine, Protea, or the Italian comedian, Foolshead, but, in Phalke's films, they saw stories they had been brought up on come to life before their very eyes. As Phalke churned out one hit after another, *Harischandra, Mohini Bhasmasur, Satyavan, Savitri, Lanka Dahan* and *Shri Krishna Janam*, audiences flocked to his shows.

In time, Phalke became an exhibitor himself and travelled widely in a bullock cart with his projector, screens and films. The audiences in this semi-rural setting paid nothing like the two rupees charged by the movie houses in the bigger cities. Phalke's rural audiences paid at most two to four annas but, such were the numbers attracted, that the weight of coins Phalke carried back home to his Nasik estate was often enormous.

Eventually the success of the Phalke films extended to all parts of India. The showing of *Raja Harischandra* in Madras brought mad rushes by the crowds waiting to see it. *Lanka Dahan* was so popular that one exhibitor had a show every hour from 7 am till midnight, with many in the audience coming back again and again to see their gods brought to life, albeit on film.

The irony of all this was that Phalke was himself very much a man moulded by Western ideas. We get a vivid portrayal of this in his one reel film, *How Films Are Made*, fragments of which have survived and where Phalke is shown rehearsing actors and processing and editing film. One scene shows Phalke, dressed in the sort of Western clothes fashionable then, wearing a shirt with a detachable collar, and a waistcoat. He is sitting on a mahogany chair, in a room full of furniture, that would not have been out of place in the West. He is examining a reel of film and the only Indian touch is that in front of him stands a man dressed in typical Indian dress, complete with turban and a long coat. Remove that man and this could well be a shot of a film-maker in Paris or London in the early part of the twentieth century.

Phalke was a special-effects genius and he explored a vast range of techniques, including animation. He experimented with colour, via tinting and toning. He used scenic models for a number of his sequences, including the burning of Lanka, for which he burned down two sets. But besides technical expertise, Phalke brought women into his movies, first his own daughter, Mandakini, and then a Mahrashtrian woman called Kamalabai Gokhale.

The introduction of Mandakini showed how daring Phalke could be and how far ahead of his time. It came in his film *Kaliya Mardan,* where he took up the theme of the god Krishna rescuing people from a snake that was terrorising them. A title tells the audience the role to be played by Mandakni, then five years old. As this was happening, we see Mandkini's face, which then slowly dissolves to form the face of Krishna. So long before the term became fashionable in the West, Phalke was using the Brechtian technique of making the audience realise that what they were watching was a piece that was not magic, but man-made fiction, all the more daring, given his audiences wanted to believe in magic.

In 1914, just before the First World War broke out, Phalke travelled to London for the second time with three of his films. *The Bioscope* noted that "Mr Phalke is directing his energies in the best and most profitable direction in specialising upon the presentation by film of Indian mythological dramas." Phalke turned down an offer from a London studio to make films in England, all the keener to return home with war having broken out.

The war added to the problems Phalke already faced in making a go of the film business. If his skills as a film-maker cannot be doubted, film business did not come that easily to him and the world war drastically restricted the import of raw film stock. He survived by getting his workers to work for half their usual salary for the duration of the war. In 1917, rising costs and the need for new equipment forced Phalke to form a new company with five partners called the Hindustan Film Company. For its first production, Phalke turned to the subject he had promised his wife he would make after watching *The Life of Christ*. This was *The Life of Krishna*, where he shows Krishna's wicked uncle Kamsa having a dream in which several figures of Krishna attack him and decapitate the head. The head then floats away but rejoins the body only to float away again, a trick that is repeated several times. This was followed the next year by *Kaliya Mardan*, which featured Manadakini.

However, within two years, he had quarrelled with his partners and retired to Benares, disgusted, as he would later tell a Government committee, by the whole film business. In this the holiest of cities for Hindus, Phalke wrote *Rangabhoomi*, a stage play which satirised contemporary theatre. But he could not keep away from Nasik and returned to resolve the quarrel and started work again, though rarely as a director. In 1921, however, he did make *Sant Tukaram,* a film about a famous poet-saint of Maharashtra.

In 1931, he tried again and made *Setu Bandhan*, an episode from Ramayana. This was the last film before the company was dissolved. Although shot as a silent film, sound, which had not arrived, was added to the film, but it failed. Phalke had one more film in him. Made in 1937, at the age of sixty-seven, it was also his first talkie, *Gangavataran,* and it showed Phalke could not come to terms with the changes in the industry.

The arrival of sound had made a big difference but his staple diet of mythological films, while they would remain popular, was no longer that dominant. Rival genres had begun to emerge. In the 1920s, social and historical films rose in importance and then stunt films, inspired by Douglas Fairbanks, became a favourite. Phalke, once the innovator, now started to feel like an outsider.

In 1927, he was the first to give evidence to the Indian Cinematograph Committee, and while his faith in films remained strong, and he denied that they were a bad influence on morals, his answers show his disillusionment with the way the medium, which he had done so much to create in India, had developed:

> Almost all productions now in India are lacking in technique and artistic merit. The acting is not good. The photography, specially, is of the worst class. Nobody knows anything about the art.

He called for a school to be set up "somewhere in India, to teach the cinema industry, photography, acting screenplay, scenario-writing etc".

It would be many decades before the first tentative steps in that direction were taken.

He died in Nasik on February 16 1944, at the age of 74, a forgotten genius.

The Indian film historian, Garga, has no doubts that Phalke was a great innovator whose, "contribution to Indian cinema cannot be overestimated. His pioneering efforts firmly established the Indian film as an indigenous product which has its roots in a rich and fertile soil".

Cinema had come to India at the same time as the rest of the world and, thanks to Phalke, India kept in step with the world—indeed was ahead of it. Phalke's *Raja Harischandra* was shown seven months before Cecil B. DeMille started shooting *The Squaw Man* and three years before D. W. Griffiths screened *The Birth of a Nation,* both great film classics.

The contrast between the Phalke and Griffiths films could not be greater. Griffiths' film is an unabashed celebration of white racism. The Klu Klux Klansman is the hero of the film, as the subtitle "The Fiery Cross of the Klu Klux Klan" makes very clear, with white actors blacked up to portray blacks as beasts preying on white women. Phalke's work is a study in goodness, resembling the story of Job in the Old Testament. But while Griffiths' film is available in its entirety, the full-length version of Phalke's great work has been lost, although after great effort the Indian National Film Archives did manage to salvage some of the original four reels. It is yet another story of how India creates and then forgets.

But that is in keeping with India's traditions: a land with a rich history but few historians and an astonishing disregard for preserving its own history.

2

The Mighty Banyan Tree

Phalke may have been the first great director of the Indian cinema but the man he invited to a preview of *Raja Harischandra* can lay rightful claim to be India's first movie mogul, and his conversion to films was very similar to that of Phalke. Phalke had been moved by *The Life of Christ*. Jamshedji Framji Madan was so besotted by Phalke's film that he started the first dominant studio system in India and became the master of the Indian film world, comparable in stature to ones in Hollywood. His emergence also set right what was an initial anomaly in the development of the Indian film industry: the absence of major Parsi figures.

As we have seen, less than a month after the arrival of the cinema in India, *The Times of India* had moaned that "our Parsi friends" were not taking an interest. This was uncharacteristic of them. Almost everything of any significance that happened in Indian life from the middle of the nineteenth century to the early years of the twentieth century had enormous Parsi influence, from politics, through business, to entertainment. If the Parsis collaborated with the British, then the early leaders of the Indian Congress which led the freedom movement against the British, were also predominantly Parsis. They were the ultimate middle-men. Slow as the Parsis may have been to get off the mark in the new medium, they were quick to catch up and were soon centre stage adding a third C, to their already established dominance in the other two C's: Commerce and Cricket.

No one did this with more style and authority than Madan, who combined both the Parsi business acumen, which had made them the first Indian bourgeoisie, with the well-known Parsi love for the theatre.

Long before Madan was born, Parsi Theatre was well established in Bombay. In 1836, twenty years before Madan was born, the Bombay Theatre, styled after London's Drury Lane, which showed plays to British soldiers and East India Company officials, had been bought by the well-known Parsi businessman, Sir Jamshedjee Jeejeebhoy. In 1853, Dadabhai Naoroji had helped establish the Parsi Stage Players, which the Indian cinema historian, Bhagwan Das Garga, says helped "determine the shape and structure of popular Indian theatre and later of the Talkie film". A decade before Madan's birth, the Grant Road Theatre was set up. While it was owned by a Hindu, the businessman, Jagannath Shankarshet, the performers were mainly Parsi amateur troupes putting on plays in English, Marathi, Gujerati and Hindi. When Madan was a year old, Jeejeebhoy started the J.J. School of Art in 1857, the same year as the Great Revolt very nearly brought an end to British rule in India. Madan was barely in his teens when Kaikushroo Kabraji established Victoria, the first professional Parsi theatrical company. It was Kabarji who first staged Ranchodbhai Udayram's play *Raja Harishchandra,* which Phalke brought to the cinema and which, in turn, inspired Madan to venture into films.

Madan brought to the films many of the traditions of the Parsi theatre. "The dominant theme of the Parsi theatre," writes Ashish Rajadhyaksha and Paul Willemen in *The Encyclopaedia of Indian Cinema,* "were the historical, the romantic melodrama, and the mythological, with a major influence being the seventeenth century Elizabethan theatre, especially via translations, and adaptations of Shakespeare, a tradition that fed into film....The Anglophile Parsi repertoire's classicism, comparable to academic naturalism in the visual arts, substantially determined the transformation of classic and popular music into urban stage (and later recording) modes, as transition assimilated into the early sound cinema."

The traditions of this theatre had been drilled into Madan from a very early age. He had, himself, started as an actor at the tender age of 17 when, in 1873, he performed in Nusserwanji Parek's *Sulemani Shamsher,* along with his brother Pestonji. Another brother, Khurshedji, was a partner in the original Victoria Theatrical Club. By the 1890s, Madan, who was a shrewd businessman, with interests that covered insurance, property, pharmaceuticals, the import of food and drinks, and film and film equipment, bought the Elphinstone and the Khatau-Alfred, two of the most prominent Bombay theatrical companies. Madan also bought their creative staff and the rights to their repertoire. But his emergence as India's first movie mogul came in 1902, when he made the cross-continental journey to Calcutta on the east coast. It was a bold move and showed the strategic sense of the man.

For a Parsi to leave Bombay for Calcutta in the early part of the twentieth century was an unusual move. Bombay then was at the heart of Parsi commercial and cultural activity; such was their dominance of Bombay business that they more than matched the British business houses of the city. Indeed they did much to lay the foundation of modern Bombay. In contrast, there were very few prominent Parsis in Calcutta and British business reigned supreme there. But Madan sensed that as the capital of British India it offered better prospects for this new medium and so it proved.

Madan's rise in Calcutta generated many colourful stories suggesting it was a rags to riches effort. One of them was that he had been a prop boy at Calcutta's Corinthian Hall, which he later owned, another that, in 1902, having purchased film equipment from an agent of Pathé Frères, he launched a bioscope show in a tent at Calcutta's Maidan.

More credible is the theory that Madan was a fairly substantial businessman when he came to Calcutta, and only got into film-making in 1905 when he presented Jyotish Sarkar's documentaries, such as *The Great Bengal Partition Movement* at the Elphinstone Picture Place, the first of many Madan-owned film theatres. Two years later he added the Minerva and the Star to his collection and through the 1910s his expansion was so relentless that by the end of the decade he had thirty-seven theatres.

Madan's skills lay in shrewdly exploiting the particular Indian conditions he had to operate under. So, well aware of the apartheid the Raj had imposed in Indian cities, he bought or leased cinemas in Calcutta's white town, what the British called the European quarters of the city—the British in India always classified themselves as Europeans, emphasising that they were a white ethnic group and their clubs, railway carriages, and other places that excluded Indians, invariably did so under the banner 'Europeans only'.

Madan appreciated that the cinemas in the European part of the town were often not only in better condition but could charge higher ticket prices, catering to the British armed forces stationed in the city, as also other Europeans and Anglo-Indians. Indians too were attracted to his cinemas, with Satyajit Ray happily going to a Madan Theatre, but not to a theatre in the Indian part of town.

While larger crowds turned up for Indian films, and also made the exhibitors of films more money, Madan was very aware of the snobbery of his fellow Indians which was openly broadcast when an exhibitor was questioned by the Indian Cinematograph Committee in 1927. The exchange between the committee members and the exhibitor went as follows:

> The type of people who like Indian pictures, their way of living is quite different and generally they chew betel leaves. Let me give you an example. I did show an Indian film, *Lanka Dahan,* and I made Rs. 18,000 in a week. But it ruined my theatre altogether.
> Q. You mean you had to disinfect the cinema?
> A. I had to disinfect the hall and at the same time I had to convince the audience that I had disinfected it. Till then I went on losing money.

The Indian public was discovering the cinema and there were various ways of experiencing this new phenomenon. Madan's fellow-Parsi, a Bombay resident, J.B.H. Wadia, of whom we shall hear much more later, describes the experience of going to the cinema in the 1920s:

> At the theatre, our strategy could not have been bettered by, say, a military officer. Kot would keep his wallet intact, so as to frustrate the likely *legerdemain* of a nearby pickpocket. Jehan would buy three tickets for us. My job was to run up to the main door of the third class and manage to push my way forward by hook or by

crook. The doors would be immediately thrown open after the entire audience of the previous show had gone out. Then there would be a veritable stampede of cinemagoers in the auditorium. Then I would try to secure the best seat possible on the wooden benches by laying myself prostrate on one of them. This was the accepted technique for reservations of seats in those days.

However, it was a very different world for the affluent classes, as Wadia again recounts:

The élite in balcony and box received VIP treatment in several first rung cinema houses. The doorkeeper would enter pompously, as if he was a superstar, coming onto the stage from the wings, holding a silver Pigani (spray) of rose water in his hand, and would then walk from one end to the other, sprinkling it liberally on and over the occupants who would go into a fitting reverie as if they had been supplied with hashish. Those enterprising Parsi exhibitors, the Wellington Brothers (Seth Rustomji and Seth Ruttonshah Dorabaji), would even present rosebuds to each of their regular patrons; and in the splendid Indian way of life not only enquire of their health but also of the entire family.

While most theatres apparently had two or more showings a day, one theatre gave twelve during melas festivals. Prices were generally in three or more classes ranging from 2 or 3 annas to 2 rupees. In cities, the top price might be 3 rupees for box or sofa seats. In the lesser cinemas, the lowest price could be 1 anna for ground seats.

The Indian Cinematograph Committee, which went round the country in the late 1920s inquiring into the state of the cinema, and has left us a fascinating insight into the Indian cinema world of the 20s, questioned theatres ranging from the Madan chain to the mofussil theatres in small semi-rural towns, and found that the mofussil [small town] theatres were in a sorry state: the lowest class of spectator had to squat on the ground and the benches and chairs in the other classes were in wretched condition and infested by bugs. There was no proper ventilation and most of the theatres were merely corrugated tin sheds. There was very little open space surrounding the theatre and no garden to please the eye and to attract the public.

The Indian penchant for officials with power, wanting things for free, caused exhibitors many problems with the local authority. "The police, the customs officials, the postal, telegraph and municipal workers, and a host of other people, have to be admitted free to avoid trouble." Women film-goers were scarce, though Hindu mythologicals brought them out in large numbers. During Western films "when a kissing scene is shown, the ladies turn their heads away".

Although this was the era of silent movies, in a country which was more of a continent, with several languages and many illiterates, it was not enough to just project the movie on a screen. Silent movies had subtitles to explain the action and in India this meant that movie houses had to provide people who could read

aloud the subtitles to those who could not read. The result was that films often
had subtitles in three or four languages. A print made for circulation in the north
might have subtitles in Hindi, Gujerati and Urdu; in the south, a print might
have subtitles in Tamil, Telugu and English. As each subtitle came up, a rumble
would sweep over the audience as people who could read proclaimed the words
for those who could not. A few theatres had official readers.

One of the theatre-owners giving evidence was asked whether this meant
cinemas had translators:

> Oh, yes. There is a man always standing there and explaining the film. He is a
> very clever fellow. He knows all about the story. Then, as soon as one scene is on, he
> explains the whole thing in Telugu, because not everybody can read what is on the
> film. He stands there throughout, he is a lecturer.
>
> Q. We were told that such a man is a nuisance.
>
> A. Not at all. He is paid 50 rupees.

Many Indian producers made three prints of films, with ten being the
maximum. The import duty on raw materials was the reason. The shortcomings
of Indian films were often mentioned by several of the witnesses. But what
emerged most clearly was, despite the shortcomings, Indian films were preferred.
One exchange at the inquiry on this subject went as follows:

> Q. You mean that ordinary people—we won't call them illiterate, but not belonging
> to the middle-class—you mean to say that they do not go to those theatres where
> foreign films are shown? Is that what you mean by your answer?
>
> A. Yes, they do not go….formerly they used to go and see fighting or any exciting
> films, or comic films.
>
> Q. Now that Indian films are produced, you think the attendance at foreign films of
> a social nature is falling?
>
> A. Yes.

But despite this, exhibitors found it difficult to show Indian films.

> Q. You find it difficult to get Indian films?
>
> A. Yes, the rates are exorbitant.
>
> Q. Have you ever taken Western films?
>
> A. Yes, they are cheaper than Indian films but they do not attract the same audience
> as Indian films.

Not surprisingly, Madan's theatres mainly showed Western movies and
until the First World War, Madan exhibited largely British films supplied by a
Rangoon-based company.

At this stage, Madan had been following established convention. In the period before the First World War, Indian theatres exhibited an assortment of foreign films, mainly from Europe. India was not unique in this. Most countries then had a big foreign influence, much of it from Europe. In 1910, for example, the features released in Great Britain included thirty-six from France, twenty-eight from the US, and seventeen from Italy, well ahead of the fifteen from Great Britain and four from Denmark, Germany and elsewhere. Before 1914, French cinema was far more developed than American and, in 1907, 40% of all films being shown in the US nickelodeons were from one studio in Paris: Pathé.

The shots in Sarajevo that led to war in 1914 would, quite unwittingly, create a cinematic revolution. It almost stopped film production on the continent, allowing the hills round Hollywood, which had begun to make films just before the war, to take over. With the audience hungry for films, and the new medium considered necessary for morale, American producers were ready to fill the void. The American expansion soon made Charlie Chaplin, Mary Pickford and others, household deities throughout the world, created fortunes, and set the stage for further expansion after the war. By the time the treaty of Versailles was signed, America was the film capital of the world, producing more than 80% of all the films then made.

Trench warfare was over, but a new one was just beginning.

With this American dominance also came a new pattern for film distribution. Britain had portents of what this might mean as early as 1915. The Essanay Company, controlling the most wanted of all films, those of Chaplin, required British exhibitors to take the whole Essanay output, not just the Chaplin films. British producers found British theatres booked up far ahead by block-booking and increasingly unable to absorb the slim output of the British film industry.

If the British, French and other producers were finding it difficult to regain a toe hold in their own countries, they found it completely impossible to regain the pre-war hold they had exercised in the US. Here, vast consolidations were taking place. Theatre chains like Loew's began purchasing studios in order to be certain of a steady flow of films. In 1919, Paramount launched theatre-buying and theatre-building programmes in order to have a secure home market. By 1921, Paramount had 300 theatres and a decade later almost a thousand. Fox and Warner Brothers also bought American theatres by the hundreds; only Universal was a bit more modest. Many theatres which were not bought came under the control of the producers via block-booking contracts. Opportunities for foreign films in the US thus became severely restricted. And with the Americans secure in their homelands, they now wanted to expand overseas.

Indian cinema owners adapted to this new reality, replacing Europe and Britain, in particular, with America as their source for imported films. Soon 90% of all imports to India were from the US and Madan, quickly adjusting to the changing circumstances after the war, began to import films from Metro

and United Artists. The Americans were not slow to sense the potential of the
Indian market. Because they were already financially secure in India, American
films could be offered at lower prices than most other films, including Indian.
An Indian film usually had to recoup around Rs. 20,000, while a distributor
showing an American film, generally paid a fraction of this. In 1927, for example,
an importer of some Columbia Pictures paid as little as Rs. 2000 per feature
for rights in India, Burma and Ceylon. American films usually appeared in
India eighteen months after release, although some came much sooner. *The
Thief of Baghdad,* starring Douglas Fairbanks, seems to have been the biggest
hit. Exhibitors almost never saw films before booking them. Outright purchase
of films—pirated in some cases—was prevalent amongst travelling cinemas, but
others rented them at Rs. 50 a night.

In 1916, Universal had become the first of the American producing companies
to establish an agency in India. By the mid 1920s, it was offering Indian theatres
fifty-two features, fifty-two comedies and fifty-two newsreels per year. Block-
booking seems to have been involved only rarely. Universal appears to have felt
that the Indian market was worth nurturing, patiently, and appeared to have
gained a reputation for being humane. An exhibitor, irate at the demands of film
distributors, declared: "The noblest exception to this statement is the Universal
Pictures Corporation, whose agent in Bombay, and several local managers, are
very considerate to theatre owners."

From fairly early on in the 1920s, American films formed the staple of most
Madan theatres and through the decade Madan Theatres imported many of the
products of American companies, often buying them in wholesale lots to secure
the outstanding big name attractions. In 1923, the year J.F. Madan died, 90% of
Madan theatre films came from the US, the remaining 10% was divided between
Great Britain, Germany and France. Such was the dominance of America that
in 1926-27, only 15% of the features released in India were Indian, 85% were
foreign, mostly American.

The Europeans did try to challenge this American dominance and in the
post-war years, Germany was the first country to strengthen the international
position of its film industry through Government action. This involved lavish
Government investments in studios, equipment and production subsidies. In
the 1920s, the German film underwent a dramatic rebirth, which had its impact
in India, with several Indo-German co-productions, the first of which was *The
Light of Asia* in 1925. German film technicians also came to work in India.

But Madan was not just an importer. He was also keen to make Indian films.
Money was clearly a factor; he realised he could make money from producing
his own movies, but he also wanted to nurture Indian talent. A year after the
end of the First World War, Madan set up Madan Theatres Limited, a joint stock
company which both exhibited foreign films and also started producing Indian
films. The Madan formula for producing films mixed a liberal helping of foreign

technical help with reliance on stories from Hindu mythology. Apart from a number of European technicians, his two most prominent directors were the Italian Eugenio De Liguoro and Camile Legrand from Pathé Studios in Paris. Before the war, Pathé had produced *The Life of Christ* which had launched Phalke, and Italy could claim to be the master of cinematic innovation with Giovanni Pasatrone's *Cabiria* and Enrico Guazzopni's *Quo Vadis.*

Madan's other innovation was that for the first time a genuine female star appeared. In Phalke's *Raja Harishchandra,* and *Lanka Dahan,* the female lead had been played by a man, albeit an effeminate one, but in Madan's films he introduced several female stars, one of whom, Patience Cooper, is widely regarded as the first great female star of the Indian screen. An Anglo-Indian, Cooper had started out as a dancer in Bandmann's Musical Comedy, a Eurasian troupe. Her distinctively Anglo-Indian looks: dark eyes, sharp features, ebony hair and light skin tone, allowed technicians to experiment with the imported technique of eye-level lighting and achieve the Hollywood look, an appearance similar to Hollywood stars of the silent era.

In 1921, De Liguor directed her in *Nala and Damayanti*, a love story from Mahabharata, one of the two great epics of Hinduism, and the following year Legrand directed her in *Ratnavali*, Harsha's Sanskrit classic where Legrand himself played the Prince opposite the Princess, played by Cooper. Three years later, in 1924, Madan Theatres went even further when they shot an entire film in Italy in what is generally considered the first co-production by an Indian film-maker. Based on another Hindu mythological story *Savitri*, where a wife successfully fights Yama, the god of death, for her husband's life, both the husband and the wife were played by Italians, Rina De Liguoro and Angelo Ferrari. The whole film was shot in Rome and when it was released in India, Madan Theatres made much of the fact that there were "scenes taken amidst the world renowned cascades of Tivoli in Rome." It was all quite incongruous and amazing but Madan Theatres knew their Indian audience for the film proved a great success.

The reason for the success of Madan films may be, as Garga says, that the basis of nearly all his films was that they "used mythology as a pretext for spectacle in which scantily clad dancing girls cavorted". By this time, Jamshedji Madan had died; he died a year before the Italian co-production, and control of his cinema empire passed to the third of his five sons, J.J. Madan. The young Madan carried on in the innovative style of his father, introducing the first Wurlitzer organ to India. Its mellifluous tones, as Satyajit Ray recalled, "drowned out the noise of the projector while heightening the drama on the screen." He also expanded the studio's activities, producing a range of films which extended from Indian epics through Persian and Arabic folk tales and historical romances, to modern love stories. This included short films which could often be educational or instructional. One was an unusual operation by a skilled surgeon, another for the Bengal Public Health Service, in addition to films on jute, tea, tobacco, and cotton and travel and newsreel footage. It is not unusual in Indian business for a son of a successful father to ruin the business but J.J. Madan built on J.F.'s legacy and the Madan empire continued to expand. Three years before J.F.'s death, the company had owned or controlled fifty-one theatres; by 1927, four years after the great man had gone, it controlled eighty-five, sixty-five owned and twenty supplied under contract. This grew to 126 by 1931. So dominant a force was it in the Indian cinematic world that it could outbid everyone. Its financial muscle meant it was less affected by the nightmarish uncertainties about foreign film supply that plagued most Indian exhibitors who, in order to get the most desirable films, often had to take foreign films they did not want.

Not surprisingly, Madan's dominance led to charges that it was a dangerous monopoly. But in December 1927, J.J. Madan gave two days of testimony in front of the Indian Cinematograph Committee and appeared to convince the committee members that charges of monopoly against his company were false and that they were simply more alert than the competition.

Soon after, he travelled to the US where, in New York, he saw first hand the effect that *The Jazz Singer*, the first feature-length Hollywood talkie, was having on the audience. He toured Hollywood to examine this revolutionary development and, unlike many others, who felt sound would not work, J.J. quickly sensed this was the way forward. Madan, having caught the fever, ordered sound production equipment and headed back for India. In 1929, Madan Theatres ushered in the talking picture in India by premiering at the Elphinstone Theatre in Calcutta, Universal's *Melody of Love*. This was not only a first for India but for the entire East and his Elphinstone Picture Palace became the first theatre to have permanent sound apparatus. A construction of a sound-proof studio was also started at Tollygunge and an ambitious sound production schedule was planned.

Hand-in-hand with such use of the best available foreign technical assistance and foreign directors, Madan continued his father's tradition of nurturing home-grown talent. Under the Madans, both father and son, many an aspiring young Indian film-maker found a home. A whole host of them worked for Madan theatres, including Sisir Kumar Bhadhuri, Jyotish Bannerji, Priyanath Ganguli, Amrit Bose, Madhu Bose and Naresh Mitra.

The Madans also had a shrewd sense of the essential ingredient required for a good film. So rights were bought up for many of the stories and novels of Bankim Chandra Chatterjee, Bengal's first great novelist, and also Rabindranath Tagore, the greatest literary figure the sub-continent has produced, and the first Asian to win the Nobel Prize for literature. One of Madan theatre's most memorable films was *Indrsabha,* screened in 1932 and based on an Urdu play which had been written in 1853 by Amanat, the court poet of Wajid Ali Shah, the last Nawab of Oudh, and considered a seminal play of the Indian theatre.

The senior Madan's grounding in Parsi theatre had always made him value playwrights and for more than twenty years his theatres employed the Indian Shakespeare, Agha Hashr Kashmiri. A descendant of Kashmiri shawl merchants, hence the surname Kashmiri, although he was more popularly know as Hashr, he had studied Persian and Arabic and, after working in Bombay, came to Calcutta in 1914 to join Madan Theatres. He soon established a reputation as a major playwright and many of his plays were adapted into silent films. He also borrowed from Shakespeare and in *Saide,* Hashr combined two of the bard's plays: *Richard III* with *King John,* the last two acts being taken from this play. As the silent movies gave way to talkies, Hashr turned to screen plays. Such was his prominence that Urdu, the linguistic product of the meeting of Islam and Hinduism, exerted a tremendous influence on early Indian films, both in terms of the language used and the techniques of the Urdu stage. Hashr also introduced an innovation that has remained to this day of having a comic sub-plot in every Indian movie, even if the film itself is far from a comedy. By the time he died in June 1935, at the age of fifty-six, his countrywide reputation was so immense that all studios and theatres closed for the day as a mark of respect.

But as the lights dimmed for an evening to honour Hashr, they were about to be permanently switched off for the company that had employed him. By 1935, Madan Theatres was in terminal decline and could not be rescued. Initially, not many Indians could believe that Madan Theatres could die. The studios had suffered disasters before and survived. In March 1925, two years after the senior Madan's death, a fire destroyed much of the company's production. But it recovered and, as we have seen, by the early 1930s had coped very well with both the coming of sound and colour with Madan Theatres appearing to give every indication that it was ready to face the challenges of the talkies. However, just as the ancient Romans believed that the hour of victory was the most dangerous, so as Madan had made history by screening the first sound film in India, wider events was casting their shadow and making their collapse inevitable.

In the autumn of 1929, soon after the screening of *Universal Love*, New York suffered its spectacular stock market crash. The Madans were already launched on their plans to convert their theatres to sound but the stock market collapse ushered in a world economic depression. The Madans, involved in innumerable enterprises, now found themselves cash-strapped. The size of the business and the casual way it was run now began to tell against the Madans. The Madan Empire, spread through Ceylon, Burma and India, which were then all one territory, had always made efficient supervision forbidding. But in days of plenty, lack of control could be masked; now, with India drawn into the world recession, the Madans paid a heavy price for their poor management.

The conversion of the theatres loomed as a major obstacle and they started reporting increasing losses of revenue. While one aspect of it might have been a drop in audience attendance, the main reason was that with the collaboration of paid inspectors and theatre managers, attendance figures were being misreported and profits siphoned off. In 1931, J.J. Madan started selling off the vast empire. Once the decision was taken, properties were disposed off very rapidly. In less than two years, the empire of 126 theatres had dwindled to just one, Calcutta's Regal cinema.

Madan still wanted to hold on to the idea of producing films and was keen to make the first Indian talkie. His hopes rested on a movie called *Jamai Sashti*, a Bengali comedy, and also on *Shirin Farhad*, a big budget musical. He did not quite achieve that, being beaten by a bare three weeks by a film produced by a Bombay rival. However, Madan did became the first Indian production company to release a whole programme of sound films. On March 14, 1931, the same day that Bombay saw the first Indian talkie, Madan Theatres put on thirty-one such films. They included a hymn chanted in Sanskrit by "lady worshippers at the Temple of Siva," a girls' chorus singing a Tagore song, a dance by the Corinthian girls, a recitation of Kalidasa and a speech by the great Indian scientist, Sir C.V. Raman. But, on the same day, in Bombay, Imperial released the first Indian sound feature, *Alam Ara*.

Madan did release *Jamai Sashti*, the first Bengali talkie, and followed it with *Shirin Farhad,* which was considered superior to *Alam Ara,* better produced, more songs and so captivated India audiences that it was said a Lahore tonga-driver—a horse-drawn cart driver—pawned his horse to see the film twenty-two times. In 1931, Madan released eight sound films, some in Bengali, others in Hindu and, by 1932, this had doubled to sixteen. In 1932, Madan also introduced colour to the Indian cinema with the film *Bilwamangal,* where, in a script written by Hashr, Patience Cooper played a courtesan with whom Bilwamangal falls in love. While the film was processed abroad, Madan's foreign technicians based in Calcutta also worked on the film and it was widely advertised as the "Madan Colour Process."

But all this could do little to stop the relentless haemorrhaging of money from the business. 1933 saw a slow-down in film production and the following year the studio was offered for rent and then finally sold. By 1936, India's first answer to a system comparable to Hollywood was history. To make matters worse, but an all-too common story in India, Madan Theatres left behind nothing tangible to recall its glories. As Garga says "not a single film to be remembered by, because studios wilfully, or through neglect, destroyed their old films, printed on inflammable nitrate stock."

Today, the rise and fall of the Madan Empire is a forgotten story, its main memorial a street in the heart of Calcutta, and its main offices now home to the Anti-Rowdy Section of the Calcutta Police. Yet its contribution to the growth of Indian cinema is undeniable. It had brought Hollywood's studio system to India, an integrated method of production, distribution and exhibition, with the collection from the box office financing Indian movies. Over the years, India was to move away from this Hollywood system but, in the early years of the cinema, it was immensely useful to have Madan. Without Madan Indian cinema might not have taken off quite so quickly.

3

Growing Under the Banyan Tree

The Madans were like a giant banyan tree; while it was dominant, under its shade, others could grow, and the story of Dhiren Ganguly, also known as Dhirendranath Gangopadhyae, or D.G., shows how some of the early pioneers of the Indian screen, first with silent movies, then talkies, developed.

Ganguly was born in 1893, in Calcutta, in a house where Satyajit Ray's grandfather, Upendrakishore Rowchowdhury, was also a tenant. He studied at Calcutta University and then went to Santiketan, the university Tagore had set up in a rural idyll near Calcutta, to study arts. After qualification, Ganguly got a job in Hyderabad as headmaster at the Nizam's art college. The Nizam of Hyderabad, who ruled a state larger than France, was considered one of the richest men in the world, but with a reputation for being a miser and whose harem was a subject of much rumour and legend. Ganguly had little contact with the remote autocratic ruler and his task could not have been onerous for he found time for other projects and in 1915 published a book of photographs, *Bhaber Abhibaktae*. In this he himself appeared in a number of roles as men and women of all ages, and all segments of society. In some photographs he appeared in several guises. For example, in one he was an orator on a soap box, as well as each of the four people listening. The book provided an outlet for his rich satirical sense and was immensely popular. It also helped launch his film career and brought him to the notice of the Calcutta Police. They were very impressed with the way Ganguly could don disguises and employed him to train detectives in the art of disguise. Decades later, he was recalled to give similar advice to the police of independent India.

Ganguly followed this with *Amar Desh, My Country* and two other books. Ganguly sent his first two books to J.F. Madan and the two men met some time in 1918. Madan, as we have seen at this time, was at the height of his powers and immediately showed his shrewdness as a businessman. When he learnt Ganguly had studied under Tagore, and thus knew the great man well, he encouraged him to get Tagore's permission to make a film based on his play, *Sacrifice*. Ganguly had no problems getting the poet's consent.

However, Ganguly, while a very inventive man, could not stick to a plan or idea for long and *Sacrifice* was postponed as, attracted by a another offer, Ganguly now emerged as a rival to Madan. A Calcutta businessman, P. B. Dutt, who had made substantial profits from the manufacture of wooden buckets, wanted to invest in films. He suggested to Nitish Chandra Laharrie, who worked for Madan, to leave Madan and help Dutt form a new group. Ganguly joined this new group which was called the Indo-British Film Company. It consisted of four partners: Dutt, as financier, Laharrie, as General manager, J.C. Sircar, as cameraman, and Ganguly, as dramatic director, which also included writing.

The story that Ganguly wrote, and which was soon being filmed, was quite remarkable. *Belat Pherot, England Returned*, achieved the unlikely dual feat of satirising both the pretensions of Indians returning home from England, trying to behave like Brits with a stiff upper lip, and at the same time the conservatism of those Indians to whom every new idea was an abomination. *The Bombay Chronicle* described it as the story of "a young Indian who returns to his native land after a long absence and is so mightily impressed with his foreign training that, at his parental home, he startled everybody with his quixotic notions of love and matrimony". A still of the picture showed Ganguly dressed as the archetypal Englishman of that time: button downed shirt, tie, the eye glass fixed to a chain, which dangled down his neck, and a pipe in his hand, looking startled as he reacted to some remark of his Indian relations. The film shrewdly balanced its digs at those Indians who were too foreign for India, with those who could not abide anything foreign. Ganguly, who played the leading role, showed such comic ability that he was instantly hailed as the Indian Charlie Chaplin. It is still considered a masterpiece of the Indian cinema and six years later, in 1927 when Laharrie gave evidence to a Government inquiry, he described it as "one of the most successful ever shown in Bengal".

The 4,000 foot film opened in 1921 at Russa, the only theatre not owned by the Madans, and soon earned far more than the production cost of Rs. 20,000 during its three month run. The Bombay rights were then sold to a Bombay businessman for Rs. 22,000. Madan, ever the businessman, overcame whatever feelings he might have had for the men who had left him and quickly bought all the remaining rights.

However, success proved too much for the partners of the Indo-British Film Company. Within a year they had parted company and gone their separate ways. Ganguly married a distant relative of Tagore and returned to Hyderabad but not before enticing several Calcutta technicians to go with him. In Hyderabad, he started the Lotus Film Company under the patronage of the Nizam. Ganguly must have been persuasive for the Nizam even gave permission to use Palace backgrounds for the production of Ganguly's films.

The company set up its own laboratory and within a short time was also operating two Hyderabad cinemas. Ganguly was very busy and soon producing a number of films. Some were comedies in the *Belat Pherot* style like *The Lady Teacher* and *The Marriage Tonic*. There was a mythological film called *Hara Gouri,* while another film, *The Stepmother,* was based on a Bengali play.

But in 1924, Ganguly realised the perils of making films in a land ruled by an autocratic Prince who brooked no dissent. Although the British owned India, not all of India was actually ruled by the British. A third of India, containing almost two-thirds of the population, was ruled by Indian princes who had treaty rights with the Raj governing their external relations, but internally could do pretty much as they pleased. And the Nizam now showed what his internal rule meant.

At one of the Hyderabad Theatres, Ganguly was showing a Bombay produced film, *Razia Begum,* based on a historical story of the only Muslim queen to rule Delhi. In Indian history this period, around the middle of the thirteenth century AD, is known as the Delhi sultanate when, for a time, former slaves became kings. Razia was the daughter of the Slave King, Shamsuddin Iltutmish. She would, herself, marry a former Abyssian slave. The historical tale was made for the cinema. The slave, Altunia, had became a warlord and initially was loyal to Razia. But, then, lured by the chance of becoming king himself, he started a revolt against her and even jailed her. But she then married him and they now joined forces against others threatening her throne. Like all such love stories this was meant to end in tragedy and did with the two lovers perishing in battle. The film was a great success in Bombay. But in other parts of India it had been refused a censor certificate on the ground that it was "immoral, indecent and offensive to Mohammedans". The Nizam, as the great protector of the faith, was furious that it was being shown and, soon after its appearance in Hyderabad, a functionary of the Nizam arrived at the offices of the Lotus Film Company and instructed Ganguly and his associates to leave the Nizam's domain within twenty-four hours.

That very day the two theatres were closed, equipment was packed and families and technicians hurriedly went to the station to take the train out of the Nizam's domains. The quickest way out of Hyderabad was the night train to Bombay and Ganguly made a brief stop there, trying to become a distributor. But he failed and soon Ganguly was back in Calcutta to organise new ventures which brought him into touch with some of the other remarkable people to grow under the Madan Banyan tree. Prominent among them was Debaki Kumar Bose.

Son of an attorney, he was born in Akalpoush, in the Burdwan district of West Bengal in 1898. In 1920, he was busy with his studies at Calcutta University and was to take exams that would make him a Bachelor of Arts, when the Indian National Congress met in a special session in Calcutta. Gandhi was just about to launch his great non-violent, non-cooperation movements against the British, and Debaki was swept into the rising tide of Indian nationalism. The following year, when Gandhi gave the call for Indians to boycott British institutions, young Debaki left college. His father, an eager collaborator with British rule in India, was furious and cut him off and Debaki went to Burdwan and opened a stall in the bazaar, selling napkins. He also became the assistant editor of a Congress weekly, *Sakti.* For some years he made a living by whatever means he could.

This was what Debaki was doing when, some time in 1928, Ganguly arrived in Burdwan to sell shares in the British Dominion Film Company, the new company he was setting up. A physician who invested in the company told Ganguly that Bose might be an interesting recruit. Ganguly met Bose and suggested he write a script. Bose sent him the script of *Flames of Flesh,* which eventually became the first production of the British Dominion Film Company. Debaki Bose started working for the company at Rs. 30 a month and, besides writing the first feature, he also played the leading role.

Despite his problems with the Nizam, Ganguly had not lost his touch with Indian princes. He soon became friendly with the Maharaja of Jaipur who allowed him to use the famous Amber Place as the background for the *Flames of Flesh,* and also loaned horses and elephants. Several dozen people travelled to Jaipur for the filming. When the film opened in Calcutta, Debaki Bose sat behind the screens directing a group who made sound effects of crowds and horses hooves. It was the beginning of a career that would span decades. A devout Vaishnavite, he used the medium of film to express love. He said "only love can bring about fruitation in all human efforts, including the making of films". As we shall see, the sound film, especially through its resources of music, was to give him the opportunity to emerge as one of India's most notable directors, though in the end he despaired of the way the industry had developed.

The same year that Debaki Bose was born so was another man, who would also have a tremendous impact on early film-making in India, except that he was born more than 1200 miles away on the west coast of India, and his achievements brought the spotlight back to Bombay. Unlike Bose or Ganguly, his senior by five years, his entry into films was more by accident but he was helped by the fact that economic changes brought about by the First World War had had a huge impact on Bombay, generating much money, some of which came into the film industry.

The film-maker was Chandulal J. Shah, who was born in 1898, in Jamnagar, not far from Porbander, Gandhi's birthplace. He studied at Sydenham College in Bombay and prepared for a career in business. After graduation, while looking for a job, he worked for a time with his brother D.J. Shah, who had written mythological films for several rising Bombay producers.

It was a time of tension and hunger but also of enterprise. The First World War had stimulated Indian business and industry. Before the war, the British had generally discouraged Indian enterprise. As a colonised country, India's purpose was to provide raw materials and a market for British goods. But the First World War forced changes. The strain on British manufacturing made it desperately important that Indian industrialisation be speeded up. An Indian Munitions Board was set up in 1917 to make India in large measure "the arsenal for the allies in the Near East." India thus became an expanding source of steel rails, clothing, boots, and tent and jute goods. All this brought economic expansion to various areas, especially to the port of Bombay. Some of this money now began to come into the infant film industry. Business had always invested in films; Phalke had got money from a textile manufacturer who funded Hindustan Films; Jagdish, another new company of this period, was funded by a cotton merchant, while Calcutta Eastern Films Syndicate was launched with money from a hair oil manufacturer. Among the Bombay investors, were the owners of theatres who were, by now, competing vigorously for new films, especially the better Indian films.

In 1924, Shah had got a job on the Bombay Stock Exchange and settled down to a life of commerce, which is what he wanted. But the following year he heard that the Imperial Theatre was desperate for a film to be launched in the week of the Muslim Festival of Id. This was still a month away and Shah, aided by his brother's reputation and by his own vague association with his brother's mythological films, offered to have a film ready. The theatre agreed to advance Rs. 10,000, half the usual budget for a 6000 feet long Bombay feature of that time. Within a few days, shooting for the film started. After a couple of weeks, the theatre made enquiries regarding the progress; Shah assured them that the movie would be ready in time. It was now that the theatre manager learnt that Shah was not making a mythological, but a story set against a modern background. He was sure that a modern Indian story wouldn't run and kept pleading for a mythological which would at least run for a month. But by then it was too late to start again. Shah delivered the movie, called *Vimla*, within the deadline and later in an interview recollected that it ran for ten weeks.

The following year, a similar crisis confirmed Shah as a film producer. He was watching a matinée at Bombay Opera House when he was called from his seat. The call was from his solicitor friend, Amarchand Shroff, on behalf of the Kohinoor Film Company. Set up by Dwarkadas Sampat, who kept a tiger for a pet, the film company had by then an extraordinary history and several rebirths. Sampat was nothing if not brave and ingenious. He was always willing to experiment, always willing to dare. In one film, *Sat Ansuya,* he had introduced a naked lady, Sakinabhai, which somehow got past the censor although when another film, *Bhakta Vidur,* touched politics and, in particular, the struggle against the British for India's freedom, the censors banned it. Then, in 1923, there was a fire which destroyed all the negative materials of the films and Sampat, who had turned some of the spacious grounds of the studio into a zoo, watched the flames billowing up accompanied by his pet, a young tiger. However, by 1926 Sampat, helped by Eastman Kodak, had regrouped and brought together several new directors, including Homi Master. It was problems with Master that had led to the summons to Shah.

Homi Master had fractured his ankle and in his agony kept asking for Shah. That evening Shah visited Master at the hospital. The latter took a script from under his pillow. He told Shah that the script was his life's ambition, the climax of his career and told Shah to finish it. Shah refused at first but was told that the beautiful

Miss Gohar was starring in it. Though he had no interest in the love story, he was certainly interested in the heroine and with the deadline twenty-one days away, he undertook to fulfil the contract with Imperial. He wrote in a new situation and started work the next day. He worked every day and, as footage became available, edited at night. In what would soon become the great film traditions of Bombay, he finished before the deadline, despite running a 104° fever.

The film *Typist Girl* featured not only Gohar but also an Anglo-Indian girl, Ruby Meyers, who later became famous as Sulochana and has been described as the first sex symbol of the Indian screen. This was followed the next year by *Gun Sundari* ('Why husbands go astray'), the script for which was written by Shah and was a milestone in the rise of the Indian social movie. Indians were just about getting used to social movies. Tackling as they did contemporary problems, they were disturbing to some, and exciting to others, but path-breaking nonetheless. The plot of *Gun Sundari* was astonishingly modern. The film dealt with a married couple. The dutiful wife slaves at home the whole day and, later at night, when the husband comes home brings the household problem to the bedroom. The husband, already burdened with work, does not want more problems and thus turns towards a dancing girl. One evening, when he is dressed to go out, the wife asks him where he is going and he says nowadays the wife doesn't ask the husband such questions. A week later she, too, is dressed, and the husband gets a similar reply. The message was that the wife need not be just a dutiful woman, but was also a companion. In 1934, Shah was to remake it as talkie in three different Indian languages and each time it was a box office success. It also began for him an association with Gohar, which was to last throughout a long professional career.

These two movies put the social movie on an equal footing with the mythological, at least for urban India. But Shah's success created jealousy and he left Kohinoor, along with Miss Gohor, first for Jagdish Films, where he made four films and then formed his own company, Shri Ranjit Film Company, with finance from Vithaldas Thakoredas. Ranjit made films for over three decades. In three years between 1929 and 1932, and the arrival of sound, Ranjit produced more than thirty films. The arrival of sound changed many things, and made Ranjit for a time even bigger. In the 1930s, it employed so many stars that it boasted, "There are more stars in Ranjit than in heaven." Shah in time would become a leading figure of the Indian film industry, the first President of the Film Federation of India, arrange both the Silver Jubilee and Golden Jubilee celebrations, and lead a delegation to Hollywood. But he never lost his love for the stock exchange or the horses. This would prove his undoing. By the time he died in 1975, not only was the Indian film industry very different to the one he had reluctantly entered – due to an accident to a director – but Shah was so poor that he was reduced to travelling around Bombay on buses and trains.

The stories of Ganguly, Bose and Shah showed how quickly things moved in those days of the Indian cinema, how individuals came together, and how new units where formed in which individuals from older companies were brought together by new capital. But there were many others who dreamt the cinematic dreams of Ganguly, Bose and Shah but did not get the chance to realise them; men who fell by the wayside, and they number in their thousands. Without sufficient funds, equipment or talent, they could not survive the vagaries of filmdom, a story that would be repeated often over the decades.

In 1926, the year Shah made *Typist Girl,* another Bombay film-maker launched a new film company which not only achieved legendary status as a producer of silent movies, but also had the notable distinction of making the first Indian talkie. This film-maker was three years older than Shah and working not many miles away from him. He can claim to have made a bigger impact and be a true giant of the early Indian screen, comparable to Phalke and Madan.

Ardeshir Irani, a Parsi like Madan, was born in 1885, and started out in his family business of musical instruments. But he grew restless, and went into the distribution of foreign films before joining tent showman, Abdulally Esoofally, in buying the Alexandra cinema in 1914; he then built the Majestic Cinema, four years later. Exhibition profits edged the partners towards production. After involvement in several other companies, they launched the Imperial Film Company in 1926 and built a studio for it on Kennedy Bridge, near Bombay's Royal Opera House. By the time the silent era had ended, it had produced sixty-two films. But its claim to history is that in 1931 this company won the Indian talkie race by releasing *Alam Ara* at Bombay's Majestic Cinema on 14 March 1931.

The conditions for making the movie could not have been more discouraging. The equipment Irani obtained from the United States was virtually junk; it was a single system Tanar recording system, unlike the later double system which allows for separate negatives for picture and sound. It also involved hiding microphones, as Irani later recalled to Garga, in incredible places to keep them out of camera range:

> There were no sound-proof studios... we preferred to shoot indoors. Our studios were located near a railway track, with trains passing every few minutes, so most of our shooting was done when trains ceased operations.

This style of film-making, making it up as you go along, had quite astonished Wilford Denning, the American technician who had come to Bombay to put the equipment together. He also gave some impromptu lessons to Irani and his assistant, Rustom Bharucha. A year later, in June 1932, Denning, interviewed about his experiences by the American Cinematographer, could barely conceal his wonder that in the conditions prevailing at Imperial, a sound picture got made:

> Film was successfully exposed in light that would result in blank film at home, stages consisted of flimsy uprights supporting glasses or cloth roof or covering. The

French DeBrie Camera, with a few Bell & Howell German makes, completed the
list of photographic equipment. Throughout, the blindest groping for fundamental
facts was evident. The laboratory processing methods, with sound in view ... were
most distressing, and obviously the greatest problem.

Alam Ara has never been described as an artistic triumph and not a single reel
has been preserved. Many of those who acted in this first Indian talkie have long
been forgotten except one, Prithviraj Kapoor, whose Kapoor clan would became
the first family of the Indian cinema and spawn four generations of Kapoor,
many of whom are still very influential in Bollywood.

The origins of the film, reflecting Irani's background, were in a Paris theatre,
where it had been a successful stage play. The story was a familiar one, dealing
with a king who had two wives, the wicked one who was childless, while the
good wife bore him a son. The machinations of the wicked queen, and how they
are ultimately defeated, leading to a happy ending, formed the plot. But if, as
Garga says, the plot was "banal", its impact was astonishing.

Irani's partner, Esoofally, would later recall the electric excitement this first
Indian talkie produced:

> Imagine our surprise when we found that on the day of the release, surging
> crowds started gathering near the Majestic Cinema right from early morning, and it
> was with considerable difficulty that we ourselves could enter the theatre. In those
> days the queue system was not known to film-goers and the booking officer was
> literally stormed by jostling, riotous mobs, hankering to secure—any how—a ticket
> to see a talkie in the language they understood. All traffic was jammed and police
> aid had to be sought to control the crowds. For weeks together, tickets were sold
> out, and black-market vendors had a field day.

The black-market price saw four anna tickets being sold for Rs. 4 or Rs. 5, a
colossal hike, and this was repeated when units went on tour with the film and
drew huge crowds outside Bombay.

For the audience, the defects of the movie did not matter. To many it proved
that India, too, could produce talkies, and as one admiring viewer put it, if the
recording of sound was not quite perfect that was only "due to the inexperience
of the players in facing the microphone and a consequent tendency to talk too
loudly."

Irani, who, six years after *Alam Ara,* also produced the first Indian colour
film, *Kisan Kanya,* had great faith in India's capacity to make sound films. He
was keen that the Government should ensure that 50% of all films shown were
Indian ones and was convinced that India could progress in the cinematic world,
not by importing foreign talent, as the Madans had done, but "by sending our
young men abroad."

Irani's faith in India's capacity to make talkies was soon being justified. The year he released *Alam Ara,* twenty-two other Hindi films appeared and all seemed to have made money. Also in 1931, three films in Bengali, one in Tamil and one in Telugu, appeared in their respective language areas. The next year brought eight films in Marathi, two in Gujerati and the following year seventy-five Hindi features were produced. Virtually all the films made money.

By 1933, trepidation over the coming of sound had given way to unbounded optimism. That year, the compiler of *Who is Who in Indian Filmland,* in a jubilant preface, gave expression to this sense of unexpected Indian achievement:

> What with scanty resources, stepmotherly Government aid, with keen competition from privileged foreign films, with few technically- qualified men, with no interested capitalists, with less interested fans, with actors and actresses scarcely able to spell their names, with no market except India, with censuring censors, with discouragement to the right, cheap sneers to the left, despair in front, and criticism from behind, the Indian film industry, thank God, has marched on and on to the field of victory, battling against a thousand other misfortunes. Has she not made a giant stride?

The arrival of sound had also brought song and dance—in part derived from a tradition of folk music-drama—and this played an important role in winning for the sound film an instant and widening acceptance. As the 1938 edition of *The Indian Cinematograph Year Book*, noted, "With the coming of the talkies, the Indian motion picture came into its own as a definite and distinctive piece of creation. This was achieved by music."

The reference to music is very important. Initially, there were some in India who were worried by this obsession with music, seeing it as a hazard to script values. As *The Journal of the Motion Picture Society of India* would put it, "Cases of singing before drawing a sword for a fight are not uncommon." But this reliance on music, which in time would make music not only integral to Bollywood movies but also sometimes its master, was in fact a preview of the change that was coming into Indian movies as a result of the introduction of sound. In time, it would lay the foundations for the very distinctive development of Bollywood, taking it away from Hollywood and marking the very different world of the Hindi cinema.

It is interesting to note how in the decade before the arrival of sound the Indian movie industry had not developed its own style and unashamedly copied Hollywood's silent movies, including promoting them as Indian versions of Hollywood movies. The arrival of Douglas Fairbanks' *The Thief of Baghdad* in Bombay, which took the city by storm, lead to much imitation. It is widely seen as Hollywood's most flamboyant silent movie, where Fairbanks leaps and grins, stealing everything except love. Released in America in 1924, it got to Bombay in 1925, and so enchanted everyone that *The Bombay Chronicle* saw it "as one of the permanent features of the city."

As it was being shown in Bombay, Bhogilal K.M. Dave, who had been manager of Phalke's Hindustan Film Company, a former partner of Irani, and a graduate of the New York Institute of Photography, was setting up the Sharda Film Company. Working with Nanabhai Desai, a well-known film-maker, and backed by funds from businessman Mayashankar Bhatt, who had also financed Phalke and Irani, Dave, a master of the camera, made some of the best silent Indian films of this era. He had no qualms about presenting his heroes as India's answer to Hollywood. So Master Vithal, who was an acrobat, but could fence, ride, fight and also play the lover, was billed as the 'Indian Douglas Fairbanks'. He featured in a number of successful silent movies of Sharda. He was also to be the male lead in *Alam Ara,* a performance that won praise from critics. As Erik Barnouw and S. Krishnaswamy have put it, "The drama lay in the transfer to an Indian world of elements of Western life—or, more accurately, of Western film."

The copying of Hollywood did not take place without debate, but this debate was taking place against a wider debate about the entire role of foreign movies in India. What to do with foreign movies was always a problem for the Indian film-makers, all the more so as India was ruled by foreigners who, while never forgetting they were foreigners, also saw India as their eternal possession and not only argued that they were better able to rule India than the natives, but that they knew and understood India better than the Indians, certainly the educated Indians. Not surprisingly these foreigners were keen to maintain their dominant economic position and their moral authority to rule the country. The rise of Hollywood as the major force in world cinema posed a threat on both fronts.

If the early British concern about Hollywood centred round the commercial effect this was having on the sale of British films in India, soon there was an even greater concern about the prestige and moral authority of the white race, so crucial in the Raj's eyes to maintaining its rule in India.

As we have seen, the rise of America as the world's cinematic super-power, was one of the results of the First World War, a war which saw no fighting in India but which had a profound impact on the Indian political world, Indian life and Indian cinema. Although essentially a European civil war, whose causes were mysterious to most Indians, Indians rallied to the help of their British masters both with money and blood. Gandhi, the pacifist, won a medal for his war effort, and Indian money helped pay for the war with £100 million given outright to Britain for the war and £20m-£30m annually for each of the five war years. 1.2 million Indians were part of the war effort, 800,000 of them as fighters, with Indians fighting on the Western front, in Gallipoli (where they did better there than the Australians and the New Zealanders), East Africa, Egypt, the Persian Gulf, Mesopotamia, Persia and the Trans-Caspian and Caucasian regions south of Russia, either defending the empire or extending it. Indian troops were decisive in the battles of the Middle

East and the creation of modern day Iraq owes much to Indian soldiers and, for a time during the British occupation in the 1920s, the rupee was the currency of that country. The end of the war also brought untold suffering to India, resulting in the biggest collateral damage of the war. Towards the end of the First World War, influenza broke out in the trenches. The Indian troops fighting there caught the disease and carried it back to India. But the war had made the British denude India of doctors and, as the returning Indian soldiers spread the disease, there was little or no medical care available. Sixteen million Indians died, almost double the numbers killed in the battlefields of the war.

Political India emerged from the war expecting the British to grant them the sort of self-dominion they had granted their white colonies. But India, a brown country, was to be treated very differently. Less than six months after the war ended, General Reginald Dyer ordered his troops to shoot an unarmed crowd of Indians that had gathered in an Amritsar garden, killing nearly 400 and wounding more than 1500, including women and children. For good measure, he forced Indians to crawl on their bellies through a street in Amritsar and had many Indians whipped. It was the worst atrocity committed by the British in the twentieth century. After that, any chance of Indians trusting the British to behave decently was gone. Tagore gave back his knighthood and Gandhi turned from a collaborator to being the greatest rebel the empire had ever seen, launching the first of his civil disobedience movements to free his enslaved countrymen.

The horrible killing-stick General Dyer had wielded had been followed by a carrot of sorts. Two years after the Amritsar massacre came the reforms of 1921 which put into place a certain amount of democratic machinery at the local level. Indians could now run the Calcutta Corporation and, in certain provinces, some departments were transferred to Indian control, in various others British officers, for the first time, worked under Indian ministers. However, these measures were combined with others, which left real power in the hands of the British Government. The system was called dyarchy and, while the essential super-structure of white supremacy was not altered, the changes reflected the paternalism of the Raj, a desire for the father, who knew everything, trying to instil some of his vast knowledge into a difficult child and get him to accept some rules of decent, civilised behaviour.

But this was where Hollywood posed such a threat to the Raj. For at a stroke it threatened to change the very ideas of what had been presented as the great virtues of white, Western, civilisation. The cornerstone of the Raj was the belief in the prestige and higher moral authority of the white races, considered essential for the continuance of white rule in India. India, after all, had only a few thousand Britons ruling a country of nearly 350 million. This could survive as long as the natives believed that the white man was always right. To control the Empire, the mystique of the white Sahib had been built up: whatever happened, all dark skins paled in front of that solitary white one. In some ways, an even greater mystique of the white woman was built up. In the British Raj, not only was the white woman put on a pedestal, but every effort was made to ensure no Indian in a public place ever saw a white woman unless she was dressed in a manner considered suitable for her status as the high priestess of the Raj. Nirad Chaudhuri, in his autobiography *Thy Hand, Great Anarch!,* describes how in 1925, when he went to Puri, a seaside resort on the Bay of Bengal, he was told off for walking too near a beach where some white women were swimming:

> It should be kept in mind that in those days swimming costumes were not what they are today. Nonetheless, a policeman was standing there to protect the modesty of these white women from our gaze. This man came up to me and said that when the MemSahibs are bathing no Indian was allowed to walk on the beaches or be within observable distance. So I must go up to the roads above. Of course, I had to.

Anything that undermined the supposed superiority of the white races in the eyes of their brown subjects was considered very dangerous. Indians watching Hollywood movies could see that the whites, back in their own homelands, did not quite behave as their British masters said they did and this alarmed the officials of the Raj. In 1922, H.L. Stephenson, the chief secretary to the Government of Bengal, discussing the need to tighten censorship of American films, wrote about scenes in which, 'white men and women [are] shown in a state of extreme drunkenness in order to portray the degradation caused by drink. Such scenes do not convey the moral idea of Western manners and ideals.' In 1926, a well-known Bishop, intimately acquainted with India, in a speech at a conference in England, had warned:

> The majority of the films, which are chiefly from America, are of sensational and daring murders, crimes, and divorces and, on the whole, degrade the white women in the eyes of the Indians.

On October 6, 1927, the day *The Jazz Singer* was released in New York, the Government of India announced the appointment of a committee of enquiry, the Indian Cinematograph Committee. The need to preserve the image of the white man and woman was paramount as the Government explained:

> Letters and articles have appeared from time to time in the British Press asseverating that much harm was being done in India by the widespread exhibition of Western films. We have seen several of these press comments from 1923 onwards. The general trend of them is that, owing to difference of customs and outlook, films are misunderstood and tend to discredit Western civilisation in the eyes of the masses in India. Such criticism was chiefly directed against "cheap American films."

The Indian Cinematographic Committee was instructed to study the adequacy of censorship as practiced in India and the need for stricter measures. But the committee had a dual role. As always with the British and their empire, anxieties about moral values were coupled with commercial considerations. If the Government hoped that the committee would make recommendations to ensure that Hollywood films did not damage the god-like status of the white man, and in particular the white woman, there was also the commercial motive of finding solutions that would help promote British films or what were called Empire films:

> At the same time the question has been raised by a resolution of the Imperial Conference of 1926 whether the various parts of the Empire could take any steps to encourage the exhibition of Empire films. As all Governments of the Empire have been invited to consider this question, it appeared to the Govt. of India that it would be appropriate that it should be examined by the proposed Committee. This extension of the scope of the Committee's enquiry would also enable it to address itself to a question which may have a far reaching influence on the development of the cinematograph in India, namely, the possibility of encouraging the production and exhibition of Indian films.

The year this committee was set up back home in England, efforts had been made to bolster the domestic film industry and try to curb the power of Hollywood. The Cinematograph Films Act of 1927 was described as "an act to restrict blind booking and advance booking of cinematograph films, and to secure the renting and exhibition of a certain proportion of British films, and for purposes connected therewith." For British theatres the quota was to start at 5% and in a few years rise to 20%. Its purpose was achieved with remarkable speed. In 1926, Britain had produced twenty-six feature films. Production rose to 128 in 1929, and to 153 in 1932.

The British did not entirely succeed in fooling Indians as to why this committee had been set up, and many Indians denounced it as trying to preserve the "Policeman's prestige." This led some English newspapers in India to try to convince Indians that the committee could prove beneficial and, indeed, might be a way of getting back against an American writer called Katherine Mayo, who had much outraged the Indians.

In 1925, Mayo had gone to India and written a book called *Mother India*. Mayo's views were what we would now call white supremacist racist, but then were considered mainstream American conservative: hostile to immigrants, blacks, and Catholics, Mayo saw American rule as bringing great benefit to the Philippines and supported the Asian Exclusion Acts, passed to encourage white European immigrants, and discourage darker-skinned people.

Mayo's book was meant to justify British rule in India and argued that the problem with India was not that it was not free, but the awful Hindu religion and, in particular, the Hindu males, who terrorised Hindu women. It later emerged that Mayo had lied in the book about not having had any help from the Raj; indeed she had plenty from the Raj's intelligence agency. The Raj saw the book as a way of attacking the Indian freedom movement and, in particular Gandhi, in America. Gandhi called it "the report of a drain inspector sent out with the one purpose of opening and examining the drains of the country to be reported upon, or to give a graphic description of the stench exuded by the opened drains." Other Indians were so outraged, that in the next two years some fifty books were written denouncing Mayo.

The English-owned *Times of India* decided to invoke Mayo in recommending The Indian Cinematographic Committee to its readers:

> There is no reason why India should take up the cudgels for the white races by banning misleading films. But there is another side to it. Indians feel grateful to English people who expose the wrong perspective of Miss Mayo's catch ha'penny bit of American yellow journalism about this country. English people would be similarly grateful to them for setting their faces against American yellow filmisms, which set a wrong perspective upon Western ways and customs.

The Indian Cinematographic Committee reflected the benign paternalism that the British wanted to project. It consisted of three British and three Indian members. One of the Indians, Diwan Bahadur T. Rangachariar, a prominent lawyer from Madras, was the chairman of the committee. The remit of the committee had been well worded. The phrase "Empire films" was elusive and the committee members were urged to consider both British and Indian films. Gandhi had raised the aspect of the threat posed to India by the West saying, "India's salvation consists in unlearning what she has learned during the last fifty years. The railways, telegraphs, lawyers, doctors and such like have all to go." The committee was now asked to consider whether "such like" did not include "Western films chiefly from America".

The committee had no power to decide, but it could study and report. The committee took this task seriously and it launched a massive study into all aspects of film production, distribution and exhibition in India, public reaction to them and the operation of Governmental supervision. There were hearings in a dozen cities, more than 9,400 miles were travelled, 353 witnesses questioned, 4,325 questionnaires issued, forty-five cinemas visited, thirteen film studios inspected, fifty-seven feature films, including thirty-one Indian films, viewed, and Rs. 193,900 spent.

The committee recorded that its witnesses had included 114 Europeans, Anglo-Indians and Americans, and 239 Indians. Of the Indians, 157 were Hindus and 82 non-Hindus, the latter included 38 Muslims, 25 Parsis, 16 Burmese, 2 Sikhs and 1 Christian. It also noted that it had examined 35 ladies, 16 Europeans and 19 Indians. The findings of the committee were published in May 1928.

Among the film industry witnesses were, apart from Phalke and Madan, many of the early giants of the Indian cinema, such as Dhiren Ganguly, Alex Hague, Sulochana and Himansu Rai, the man who founded one of India's greatest-ever studios. Other witnesses included representatives of American companies, censorship officials and Indian exhibitors.

The problems of Indian film producers were illuminated by many witnesses. Several film-makers were producing, or trying to produce, a schedule of a dozen productions a year. A six week production schedule was considered normal for a feature. Bombay considered Rs. 20,000 a proper budget, although some films had cost more. Calcutta and Madras felt that Rs. 10,000 to Rs. 15,000 was the practical limit. Companies were paying actors between Rs. 30 to Rs. 1,000 per month. The Rs. 30 salary was for extras; average actors got Rs. 200-Rs. 250 per month. A normal star's salary was Rs. 600-Rs. 800, while a few received a bit more.

In Bombay, producers were already beginning to consider Punjabis the most suitable specimen for film acting. Phalke had talked about the looks required for acting, saying that the Punjabi, upper-class Hindu male is the most suitable and this trend continued throughout. Heroines, of course, could be from all over, especially Bengal and the South.

Stars were rapidly becoming idols. One woman star, Sultana, used to receive baskets of fruits from distant admirers. In Calcutta, a few ladies "of better classes" had acted in movies but most producers drew on "prostitute and dancing girls" who had lost their early reluctance to enter the cinema. The committee, concerned about the well-being of the industry, pursued this matter at every stop. One exchange with a witness on this subject went as follows:

Q. Do you think that the present conditions in your studio are satisfactory, and sufficient to attract respectable actors and actresses?

A. Oh yes, we are catering for respectable actors and actresses.

Q. I mean what arrangements are made to house them?

A. We keep the respectable characters in separate rooms and they remain quite aloof from the others.

The relation between the press and cinema also received attention. The committee noted that while newspapers carried critiques of foreign films, there were hardly any of Indian films. And it was very clear that film reviews were not independent critical assessments but puff pieces, masquerading as reviews. An exchange with a Bombay editor went as follows:

If I may frankly confess to you, all newspapers get critique paragraphs typewritten from the exhibitors themselves. That is my frank confession.

Q. In the case of foreign films, they get it from the foreign producers, ready-made?

A. Ready-made, cut and dry, only to be sent down to the printer.

Q. Suppose you criticise a picture honestly?

A. Our trade is so closely interwoven with the interest of the producers and exhibitors that we cannot possibly think of doing so.

The working of censorship of course got major attention. Under the legislation of 1918—the Indian Cinematograph Act—and the amendments of 1919 and 1920, the control of cinemas and the censorship of films had been made provincial "reserved" subjects, and placed under police jurisdiction. In Bombay, Calcutta and Madras, boards of censors had been set up in 1920 to assist the Commissioner of Police in this censorship. A Punjab board had been organised in 1927. Each of these boards could license a film to show throughout India or at anytime "uncertify" it. A film could also be uncertified at any time for any city by its police commissioner or for any province by the provincial authority. As we have seen *Razia Begum,* which had angered the Nizam of Hyderabad, was banned in several cities.

The make-up of the Boards and their procedure reflected the communal balance which the British were so keen to maintain. The Calcutta Board, for example, had a Hindu and a Muslim member, along with a British military man and a British woman. The chairman was the Police Commissioner of the City concerned, and he was always British. The result was that in a British versus India clash, the British members had a majority.

The work of censorship was largely done by two inspectors, an Indian and a Briton. Each film was seen by one Inspector. The board generally certified on his recommendation. If he foresaw problems, members of the board had a look at the film. The paid inspectors, before recommending a license, often asked for cuts from the producers or distributors and quite often this had to do with subtitles. But most producers said little by way of protest.

Indians already had experience of how censorship could work. So, back in 1921, the year Gandhi launched his first civil disobedience campaign, Sampat had run into problems with his film, *Bhatka Vidur.* The main character, played by Sampat himself, resembled Gandhi in appearance and was portrayed as a man who survived the oppressions inflicted on him. But, while the film was a success in Bombay, it was banned by the District magistrate of Karachi, who concluded, "It is likely to excite disaffection against the Government and incite people to non-cooperation." He saw it as "a thinly-veiled resumé of political events in India, Vidhur, appearing as Mr Gandhi, clad in Gandhi cap and *khaddar* (Indian home-spun cloth that he had urged Indians to wear instead of Lancashire cotton) shirt. The intention of the film is to create hatred and contempt and stir up feelings of enmity against the Government." In other cases some censors had banned films for being vulgar and too American.

The European witnesses argued strongly for stricter censorship, particularly of films that were bringing Western society into contempt and undermining Indian respect for Western women.

Indian witnesses also felt that it was essential to have strong censorship in India but their reasons were different. One reason given was communal tension, the other was that many felt that foreign films were encouraging crimes in India. A recent rise in "motor car dacuites" were mentioned by several witnesses. Still others spoke about the "hugging and kissing" in Western films as demoralising. Many favoured censorship of "love scenes".

But there were odd voices in favour of freedom, in particular a spirited statement made by A. Venkatarama Iyer, B.A. LLB., of Madurai who, like many Indians educated in the English system, showed how much Indians relied on British models to argue their case:

> I think every member of this committee believes in the freedom of speech and freedom of opinion. I believe that all must have read John Milton's *Aeropagitica*. I believe also that British citizenship is a thing founded upon liberty. I think that classical works are characteristically great because there is freedom of expression and boldness of conception. Fetters, even though they are made of gold, are still fetters. Censorship is cold, critical, routine-like, and tyrannous and inspires fear in the budding genius to express himself. The business of censor is more to prohibit rather than appreciate a work of art. The very name savours of a sickening restriction, and it is the hand of death if it touches a work of art.

But there were views opposed to this:

> Unduly interfere with the artistic and inspirational development? This is bosh. There is neither art nor inspiration in such pictures. They are gross and vulgar.

In May 1928, the committee submitted its report. As instructed, it made recommendations on:

The adequacy of censorship
Imperial preference

On the matter of censorship, it took a calm tone, expressing the opinion that Indian youth was not being demoralised and that the alarms about the impact of the cinema was exaggerated. It emphasised that many of the expressions of alarm had originated outside the country, and suggested that they had come to a large extent from people motivated by their own special interests and perhaps not fully in touch with the facts. As to the adequacy of censorship, the committee expressed itself satisfied. It made the cautious comment that "too much tenderness is bestowed on communal, racial, political and even colour considerations". It suggested "that over-much tenderness to frivolous objections is more likely to encourage dissensions".

On the matter of "empire films" it noted:

> If too much exhibition of American films in the country is a danger to the national interest, too much of other Western films is as much a danger. The British social drama is as much an enigma to the average Indian audience as the American.

With these words, the idea of imperial preference was pushed aside. But the committee went further. It suggested various measures including a cinema department under the Indian Ministry of Commerce to look after the industry's interest, a Governmental film library, to utilise the educational values of films, a Governmental film finance fund, and a plan to encourage building of cinemas.

But the committee's recommendations were not unanimous. The British members of the committee were under constant pressure from their fellow Britons, or Europeans, as they styled themselves in India. A certain Captain Malins, who was on a worldwide mission to promote British films, had got a resolution passed at a meeting in Calcutta that "the American film monopoly constitutes a menace to India". This had prompted the classic riposte from Rangachariar, the chairman: "If too much exhibition of American films is a danger to national interest, too much exhibition of other Western films is as much a danger."

The result was that the British members penned a dissenting minute, fearing the Government might otherwise have to act on the report. This provided the perfect excuse for the Government of India to completely ignore the report. Not one of the recommendations was enacted into law. However, some of the ideas would be reincarnated many years later by the film enquiry committee set up by Independent India.

The inquiry did have one significant impact. Nearly all the prominent men in the Indian film industry had given evidence. They had heard what George Mooser, the Universal Picture Company representative for South Asia, had told the committee. He had dismissed the idea that India was important for Hollywood, only 2% of Hollywood's overseas earnings coming from India. He was scathing about the primitive film-making techniques used, the poor standards of acting and scenarios, and the wretched standards of Indian films. None of this would have surprised the Indians. What they found more interesting was Mooser's advice: establish an infrastructure similar to Hollywood and create a well-organised distribution network. Ardeshir Irani, and others from Bombay, who heard this advice, clearly took it to heart as they sought to create a studio system in Bombay, similar to the one by then flourishing in Los Angeles.

And, if the inquiry achieved nothing, it had come at a seminal moment for the Indian film industry. The coming of sound not only changed what the audience saw but also the way films were made and Indian cinema, for all the British warnings about the evils of Hollywood, was set to follow the Hollywood model of making films, at least for some time.

Part II

When Bollywood was like Hollywood: The Studio Era

4

Mavericks, Eccentrics, Bigamists

In 1933, a book was published called, *Who is Who in Indian Filmland*. This listed the number of companies that had sprung up, a handful of which still remained. They had come up all over India: Bombay, Calcutta, Kolhapur, Madras, Hyderabad, Lucknow, Gaya, Delhi, Ahmedabad, Peshawar, Secunderabad, and Nagercoil.

In listing the vanished companies, the editor had great fun putting a cryptic comment after the name. For Bombay, it listed Oriental Pictures Corporation (this had a short life), Young Indian Film Company (one picture and then it died), Jagadish Films (defunct), Excelsior Company (shut down), Suresh Film Company (liquidated). For Calcutta, it listed Ganguly's Indo-British Film Company (broke up), Taj Mahal Company (short-lived), Photo Play Syndicate of India (flashed like lightning and as quickly disappeared after their first picture, *Soul of a Slave*).

Many of these enterprises had started with only the sketchiest technical preparation. A few had even started on the basis of correspondence courses given by one or another institute in the US. Some started on the basis of one man's travels and observations abroad. In 1921, a young Indian in London, sought permission to watch production at one of the studios but was asked to pay a premium of £1000, which he could not afford. He travelled to Germany, where he secured the same privilege for a more modest £15. Another had travelled to the US in the hope of making such observations but could not gain entry into the studios, and finally managed it as an extra. And, on the basis of another man's camera experience in the US, a Bombay company was formed which was liquidated after the man died suddenly.

Nevertheless, excited by the medium of film, these enterprises were launched. Their failure, however, made many observers comment that if, during the 1920s, Indian films were getting worse, and not better, then by the end of the decade capital, too, seemed to be drying up.

Amongst exhibitors, too, there was birth followed by a very quick death. The number of theatres in India increased from about 150 in 1923 to about 265 in

1927. This brought a sharply-increased demand for Indian films, a demand which could not be met. The dominance of Madan did not help, and exhibitors were often faced with nightmare uncertainties about film supply and sometimes took foreign films they did not want.

But, despite this, by the end of the 1920s, India was making a hundred films a year and in two years, at the end of the decade, raw film imports increased from 12,000,000 feet in 1927, to 19,000,000 in 1928-29. By the early 30s, despite the mournful list in *Who is Who in Filmland,* there were several Indian film studios which could claim to be like the studios that had begun to dominate Hollywood.

It is important not to exaggerate the similarities of the studio system in the two countries. There was no Indian equivalent of Adolph Zukor. This Jewish immigrant from Hungary, who owned a New York nickelodeon, invested in a film distribution company named Paramount Pictures in 1913, and three years later merged with the Jesse L. Lasky Company, which was producing films in Hollywood. The merged corporation consolidated its production and distribution divisions, and audiences began seeing "Paramount Pictures." In 1919, Zukor floated Paramount on the stock exchange. As Neal Gabler in his book, *An Empire Of Their Own,* says, Zukor "had helped establish the industry's *bona fides* with finance". Paramount's early artists included directors Cecil B. DeMille and William S. Hart, and stars such as Mary Pickford, Rudolf Valentino and Clara Bow. *Wings,* the studio's 1928 release, received the very first Academy Award for Best Picture. And the vast new studio on Marathon Street, in Hollywood, constructed by Zukor and Lasky, has been the home of Paramount since 1926.

The link with finance that Zukor established in America never developed in India. Some of this can be traced to Phalke. The historian, Brian Shoesmith, has identified three eras in the Indian film industry: the cottage industry period from 1913 to 1924, the studio era from mid-1920s to 1940s, and since then up to the present times with the star as the main commodity. At various times the Indian film industry came close to being exactly like Hollywood, the closest being during the studio era of the 30s and 40s. Indeed, as Shoesmith shrewdly observes, while Phalke's Hindustani Film Company had all the trappings "of a proto-studio", this did not represent a stake in the development of the studio era in India. What Phalke developed was a variation of the Hindu joint family, with himself as the patriarch. Phalke was responsible for all aspects of the film-making process and there is little evidence of him developing any sense of continuity or of any of the people who worked for him going on to develop their own companies or products.

More significantly, Phalke's ways of raising money, reflecting the very different circumstances prevailing in India, was not remotely like that of Zukor. Ardeshir Irani was later to say that while Phalke may have started the relationship between finance and film by trying to get funds from traditional Indian sources of money, a relationship that lasted for much of the first decade, he did not pay any attention to the distribution and exhibition side of the film industry. Irani, and

other Bombay film producers, reacted to this and sought to be masters of what
they produced. This led to the rise of the studio system. But unlike America,
no corporate structure of ownership of studios developed and it was largely the
work of individuals.

In our story so far we have already seen the impact studios have made but, in
the overall history of the Indian cinema, three studios of the studio era stand out.
These are Prabhat in Poona, which started in 1929, B.N. Sircar's New Theatres
Ltd, which started a year later in Calcutta, and perhaps, the most evocative of
them all, Himansu Rai's Bombay Talkies, which opened its doors in Bombay
in 1934. Various factors went into the creation of these studios but at the end
of the day they reflected the personal styles of their founders and the fact that
more often in India personality, rather than wider economic or social factors,
direct change.

New Theatres is a classic case in point. The man who founded it could be
said to have had one thing in common with a Hollywood movie Mughal like
Zukor. Zukor had started by owning a nickelodeon. Birendranath Sircar fell
in love with the idea of owning a cinema, while constructing one. He was the
son of Sir Nripendranath Sircar, the Advocate General of Bengal and, later, Law
Member of the Government of India, whose title and position indicated his close
collaboration with the Raj. Young Birendranath qualified as a civil engineer
from London and when he returned to Calcutta he busied himself constructing
various buildings in the city, taking advantage of the construction boom in the
city then. It was while he was constructing a cinema in the city that his thoughts
turned to building one for himself, which eventually led to the creation of a
studio. Ironically, the cinema he built for himself, Chitra, was inaugurated by
Subhas Chandra Bose, then the Mayor of Calcutta, and a radical firebrand. He
wanted freedom from British rule and would escape from the country during
the war to seek German, and then Japanese, help to evict the British from India.
Birendra's father was a political opponent of Subhas but a mentor and personal
friend of Subhas's brother, Sarat, and he often gave financial help to the Boses
when Subhas was imprisoned by the British as he often was.

It was against this complex Indian background of the 1930s that Sircar, having
first formed International Filmcraft, which produced two silent movies, set up
New Studios on February 10, 1931.

Sircar, impressed by *Alam Ara,* acquired Tamar recording equipment and also
got the services of Wilford Denning, who was much more impressed with the
order in Calcutta, compared to the chaos of Bombay and Irani's studios. In the
same issue of *The American Cinematographer*, where he had been so scathing of
Bombay, Denning wrote:

> Calcutta proved a complete surprise...contrasting the rushing, haphazard methods
> of Bombay. Here, I was presented with the nucleus of what has became a real

production, well-financed and with an ambitious programme of producing pictures for India actually comparable to those of the independent Hollywood companies.

Sircar, a kindly man, who loved playing billiards, created a friendly family atmosphere in the studios. Kanan Devi, a leading actress of the time, felt that the studio made everyone feel they were part of one big family. Many years later she would tell Swapan Mullick:

> The studio car collected us in the morning, as if we were on our way to school. We worked the whole day and took music lessons. If there was not much work, some of us would get together for a game of hide and seek or badminton before we were dropped off home.

Sircar's great skill was in spotting and gathering round him talented people. One of them was Ganguly's old friend, Debaki Kumar Bose. Another was P.C. Barua, one of the most remarkable directors in the history of the Indian cinema. Pramathesh Chandra Barua, son of Raja of Gauripur, was born in 1903 in Gauripur, Assam. After graduating in 1924 from Calcutta's Presidency College, the young Prince left on a European tour during which he took interest in the arts, especially films, delighting in the works of René Clair and Ernst Lubitsch. After returning to India, he, like many a son from a rich family, had time on his hands but no idea what he would do with it.

He had innumerable interests and everything came easily. An avid reader and music lover, he was also considered outstanding as a horseman, marksman, dancer, tennis and billiard player—he was billiard champion of Calcutta—and a hunter. In his native Assam he had already bagged several dozen tigers and innumerable boars—although it was said he blanched at the mere sight of a cockroach. He was so scared of cockroaches that he once jumped out of a moving car to hold up a train rather than suffer their presence.

During the dyarchy period, he served for a time by appointment in the legislative council of Assam. But the heady life of Calcutta was what he liked best. He loved driving his Italian sports car at 90mph through the streets of the city and he soon settled there to become involved in the film world. He acted the part of a villain in *Bhagyalaxmi,* made by a newly- formed production company, Indian Kinema Arts. He had also been involved with Ganguly, having made a small investment in Ganguly's British Dominion Films. When the British Dominion Films collapsed, Barua hired Ganguly to work for him. These experiences made film an incurable obsession. Returning to Europe, he got permission to observe production at London's Elstree Studios and then, after a trip to Paris, where he purchased lighting equipment, he returned to Calcutta to form Barua Pictures Ltd., and built a studio. It was Barua Pictures that produced *Apradhi* (The Culprit). This first Calcutta production, using artificial lights, starred Barua, and was directed for him by Debaki Bose. It was a critical success in the last days of the silent film.

Barua could sense that the film world of Calcutta was disintegrating and he clearly wanted to rally around him various talents set adrift by this. The problem was Barua was no more ready for sound than Ganguly's British Dominion had been. His father, the Raja, angered by his son's dalliance with the film world, which upper-class India then considered as very low grade work, not far above being associated with prostitutes, refused to support him financially. The Prince's ample allowance, help from friends and loans, had given him a start, but the company needed firmer financial footing and, in the end, Barua decided to throw in his lot with New Theatres. Sircar was quick to ensure that the Prince had the budgets required.

Barua proceeded to justify Sircar's judgment in a sensational fashion. In 1934, he had directed *Rooplekha,* but it was his 1935 production of *Devdas* that set the Indian cinema world alight and to this day remains an iconic movie. Its status derives not only from the quality of the film but, because of the men Barua involved in the production of the movie, which would go on to have a dramatic effect on Indian cinema for many decades to come.

Based on a novel written in 1917 by the great Bengali writer, Sarat Chandra Chattopadhyay, *Devdas* had been made as a silent movie in 1928 but this first talkie version, adapted and directed by Barua, proved so successful that, as M. and N.K.G. Bhanja put it in their essay, *From Jamai Sasthi to Pather Panchali* it "revolutionised the entire outlook of Indian social pictures". *The Bombay Chronicle* was ecstatic in its review calling it "a brilliant contribution to the Indian film industry. One wonders as one sees it when we shall we have such another." In fact, over the decades that followed, Indians continued to see remakes of this film. In 1936, the film was remade in Tamil by New Theatres and almost every generation of Indian film-maker has made a new version of *Devdas,* some in several Indian languages, including Bengali, Hindi (thrice), Telugu (twice) and Tamil. Some of the biggest names in the Indian cinema have played the leading role and when it was remade again in 2002 , it became one of the most expensive Bollywood movies ever made. All the *Devdas* movies have been box-office hits.

Sarat Chandra's novel of a tragic love affair between a rich landlord's son and a poor woman in rural Bengal had long been a literary classic. The childhood friendship of Devdas and Paro (Parvati) blossoms into love as they grow up. Devdas' father does not approve of the relationship and breaks off relations between the families. Devdas, prevented by his family from marrying Paro, drifts in life, agrees to go away to Calcutta, where he seeks comfort with a prostitute, Chandramukhi, and the bottle, but finally returns to his village, where he dies.

Barua's genius was the way he adapted this very literary novel to the cinema, showing an unexpected and wonderful mastery over the new medium. He used both sound and vision to convey emotions and feelings and there was none of the over-the-top flourishes in showing love scenes that were so common in the Indian cinema then.

Although a romantic-tragedy, the script for *Devdas* achieved a naturalness of tone that was, in its day, almost revolutionary. When Kidar Sharma completed the Hindi version of the Barua scenario, one comment was "This isn't dialogue, this is the way we talk." This was precisely the reaction Barua wanted.

Until then, Indian cinema's dialogue was far removed from the way common people talked. Dramatic literature had long been associated with the language of the courts. Perhaps, for this reason, dramatists in the vernacular tended to write in a florid style, reaching for a remoteness associated with what they perceived the status speech should achieve in film. But Barua had been exposed to European naturalistic trends and wanted to discard such language. He also demanded from his actors a quiet, natural tone. The actress Durga Khote was astonished when she joined New Theatres to find how quietly actors delivered their lines.

There was one other major innovation in Barua's *Devdas*. Its 'tragic' ending was at variance with Indian classical tradition, which permitted tragic scenes to be depicted but insisted that every play could only have a happy ending. Indian drama had nothing to match the concept of tragedy as found in Greek drama. Tragic endings were not used in Sanskrit drama and were even considered to be at odds with the Hindu view of existence. The argument was a life can hardly be interpreted as a tragedy when life is itself a transitional state. But in Bengal, influenced by European ideas, the tragic ending was not unknown both in Bengali literature and drama. Now Barua brought this concept to films. While some Barua productions introduced into Indian films a note of sophisticated humour, his major successes were romantic-tragic dramas.

Barua demonstrated how far ahead of his time he was in having such a tragic ending for his film. Even today, Indians are not always comfortable with a film that ends tragically. As the film director, Shyam Benegal, told me:

> There is no Greek style tragedy. In *Shakuntala* (classic Sanskrit's greatest play), the tragic part is in the middle but it all ends well. Mahabharata has tragic parts but it also ends well. There is no inevitability of tragedy that you can get in Greek drama, that sort of thing we have never had. That does not mean we don't have tragedy. And we do have audiences that love tragedy but there are regional variations. I can give you an excellent example. There was a time in South India when they made two versions of the same film in different languages—Tamil and Malayalam, for instance. The Tamil version would have a happy ending while the Malayalam version would have a tragic climax. It was perceived that Malayalees preferred sad endings while Tamils wouldn't see the film if it did not end happily. Kerala, as you know, has a very high level of literacy (almost 100% by now).

Barua made the film in two languages. In the Bengali version, which was made first, Barua played the lead; in the Hindi remake that followed, again directed by Barua, Devdas was played by a new recruit, Kundanlal Saigal. Both versions were released in 1935.

Saigal had acted before in films and he would act again. He played many a lead role in New Theatres films until the end of the decade but *Devdas* was significant, not so much for Saigal's acting but for his singing. That made him one of the great singing stars of India and introduced a new kind of singing style. In the process, it completely transformed Indian film music.

Saigal, who was born in Jammu of Hindu parents, had always been interested in acting and singing, even playing the female Sita in amateur productions as a young child. But this remained a hobby, while he first worked as a timekeeper for the railways in Delhi and then sold Remington typewriters. It is said that he was so fond of singing that he would burst into song while demonstrating the typewriters, and customers would often ask him to sing before they decided whether to purchase his typewriters. A friend took him to Calcutta and introduced him to Sircar who, impressed with his singing voice, offered him Rs. 200 to join the New Theatres. This was riches for a man who at that time earned Rs. 80 a month lugging Remingtons round the streets.

However, when the songs of *Devdas* were being filmed, an unexpected problem arose for Saigal. He had developed a sore throat. As he began to sing his voice cracked. The recordings were postponed but the sore throat persisted. Finally he tried to sing the songs in a quiet, soft tone. It fitted the acting style Barua wanted, as well as the volume limitations of the microphone and soundtrack being used. So, in the classic way of Indian cinema, quite by chance, was born a singing style that soon spread all over India, and that also resembled what was then a new Western development: the microphone crooner.

Saigal's songs in *Devdas* were made into phonograph records and are still played on radio stations across India. Soon the Hindusthan Recording Company got him to record two other songs, *Jhoolna Jhulao ri* on one side, and *Bhajan Hori ri Brij rajdulari* on the other, and to their delight found they had a winner. The record sold 50,000 copies. Although Saigal died very young, at the age of forty-two, of diabetes, caused by excessive drinking, just twelve years after *Devdas* was made, his voice inspired a whole host of Bollywood singers and he is rightly considered the father of Hindi film singing. Many of the ones who would dominate Hindi singing over the next four decades modelled their singing style on his. Talat Mehmood, who was himself one of the most celebrated singers in Bollywood for almost three decades between the 50s and 70s, when asked who had inspired him said:

> Oh, K.L. Saigal, easily. It was unbelievable how effortlessly he sang, with such *talaffuz* [pronunciation], a beautiful throw of voice and depth of feeling. What voice control! It used to make my hair stand on end listening to him. I could never touch him.

For years, All India Radio would end its morning musical programme with a Saigal song and, as Manek Premchand puts it in *Yesterday's Melodies, Today's Memories,* "this was the way many people started their day, getting out of bed, not to the sound of twittering birds, but to the sound of Saigal's voice".

Saigal, himself, remained a great eccentric, as his colleague of New Theatres, Phani Majumdar, would later recall:

> K.L. Saigal once bought a motor-bike but refused to ride it himself. He actually hired a chauffeur to take him around. Finally, he decided to get a licence, but he could never gain any real mastery over the bike. He was always looking forward to an opportunity to show it off to his friends. The New Theatres Studio was just a few furlongs from the old tram terminus in Calcutta. Saigal would wait at the terminus every morning so he could offer someone a lift. But most of us preferred walking. One day, I asked him to give Pankaj Mullick [a noted music composer], who was just alighting from a tram, a ride. As I reached the studio, there came Saigal chugging away. He was alone. I asked him where Pankaj was, and Saigal looked stunned. He had given Pankaj a lift all right but the man had fallen off the pillion somewhere midway. Not only had Saigal not noticed that his companion had fallen off, but he'd quite forgotten that he'd given Pankaj a lift in the first place.

Saigal's emergence as Hindi cinema's first great singer also coincided with an important technical development that was to revolutionise Indian cinema. In another New Theatres film of that same year, *Dhoop Chhaon* (Sun and Shade), songs were pre-recorded for the first time. Indians call this playback singing and soon Indian films had produced a new twist to the way songs were sung. In the 1930s and 40s, it was the norm for actors and actresses to both sing and act. Saigal played opposite Kanan Devi and both of them also sang. Although Kanan Devi is now known as the "First Lady of the Bengali Screen", she came from a musical family and was in many ways much more of a singer. This ability both to act and sing was common to almost all the actors and actresses of Saigal's era. But within a decade this breed completely vanished, so totally that cinemagoers of today's Bollywood would struggle to believe they ever existed. From the late 40s, just about the time Saigal was dying, the actors and actresses who began to emerge could not sing and did not have to sing. And the singers who took Saigal as their role model, like Talat, could not act and merely sang. They recorded the songs in a recording studio and on screen, actors and actresses mimed these songs while the pre-recorded tape was played.

Not that there was any deception involved. This was not like the scenes in the Gene Kelly musical, *Singing in the Rain,* which shows how a Hollywood actress of the silent era, determined to continue working in talkies despite the fact that she had a dreadful voice, forces a little known but highly talented actress, played by Debbie Reynolds, to voice her lines and even sing her songs while she mimes in front of the screen. In the end her attempt to fool the public is exposed and we have a happy ending with the two characters, played by Gene Kelly and Debbie Reynolds, joyously united.

In Bollywood, once playback singing took hold, it was made clear that the stars were not singing and the playback singers, who were never seen on the screen, became celebrities in their own right through their songs. It marked a major innovation of Indian cinema and another step that would take it away from the Hollywood tradition of making films. Bollywood had created a divide between singing and acting which has never been bridged.

Two other men involved in Barua's *Devdas* are worthy of note. The cameraman was a young Bengali called Bimal Roy. Roy would became a legend of the Hindi cinema, eventually leaving Calcutta for Bombay to became one of the leading directors of Bollywood. Just over twenty years later, he would produce his own version of a Hindi *Devdas*. This 1956 version contributed to the rising fame of its two stars, Dilip Kumar and Vyjayanthimala.

The songs for *Devdas* which Saigal had sung were written by Kidar Sharma. A decade later; now a film-maker, his film *Neel Kamal* introduced Raj Kapoor and Madhubala to the screen, two of the greatest names of Bollywood.

Barua went on to make numerous films but *Devdas* was his defining film and in Indian cinema he is always referred to as the man who made the first *Devdas*.

Barua wrote most of the screen plays he directed. He left notebooks full of carefully-pencilled notes, plots, and character sketches. Many seem to have been projections of his own concerns and conflicts and he seemed deeply anguished by the dilemmas of his native land, its almost unbelievable extremes of wealth and poverty, of spirituality and cruelty. His plots often touched on these dilemmas but in the end were constructed to evade any dramatic confrontation.

An example was *Adhikar*, voted by the Film Journalists Association as the best film of 1938. Besides writing and directing it, Barua appeared as Nikhilesh. The story tells of Radha, a girl of the city slums, who longs for wealth and happiness. When she learns that she is the illegitimate daughter of a rich man, whose only daughter, Indira, born of wedlock, is living in utmost luxury, she goes to Indira and claims half her father's estate. Indira, shocked at what she learns, gives her shelter and money. Not content with this, Radha now brings about an estrangement between Indira and her fiancé, Nikhilesh, and then persuades her half-sister to give her the whole of their father's estate. However, her unscrupulous ways turn everyone against her and in the end she learns that even her boyfriend, Ratan, no longer cares for her.

By making Radha, in the latter half of the story an increasingly unscrupulous character, the dramatist manages to move the spotlight away from the problems of social and economic disparity with which he confronts us in the beginning. In the end, he leaves matters weighted on the side of the *status quo*.

Yet for all his panache and the confident way he handled films and people,

Barua feared failure and, after he had finished a film, he seldom attended the première. He would predict its utter failure and then be off to the forests of Assam, Europe or America. In time, he would be back with notes for a new film, only to find that the film whose premier he had not seen had been loved by the critics and the public. Almost all his films were successful at the box office.

Admiration for him took extravagant, gushing tones. In an "open letter to Prince Barua" published in a Calcutta paper, in 1939, a fan wrote:

> We are inclined to include you in the category of the great thinkers of the present day. By producing the immortal *Devdas* you opened a new way for the Indian film industry and since then you are looked on as a great philosopher...

The tone of this letter was hardly unusual for that period. In the same year, 1939, an observer wrote about the influence of stars on clothing fashions:

> Who can deny that Kanan's novel way of hair-dressing in *Mukti* has been 'the method' of dressing for modern girls?...that Barua's curious cap in the same picture has won Calcutta-wide recognition as the most up-to-date' headwear? that Lila Desai's dancing sari in *Didi* is in vogue as 'Lila sari?'

In the film, *Mukti* (Liberation), Barua had played the role of a young romantic artist, who allowed his wife, played by Kanan Devi, to marry again, then carries out a perfectly simulated suicide and vanishes into the forests of Assam. The scenes in Assam were shot on location and when the wife and her new husband go there on a vacation, they meet Barua again. This time, Barua rescues her from a band of dacoits but is killed in the process. Thus, he again gives her *mukti*.

Barua, himself, had two wives—multiple marriages were still legal in India, even for Hindus—they remain legal for Muslims to this day. The two wives lived in adjoining villas in Ballygunge Circular Road, a posh area of Calcutta where the richer Bengalis lived. Each of his wives bore him three children.

Barua was an unrelenting workaholic but was said to be considerate, never ruffled and debonair. He planned his work minutely. Unlike most Indian directors, he never told an actor how he wanted a scene played. He felt this would convert an actor into a mimic, trying to copy what the director wanted when the actor should be an interpreter and arrive at his own concept of what his role should be.

Barua's best work was done during his first decade with New Theatres. In the 1940s, he planned an ambitious Indian version of *The Way of All Flesh,* but this never came off. His health declined rapidly and he underwent an operation in Switzerland. He returned full of plans, but soon collapsed. He lived to see India free but did little work during the rest of the 40s. When he died in 1951, *The Journal* of the Bengal Motion Picture Association recorded: "Pramathesh

Chandra Barua, creator of *Devdas,* died at 4 pm on Thursday, November 29 last, at his Calcutta residence, after protracted illness. He was forty-eight."

In the last few years of his life Barua fell out with Sircar but, before his death, he requested that his funeral procession should stop at New Theatres before going towards Kalighat, where he would be cremated. When the procession reached New Theatres, Sircar, by then confined to his chair, because of illness and gout, hobbled across the room to watch the procession and pay his last homage to Barua. Clearly in death, Barua wanted to roll the years back to his early triumphs, to the years of the rise and influence of New Theatres, when he was the great star of the Indian cinema.

If Barua was the brightest star there were others, and the two most interesting ones were the two Boses, Debaki and Nitin, not related. Debaki Bose, Ganguly's old colleague, favoured historical subjects drawn from India's mythological past and, unlike Barua, worked slowly, shot far more than was needed and New Theatres was always having to cope with the problems caused by a Debaki Bose film running late. He was, however, too highly regarded a director for Sircar or anyone else to say anything. So much so that he was the only one allowed to work for rival producers. Indeed it was for the rival East India Film Company that he made *Seeta,* which is rated as the best Indian mythological film and was screened at the 1934 Venice film Festival. He eventually left New Theatres, just after the Second World War broke out, to start on his own and was making films until the 1950s.

Not everyone was impressed with Debaki Bose. Durga Khote had come from Kolhapur in western India to work in Calcutta and in her memoir, *I, Durga Khote*, she was damning about Debaki Bose, "The sets were smaller, recording was in natural voices, and the film's pace generally very slow. The working hours were also irregular. One felt a lot of time was being needlessly wasted. Our director Debaki Kumar Bose was very caustic. He used the harshest words for the smallest mistake – in English, of course."

Debaki Bose also spoke in Bengali, and Khote went on a crash course of Bengali to work out if he was criticising her in Bengali.

Nitin Bose's love was the camera and he had come to New Theatres as a cameraman. His infatuation with the camera went back to the time just before the First World War when his father presented him with a Houghton Butcher as a birthday present. Bose would later tell Govind Nihalani the effect that this had on him:

"For several nights after everyone was asleep I would quietly bring up my camera to my bedroom on the second floor. I would place it on the pillow by my head and sleep with the hand on the camera and the feeling that it is my camera, and the camera was me, as if we were twins. That was my attitude right from the very beginning; that was my attitude throughout life."

At New Theatres, he trained other young camera men such as Yusuf Mulji and Bimal Roy. Nitin Bose directed his first film, *Chandidas*, for New Theatres in 1934, and after that made a number of movies. If Debaki liked mythologies, then Nitin's fondness was for love stories. But his romances were not of the gushing kind, his characters were believable men and women not fantasies and in his films he showed a sure grip in displaying everyday scenes which conveyed the tensions and realism of ordinary life. Garga writes, "Characters in a Nitin Bose film are no cardboard cut-outs; they are flesh and blood incarnations, revealed in all their diversity. Nitin's impeccable craftsmanship was achieved with a strong romantic-humanist streak which set his films apart and earned him a special place of his own."

In 1941, Nitin Bose decided to move to Bombay, which he would later bitterly regret, "the biggest blunder of my life". The move indicated that Sircar's studio was in decline.

It did not die quite immediately. Three years later, in 1944, New Theatres produced the first film of a man who was to become a major Bollywood director, Bimal Roy. Belonging to the Bodhi Hindus of Bengal, his family came from well-off Zamindari stock, as the landlord class in India is known. Educated in Dacca, at a school which had Armenian influence, being called Armani Toli High School, he grew up very socially aware of the plight of his fellow Indians.

His first movie, *Udayer Pathey,* whose Hindi version was called *Hamrahi,* was the story of love between the daughter of a rich businessman who employed a Marxist as a ghost writer for his speeches. Roy added to the tension between the man, who lived to make money, and the idealistic Marxist, by shooting scenes on actual locations rather than in the studio and had two songs by Tagore, one of which became the national anthem for India when the country won its freedom.

The film proved a minor classic and its dialogues proved so popular that a booklet containing them became one of India's best-sellers. The writer, Nabendu Ghosh, then living in Patna, having seen the film and loved it, now found booklets of the dialogue had been printed and were being sold by street vendors all over the town.

The film's success provided some relief to New Theatres, but could not prevent its ultimate demise.

Many who worked here have said it imploded due to internal tensions. Khote says New Theatres' fall was due to the kindness of Sircar who, while making great films could not control his directors who formed cliques and ruined him financially. Kanan Devi may have enjoyed the early family atmosphere but left because she could not get a rise. Then, there were tensions between Pankaj Mullick and R.C. Boral, another composer, with Mullick feeling Boral always tried to steal the limelight. While Mullick remained faithful to Sircar, Boral joined Nitin Bose on the train to Bombay.

But in many ways, New Theatres' fall was inevitable, for it represented the last great hurrah by Bengal's film world to be the centre of Indian cinema.

We have seen how Madan, moving from Bombay to Calcutta at the beginning of the twentieth century, had dominated early Indian cinema. By the time Nitin Bose made the journey in the reverse direction, Calcutta had long ceased to be the centre of the Indian world. It had assumed this unexpected position in 1757 following Robert Clive's victory in Plassey, which established the British Empire in India. The British made it the capital of their Indian empire, the first time a coastal town in India had occupied such a lofty position. The seeds of its decay were laid in the Raj decision in 1911 to move the capital of British India to Delhi, although it was some years before this became evident. This was because it took Edward Lutyens and Herbert Baker some time to build what is called New Delhi, and it was another decade before the Raj abandoned Calcutta as the capital. Once the capital had moved, Calcutta was doomed. True, Sircar had established New Theatres after the capital had moved and, with British businesses houses in the city still strong and dominant, the decline was masked.

However, the city's fall became very evident in the 1940s which was an awful decade for Calcutta and Bengal. In 1942, the British defeat at the hands of the Japanese and their conquest of Burma brought many refugees. In 1943, came the Bengal famine when three million Bengalis died, the worst famine to hit south Asia in the twentieth century, and the British administration callously abdicated responsibility. Calcutta was so little regarded by the highest British officials that the then Viceroy, Lord Linlithgow, did not visit the city during the famine. By the late 40s, Hindu-Muslim tensions were so high that in 1946 there was the Great Calcutta killings, with first Muslims targeting Hindus, then Hindus retaliating. In 1947, Bengal was partitioned. Calcutta, which little over twenty years earlier had been the capital of all of India, and was considered the second city of the Empire, was now the capital of a divided province, and crammed with some ten million refugees, mainly Hindus from Muslim-majority east Pakistan. In 1911, Lord Hardinge, then Viceroy, who took the decision to move the capital, saw it as an indication that the British would always rule India. In less than twenty years after the move, the British were gone from India and Calcutta was set in a decline from which it has not yet recovered. New Theatres was a cry against the dying of the Bengal light, a marvellous cry but, in the end, doomed to failure.

Not that the art of the cinema vanished from Calcutta. In the 1950s, it was to produce many great directors, actor and actresses and, above all, Satyajit Ray, one of the world's greatest film directors. But the demise of New Theatres meant the city's chances of rivalling Bombay as the centre of Indian cinema disappeared. After that it remained an important regional centre but not the capital that Bombay became. However, in the 1930s, while New Theatres flourished, Bombay was worried.

Bombay had watched New Theatres' rise with great anxiety. The magazine *FilmIndia,* produced in Bombay, had warned, "It is not a provincial competition.

It is New Theatres against the entire lot of producers, whether from Bombay Calcutta or the Punjab. It is sheer quality against such quantity." During that decade, Bombay financiers had repeatedly offered Barua substantial sums of money to produce such films in Bombay. Pahari Sanyal, a star actor at New Theatres, was often an intermediary in such offers. Barua waved them aside stating, "It is not my field. It is a bazaar."

Bombay's answer came from some very enterprising men, although these men worked not in Bombay but in small towns some distance from Bombay, first in Kolhapur and then in Poona, now known as Pune. In their own ways, they were to exert almost as great an influence on Indian cinema as New Theatres. Launched in 1929 in Kolhapur, Prabhat Film Company moved to Poona in 1933, both cities very firmly in the Marathi-speaking area of the state, Bombay then being a state that combined both present day Maharashtra and Gujerat. If New Theatres was remarkable for the educational level of its leaders, the Kolhapur group was remarkable in exactly the opposite way. Rich in talented directors, it had few with formal education.

One of it leaders, Rajaram Vanakudre Shantaram—known professionally as V. Shantaram—was born in Kolhapur in 1901. In his early teens he got a job in a railroad repair and maintenance workshop, where his working day was 8am to 6pm and his salary Rs. 15 per month. At sixteen he acquired an additional job. Each day he went from the railroad shop to a local tin-shed cinema. Here, at a starting wage of Rs. 5 per month, he did odd jobs, eventually graduating to be a door-boy and then becoming a sign-painter.

His education came from this cinema house where he watched films as often as he could. Shantaram became saturated in the lore of the film world and closely studied film personalities. As a boy he was admired as a mimic of Western screen favourites: the French Zigomar, Max Linder, Protea and the Italian Foolshead. His Foolshead portrayal—his speciality—included not only the comedian's mannerisms but the quivering primitive screen image. This fascination with the Western world was, however, overshadowed by something else. Among the great events of his childhood was the periodic arrival of a Phalke film. In the manner traditional to travelling shows, it would be promoted by a parade through the streets with proclamations heralded by the beating of drums. It was not by accident that Shantaram's first sound film, years later, was *Ayodecha Raja*—the story of King Harischandra, the tale that had launched Phalke.

The theatre job that the boy Shantaram got meant he was now in the midst of an exciting world and this soon led to a job as an assistant to a photographer. Then, in 1921, he was hired by a new film company just starting in Kolhapur, the Maharashtra Film Company, having been introduced to its owner by a cousin. At the moment of introduction, the owner was painting. He looked up absentmindedly said, "Huh," which was taken as 'Yes', and Shantaram was accepted.

Spurred by Phalke's success, Maharastra Film was producing mythologicals and historicals based on regional history. The proprietor, who had so casually said yes, was called Baburao Painter. This was not his real name. His real name was Baburao Krishnarao Mistry, who had been born in Kolhapur in 1890. The Painter name was given to him because of his skilful hands which produced marvellous paintings, sculptures and woodworks, having taught himself to paint and sculpt in academic art school style. Between 1910 and 1916, he and his artist cousin, Anandrao Painter, were the leading painters of stage backdrops in western India, doing several famous curtains for Sangeet Natak troupes and also for Gujarati Parsi theatres.

Painter had set up the Maharashtra Film Company with support from the local nobility and, apart from V. Shantaram, and the group that later left to set up The Prabhat Film Company, he also introduced two female artists, Gulab Bai and Anusuya Bai, renamed as Kamala Devi and Sushila Devi, respectively. Since acting was looked down upon, the two ladies were excommunicated by their community and had to find refuge in the studio premises. As well as acting in films, they would often cook and serve food to the entire unit.

Like Shantaram, Painter had had little education but, like many others, he had been inspired by Phalke's *Raja Harishchandra* and, starting with a camera he had picked up in Bombay's Chor Bazaar (literally Thieves' Market but, in reality, a flea market), he became an innovator of the silent era.

A man who wrote his own screenplays, he changed the concept of set-designing from painted curtains to solid, multi-dimensional, lived-in spaces and understood the importance of publicity. As early as 1921-22, he was the first to issue programme booklets, complete with details of the film and photographs. He also himself painted tasteful, eye-catching posters of his films.

But another innovation, artificial lighting, proved so successful in the film *Singhagad* that it turned out to be double-edged. Its box office success made the Bombay Revenue Department decide the Government should have some of this money and the Entertainment Tax was introduced.

If the tax men were drawn to films through Baburao, then his first film, the 1920 *Sairandhri,* did not please the censor board for its graphic depiction of the slaying of Keechak by Bhima. The scene had to be deleted but the film won both critical and commercial acclaim.

Baburao also made the first realistic Indian film, the 1925 *Savakari Pash,* dealing with money-lending, a problem that blighted the lives of countless illiterate, poor farmers. However, for audiences that loved mythological fantasy and historical love, this was too strong a dose of realism and the film did not do well, forcing Baburao to return to costume dramas.

Painter gave Shantaram every conceivable job in film production: cleaner, errand boy, scene painter, laboratory assistant, special effects man, camera assistant, and performer.

In 1929, Shantaram, at the age of 28, along with four partners, decided to launch the Prabhat Film Company. His partners were Vishnupat Damle, Keshavroa Dhaiber, S. Fatehlal and Sitaram Kulkarni, with Kulkarni the financier of the group. They began in a canvas studio, acquiring a tin-built studio only years later, after the move to Poona. For actors, they relied heavily on local performers and soon had a roster of a hundred local people. The spirit of community participation was clearly infectious. As Fatehlal recalled in *Indian Talkie*, "They accepted a rupee or two if we offered. When we needed elephants, horses or soldiers, the Maharaja of Kolhapur lent us as many as we needed. He even arranged mock battles and supervised the shooting."

The emphasis, however, gradually shifted towards professionalism and the group transformed itself into a large, self-sufficient organisation of several hundred artists, technicians and assistants. After a few silent films, the young company began, in 1932, to release a stream of sound films in the Marathi language, some of which were also made in Hindi. Some Tamil films were also made. It was many years before Shantaram's studios made films only in Hindi.

The three releases of 1932, including Shantaram's *Ayodecha Raja*, were produced in Hindi and Marathi. The role of Taramati, played in the Phalke film by the male actor Salunke, was now played by a high-caste girl of Kolhapur, Durga Khote, who was hailed as "the most spectacular new-comer of the year" and was to become one of India's most celebrated actresses.

Shantaram had to work hard to get Khote. Her father was a solicitor who liked the theatre but was appalled by the idea of his daughter becoming a screen actress, sharing many of the prejudices of the higher Indian classes for this medium. When Shantaram came to Bombay to scout for actresses Durga, who was by then a married woman with two children, he had to plead with her father to let her act. He insisted on vetting everything and Durga had to fetch Shantaram to come and see her "Papa". In the taxi that took them to her father's house, Durga was so nervous she incessantly spoke in English, making Shantaram wonder if she could speak Hindi or Marathi, the languages of his films. Shantaram persuaded Papa Laud (Khote's maiden name) to let his daughter travel to Kolhapur but Papa sent a retainer along with his daughter. Though studio facilities in Kolhapur were primitive, the company worked with precision and a sense of organisation. Khote was supplied with complete ready-to-shoot scripts, well in advance, and told what songs and what dialogue to deliver. In her memoir, *I, Durga Khote,* she recalls:

> Shantarambabu was a strict teacher. Nothing was allowed to pass on the basis of 'It will do.' He took immense pain, observed my walk, speech, gestures, posture, the way I moved before the camera, and every other detail, with a minute eye to get exactly what he wanted out of me. Though I loved music, I was not a trained musician. So my singing was nothing to write home about. But he [Govindrao Tembe, who looked after the

music] somehow managed to make my songs more or less acceptable; but that was about all. The fact that they became popular was undoubtedly on account of their melodious tunes, their beautiful picturisation and their perfect placement in the scene. I was busy almost twelve hours a day in Kolhapur, working on something or other connected with the film. There was no electricity in Kolhapur in those days. We had to be in the studio at the crack of dawn because all the shooting had to be done in natural light. Make-up, costume, hairstyles, all had to be completed by half-past seven, when the shooting began. It went on till about five o'clock when the last rays of the sun were fading. The next morning the day's routine would start again from five o'clock onwards.

Shantaram's first sound film, *Gopal Krishna,* won him wide recognition. From the start he struggled against the staginess of early sound films and tried to make much of the mobility that the use of camera gave him. In 1936, his impressive spectacle, *Amar Jyoti,* made in Hindi, was shown at the Venice Film Festival. But it wasn't Shantaram alone who made Prabhat, as was demonstrated when a year later, in 1937, *Sant Tukaram,* made by Fathelal and Damle in Marathi, became the first Indian film to win a Venice Film festival award.

To Prabhat, as with New Theatres and other studios, well-known mythological and devotional stories seemed the safest starting point in the sound era. For decades an Indian producer, when asked why a film was popular, seemed likely to say that it was because the people knew the story. Familiarity, not novelty, was long considered the safest investment. For example, the first five years of sound brought three different versions of the Tukaram story, all in Marathi, and eight versions of the Harischanadra story, in five Indian languages.

Shantaram and his fellow directors of Prabhat, were keen to experiment with social films and the most notable of these came from Shantaram. In 1937, he produced *Duniya Na Maane*, first in Hindi and later in Marathi, under the title *Kunku.* In the film we learn of a bright young girl, Nirmala, who is married to an elderly man through negotiations conducted by her uncle. In a series of deftly-treated episodes, the old husband becomes aware of the wrong done to her. Finally, in his eagerness to restore to Nirmala the freedom taken from her—divorce was not possible in those days—he kills himself.

Bapu Watve in *Ek Hoti Prabhatnagar* has described how the suicide scene was filmed:

> The suicide of the heroine's aged husband was filmed with sensitivity. An antique clock symbolises his advanced age. He removes the long pendulum of the clock, signifying taking his life himself, and uses it as a paper-weight for the suicide note he leaves for his wife and daughter.

In 1939, Shantaram's *Admi* again carried an implied challenge to traditional Hindu society. It told of Moti, a police constable, who is assigned to raid a gambling den and brothel. Here he meets Kesar, a prostitute, and finds her eager to escape the vicious atmosphere of her life. He lends her a helping hand and eventually comes to love her but the religious atmosphere of Moti's house drives the girl away.

Shantaram did not make too many more movies with Prabhat. In 1941, he made *Padosi* (Neighbour), which tried to deal with the growing Hindu-Muslim tension by showing that what divides people is not religion, but money. The film also had a Marathi version called *Shejari*. The lead actress was a woman called Jayshree and she now came between Shantaram and his partners.

In many ways the break-up of Prabhat would have made an ideal Shantaram script. When the partnership was formed, the partners had a strict code that they should not get involved with actresses who worked for them. If they did, they had to leave. This was what forced Keshavrao Dhaiber to leave when he married Prabhat actress, Nalini Tarkhad, Baburao Pai coming in as the fifth partner.

Shantaram, although married to Vimal, who was mother to his three children, had fallen in love with Jayshree and wanted to marry her. The romance between Shantaram, by now in his 40s, and Jayashree, a good deal younger, had started off in the classic tale of the older man and the younger woman, in this case the older man summoning the younger, high-spirited, woman to his office for a ticking off. Jayshree liked to play pranks and since Shantaram was keen on tight discipline in his studios, she was called to his room for a chat. His biographer says "no one knows what transpired", but clearly a bond was established which developed into love.

The effect was very noticeable. Shantaram had so far dressed more like an Indian. Although he wore trousers when shooting, he wore the Indian dhoti-kurta when not working. And his work clothes were simple: always white, a short-sleeved shirt, a pair of trousers. Jayshree made him dress the way a well-off Western male of the 30s would have dressed: bow tie, sports jackets, expensive trousers, and boots. A photograph of him with Jayshree shows him looking like quite a Westernised Indian dandy, while Jayshree, in a sari, gazes at him admiringly.

But his partners were not looking on admiringly. They did not approve of his dalliance with Jayshree and Shantaram refused to follow the law he had himself laid down that any such affair meant the partner had to leave. By this time his relationship with Damle had broken down. The two men were not even on speaking terms and the soft-spoken Fatchlal had to try and keep the peace. Even then, when Damle and Fatehlal had their *mahurat* for *Sant Sakhu,* they did not invite Shantaram, an insult that could not be more pointed.

Shantaram could not stay away from Jayshree and they got married without, of course, divorcing Vimal, a situation she reluctantly accepted. The partners had, in the meantime, forced Jayshree to resign but this could not heal the rift. Shantaram had to go. The parting could have been more acrimonious, as Prabhat was then worth Rs. 60 lakhs but, Shantaram, according to his biographer, Jayshree's son Kiran, "agreed to give up the partnership for a mere Rs. 2.5 lakhs (Rs250,000), knowing fully well that if he demanded his rightful one-fifth share, the company would close down immediately".

Shantaram moved to Bombay, and although he hated Barua, and the movies he made, the two men's life styles now converged. Like him, he had two wives who lived near each other. Jayshree, producing more children for him, including Kiran, lived opposite Vimal and her family, Jayshree and her children in Cambridge Terrace at Pedder Road, Vimal and her brood at Shahbaug, across the street. The two families often met during Hindu festivals and other occasions. In time, Shantaram even bettered Barua and left Jayshree for a third wife.

Initially, in Bombay, he worked as Chief of the Film Advisory board set up by the Raj to make war propaganda films, a job he had been offered by J.B.H. Wadia, a man who will figure later in our story. Shantaram was not too keen to work for the British but this solved the problem of what he would do when he moved to Bombay. However, in 1942, when Gandhi gave his call to the British to quit India, he resigned and formed his own studios, Rajkamal Kalamandir, Rajkamal being an amalgam of his father's name Rajaram and his mother's Kamala, with money for the studio coming from a Delhi financier called Gupta.

Shantaram, like most Indians of that period, wanted to see India free; pictures of him show him wearing the Gandhi cap and, inevitably, he had to cope with the British censors being sensitive to anything that they thought promoted the idea of India's freedom. One of his early films for Prabhat in 1930 was *Shivaji*, about the sixteenth century Maratha leader who challenged the Mughals and established the Maratha Empire. A great hero in Maharashtra, Shantaram originally called the film *Swarajya Torna* (Flag of Freedom). The British saw this Shivaji v. Mughal fight as a thinly-disguised reference to Gandhi's campaign against the Raj, then gathering renewed force. Gandhi had just made his historic march to the sea to demonstrate the inequities of British rule that led, in the summer of 1930, to the launch of his second major civil disobedience campaign. The censor had the film renamed *Shivaji* and demanded that "its patriotic fervour be diluted." In 1935, inspired by Gandhi's call for Hindus to reform their wretched caste laws, in particular the way higher castes treated untouchables, Shantaram produced a film he originally called *Mahatma*. But this was the name Indians called Gandhi and the censors objected, saying it had "association with a certain political leader". It also did not like the film's "controversial politics". Shantaram was not happy to make the cuts but the distributors agreed and the title was changed to *Dharmatma*.

Like Barua, Shantaram was a pioneer of the Indian cinema, and can be credited with innovations such as the first film-maker to use a trolley shot, and the first to use a telephoto lens for close-ups. But, unlike Barua, whose *Devdas* appalled Shantaram—he felt it was too pessimistic and affected audiences badly—Shantaram was more interested in the evolving political world round him. During a 1933 visit to Germany, where he had gone to use the Agfa laboratories to help develop his colour film *Sairandhir,* he was impressed by the order and discipline that Hitler, who had just come to power, had brought, a not uncommon view of the early years of Nazi rule. But even more than that he was taken by the then giants of the German cinema: Pabst, Lang, Lubitsch and Max Ophuls.

Interestingly, the German influence also weighed heavily with two other Indians who were responsible for creating the greatest Indian film studio which, even more than New Theatres and Prabhat, was to mould and influence Indian cinema long after it had ceased to make movies. This was Bombay Talkies and, in a story all too Indian, the road to Bombay Talkies was through Berlin and London.

5

The Road to Bombay via Munich and London

Late in 1933, two young people arrived in Bombay from London, bringing with them a completed film which had been finished in London and already shown there. Along with its English version, they brought a Hindi version, which was yet to be seen by the public. The two young people were Indians, though both had been absent from India for much of their lives. In their plans, much depended on the reception they would get in Bombay for their Hindi film. For both, long journeys via Germany and England had led to this moment.

Devika Rani Chaudhury—better known as Devika Rani—was born in Waltair in southern India. Her father, Colonel Chaudhury, soon afterwards became Surgeon-General of Madras. A great-uncle on her mother's side was Rabindranath Tagore. When she was nine, her father shipped her to England to be educated, telling her she must learn to take care of herself. The Colonel was like many an upper-class Indian who believed that an English upbringing from an early age was the best education there was; the English rulers of India sent their children to be educated back in England and Indians of this class were very keen to imitate that. Devika's early years were spent in north London's South Hampstead School.

When she finished school, she won a scholarship to the Royal Academy of Dramatic Art. She also earned surprisingly large sums of money making Paisley designs for a British textile company, and wrote to her father that he need not send her any more money since she could take care of herself. But she was not quite sure what career she should follow. London seemed to offer so many opportunities. Already showing rare beauty, she had, by this time, been befriended by an international crowd, which included Anna Pavlova, and discussed her career problem earnestly with them. Should she be a dancer, as Anna Pavlova urged? A singer? A doctor, like her father? Or, even, perhaps an architect? Interested in architecture, she enrolled on a course. Then she met Rai, an Indian film producer, and asked him the same question she had been asking her other friends.

Three fields, he said, would grow in importance, and in any of them she would be able to serve India: the press, radio, and film. He then offered her a job as consultant on costumes and sets for his next film, to be shot in India. This was the start of a friendship that soon blossomed into love and the following year, after the shooting was finished, they were married in southern India. Devika was still in her teens.

Rai was at this time in a crisis in his own career. Born in Bengal, where he was part of a large family that had its own private theatre, he had studied at the University of Calcutta, acquired a law degree, and also studied under Tagore at Santiniketan. During his time there, Gandhi visited the school. The young man was inclined to the arts, but the family's plans now called for him to go to London for training as a lawyer at the Inner Temple—as Gandhi had done. Rai gladly went.

In London, while he did his law studies, he could not keep away from the theatre, and got a small part in the fabulously successful musical, *Chu Chin Chow*, when he was asked to carry a spear. Then he played a role in a London production of *The Goddess*, a play by a young Indian writer, Niranjan Pal. Meanwhile, he was formulating other, grander, plans.

He wanted to make a series of films on the great world religions. One would deal with the Buddha; another would be based on the Oberammergau Passion Play. Soon Rai journeyed to Munich, to promote his plans.

He was a skilful pleader and, early in 1924, persuaded the Emelka Film Company of Munich, to take part in an ambitious project: an international co-production, the first such co-production in Indian films. Rai wanted to tell the story of Buddha, basing it on *The Light of Asia*, the poem by Edwin Arnold. Emelka would send to India a director, cameraman and assistants, and would provide all the equipment. Its laboratory in Munich would process the film, and would do all the editing. Rai for his part would provide an Indian cast and raise funds in India to pay them, and other location costs. Emelka would own all European distribution rights. The Indian investors would own Indian distribution rights and would receive from Emelka two prints to exploit these rights.

Rai's visit to India worked according to plan and he raised an unusually large sum—eventually about Rs. 90,000—for the production outlay. Work quickly began, with Buddha played by Rai and the feminine lead by a thirteen-year-old Anglo-Indian girl, Sita Devi, whose real name was Renee Smith. The screen play was the work of Niranjan Pal; Frank Osten, a German, directed the film, while Rai produced. The film had gala openings in Berlin, Vienna, Budapest, Venice, Genoa, Brussels, with personal appearances by Rai and toasts to this unique production by various international notables. The film was a success throughout Central Europe, providing a great financial triumph for Emelka. In London, it had a Royal Command Performance and ran for over four months at a concert hall, though not profitably.

In India, the film received favourable criticism but only limited success at the box office. The trade persisted in considering it "foreign". The backers, moving their two prints from city to city, experienced mounting disillusionment. After two years, Rs. 50,000 remained un-recovered. What Rai had hoped would launch a series of international productions did exactly the opposite and closed the door to Indian capital.

But what had closed doors in India opened them wider in Germany. The continental success of *The Light of Asia*, (a print of which has been preserved by the National Film Archive of the British Film Institute, London) brought Rai offers that resulted in two more Indo-German productions, both shot in India, both performed by Indian casts including Rai and Sita Devi, both written by Niranjan Pal, directed by Franz Osten, and produced by Rai—this time with German capital.

The first was *Shiraz,* made in 1926 under the Emelka banner, and telling a story of the designer of the Taj Mahal. The second was *A Throw of Dice*, produced under the banner of Universum Film Aktiengesellschaft, Ufa—the giant Government-subsidised organisation with studios at Neubabelsberg. It was this film that involved Devika Rani.

When the shooting was completed for *A Throw of Dice,* Rai and his bride hastened to Neubabelsberg, Germany, for the editing. The world of Ufa was thrown open to them. As the editing progressed, Devika Rani became a trainee in the Erich Pommer unit. She got advice from Fritz Lang, watched the shooting of *The Blue Angel,* held the make-up tray for Marlene Dietrich, and engaged in intensive seminars with the great director G.W. Pabst. Pabst, in one exercise, would place a trainee before the camera and, while the action was shot, ask a series of questions to be answered with "yes" or "no". Then, Pabst would review the film in minute detail. "Never use that one," he would say. "See what an ugly thing it does to your mouth there? Remember that, eliminate it."

The Ufa training created exciting vistas. But it could not last. Sound was coming and along with that other changes in the wider economic and political life of Germany. Suddenly, one day, Ufa issued a barrage of dismissal notices. The arrival of sound had forced a complete Ufa reorganisation. Indian co-production no longer seemed feasible and the German career of Rai was ended. Not long afterwards, Ufa came under Nazi control. Lang and others were ousted in the interest of racial purity. Pommer and Pabst went into exile. Meanwhile, Emelka of Munich, which had given Ufa some competition, became a victim of the spreading financial depression.

But if the doors in Germany were closing for Himansu, doors in England were still open to him where both *Shiraz* and *A Throw of Dice* won sufficiently favourable reception for British capital to show increasing confidence in Rai. There were critics of the films in England, some found the *films* "singularly uninteresting", but many others were enchanted. A British distributor had already guaranteed the German backers £7,500 for British rights in *Shiraz,* another had also given Ufa an advance guarantee on *A Throw of Dice.* Rai found that British capital was ready to take the full risk on his next venture. Rai made the most of this and launched an international production.

This Anglo-Indian co-production with both English capital and technical assistance (an Englishman, J.L. Freer Hunt, directed the film), was the beginning of *Karma* (Fate), in which Devika Rani co-starred with Rai.

The film marked Devika's rise as the lead actress, *Karma* having marked the end of Sita Devi's association with Rai, who did not appear in the film. Her success in three Rai films had won her a starring position with the Madans. Not having mastered Hindi, she slipped from the public eye after sound arrived.

In 1930, the Rais were back in India for many months of exterior shooting and intensive study of Hindi; then they returned to London's Stoll Studios for the interior shooting, including the recordings of the songs. For every shot, two takes were made: one in English, one in Hindi. Because of a limited budget, two takes for a shot was usually the limit, except for the songs.

The film took over two years to complete. It was a modern story about a beautiful young maharani (Devika Rani) who wanted "progress"—it was never quite explained what this meant—and her love for a prince of a neighbouring Indian state (Rai), who also wanted "progress", but whose father, the maharaja, did not. Marriage brought her, by the rules of Hindu society, under her father-in-law's authority, and this created the conflict of the film. It was premiered in London in May, 1933.

Critics had some reservations about the story, which a few considered naïve, but Devika won all of them over. The critics gushed over her beauty. "A glorious creature," the *Eva* called her, "Devika Rani's large velvety eyes can express every emotion."

On May 11, 1933, *The News Chronicle* declared that "she totally eclipses the ordinary film star. All her gestures speak, and she is grace personified". Four days later, on May 15, 1933, *The Star* reported that "her English is perfection." Fox Film Corporation now wanted Devika Rani to star in a film about Bali, and a German producer wanted her for a film about a snake-charmer. But Rai had no desire to became an Indian exile in Europe and told Devika, "Let us learn from these people, but let us put the knowledge to work in our own country."

The couple knew that their film future was in India. With the advent of sound, this was more certain than ever. Rai now staked everything in the Hindi version of *Karma* which had its Bombay premier on January 27, 1934. Its reception once more opened doors for Rai and made Indian investors look on him with sympathy and some of them even brought out their cheque books.

That year, Bombay Talkies Ltd., was formed as a joint stock company with an authorised capital of Rs. 25 lakhs, around £192,000, a colossal sum of money for India in those days. Rai showed foresight in his choice of the place for the studio. Until then film activity in Bombay had been in south Bombay but he chose Malad, then a remote suburb of Bombay, indeed, almost part of the wilderness that surrounded Bombay. It seemed to suggest he knew the direction in which the city would develop and where its future film facilities would be built and over the next few decades he was to be proved right. He located the studio at the summer mansion of F.E. Dinshaw, a rich Parsi, and got some of Bombay's most prominent businessmen, all of them knighted by the King-Emperor, to serve on his board. They were: Sir Chimanlal Setalvad, Sir Chunilal Mehta, Sir Richard Temple, Sir Pheroze Sethna, Sir Sohrabji Pockhanawala and Sir Cowaji Jehangir, three Parsi knights, two Gujarati knights reflecting the then economic and social power of both communities with Temple, the solitary Brit, being the son of a former Governor of Bombay.

It could not have been more establishment and it said much for Rai's powers of persuasion that he got such a group together, in particular Sethna, who was then the dominant figure in Bombay business and national politics. A director of Tatas, the giant industrial house of India, he was also chairman of the Sun Insurance company and had been the first choice of the British to head the inquiry into the cinema; just before he joined Rai's board, he had become the first head of the newly set up Motion Picture Society of India. Rarely in the history of Bollywood has such a glittering board of directors graced a film company; it was a first and remains an exception; Rai had come to Bombay at just the right time. Bombay was still a sleepy, colonial town, as it would remain for some time to come. However, the 1930s was a time of expansion for Bombay, a city made up of seven islands joined together by nature, was now seeing vast efforts to reclaim land. This was when Marine Drive, the promenade in south Bombay that defines the city, was built, as was also Brabourne Stadium, its historic cricket ground. Bombay was not yet the commercial capital of India—that distinction still belonged to Calcutta—but it was getting ready to take over from its historic rival.

Rai built the studio with painstaking care, supervising the purchase of the most modern equipment. In 1935, a stream of Hindi productions began to emerge from Bombay Talkies Ltd. Rai realised he needed foreign technical help and turned to Germany and Britain. Franz Osten, director of *The Light of Asia, Shiraz,* and *A Throw of Dice,* joined him. The cameraman was also a German, Carl Josef Wirsching, as was Carl von Spreti, the set designer, while Len Hartley, the sound recordist was British, with Zolle, the laboratory technician. Rai felt this leavening of foreign help was necessary in order to teach and guide his other staff of whom there were more than four hundred—artists, technicians, assistants, and others—and all of them were Indian. It became, like New Theatres and Prabhat, a largely self-sufficient organisation.

Rai's desperate efforts for international co-production had been ahead of its time. For years to come, with the difficulties of sound, film producers in most countries would concentrate on home productions. Bombay Talkies Ltd would do likewise. But co-production would, in later decades, once more emerge as a challenging and necessary idea, and in India the pioneering work of Rai would remain a reference point for all such ventures.

Mindful of the exhilarating days with the Pommer unit, Rai and Devika Rani soon instituted a trainee programme. Each year Rai interviewed scores of job candidates, many sent by Indian universities. Within a few years the names of a number of younger Bombay Talkies staff members were to become the legends of Bollywood.

The first, and in many ways the greatest of them, was Ashok Kumar. The way he was discovered and made into a star illustrated how Rai worked and how film stars emerged in India. There could not have been a more reluctant film star, a man who was given his first chance despite the fact that the director thought he could not act and he himself had studied to be a lawyer and wanted to be a film director.

Ashok Kumar Ganguly was a Bengali Brahmin who claimed his family were not really Brahmins. The story went that his great-grandfather was the dacoit Raghunath who, seeking shelter from the Raj's police, took refuge in a temple and posed as a Brahmin there. The police, taking him to be the temple priest, left him alone and Rogho, as he was known, celebrated his escape by giving thanks to the gods, deciding to give up dacoity and become a Brahmin priest. This made Ashok Kumar an Amathe Brahim, who Ashok always claimed were not real Brahmins at all. Ashok Kumar was also not a Bengali from Bengal but, what Bengalis called Probashi Bengali, an "overseas" Bengali.

He was born in Bhagalpur in Bihar, where his father was a lawyer. Ashok set out to become a lawyer, but in Calcutta, where he was sent to study, he started showing an interest in films and set his heart on becoming a film director. Keen to study film direction at Ufa, and having heard about Rai's connections with Ufa, he decided to seek the help of his brother-in-law, Sasadhar Mukherjee, who was already working for Bombay Talkies. Ashok asked him if he could get him an introduction to Rai, which he thought might help him get to Ufa. Ashok Kumar dared not tell his parents that he was going anywhere near films, as well-brought up, middle-class boys and girls were warned to keep away from this dangerous medium. He secretly used the money given for his examination fee for the law college—all of Rs. 35—to buy a ticket to see Sasadhar in Bombay, arriving in the city on the morning of January 28, 1934.

But the first meeting with Bombay Talkies went badly. When Himansu asked Franz Osten to give Ashok Kumar a test, the German was distinctly unimpressed with the latest recruit of the producer. Their conversation went as follows:

"Mr Ganguly do you act on stage?"
"No. Sir"(he had, but as child in amateur theatricals)
"Do you sing?"
"Yes. Mr Osten. I can sing."
Ashok then sang a classical Bhajan, a devotional Hindu song.
Osten said nothing and asked him to take a screen test.

At the end of it, he told Rai, "No, Mr Rai, no good" and turning to Ashok Kumar said, "You have a square jaw, you look too young and girlish."

Osten advised him to return to Calcutta and his law studies. Rai, however, had other ideas. He was keen to hire educated people. Both he and Devika had made this their aim when they started Bombay Talkies. Sasadhar, himself, was a good example of this. The scion of a rich Bengali family from Allahabad, he had an MSc. in Physics, having studied under the great Indian scientist, Dr Meghnad Saha, who believed Sasadhar had a brilliant future as a physicist. Rai reassured Ashok that, as he wanted to be a film director, this setback did not matter, and hired him as trainee technician. His first job was to be a camera assistant. He was to be paid Rs. 150 a month, a just about liveable salary. His father, who had dreamt of his son becoming the Chief Justice of India, was distraught, while his mother worried if she could ever marry him off to the daughter of a respectable family. Eight months later, Ashok Kumar's life was changed through a disastrous love affair involving Devika Rani, with the result that Hindi screen's first matinée idol, the man who was always called "the Evergreen hero," was born.

Himansu Rai was shooting *Jeevan Naiya*, The Boat of Life, when Devika, as usual playing the leading lady, decided to change boats and run away with the leading man, Najmul Hussein, to Calcutta. Himansu got his wife back through the efforts of Sasadhar who, according to the Urdu writer Saadat Hasan Manto, took pity on Himansu and on his own initiative persuaded Devika to return. Najmul stayed on in Calcutta to become part of New Theatres and now vanishes from our story. But this still left Himansu with the problem of getting a leading man. Then he recalled the young man who wanted to be a director, who Osten thought would never make an actor but whose good looks had impressed Himansu.

One day he went to the lab where Ashok was working and asked a startled Ashok to walk, while Himansu watched. After watching for a few minutes he told him he would be the hero of *Jeevan Naiya*.

Ashok was terrified by the idea of acting. He had just heard that his parents were about to choose a bride for him and told Himansu he could not act, as this would jeopardise his marriage prospects. "Sir, those who act belong to the lower strata of life." Himansu was not best pleased. "You know my wife acts. Does that mean she belongs to that class?" Right till the first day of shooting, he kept raising objections. Before the first day's shooting he had his hair cut very short, which meant a wig was required. Then, just before the shooting began, he pleaded with Himansu, "Please sir, don't ask me to embrace any heroine or girl. I won't be able to do that." Many years earlier on the Calcutta stage he had seen such an embrace and it had filled him with embarrassment, the memory of which still haunted him. Then just as the shooting began, he noticed Sasadhar adjusting the microphone as part of his job as sound engineer. He told Himansu he could not possibly act in front of his own brother-in-law. Himansu assured him Sasadhar would be in a booth and not visible on the set.

The first day's shooting was a disaster. The film, a love story, involved Ashok having to put a gold necklace round Devika's neck. But he was terrified of touching her and made such a ham-fisted job of it that the necklace got tangled in her hair and it broke. Devika tried to reassure him in Bengali but this made him all the more nervous and made him want to run to the toilet.

In another scene, he was required to jump through a window to stop the villain molesting Devika. Osten had told him to count to ten before he jumped. Ashok forgot, jumped too early, and landed on top of Devika and the actor playing the villain, who broke his leg in the fall.

Osten despaired of the man, who he was sure would never be an actor. But Himansu brushed aside the accident saying to Ashok, "So you broke the villain's leg," and remained convinced he could act. On that terrible first day's shooting he also gave Ashok Kumar his screen name although he was unwittingly inspired by Osten. During the first day's shooting Osten, never quite able to cope with Indian names, called Ashok "Mr Kumar". As he did so, Himansu said, "You have helped me give a new name to the new hero Ashok Kumar Ganguly. Tear apart Ganguly from his full name. Make him a casteless hero loved by all castes and classes. He shall simply be Ashok Kumar." This was a shrewd choice. Kumar is a common middle name in India (it means young prince in Hindi) and soon new actors coming to Hindi cinema also dropped their surnames and used Kumar as their surname, seeking to bridge the many divisions in Indian society.

Jeevan Naiya was a success although Ashok Kumar was so embarrassed by his acting he did not want to attend the première. Himansu gifted him a suit and persuaded him to attend; at the end, he found himself being summoned by the Maharaja of Gwalior, who was in the audience and had been impressed by the film. This started a friendship between the actor and one of Indian's most important royal families. The audience's reaction reassured Ashok Kumar but it was still not certain he would remain in acting. His father, determined to rescue him from films, had got him a job as a tax inspector which paid more than Bombay Talkies then paid him. Ashok Kumar would have had good reason to leave films then. Osten had been dismissive, film critics had called him a "chocolate hero" and as Saadat Hasan Manto, who got to know him well, wrote in his memoir, "I had seen some of Ashok's films but as far as acting was concerned Devika Rani was streets ahead of him."

However, Ashok Kumar was slowly being infected by the film bug. It did not take him long to reject life as a tax inspector and sign up for another film *Achhut Kanya* (Untouchable Girl) in which he would play the lead male role opposite Devika. In 1955, talking to Bunny Reuben, he would say he wished he had become a tax inspector. What pleasure he said it would have given him to summon the stars to his cubicle and shout at them for not paying their taxes but this was a tongue in cheek remark. He never really regretted going into films and *Achhut Kanya* was to prove a seminal film both for Bombay Talkies and for Ashok Kumar.

The Hindu, the highly respected but deeply conservative Madras-based paper, which had begun a weekly page of film, news and comment—itself an indication of the growing power of the new medium—summed up the film as follows:

> She, [Devika], appears as a Harijan girl, in love with a Brahmin youth, portrayed by Ashok Kumar. Caste barriers and religious bigotry stand in the way of their union. The boy is forced into a marriage to a wife he cannot love and the girl to one of her own class. Wisely, afraid of their love, they keep out of each other's way, till chance throws them together at a village fair. Inflamed by jealousy and egged on by neighbours, the girl's husband mistakes this meeting and a fierce encounter ensues between the Brahmin youth and the untouchable husband at a level-crossing. A train comes along. The girl, in an effort to part the combatants, is run over and killed, a human sacrifice at the altar of bigotry.

Ashok Kumar was far from happy with his acting. In one scene when Devika tells him they could never marry as she was an untouchable girl, Ashok was required to clasp his hands in agony and cry out, "Oh, God! why did you not make me an untouchable?"

After the shooting was completed, Osten came over and said "Mr Kumar, your two hands clasped each other so hard that it seemed they would break into pieces."

Osten had bluntly told him that his acting did not matter, and while he must try to do his best, the story would pull the film through. *Achhut Kanya* was a good example of this. This was a time when law and precedent obstructed intercaste marriages and firmly supported the ostracism of the untouchable. But Indian politicians, and all the leaders of the Indian National Congress, had called for an end to this dreadful, age-old scourge of Hinduism, with Gandhi going so far as to denounce untouchability as "a plague." Other leaders like Nehru were warning that independence in itself would not be enough, that Hindu society must also reform itself from within. Against this background, this was the right film, made at the right time. It showed that Hindi films had a conscience; it was not just about neat plots, the ready-made ironies, the popular yearning for doom; Indian film-makers, like their counterparts in the West, did not shrink from stories that attacked implicitly, and often, explicitly, the canons of Hindu society.

The film's success was also due to the acting of Devika Rani, which was compared by some critics to that of Garbo. *The Hindu* considered it "easily the best Devika Rani film to date".

The Indians also took to the songs in the film. This being before the days of play back singing, both Devika and Ashok sang their own songs. Their duet

"*Mein bun ki chirya, bun bun boloun re*" (I am a forest bird who sings from grove to grove), became a great hit song (and remains a classic) which, long after the film had become history, was being sung by Indians. What was not known, and only emerged later, was that the music director, Saraswati Devi, had enormous problems during the recording of the song and almost despaired of getting the pair to keep in tune.

Himansu was very keen for politicians to see the film but, despite a plea by Himansu, Gandhi showed no interest in the film; this was one of those foreign Western ideas he never came to terms with. But Jawaharlal Nehru, his daughter, Indira, and Sarojini Naidu, a famous poetess and a leading Congress politician, came to see a special screening of the film at Bombay Talkies. Sarojini did fall asleep during it but woke in time to hear Ashok Kumar sing. "Who's that boy? He's singing so well," she exclaimed in wonder. Ashok, sitting next to her, beamed with pleasure as he said, "That's me, up there on the screen." Nehru not only stayed awake but liked it so much that after that, whenever he saw Ashok Kumar, he would say, "Hello, hero, Kaise ho?" (how are you?). Osten managed to screen the film at Josef Goebbel's Ministry of Propaganda in Berlin, although, what the Nazis made of a film preaching universal love cutting across caste barriers, is hard to say.

The success of the film meant the Indian screen had a pairing that could rival the ones in Hollywood, at least in the eyes of the Indian audiences. Ashok Kumar, though, was all too aware of his own inadequacies as an actor and, advised by Himansu, he began to watch Hollywood movies to try and study voice control, gestures, and postures. He was dreadfully worried about what to do with his hands. What, he wondered, should he do with them when he was talking, standing still or playing an emotional scene? He closely studied Hollywood actors to find a formula that would work for him.

Himansu had first advised him to study Ronald Coleman; soon Ashok moved on to films by Spencer Tracy, Leslie Howard and Charles Laughton. But his best acting coach, as he would later confess, was his own brother-in-law, Sasadhar, who urged him to consider the scenes he was acting in, study the dialogue, and personalise it so he could convey emotions and feelings.

By now Bombay Talkies had settled down to a schedule of about three films a year, although in some years, like 1938, only two were made. If films like *Achhut Kanya* were path-breaking social films, Bombay Talkies did foray into the staple diet of Indian cinema mythologicals, although it only made one movie of this genre, perhaps because the studio's fortunes were then in decline. This was *Savitri,* produced in Hindi in 1937, with Devika Rani and Ashok Kumar in the lead.

This story from the *Mahabharata* had already been the basis of five different sound films in four Indian languages, but the Bombay Talkies version was admired for its unique delicacy. The story tells of Savitri, daughter of King Ashwapati, who ruled thousands of years ago. Savitri marries a man fated to die.

But she loves her husband so much that by her piety, penance, and devotion she wins back his life from Yama, the god of death. The story has a quality akin to that of the Orpheus story—but with a happy ending.

However, the Bombay Talkies story could not have a happy ending. War was coming and with it changes that would overwhelm the studio. In 1939, the studio had every reason to feel satisfied. After a few films, which had failed to make much of an impression, it found a new female star, Leela Chitnis, and paired her opposite Ashok Kumar in *Kangan*. The film was a hit, reviving the studio's fortunes. Ashok and Leela radiated chemistry on screen, helped by the fact that there was competition between them. Leela, making her début, was determined not to be outshone by the man who was already a screen idol. "I used to say to myself," she later wrote in her autobiography, *Chanderi Duniye*, "He should not surpass me... And he thought likewise about me. It was a secret competition between us."

Not that Chitnis was overly impressed with Ashok Kumar's acting ability. She accepted he was good-looking but found his voice more seductive than his acting, "As an actor his personality seemed unimpressive. And there was no liveliness in his eyes." Ashok, on the other hand, was much taken by how Leela used her eyes to 'speak' and he decided to try and bring some of that quality to his acting. India's first great screen hero was learning on the job.

Kangan was to be the last movie Osten directed and he could not even complete the film before war intervened. Within days of Neville Chamberlain announcing Britain was at war with Germany, Linlithgow, the Viceroy in Delhi, without consulting a single Indian, announced India, too, was at war. This had an immediate impact on the Germans at Bombay Talkies. Osten, Wirsching and all the others were interned and *Kangan* had to be completed by Osten's two assistants, N.R. Acharya and Najam Naqvi. That was the end of the foreign era in Indian films, and Garga perceptively points out that while Osten and Wirsching, who remained in India after the war, and died there, brought much technical expertise, the films "lacked the elusive spirit and insight into the everyday incidents of Indian life."

All of Osten's fourteen films were made by the same production team, so they tended to be repetitive. Eight months after war broke out, and just as Hitler launched his Blitzkrieg, Himansu, himself, was dead. He died of a nervous breakdown in May 1940, just forty-eight years old. If Phalke is the father of the Indian cinema, then Rai must be credited with not only having the ability to bring together great artistic talent under one roof but, also, with making sure that Bombay, not any other centre, and certainly not Calcutta, would be the home of the Indian cinema.

On Ashok Kumar's first fraught day of shooting, in order to calm the nerves of his new star, Rai had sent him a special lunch from his own lunch pack to his room. It was chicken soup, roast chicken, pudding and sweets. This was special treatment for a man he knew was crucial to his movie. But, in general, and in contrast to what happened in the rest of the country, Rai practised the social equality his movies preached. So all company members, of whatever caste, ate together at the company canteen, a huge statement in India for the 1930s. It was even said that top actors, on occasion, helped to clean the floor. Rai, perhaps with memories of Gandhi's visit to Santiniketan, insisted on this.

Was this symbolism or did it have a wider impact? Many historians and sociologists have tried to come to a judgement. P.R. Ramachandra Rao, reviewing the achievements of the Indian film at a twenty-fifth anniversary celebration of the industry, and with Bombay Talkies very much in mind, felt that Indian films had made a great contribution in this regard. "It has unsettled the placid contentment of the Indian masses, it has filled the minds of youth with new longings and it is today a potent force in national life."

In few places round the world would a film industry have been praised for unsettling public contentment. Yet it is possible that film was indeed shaping Indian attitudes, and doing so in a variety of ways. Bombay Talkies played a major part in this, a fact recognised years later when the Government of independent India was to bestow on Devika Rani the title of *Padma Shri*, one of the titles independent India bestows on its people. The magazine *Filmfare* in its issue of May 14, 1958 used the occasion to look back to the 1930s and the first days of Bombay Talkies, declaring: "It was but natural that Bombay Talkies soon came to stand for new values."

Bombay Talkies carried on for many years after Rai's death but in many ways its most remarkable period had ended with its founder.

6

Making a Nation Through Films

In 1939, a few months before Rai died, Indian cinema marked twenty-five years of its existence. The Silver Jubilee celebrations were lavishly organised in Bombay. Several souvenir brochures were brought out and the All-India Motion Picture Congress was held. It was opened by S. Satyamurthy, which was significant in that it showed that at least some people in the Congress were interested in films. Gandhi clearly was not, but Satyamurthy was a powerful figure in the party and the party was just then in a position of some power. If its goal of freedom for the country had still not been realised, it did now hold ministerial office in provincial Governments under the limited regional autonomy, granted to the Indians by the British in the 1935 Act. Through many negotiations, and round table conferences, the 1935 Act had been the end product of the 1930 civil disobedience campaign of Gandhi. Indeed, a Congress ministry ruled the provincial Government of Bombay. If real power still rested with the British governor of the province, the local Indian ministers did have some power to affect change.

The conference was meant to demonstrate that cinema had arrived as an important social force to help with this change, although it was recognised that deep problems remained. Chandulal Shah, who chaired the conference, highlighted the problems, rather than the successes, in his opening address, and bemoaned the continuing lack of finance, the failure by banks or other organised sources of finance to provide money, and also the internal dissensions within the industry.

Shah's analysis was reasonable and these problems would never be solved, but he was also making a point in front of a political audience and, in that sense, being unduly pessimistic. He down-played how far the industry had come and, in particular, Bombay. Indeed, it was Bombay's ability to move quicker than any other Indian city that had helped Rai make Bombay Talkies so prominent, an ability the city had demonstrated even before Rai had chosen Bombay as the home of his studio. Back in 1927, when Rai was still in London, no sooner had the Government announced it was setting up the film inquiry, than a quickly-convened Bombay Cinema and Theatre Trade Association was formed to give unified evidence. This led, in 1932, to the creation of The Motion Picture Society of India and then, in 1939, to The Indian Motion Picture Producers Association of India. Calcutta and other centres viewed this Bombay activity with alarm, but they could not get their own act together. The Bombay-based organisations made representations to the Government on behalf of the industry. The existence of these organisations also meant that Bombay became the place where industry data was gathered and Bombay was able to write the narrative of how the movie industry was developing. Members of these organisations brought out publications that emerged in the 1930s and which have formed the basis of all subsequent interpretations of the role of the studios, such as Y.A. Fazalbhoy's 1939 *The Indian Film: a Review*, collations by B.V. Dharap, and other souvenir publications.

Shah himself had been busy making films during this period. His Ranjit Movietones, as the studio had been renamed after sound was introduced, was producing twelve movies a year, as opposed to three by Bombay Talkies. In terms of the sheer number of films made, Ranjit made more films than its two main rivals in western India, Bombay Talkies and Prabhat. Up to 1940, Bombay Talkies had made eighteen films in six years, Prabhat made thirty-one and Ranjit made sixty-six. By the time Ranjit finally finished making films in 1963, over 150 films were made. However, in a common story of Indian cinema, the entire original material of these films was lost in two fires in the studio's vaults and laboratories.

Ranjit Movietone was well equipped, with four sound stages, its own laboratory, and a staff of 600. By the late 30s, Ranjit was being called 'the film factory', and like a factory it churned out thrillers, musicals, and comedies. However, Shah was always on the look out for new things. His 1939 film, *Achhut*, was another look at 'the untouchables', but, unlike *Achhut Kanya*, this was not a love story on the practices of Brahmins and other higher Hindu castes considering the lower caste as unclean. Shah, who wrote and directed the film, took the bold step of showing how, in order to get out of this 'Hindu hell', the 'untouchable' in the film coverts to Christianity and his daughter, played by Gohar, is adopted by a well-to-do family. She soon, however, finds herself back among 'the untouchables'. The reaction to this situation is the central drama of the movie.

Shah also had directors, such as Abdul Rashid Kardar, make *Thokar* in 1939 and *Pagal* in 1940, where Prithviraj played a doctor who ends up in the lunatic asylum he was meant to manage. These films are both regarded as the best films of this highly-regarded director. Kidar Sharma, Nandlal Jaswantal and Jayant Desai, who made the much praised *Sant Tulsidas* in 1939, also made significant movies for Shah.

Shah was not the only Bombay rival of Bombay Talkies. Four years before Rai set up in Malad, Sagar had been set up by Chimanlal B. Desai and Dr Ambalal Patel, with help from Ardeshir Irani. They had brought Ezra Mirza, who had started as an actor with Madan in Calcutta in 1923, and had a stint in the Hollywood cutting-room of Carl Laemmle's Universal Pictures Corporation. Sagar made *Zarina* in 1932, which was about a gypsy girl who was clearly influenced by Hollywood. The movie was debunked as an "occidental transplantation", but it showed some fine touches and much technical merit.

Sagar was no less active compared to Ranjit. Between 1931 and 1940, Sagar made only one less movie than Ranjit. What all this indicates is that if Bombay Talkies, New Theatres and Prabhat were pace-setters and moulders of fashion in the first decade of sound, there were a number of other companies of a similar structure that achieved success and had influence in shaping India's cinematic taste in this period. Of course, there were also success stories in the various regions reflecting the fact that India was more of a continent, rather than a country.

A listing, by location, of the production companies as printed in the 1938 *Indian Cinematograph Year Book* illustrates this point well:

Bangalore	2
Kolhapur	6
Poona	4
Bezwada	2
Kumbakonam	1
Rajahmundry	2
Bombay	34
Lahore	4
Salem	6
Calcutta	19
Lucknow	1
Tanjore	1
Coiambatore	8
Madras	36
Trichinopoly	2
Dharwar	1
Madurai	7
Tirupur	2
Erode	2
Nellore	1
Vizagapatam	1

That India's coastal regions should have taken a lead is not surprising. The British conquest of India had meant that the coastal towns of Calcutta, Bombay and Madras, towns the British had either created or, like Bombay, received as a present from the Portuguese and then developed, had usurped the historic position of places in north and central India, which had been the birthplace of Indian culture and civilisation over the centuries.

However, this conquest also created a dilemma. There was no common language spoken in these three centres. Most of the people in Bombay, Calcutta and Madras had their own mother tongues, which were very distinct from Hindi. It was Bengali in Calcutta, Tamil in Madras and Marathi in Bombay. And, while Bengali and Marathi shared some common roots with Hindi, Tamil did not. Nevertheless, a picture made in Bengali or Marathi would make little sense to a Hindi speaker. In contrast, there was little or no film activity in the heartland of the regions where Hindi was the mother tongue. Lucknow, the capital of the United Provinces, as it was called then had, as our 1938 list shows, a solitary film company. Otherwise, the Hindi belt of the north of India barely registered. Lahore did but Urdu was the main language there, not Hindi.

Rai's decision to choose Bombay, and to make films in Hindi, had highlighted this aspect of the Indian cinema. Indians had to find a language to make films and then make it acceptable to all Indians. Neal Gabler in *An Empire of Their Own* has explained how "the Jews, in building Hollywood, imposed their own version of America". These were Jews, immigrants from Eastern Europe, keen to be accepted by mainstream America. However, one thing that Hollywood did not have to worry about was to find a language. The language was English.

The British had imposed English on the Indians but this was spoken at best by a tiny minority, a figure of 2% was much quoted. It could not be the language of an Indian film. Indian film-makers had to figure out which of the many Indian languages they should use. Although Sanskrit is the mother language of most Indian languages, it had been a dead language for centuries, only used by Hindus for prayers. A film in Sanskrit would make little sense. Subhas Bose, impressed by how Ataturk had Romanised the old Turkish script, had argued that the common language should be in the Roman script. This would never be accepted.

A common language for India had long been a very controversial political issue in India. The British, seeking to justify their occupation of India, had debunked the Indian nationalists' argument that India was a nation by pointing out that there wasn't even a language common to all Indians. The Congress decided that once India was free, Hindi would become the national language. It was the mother tongue of more Indians than any other language, and was generally understood in most parts of the country, apart from the south where it is still not spoken. There would be a reorganisation of the provinces along linguistic lines once the British left. The British had put together huge provinces that suited the administrative convenience of a conquering power. The Congress planned to divide the country into many more states according to the language spoken in a particular region. The idea was that every Indian would speak two languages: his or her own mother tongue and Hindi.

But all this was in the future. The linguistic reorganisation of India did not start until the 1950s, and it is still going on, with the result that India is forever creating new states. In the 1930s, with the arrival of sound and film-makers seeking to appeal to a very diverse country, a decision had to be made on the language of an all-Indian film. Despite the fact that the heartland of the Hindi speakers in the north made little or no contribution to the development of the new medium, Hindi was chosen. But this left the film-makers with a huge problem—it meant most of them were working in a medium which was their second language at best, and sometimes their third. It also meant that making a film involved shooting it in more than one language.

The great film-makers of the 1930s were always having to work in a language which they had learned fairly recently. So, in Calcutta there was Prince Barua, whose native tongue was Assamese, and who also spoke fluent Bengali and English; in Poona, V. Shantaram, whose native tongue was Marathi; and the two partners of Bombay Talkies, Rai and Devika Rani, were both products of Bengali culture. It is interesting to note that when in 2003 V. Shantaram's son, Kiran, wrote a joint biography of his father, he used the Marathi term for mother 'Aai' throughout the book. Yet film-makers all had to try and make films in Hindi. Even in Madras, speakers of Tamil were becoming producers of Hindi films.

It could not have been easy for the film-makers of Calcutta, Bombay and Madras to accept Hindi. Bengal prided itself on a long tradition of Bengali culture which had already thrived for four centuries going back to the era of Chandidas and Vidyapathi. The Marathi language also had a long literary heritage, including revered poet-saints of the thirteenth century, and the beloved Tukaram of the seventeenth century. As for Tamil, it claimed a literature going back at least to the fourth century.

In comparison to all this, Hindi was a new development with a very limited literary hinterland. For many producers it was as devoid of associations as Esperanto. Yet the complex nature of the Indian linguistic map meant a film that wanted to reach out beyond its regional borders had to be in Hindi. It did, however, leave a legacy. If many observers have found in Indian films an increasing rootlessness, one reason may be that many of its finest talents have had to exert themselves in a language not of their own, and spoken by people from whom they were both physically, and culturally, removed. This became, and remains, one of the great agonies of Hindi films.

The nature of the country as a continent with many languages, dictated the way the film industry developed, and throughout the 1930s the geographical pattern of the Indian film industry underwent many changes. Almost from the beginning, two opposing trends were at work. One tendency was for each language area to develop a production centre or centres of its own. This trend appealed to regional pride, made efficient use of talent speaking the local language, and created regional stars. It had the disadvantage that a wide range of technical services could barely be supported by every language area.

A concentration in three large centres emerged—Bombay, Calcutta and Madras—each producing in the language of its area but also attempting, often through imported talent, to reach into and exploit other language areas. From the beginning, the larger centres felt that they needed to work in more than one language and to spread their wings beyond their immediate geographical area. The smaller centres, on the other hand, concentrated on one language.

Sometimes, a film script, after proving a success in one language, would be acted in another language, with an entirely new cast. *Devdas*, after its success in Bengali, was repeated by New Theatres in Hindi and later in Tamil. A producer, however, could save costs by shooting two or more versions simultaneously. The 'double versions' began almost immediately. Each separate shot was done first in one language, then in another. The operation sometimes called for two complete casts, although dance numbers often served both versions.

On the studio floor, the shout of 'Bengali take!' would be followed a few minutes later by 'Hindi take!' It became a very common cry in New Theatres and in other Calcutta studios. Occasionally, a bi-lingual actor would appear in both films of a double version. But the prevailing tendency was to use double casts, and this was one reason why film companies grew rapidly in size. The large companies acquired acting staffs representing two or more major languages.

Calcutta almost immediately achieved a monopoly over Bengali production, using this as a base for forays into other language markets, especially Hindi. The Bengali-Hindi double version became a standard activity at New Theatres and other Calcutta companies—such as the East India Film Company, which was launched in 1932.

Bombay and nearby cities, including Poona and Kolhapur, meanwhile took charge of Marathi production, using this as a base for incursions into Hindi and other language areas. In theory, Calcutta should have cornered the Hindi market. Bihar was the neighbouring state, and beyond that was Uttar Pradesh, both strongholds of Hindi. But Calcutta was a more distinctive Bengali city, while Bombay did not quite belong to the native Mahrastrians. The Mahrastrians were not a majority in the city; there was a large Gujarati and Parsi population which spoke Gujarati, and the city boasted of being cosmopolitan. Bombay even had its own cricket team, distinct from the Maharashtra team. As Bombay grew in prosperity, and more Hindi-speaking people were attracted to the city in the form of villagers, who migrated from the rural areas to the urban areas of Bombay, the city began to take a more prominent role in Hindi production and also to develop its own brand of Hindi, which became known as 'the Bombaiya Hindi.' In time, Hindi films would take this film language nationwide and make it almost a distinct language.

The two leading languages of southern India, Tamil and Telugu, were for some years the focus of mighty struggles. When sound was introduced in Bombay and Calcutta, there was no sound-production equipment in Madras, the centre of the Tamil area. The large Tamil market looked open to others. In 1932 and 1933, Tamil films were produced in Bombay by Ardeshir Irani's Imperial Film Company and by Sagar Movietone; in Calcutta, by New Theatres and the East India Film Company; and in Poona, by Prabhat. For these films, the companies usually arranged junkets of Tamil-speaking actors from Madras to come to Calcutta and to Bombay or Poona for the shoot. This sort of activity stirred southerners into action.

Among those in Madras who had some film experience was K. Subrahmanyam, a young criminal lawyer with a passion for the arts. In the late 1920s, while getting a foothold in law, he had earned money on the side selling stories for silent films to a newly-formed company, Associated Films. This company had been started by a professional strong man, Raja Sandow who, after playing hero roles for Chandulal Shah in Bombay, decided to take up production in his native province. Associated Films soon "failed for want of business-like instinct" as stated in *Who Is Who in Indian Filmland*. Meanwhile, the young criminal lawyer had won local notoriety as a film expert. In 1934, a Madras financier, intent on producing a Tamil-language film, invited Subrahmanyam to write and direct it.

There were still no available facilities other than three glass-roofed studios, and it was decided, therefore, to shoot in the open air. One difficulty was that the financier had had a quarrel with a former business associate who came each day and parked his baby Austin close to the production. As soon as he heard "Silence, please!....sound....camera!" he would start honking his horn. This forced the financier to settle with his former associate. And, although *Pavalakkodi* was completed, and was a box-office success (it had fifty songs), it persuaded Subrahmanyam that there were better ways of making films.

That same year an entrepreneur in Salem, T.R. Sundaram, took a group of actors to Calcutta, rented the Madan studio in Tollygunge for three months at a cost of Rs. 25,000, and completed a Tamil language film that proved so profitable in the south that he went north for six more junkets, all being profitable. Meanwhile, Subrahmanyam was offered financial backing for similar junkets, for which he rented the East India Film Company studio in Calcutta. On the first such junket he took sixty-five people, renting a three-storey house for them for three months, and a car to shuttle them to and from the East India studio. The studio supplied all technical personnel, including its editors. All the films were financial triumphs. Other producers arranged similar trips to Bombay.

The visits, leading to expanding profits, spurred construction of modern studios in the south. Several such studios were built during 1935-36—in Madras, Salem, and Coimbatore. These included a studio built jointly by several Madras producers, organised as the Motion Picture Producers Combine. Thereafter, Madras was never dependent on the studios in the north. The producers in the Madras area now began to take charge of Tamil production, and gradually also took control of production for the nearby Telugu area, as well as the important

Kannada and Malayalam language groups. By the 1940s, Madras, having grown powerful through its grip on these markets, also began to make astonishingly successful forays into Hindi production. This success was also helped by the decline of Calcutta, particularly following the partition of Bengal.

Vasan had been knocking at the doors of the film world for some time. Born in Thiruthuraipoondi, a small town in Madras state, he came to the big city of Madras to study, and then started an advertising agency. He soon had enough money to buy a small printing press and launched *Anandavikatan*, a popular weekly. His first forays into films were when his novel, *Sati Leelavati*, was made into a film in 1936. In 1938, he took over the distribution of films of the Madras United Artists Corporation. In 1941, there was a fire in the studio of the Motion Picture Producers Combine. Like most studios in India, it was uninsured, as no insurance company would take the risk. When the partners decided to sell the charred premises, Vasan bought it, did some rebuilding, and launched the production company, Gemini Studios. During the war, the firm made a number of films, not knowing what the best kind of film was, including a mythological film, a stunt film and a couple of love stories. However, all this was a prelude to *Chandralekha* in 1948.

It cost Rs. 3 million to make *Chandralekha*, but grossed Rs 20 million at the box office. The film, where two princes fight over a royal dancer, had taken seven hundred days to shoot and Vasan would borrow heavily for it. Vasan was persuaded to make the film in Hindi and to "retain the long and mid-shots intact, and retake the close-ups along with the songs and comedy scenes".

The film proved such a success—its drum dance is remembered even today—that 603 prints of the Hindi version of *Chandralekha* were made. The film was even released in the United States—'*Chandra*'—with English subtitles! Vasan believed that films were meant to entertain and were meant to be tailored to the ordinary man. Colossal production values, huge sets, mammoth dances, and thousands of extras were his hallmark. Thus, his films were more akin to variety entertainment programmes rather than true cinema.

In the 1950s, Gemini Pictures came out with films both in Tamil and Hindi and these Hindi films included *Mr. Sampat* (1952), *Insaniyat* (1955), *Raj Tilak* (1958), and *Paigam* (1959). There were others from Madras and elsewhere in the south, who were also attracted to Hindi movies. A.V. Meiyappan Chettiar of AVM Studios, and Venus Krishnamurthy, both from Madras, and S.M.S. Naidu of Coimbatore's Pakshiraja Studios. Then, in the 1960s, came B. Nagi Reddy of Vijaya Vauhini Studios. Through the 1950s, by making films both in Tamil and Hindi, Madras would in some years surpass Bombay in terms of the volume of film production.

The rise of Madras in the 1950s meant, of course, a reverse flow of the journeys made by film people in the 1930s to Calcutta and Bombay to make films. At that time, they had taken their actors and actresses across India, camped in these cities, and made the films. Now, southern executives would journey to Bombay, sign up stars, supporting actors and actresses, music directors and singers, and fly them out to Madras, set them up in hotels and shoot the film on the sort of tight schedule which was becoming very foreign in Bombay.

Pran, who by then was being permanently cast as the villain of Hindi cinema, recalls how there was a method, and a plan for a film shoot unlike the casual style that Bombay had increasingly come to adopt. "Everybody was totally work-oriented. Much more work was accomplished day-to-day in Madras than was ever being done back in Bombay. They were serious about film-making—the south Indians used to work more and gossip less. We learnt discipline from them, and to be punctual also."

The southern Hindi movie became known as 'made in South India' Hindi films, but there was never any danger that Madras would take over from Bombay as the movie capital of India. The southern Indian movie-makers had shrewdly judged the money to be made out of Hindi movies. While they could retain their own language specialties, the Hindi market provided the more lucrative target. This was where the big stakes were and this was the language that could describe itself as truly Indian. Bombay was so firmly entrenched as the headquarters of the all-Indian movie that it could not be displaced as the capital of Hindi movies.

There was also a problem for regional centres, and Madras in particular,. The drive by independent India to make Hindi the national language was not welcomed by the regional centres, such as Bengal. It was most actively resented in Madras, where a political party called the Dravida Munnetra Kazhagam (DMK) was set up. Hostility to Hindi was only one of the many motivating factors for the party. It also fed on the strong anti-Brahmin feeling in the region. The Congress leaders tended to be Brahmins, and there was also some talk of secession from the Indian Union, although this was discarded in later years. Films proved very useful for the party with many of its leaders, including the charismatic C.N. Annadurai, being from the film world. Tamil films were used in spreading the message so effectively that, in the 1960s, the DMK became the dominant political party of the state of Madras and came to power. The state was renamed Tamil Nadu, the land of the Tamils. Himansu, even before he had come back to India, knew Hindi had to be the language of the all-Indian film and by the time he died nobody would question Bombay's right to be the movie capital of India, or that Hindi would be the language of what became known as Bollywood.

Compare this with how easy it was for Hollywood to become the movie capital of America, and then the world, and the reasons which prompted films to decamp from the eastern seaboard of America for the west coast. The move from New York and New Jersey in the early 1900s was dictated by the weather, Californian sunshine ensuring natural light at a time when electric lights were not powerful enough. California movie-makers could also escape Thomas Edison.

Edison owned almost all the patents relevant to motion picture production and in the east, movie producers acting independently of Edison's Motion Picture Patents Company, were often sued by Edison and his agents. Edison did send his agents to California, but a movie-maker in Los Angeles could easily slip away to Mexico before the agent arrived.

Rai and other film-makers of India had a much trickier task. They had the task of nation-building through films and that at a time when India was still not free, and when there was no certainty when it might be free, or what shape this freedom would take. In India, films were an agent of a much wider social change, of making a new country from a very old one.

7

The Children of Rai

Rai's death saw his wife, Devika Rani, take charge and she quickly appointed Sasadhar Mukhjerjee and Amiya Chakraborty, who had started as an extra and then caught Devika's eye and moved up the ladder, as the producers. For a time this appeared to work very well and, in the early years of the war, Bombay Talkies produced a number of successful films, many of which even charted new territory. *Naya Sansar* in 1941, set in the newspaper industry and scripted by Khwaja Ahmad Abbas, who was himself an assistant editor at *The Bombay Chronicle*, was a critical success, if not quite a commercial one.

Two years later, in 1943, came a movie which closely resembled Walter Wagner's 1938 film, *Algiers*, which was itself a Hollywood remake of the Jean Gabin classic, *Pepe le Moko.*

Ashok Kumar's biographer, the script-writer, Nabendu Ghosh, says Sasadhar, Ashok and Gyan Mukherjee, another science student of Meghnad Saha, who had been lured into films, devised the script after studying a book on Hollywood script-writing by Francis Marion, which had a scene-by-scene analysis of some twenty early Hollywood classics.

The result was *Kismet,* the first classic Hindi thriller, where Ashok Kumar played a crook with a heart of gold who robs, in order to help a once great actress – played by a new heroine, Mumtaz Shanti – who had fallen on hard times. After many ups and downs, it all ends well.

But, as *Kismet* was being completed, the tensions latent in Bombay Talkies burst open. This appears to have been based on intense personality differences rather than any great ideological or economic reasons. In the years immediately after Himansu's death, Devika had allowed Sasadhar and Ashok to run the show but, slowly, she began to rely almost exclusively on Amiya Chakraborty, and made it clear he was the man who had her blessing. Sasadhar and Amiya did not get on and one day Sasadhar gave Devika an ultimatum: either Amiya goes or I go. Amiya stays, said Devika, so Sasadhar walked out.

Soon after came Ashok Kumar's turn. He was doing the final editing of *Kismet* when Amiya asked to see the rushes and also told Ashok to leave the editing suite. Ashok left but in such a temper that when he returned to his office he punched the wooden partition with his fists and drew blood. He decided to leave for good and would have left immediately but security guards prevented him from seeing Devika Rani that day. Soon after, he left, as did Rai Bahadur Chunilal, the general manager, Dattaram Pie, editor, and Gyan Mukherjee, the director of *Kismet;* they all joined Sasadhar in setting up a new studio, Filmistan (the Land of Films). It is interesting to note that in this clash of personalities the leading persons of Bombay Talkies were all Bengalis, illustrating the well-known Indian saying that four Bengalis produce five arguments.

However, perhaps there was more to it than just personality clashes. Money clearly played a part—after all, Bombay Talkies had rivals. There was Chandulal Shah's Ranjit Movietones, and Shah was always willing to offer stars from other studios large increases in their salaries, if they joined him at Ranjit.

Saadat Hasan Manto's memoir *Stars from another Sky* describes how Ashok Kumar became aware of money to be made as he became the great star of Indian cinema. When Himansu Rai gave him a film start, he trebled his salary to Rs. 250. Ashok Kumar trembled as he took the salary packet home and was so nervous that that night he had nightmares of being robbed. Malad then was the back of beyond and a terrified Ashok kept the money hidden under his mattress. But, as Manto says, "While Ashok was telling me this story, outside a film-maker from Calcutta was waiting to see him. The contract was ready but Ashok did not sign it because while he was offering Rs. 80,000, Ashok was insisting on Rs. 100,000. And to think that some years earlier he was at a loss to know what to do with Rs. 250". Certainly, going off with his brother-in-law to make movies meant more money all round.

Ashok Kumar doubled his salary from Rs. 1,000 to Rs. 2,000 by joining Filmistan and he now had the freedom to work for other film-makers. Following *Kismet*, Ashok Kumar could literally name his price. Mehboob Khan, who had made a reputation with several films, offered him one lakh (Rs. 100,000), a magic figure in India then, for the film *Najma*. By 1945, Debaki Bose was offering Rs. 2.5 lakh (Rs. 250,000) for *Chandrsashekar*, a film in which he was cast opposite Kanan Devi. In that sense *Kismet,* and the split from Bombay Talkies, could be said to have marked the start of the end of the studio system in Bollywood. Studios continued to exist for some time but Bombay Talkies-style studio system, and its very firm principle of an actor being wedded to one studio, was slowly dissolving. Actors and actresses could work for different studios and the big names, like Ashok Kumar, demanded very large sums of money. Ghosh marks the moment as the one "where black money entered the film industry and the studio system died out. All this happened in 1943."

Indian film historians agree that the collapse of the system was due to the laundering of black money earned by war-time profiteers, although a similar thing had also occurred, but on a much smaller scale, at the end of the First World War.

In the previous decade there was limited money in movies and it was fairly well regulated. Ruby Myers, who acted as Sulochana was, perhaps, the biggest star, and was paid Rs. 5,000 a month. The cost of a completed picture was around Rs. 40,000, and the profit-sharing ratio between producer and distributor was 60-40. The country had around 2,000 cinemas and overseas sales meant nothing, round about Rs. 2,500 per picture.

Burjor Karanjia, who for many years edited the leading film magazines and was active in the industry, in his memoir, *Counting Blessings*, has no doubt that the Second World War changed everything:

> The shortage of raw stock led to the pernicious licensing system, which in turn became the breeding ground of corruption and indiscriminate freelancing by film stars. When C.M. Trivedi, a producer, signed up the green-eyed Chandramohan (who was then on the staff of New Theatres) for a film titled *Apna Ghar* (Our House), the freelancing system was born, with all the ills that came in its wake. The new money that flooded the film industry included black market money, which coloured not only the mode of payment, but the very mentality of film making. Realising that the idolised stars were the key to immense profits, the new independent fly-by-night producers, without a stake in the film industry, began to make offers to stars on a per picture basis. The stars began to discover that they could earn more in a one picture contract than they could in a year of employment in a studio. They began to leave the big companies that had studios of their own. Freelancing became the practice, rather than the exception it had hitherto been. By the end of 1941, various stars were working in three or four films simultaneously. The number rose to seven or eight films and, in the case of one particular star, a dozen films.

The split meant *Kismet* was released with its creative team no longer at Bombay Talkies, but they drew much comfort from the fact that the film was one of the great commercial successes of the Hindi cinema—in one Calcutta theatre, Roxy, it ran for three years continuously. And, as we have seen, Ashok Kumar, and the others involved in its making, could use *Kismet* to make the sort of money no actor had previously made in the Indian cinema.

Devika Rani was determined to carry on and, while Bombay Talkies did not produce many more outstanding films, even as *Kismet* was being made she had managed to follow the example of her dead husband and discover a young actor who would became one of the greatest of all Indian actors: Dilip Kumar. And like so much of the Bollywood story it came by chance, and in the most unexpected of places, far from Bombay in the north Indian hill station of Nainital.

Devika had gone there with Amiya to look for suitable locations. Dilip Kumar, whose real name was Mohammed Yusuf Khan, had come to buy fruits for his father's fruit business. A Pathan from Peshawar, not far from what today would be Taliban country in north West Pakistan, he had come to Bombay with his father,

Mohammed Sarwar Khan, when he was a young boy. He had been schooled in the city, and his great ambition was to play Test cricket. By the time he met Devika Rani, not yet twenty years old, he was the mainstay of his father's fruit business in Bombay, and was looking to expand it.

Yusuf Khan, despite his age, was no callow youth. Not long before his meeting with Devika, a quarrel with his father had taken him to Poona where he had got to know British soldiers and often played football with them. They called him Chicko or Genghis, being the only type of Khan they knew. While Yusuf got on socially with them he, wearing his nationalist shirt, also argued with the soldiers about the hypocritical British position during the war: they said they were fighting the war for freedom yet were denying India its freedom. He even spent a night in jail, although this does not appear to have been due to his nationalist activity. But while he was in jail Gandhi observed a fast and Yusuf refused to eat the prison breakfast.

Now reunited with his father, he had come to Nainital on the annual search for fruit that took him to the Himalayan foothills of India where some of the best fruit of the sub-continent can be found.

It is not quite clear how he met Devika Rani. A psychiatrist who Devika was indebted to, Dr Masani, played a part, but whoever introduced them, meet they did and she asked him to come and see her at Bombay Talkies.

Yusuf Khan's biographers cannot agree what made Yusuf go to Bombay Talkies. He was well aware of how his father disapproved of films. Sarwar Khan was a close friend of Lala Baseshwarnath, father of Prithviraj Kapoor, both families hailed from Peshawar, and Sarwar would often chastise his friend saying "Baseshwarnath, how can you allow your son to act with *naachenealis*?" (The word for professional dancers who are held in very low esteem in India).

Yusuf Khan would tell one biographer that while the business was making money he felt his life lacked something. Whatever the reason, he was so eager that he turned up at Bombay Talkies on a Sunday morning and, finding it closed, turned up the next day, although the meeting with Devika did not go well, or at least that is what Yusuf thought. This was very understandable.

She asked him four questions: did he act, would he like to act, did he smoke, and did he speak Urdu. The answers were no, yes, no, yes. After which he was imperiously dismissed from her presence. But, then, she wrote to him, asking him to come back, although she was still not sure what to do with him. Fortunately for Yusuf Khan, Amiya Chakraborty took a shine to him, and so did Hiten Chowdhury, another import from Bengal who was soon to become Controller of Productions at Bombay Talkies.

But before he could act, Devika decided Yusuf Khan needed a new name and gave him a choice of three: Jehangir, Vasudev or Dilip Kumar. It is not clear why she felt Yusuf was not suitable. This was a time of growing Hindu-Muslim tension and she may have felt Yusuf would not go down well. Yusuf Khan told Bunny Reuben, one of his many biographers, that, when presented with the choice, out

out of sheer nerves he chose Dilip Kumar, even though he liked another name. Another biographer says he liked Jehangir but an adviser to Devika suggested Dilip Kumar and this appealed to her as it was similar to Ashok Kumar.

Amiya Chakraborty cast Dilip Kumar in the film, *Jwar Bhata,* which was shot in May 1942, with Dilip just nineteen years and five months old. Ashok Kumar, in his first movie, jumped before he was meant to; Dilip Kumar, in his first, ran so fast when he was asked to rescue a heroine, that the director shouted 'Cut!' before he could reach the heroine. The camera could not follow him and, the director told him, this is not a sports race but a movie. Like Ashok Kumar, but perhaps even more so, he taught himself acting, and eventually became the consummate movie actor of his time.

The film though proved unmemorable and *FilmIndia* described him as "an anaemic addition to our film artistes. He needs a lot of vitamins and a prolonged treatment of proteins before another picture can be risked with him." But the film has a footnote in Bollywood history. A bit part was played by an eighteen-year old called Raj Kapoor, the son of Prithviraj, who had joined Amiya Chakraborty as an assistant. This meant the two men, who would became the biggest stars Bollywood has ever produced, were both in the same movie at the very start of their parallel, and often contrasting, careers.

Jwar Bhata was not released until 1944 and, by 1946, Dilip Kumar had acted in two more films. By now, however, Devika Rani was tiring of films. In 1946, she married the Russian painter, Svetoslav Roerich and, in one of the great ironies of the Bombay Talkies story, she sold the studio to Ashok Kumar, who bought it in partnership with Savak Vacha, a colleague from Bombay Talkies with whom he had just made a film for Filmistan called *Shikari*. They returned to find their old company had debts of Rs. 28 lakhs (Rs. 2.8 million) and various frauds had been committed, some of them by the directors themselves.

Even more worrying was the overall political situation. The war had ended but India, which had seen little war fighting, was now in turmoil as the pent-up feeling for independence erupted. Gandhi's Quit India movement of 1942 had been put down with savage force by the British, turning India into, as a British official put it, "an occupied and hostile country". The British and their allies had won the war, but the stunning defeats suffered by the British, and other white empires in Asia at the hands of the Japanese, had destroyed the mystique of the white races in the east. No longer could a handful of whites rule over millions of browns. Even those Indians who had been the most reliable collaborators of the British wanted the British occupation to end. Immediately after the war the British Indian Navy, based in Bombay, had revolted, and for a few days there was a near revolutionary situation in the city. There were also growing Hindu-Muslim tensions.

Ashok Kumar and Vacha seemed impervious to all this and when they took over Bombay Talkies, they employed mostly Muslims while dismissing many Hindu employees who were redundant.

Saadat Hasan Manto, himself a Muslim working for them, feared a Hindu backlash and warned them of the growing Hindu anger. Vacha received hate mail from Hindus saying they would set fire to the studios, but he defiantly promised to push anyone who dared into the burning studio. Ashok Kumar was just as nonchalant about any religious strife and saw it as a passing madness that would soon blow over. But as Manto says, "However, it never went away, this madness. Instead, as time passed, it became more and more virulent."

Ashok Kumar was right in the sense that for all the murderous violence between Hindus and Muslims, film stars were different. This was graphically illustrated one night when Ashok Kumar, giving Manto a lift, took a short cut through a Muslim neighbourhood of the city. Manto was petrified the Muslims would recognise Ashok Kumar and kill him and he, a Muslim, would carry this guilt to his grave. Crowds did indeed stop the car but, when they recognised Ashok Kumar, instead of violence they offered brotherly greetings. So much so that they helpfully pointed out that Kumar had literally taken the wrong turning and indicated the road he needed to get home. As they left the Muslim area, Ashok Kumar told Manto, "You were worried for nothing. These people never harm artistes. They are neither Hindus nor Muslims."

This was a perceptive recognition of how Hindi films could rise above such divisive barriers, barriers so deep that the sub-continent was about to be partitioned along religious lines resulting in one of the biggest, and most violent, migrations across the newly-created borders of the two countries.

And it was a Muslim director that Ashok Kumar had hired, Kamal Amrohi, who was to produce Ashok Kumar's Bombay Talkies biggest hit and a film which is still seen as a landmark Hindi film, *Mahal*. The word means mansion and Ashok Kumar had lived with the idea of the movie for a long time. He had always been intrigued by ghost stories. Some time in the summer of 1948, workers of Bombay Talkies told him that they had seen the ghost of Himansu Rai. This set Ashok Kumar thinking and when later that summer he hired Jeejeehoy House, a supposedly haunted house in a hill-station near Bombay, he had an experience which made him feel ghosts may be real. One night, as he was about to go to sleep, a woman knocked at the door asking for help with her car. But the car could not be fixed and she abandoned it outside the house. Later that night, Ashok was woken up by shouting and went to find that the car was still there, with a man dead inside it, his throat having been cut.

Next morning he summoned his servant but the servant assured him he must have had a nightmare for there was no car outside. Ashok, not satisfied, went to the police to report the incident only to be told by the inspector "This murder took place fourteen years ago. A woman murdered someone and fled. Then she died in a car accident."

On his return to Bombay, Ashok Kumar narrated the story to Amrohi who took the idea of the haunted house but added the necessary love ingredients, essential in a Hindi film. The result was a taut, atmospheric film made haunting by both the visuals and the music. The film was shot by a ghost, but a living ghost in the shape of Wirsching, who had not set foot in Bombay Talkies for a decade but, now, after the war, was a free man and had decided there was no point in going back to Germany and would live his life out in India.

Ashok Kumar, himself, played the male lead opposite an actress who was barely sixteen years old but already a very experienced one. *Mahal* was her seventeenth film and that year, in 1949, she was to star in no less than nine films. She had come to films as an eight-year-old in 1942, the same year Dilip Kumar made his début and, like Dilip Kumar, she had a Pathan father, Attaullah Khan who was, if anything, even more fierce than Sarwar Khan, and certainly more determined to make the most of the gifts of his beautiful daughter.

The Khans were poor, lived in a slum near Bombay *Talkies's* studio and Attaullah, having left his job at Imperial Tobacco over some tiff, had got his eight-year-old, called Mumtaz Khan, an audition with Devika Rani. She gave her a new name, Madhubala, a part in the 1942 film *Basant,* and by the time she played in *Mahal,* she had acquired that touch-me-not beauty that Ashok Kumar felt the main actress in *Mahal* ought to radiate. The film required her to sing a song which was to became one of the most successful ever in the history of the Hindi cinema *"Ayega ayega, ayega, aanewla ayega ... a ....a"* (he who is meant to come will come).

Of course, by this time, unlike when Ashok Kumar had made his début, actors and actresses were not required to sing: they mimed; playback singing was becoming the norm and the song was sung by Lata Mangeshkar who herself was only twenty but with this song became the first great female singer of the Hindi screen, matching, and then surpassing, the father of Hindi film singing, Saigal.

By this time, in the true traditions of Bombay Talkies where the producer always discovered the next big star, Ashok Kumar discovered his, at least made him feel that he had a future as an actor. In 1948, Ashok Kumar chanced on Dev Anand in the garden of Bombay Talkies, Ashok having gone there to have a cigarette break while discussing who should play the lead role in the next film his studio was planning. Dev Anand had every reason to feel despondent.

Devdutt Pishorimal Anand, to give his full name, was then twenty-four years old, yet another immigrant from the north like Dilip Kumar and Raj Kapoor. Like Ashok Kumar, his father was a lawyer, and after graduating in English Literature, Dev Anand had come to join his elder brother, Chetan, already a prominent member of the Indian Peoples' Theatre Association (IPTA, a leftist cultural organisation in the city). As he puts it, he wanted to be known to the world and so packed his bags and came to the city, determined to tramp the streets until he made his presence felt. But despite Chetan being there, and also getting to know K.A. Abbas, the film world was proving very difficult, and he worked for some time in the Military Censor's Office, reading letters written by soldiers to their families. Eventually, he barged through yet another door, literally gate-crashing into the office of Baburao Pai, the financial consultant of Prabhat Studios who asked him to go to Pune for an audition. Much to Anand's surprise, he also gave him a first-class ticket on the Deccan Queen, which took him in three hours in some comfort from Bombay to Pune. There, after an audition by director P.L. Santoshi, he got a three-year contract on a monthly salary of Rs. 350.

The film, *Hum Ek Hain,* made in 1946, could not have been more idealistic. The title meant 'We are One' and stood for Hindu-Muslim unity where Dev Anand, a Hindu, played the Muslim in the film, while a Muslim actor played the Hindu. However, the film flopped and the Prabhat experience was more notable for the friendship he formed with the choreographer of *Hum Ek Hain,* Guru Dutt.

It came through their common washerman, the ubiquitous Indian dhobi, who would often hand Dev's shirts to Guru and *vice versa.* They made a promise to each other that if, some day in the future, Guru Dutt were to turn film-maker, he would take Dev as his hero, and if Dev were to produce a film, he would take Guru Dutt as its director.

Then, a chance encounter on a train took him to Bombay Talkies and the fateful meeting in the garden with Ashok Kumar. According to Ashok Kumar's biographer, their conversation went as follows, with Ashok starting off by asking:

"Why are you seated here? What do you want?"

"Sir, my name is Dev Anand. I am an actor and I want a job."

"Have you acted before? Are you acting in any film right now?"

"I have acted in one film, which did not do well. I have no work now."

"Come with me."

This conversation has echoes of the conversation Ashok had with Himansu and that Devika had with Dilip Kumar, which may mean that, in recollection, the careers of Hindi film personalities follow the same pattern as if they are reading from the same script.

Like Himansu with Osten, Ashok Kumar had great difficulty convincing his director, Shahid Latif, to take on Dev Anand. Shahid protested that, "He looks like a chocolate bar," the same criticism that had been made of Ashok Kumar when he started. Latif had set his mind on having Ashok Kumar play the lead in his film and did not see any reason why he should have to settle for this newcomer.

But, like his mentor Himansu, Ashok Kumar proved stubborn, which was appropriate as the film was called *Ziddi,* Hindi for stubborn. Determined to save his energies for *Mahal,* the idea for which he already had, he had his way. Dev Anand suddenly found himself earning Rs. 20,000 and was launched into stardom.

The film was to prove crucial to Dev Anand's career for another reason. Apart from being a commercial success, it introduced Dev Anand to Kishore Kumar, Ashok's younger brother, who was making his début in the film as a playback singer. It was the beginning of a lifetime of friendship, one that would shape the course of both their individual and professional lives.

In the decades that followed, much of Dev Anand's success as a film star owed a great deal to the number of super-hit songs which Kishore sang for him in the 1950s, even as Dev's screen presence helped establish Kishore's career as a singer. They produced a wonderful chemistry, with Dev Anand insisting on Kishore singing for him, and Kishore lending his voice as a playback singer to Dev in the 1950s and 1960s.

So, in a short space of time, Dilip Kumar, Raj Kapoor and Dev Anand—all born within a year of each other—along with Madhubala, were launched as stars. Not long after the 1950s had started, the Big Three of Bollywood, as Dilip Kumar, Raj Kapoor and Dev Anand are called, had ushered in the new era of Bollywood, the star system. Despite the fact that this was done against the background of post-war, independent India, when the world was changing, and the Indian world was changing even faster, the star system that these three helped cement—Ashok Kumar, in a sense having launched it—has proved more enduring than the Hollywood studio system that Himansu and Devika had tried to foster in India. The studio system had barely lasted two decades, whereas the star system has been around for more than sixty years and shows no sign of being challenged.

In the history of Bollywood, much is made of the Big Three and when, some years ago, Stardust published *100 Greatest Stars of all Time,* the cover showed a photograph of Raj Kapoor in the middle, flanked by Dev Anand and Dilip Kumar. It was a rare photograph and a somewhat misleading one. The Big Three never acted together, although Raj and Dilip did, and Dilip and Dev did, but never Dev and Raj. Although Dilip Kumar and Raj Kapoor followed very different paths, Dilip Kumar being widely seen as the great actor and Raj Kapoor not paying much attention to acting, but wanting to be an impresario, they were and remained close friends. Their families had known each other from Peshawar and Dilip Kumar intervened to try and sort out Raj Kapoor's marital problems. When Dilip Kumar got married, Raj Kapoor crawled on his knees up two floors to see Dilip's elder sister.

Dev Anand was never part of this circle. Fairly early in his acting career he and his brother Chetan started Navketan, a film production company for which Dev acted and also later directed his own movies. Some of his best moments as an actor came when being directed by his brother, Vijay.

In 1949, while making *Jeet,* Dev Anand fell hopelessly in love with his leading lady, Suraiya. She was of the old school in that she could sing, as well as act. But she was also a Muslim, and the woman she called her grandmother (she was, Manto says, really her mother) would not hear of her marrying a Hindu. The pair went on acting together for another three years but in the end it was clear there could be no happy ending to this story, as Suraiya's mother refused to consent to an inter-religious marriage. Suraiya, whose own career declined as singing stars went out of fashion, lived out her life, unloved, and unnoticed, meeting a sad, lonely, end.

In 1954, during the making of *Taxi Driver,* which his brother Chetan Anand had directed, Dev Anand did find love when he married the film's leading lady, Kalpana Kartik, who had been discovered by Chetan Anand when she had essayed a small role in *Baazi.*

In contrast to Dilip Kumar's masochist lover boy, and Raj Kapoor's Charlie Chaplin style 'tramp', Dev Anand personified a sense of fun. Yet unlike these two actors, he did not evolve. A certain Dev Anand style developed: a sing-song, rat-a-tat-a-tat dialogue delivery, his puffed-up hair, exaggerated motions of the hand, and the swaggering gait remained the same. Whatever the character or the plot, the mannerisms rarely changed, which meant he was never rated too highly as a performer. Not surprisingly, he did not have too many award-winning roles, *Kala Paani* and *Guide* being exceptions. However, he knew the secret of Bollywood success was entertainment value. This explained his popularity over the next two decades as Dev either acted in or directed a series of musical blockbusters, where the plots were often the same but the emphasis was on entertainment on a scale not seen in Hindi cinema of that era, with some of the best Hindi film music ever heard.

Ashok Kumar continued to make films at Bombay Talkies until 1953, searching for new talent both on the screen, and as a director. The process of discovery was often quite remarkable. In early 1951, Ashok Kumar agreed to work in a film with an unknown young man. The man had been pestering him for some time saying that he was a refugee and had a script which had a double role for Kumar. In the end Ashok relented. On the first day of the shooting Ashok Kumar was irritated to find a crowd of people, some forty-odd journalists, gathered around, but the new director promised to quieten them down. But soon after the first shot was taken, he annoyed Ashok Kumar by suggesting he should do it differently. For an unknown director to suggest this to the great Ashok Kumar was unheard of. Kumar agreed, but said, "Develop both the takes tonight so that I can see them at 8am tomorrow. If my shot seems right, then you will let me work according to my reasoning and never bother me in future."

At eight the next morning when both shots were projected, Kumar had to accept that the new director was right. Until then Ashok had not known the man's full name, an indication of the informal way Bollywood works. Now he asked him and the man replied, "Baldev Raj Chopra."

Like providing Dev Anand with his first hit, Ashok Kumar had helped discover a man who would soon establish himself as one of Bollywood's great directors, he was generally known as B.R. Chopra, and a Chopra dynasty would develop with his brother, Yash Chopra, also becoming a famous director.

The actress Nalini Jayant got her break with Kumar's Bombay Talkies in *Tamasha* which brought Phani Majumdar from New Theatres as a director in Bombay. Nitin Bose had already arrived to make *Samar* in 1949 and *Mashal* in 1950.

That was also the year when one of the most important Bengali directors came to work for Bombay Talkies, making a seminal contribution to Bollywood. Bombay Talkies were making a film called *Maa* which would provide a launch pad for Bharat Bhusan, who had been struggling for some time. Savak Vacha decided that the film needed a strong director and decided to ask Bimal Roy to come from Calcutta to direct the movie.

The young director, accompanied by his family and a small tight group of colleagues, left Calcutta's Howrah station for the thirty-six hour train trip that would take them west to Bombay's Victoria station. His young daughter, Yashodhara Roy, who was then six, was on the train:

> We travelled first class. In those days you had a bogie all to yourself; it was not a corridor train. We would have travelled on the BNR, Bombay Nagpur train. My father brought a group of people with him; all of us were in the same compartment. The people who travelled with us included Asit Sen, my father's assistant and a great comedian, Hrishikesh Mukherjee, who was my father's editor, Nabendu Ghosh, a writer and Paul Mahendra, a Punjabi, who grew up in Calcutta. He had acted for my father and was my father's dialogue writer. Father would write in Bengali. Bengali and English were the two languages he knew. He hardly spoke Hindi. Hindi dialogue was difficult for him. Nazir Hussein was also in that compartment. He was an actor who had acted in a film for my father. He also helped with the translation from Bengali to Hindi. The house we were given in Bombay was Devika Rani's house, about ten houses away from the studio in Malad. Malad then was very rural: a lot of trees; I would not say jungle, but it was very green, and not developed as now, and with the roads not paved. It was a quaint little cottage, single storey, with a stone exterior. We all camped together. There were three bedrooms and a drawing-room, kitchen and a store-room. People slept in the drawing-room, five of them sleeping on the floor. I remember, they would go to the studio and then come back and tell my mother "*Bowdi* (a term of respect), we are hungry." My mother was pregnant with my younger sister. In those days Malad was so far away that when my mother would go to the city, my father would tell my mother to please come back before dark. Savak Vacha had called him over to Bombay. He came to do *Maa* and the plan was to go back to Calcutta.

Roy never did return. He made his home in Bombay and became one of the great directors of Bollywood with his 1953 film, *Do Bigha Zameen,* a film about rural poverty—the title means two acres of land—and the terrible burden it imposes, arguably one of the most powerful social dramas Bollywood has ever made. The movie, in many ways, represented all that was best in the New Theatres Bengali school of film-making, for Roy was a quintessential Bengali film-maker. His films were a blend of good cinema and commercialism, the sort of films rare in Bollywood today. Like many Bengalis of his generation, he saw himself as a progressive man of the left, probably a bit ahead of his time, who would have been happiest making films in Bengali. But because of the dominance of Hindi and Bombay he had to make films in Hindi, a language he did not speak much.

Yashodhara recalls:

He was a Bengali and proud of it. He hardly spoke Hindi. He never spoke Marathi [the local language in Bombay]. He only knew English and Bengali. He wrote by long-hand, paper and pen, using a Parker pen, writing in Bengali and that would then be translated into Hindi. Baba's work-clothes were white cotton shirt and black trousers or dark brown trousers, but at night he used to wear a white lungi and a white kurta. And on formal occasions, he would always wear dhoti, Punjabi and chaddar: formal Bengali dress. He took us to Russia in 1959 and I still remember in Moscow, in the cold, he was wearing dhoti, kurta and chaddar. Because of him being a Bengali, there was a certain resentment my father faced on several occasions. They resented the fact my father felt and acted like a Bengali. This came out when my father won the awards for *Do Bigha Zameen*. *Do Bigha Zameen's* original idea was that of Salil Chowdhury (another Bengali who provided the music). My mother was sitting at the *Filmfare* award ceremony next to some people who were Punjabis. She told us this story. My father went the award that night dressed like a Bengal babu wearing dhoti, Punjabi and chaddar. As he won the awards, he took away the Best Picture and the Best Director award, she heard them say, 'Who is this dhoti-clad fellow who has won the award?' *Do Bigha Zameen* was the first Hindi film released in Metro, an epoch-making occasion. Radio Ceylon interviewed everyone after the film asking the crowds for their reaction. The man carrying out the interviews outside Metro was Sunil Dutt; he was called Balraj then. My father was a man of very few words. He never talked loudly. A chain-smoker, he smoked his last cigarette one and half hours before his death. He always smoked Chesterfield. He did not drink at all but he was addicted to tea. Later, when we lived in Godiwalla Bungalow, a two-storey bungalow with a portico and a garden, I would witness script sessions. Baba preferred them all to come over to the house. I remember seeing Guru Dutt uncle, S.D. Burman, Salil Chowdhury, Uttam Kumar, Dev Anand and Suchitra Sen. I remember when he made *Madhumati*, Dilip Kumar came over. They would sit round outside and there would be heated discussions and arguments. Later, Gulzar came over and my father, recognising he was a good poet, asked him to do the lyrics for one of the *Bandini* songs.

Gulzar, a Sikh, who at birth was named Sampooran Singh Kalra, had come to Bombay just a year before Roy, part of the migration of partition from north India to the city, but he could both speak and understand Bengali, and it was a Bengali friend who introduced him to Roy. However, initially this led to an interesting misunderstanding. Roy thought he was a Muslim and asked his fellow-Bengali "Bhodrolok Baishnow kobita ki kore bujbe." (How will the gentleman understand Vaishnav poetry? Vaishnav being highly regarded Bengali romantic poetry?) He was told the gentleman was a Sikh, who knew Bengali. Like everyone else in Bollywood, Bimal Roy would became Bimalda for Gulzar, the term of respect used in Bengal. As Gulzar himself became a successful director he never stopped acknowledging the role that Roy played as mentor for a whole generation of Bollywood film-makers.

If this shows the influence the Bengal school had on Bollywood then the exodus from Calcutta to Bombay also created an extraordinary Bengali colony in Bombay.

I had personal experience of this when, in the late 40s, the Bengali singer Hemant Mukherjee, came to Bombay seeking work and lived in our home in Bombay for some time. My father, a prominent businessman, introduced him to a few people and Hemant Kumar, as he became known, went on to build a very successful career as a playback singer. New Theatres had all but gone, but the Bengali influence in Bombay was to remain strong for many decades.

In 1950, Ashok Kumar tired of always playing the goodie, decided he wanted to play a bad character and got Gyan Mukherjee to direct *Sangram,* but this was to prove too controversial for independent India. Ashok Kumar portrayed a rarity in Hindi cinema then: a bad police officer, who murders a girl he loves, extracts money from traders to gamble, shoots down a policeman who has come to arrest him, and is finally shot by his own father.

The audiences loved it and it was well on its way to the much-coveted silver jubilee—twenty-five weeks continuous showing in theatres—but the idea of the Indian cinematic public taking to a dishonest cop proved too much for the then Bombay chief minister, Morarji Desai. He summoned Ashok Kumar and told him, "You have to do two things, Mr Ashok Kumar. First you have to withdraw your film from the cinema houses and this you must do tomorrow. The second is my request to you—play the role of the honest police inspector." *Sangram* was banned as it entered its sixteenth week.

What Ashok Kumar did not know was Bombay Talkies could have done with honest employees. Although the debt of Rs. 28 lakhs had been reduced, despite the success of the films, there was still a three lakh debt. When the books were examined, it was discovered that the accountant had been less than honest; he had got Ashok Kumar's signature on blank papers and siphoned off money, even remitting money every month to someone's mistress. In 1953, Ashok Kumar had had enough and sold off Bombay Talkies, taking a huge loss. The new owners could make nothing of the company; it was soon liquidated and today, heaps of rubble and garbage, and a public toilet, conceal the dilapidated studio that once showcased the best acting talent in the country.

The Bollywood studio era did not produce a Joseph Kennedy or a Howard Hughes style figure and Benegal points to the difference in the style of the producers between the two cinematic worlds:

> A lot of studio owners of the pre-war time in Bombay were people who had made a lot of money on the stock exchange: grain merchants, sattaria, and speculators on the stock exchange. In Hollywood, the producers became far more important than the director. The director was a hired hand. The producer was a person who conceptualised something and got writers to write.

In Bombay, a man like Ardeshir Irani, who was known as Seth (the local word for boss), combined both roles and Saadat Hassan Manto, who worked for Irani's Imperial as a *munsi,* meaning resident writer, recalls an occasion which suggests the Seth was a sort of Bombay Joseph Kennedy figure, very keen to increase his harem of women:

> One day I went to Imperial Film Company to meet Seth Ardeshir Irani. As I walked into his room, through the swing door, I found him pumping one of Sheedan's breasts (Sheedan was a rather plump actress), as if it was one of those old-fashioned car horns. I turned right round without saying a word.

This is not quite the romantic interest Brian Shoesmith has in mind when he says that "In many respects the studios represent a romantic moment in capital formation in contemporary India." It certainly did not succeed in its stated purpose of bringing bank finance to the industry or even Government assistance. In fact, the success of the movies made the Government tax it more. But the studios, says Shoesmith, "also created the beginnings of a truly Indian film form: the *masala* film, which combined drama, song, dance and action".

The film historian and writer, Iqbal Masud, has said the forties laid the foundations of Indian cinema's themes and ideas. Concepts of the cinema sown in this era would replicate themselves in any number of variations in films from that moment on. In the process, the studio era of the forties also helped define an Indian nation, a definition that at the beginning of the decade seemed difficult, if not impossible.

8

Blondes and Brunettes: Bollywood's White Women

In a country which has an ambivalent relationship with women, worshipping them as strong mother goddess figures but, also, in other respects, treating them as possessions, one of the remarkable features of the Bollywood story is that from the mid-30s until well into the late 40s, there was a galaxy of female stars who dominated the film scene, overshadowed their male stars and defined the emerging Bollywood movie. Rarely in the history of film anywhere in the world have the female stars taken such a central role or come from such a varied background. What was even more astonishing was that this happened just a decade after no director could find women to play female roles and had to use men for this purpose.

We have already seen the impact of Devika Rani, but even as Bombay Talkies was up and running, another female star had emerged who had an even more exotic background and whose deeds, looked at now, sixty years after she wowed the Indian cinema audience, have a ring of fantasy and wonder about them. In strict cinematic terms, the movies this actress starred in were B movies; pretty low-grade, cheap entertainment stunt films, but her rise and dominance during the 30s tells us a great deal about Bollywood and the Indian cinema world. 'Fearless Nadia', the name by which she was known on the screen, was born Mary Evans, to a Greek mother and a Welsh father. A large blonde, her movie roles involved beating up Indian men and then bursting into loud laughter and who, despite an illegitimate son, ended up marrying one of the owners of the studio which made her into a star.

Her films were shunned by the Indian intellectuals but they appealed to the uneducated urban masses increasingly drawn to the cities, factory workers, tonga drivers, and they also reached beyond India to Africa and the Far East, where her blonde looks and rebellious on-screen behaviour carried an enormous sex appeal. The irony here was that the films were made for Wadia Brothers and the older Wadia, the man who had started the studio and gave Evans her break in films, was one of the great intellectuals of the Indian cinema and played a leading part for many years in the politics of the Indian film industry.

Jamshed Bomanji Wadia could not have been more educated, with an MA in English literature and a law degree, or better connected to the Parsi upper crust of Bombay. The name Wadia meant master builder and it was a title given to an ancestor, Lovji Nusserwanji when, in 1735, as foreman at the East India Company's shipyards, he was asked to build ships in Bombay and modernise the shipyards. Lovji's success led to a migration of Parsis from Surat, and other west Indian towns, to Bombay, leading to the growth of the city and of Parsi dominance. J.B.H, as he was known, and his younger brother, Homi Wadia, ventured into films with Homi directing the 1931 silent movie *Diler Daku*. They had originally called themselves Wadia Brothers Productions but the success of the silent *Toofan Mail* (Fast Train) in 1933, made then launch Wadia Movietone. They now had backing from the Tatas, a financial partner in M.B. Billimoria, and bought the former family seat, Lovji Castle, in Bombay's Parel district for this purpose. Keen to preserve their family history, the studio emblem was a sailing ship. There was no hint in their early films that they would bring a Nadia-like creature to the screen. Their first sound film, *Lal-e-Yaman*, made in 1933 was a story of romance and princely intrigue, the central ingredient being Persian-Arabian fantasy, scripted by Joseph David, who had written *Alam Ara* and long been part of Parsi Theatre. But the Wadias were toying with the idea of stunt movies and this is where Mary Evans, then a twenty-five year old, fitted in very well. She would emerge as a sort of Indian Robin Hood, albeit female, as if all her life had been destined for this moment.

Before that, Mary Evans's life had been like that of many a young white woman in India of no great means, who was hoping to exploit as best as she could the fact that the British ruled the country. Born in Perth in 1909, she had arrived in India in 1911, when her father's army unit was posted to the country. Her father died in the trenches of France in 1915 and Margaret, her mother, a one-time belly dancer, settled in Bombay where Mary, a Catholic, went to a convent school.

Like all English children in India, she was brought up totally ignorant of Indian history or culture, let alone what Gandhi and his followers were getting up to, sometimes literally, outside the walls of the convent. But at the convent, the nuns discovered she had a nice voice and gave her some solo parts in the church choir. However, Mary's ambitions were aroused by films; she watched them avidly, being allowed by her mother to go and see this cheap form of entertainment.

In 1922, Mary and her mother left Bombay for Peshawar making, in effect, the journey in reverse that not long afterwards many of the stars of the Indian screen, like Prithviraj and Dilip Kumar, would make. Mary was enthralled by her journey on the Frontier Mail to Peshawar and, throughout the trip, stayed glued to the window of her carriage as the train sped across western India to the northern borders of British India. Margaret and Mary arrived at what was described as an 'uncle's' farm an hour away from Peshawar, complete with horses, dogs, chickens and ducks. Nothing could be more different from Bombay: neither cinemas nor theatres, nor other places where a teenager, white and female, could linger carefree.

Mary, of course, was subject to the code the British had imposed on themselves in India: no social mixing with the Indians. So while Peshawar was not a big place, and Hindus and Muslims mixed with each other, the Europeans remained a separate caste. This meant that Mary Evans missed getting to know the families of Sarwar Khan, father of the film star who assumed the name Dilip Kumar, or the family of Bashesharnath Kapoor, whose son was Prithiviraj. The Khans and the Kapoors knew each other well and were good friends.

The odd English man and woman did have contacts with Indians and even encouraged them. Norah Richards, wife of the Professor of King Edward College in Peshawar, played a crucial role in developing Prithviraj's interest in the theatre and, as Zohra Segal has written, "Norah nourished his dream about a theatre of his own. She initiated him in the world of Western plays." But this was a world removed from Mary.

She continued to sing and learnt to ride, being presented on her fifteenth birthday with a chestnut-brown male pony called Tommy. Then something mysterious happened. Mary had a love affair with a British officer but whether this led to something or not is not clear. What is clear is that is on 26 November, 1926, Robert Jones was born, known from then on as Bobby. He would later become a hockey player in India and go to live in Australia, where he retired. Mary Evans's biographer, Dorothee Wenner, says that it remains unclear who Bobby really was. Sometimes he was called Mary's brother, at other times her cousin, while in all probability Bobby was Mary's son. It was not until 1972 that Mary and her husband, Homi Wadia, officially adopted Bobby as their 'son'—and nothing further was stated. Homi Wadia would later tell a story that suggested that the child was not that of Mary Evans but had been adopted by Mary and Margaret during a visit to England. Mary had gone home hoping to get to drama school but was told that there were any number of pretty English girls bursting to get into the cinema and she would be better off trying her luck in India. During the visit they met an acquaintance of Margaret, who was even poorer than the Evans, and Margaret took pity and decided to adopt one of the young boys and bring him back to India. Wenner cannot say how true this version is. What is true is that from 1926, Margaret, Mary and Bobby formed a very tightly-knit family.

Clearly, Mary had to earn money; Peshawar hardly provided many opportunities, and in May 1927 she was back in Bombay, once again journeying on the Frontier Mail. A year later, Prithviraj would take the same train and arrive at the same station in Bombay and his first words to the tonga driver were "Take me to the sea!"—he had not seen the sea before. Mary knew all about the sea and went to the accommodation arranged for her by friends.

In Bombay she worked in the cosmetics department of the Army and Navy Stores, the former Watsons Hotel, where India's first cinema show had been held. The belief among the poorer whites and Anglo-Indians in Bombay was that work in this, then the most prestigious department store of town, could result in a meeting with a British officer, who might come shopping and, possibly, lead to marriage. It had happened to an Anglo-Indian friend of Mary's. But she was not much of a cosmetics counter girl and soon became a secretary in a law firm before, through an advert in *The Times of India*, she met the Russian ballerina, Madame Astrova. Madame Astrova, like many Russians of her class, had fled her country after the revolution, and was looking for new students for her dance school. Mary joined her and soon acquired a new name when, after a visit to an Armenian tarot card reader, she was told she would be very successful but would have unhappiness in her private life. Take on a stage name, advised the Armenian, and after much looking at the cards Mary looked for a name beginning with 'N' with five letters and chose Nadia.

Madame Astrova's troupe toured the country, performing in front of diverse audiences from soldiers at military bases, to open-air shows in front of villages, in small towns, and in Maharajah's palaces. The audiences were generally men and soon Nadia had graduated from the chorus to her own solo number, a gypsy dance demonstrating her mastery of the cartwheel and the splits. She was now the star of the show.

But feeling underpaid, Nadia had a fight with Madame Astrova while the troupe was in New Delhi and she left the show. There was a brief sojourn with the Zarko Circus, performing as part of their Asian tour, but this did not work and Nadia tried her hand with the management of the Globe Film Theatre, a new cinema chain. Sound had not yet arrived so every movie hall showing a silent movie had an orchestra. Nadia wanted to perform little vaudeville sketches on the stage, before the main film, to draw a larger crowd. Soon she joined a Russian-German dance troupe specialising in gypsy dance which performed in cinemas and Nadia learnt a new trick, offering off-screen noises and songs during the silent movies. As the heroine began to die, Nadia was supposed to sing a sad song. She often got her timing wrong with the result that even as she finished singing the heroine was still alive, causing much mirth in the audience. It suggested she had an ability to provoke laughter, even if unwittingly, and this would prove useful.

During her travels, Nadia had got friendly with Eruch Kanga, the manager of Regal Theatres in Lahore, who had told the Wadias in glowing terms about her. Soon she was on her way to Parel for an interview. Nadia would later recall the first meeting, "When the day came I took the train from Wellington Mews in Colaba, not far from my home, and rode out to Parel where the studio was located right next to the house of the Governor of Bombay. In those days, the areas were on the edge of town, and behind the studio were lots of paddy fields, and you could look over to Antop Hill and out to Borivili—no skyscrapers blocking the view. I remember I had treated myself to a sweet, sky-blue dress for the interview, along with a pretty little hat, complete with sunflowers. When I alighted from the tram, Mr. Kanga was there, waiting for me in his red Chrysler, and we drove through the wrought-iron studio gates together. I had rather anticipated some sort of tin shed structures, as I had seen in Imperial Studios, where I had sometimes watched filming in the silent-movie days. But, suddenly, we were driving up to a grand villa! The whole atmosphere led me to prepare myself for a meeting with some respectable elderly gentlemen. As we entered the lobby, all I could see were some actors hanging around, dressed as monkeys. It was quite funny."

She found J.B.H. Wadia chain-smoking behind his desk. His first look at her horrified him. Kanga had not told him how white Nadia was or how large. JBH would later admit that he thought Kanga was playing a trick on him. Nadia, never lacking confidence, told him she was famous in the world of cinema. JBH replied he had never heard of her. "To which I said that until now I hadn't heard of him either!" Both laughed. Nadia then advertised her qualities: a horse-rider, a dancer, very athletic, she could even do the splits.

But while she could speak Greek—the influence of her mother, who spoke accented English—she did not know any of the Indian languages—no Hindi, Urdu, Marathi or Gujarati. Nevertheless JBH was impressed but wanted Homi's advice. Nadia just laughed when she saw Homi and, turning to JBH, asked, "What? This man decides such matters?"

There is conflicting evidence as to how much Nadia was paid; it was either Rs. 60 a week or Rs. 150 a month. Homi thought JBH was mad but went along with him. Nadia had to learn a Hindi scene by heart. Since she could not read Hindi it was written for her in the Roman script and she was asked to return in a week, after which Homi would give her a screen test.

The result was predictable. Nadia could not master the new language, mispronouncing words in the way that advertised her as an alien. She spoke Hindi like almost any other Briton trying out the language for the first time, and this sounded very comical to the Indians. But the Wadias soon saw she could be an ideal stunt woman. She had tiny, three minute roles in *Desh Deepak* (Light of the Homeland), which JBH directed. A more substantial part followed in *Noor-e-Yaman* (Light of Yeman), where she sang and danced, and also shed a few tears.

Nadia, of course, was an odd person at the studio. Most of the employees spoke Gujarati, which was also the mother tongue of the Wadias, so Nadia could not converse with them. She learnt her Hindi from texts that were transcribed into Latin letters and her pronunciation had to be endlessly corrected. Wenner says Nadia wasn't really taken seriously and, in any case, in the hierarchy of those days, actors were by no means at the top of the business and would never have thought of demanding special treatment.

The Wadias, like Rai, ran their studio as a patriarchal family unit where every one of the 600 people on the payroll was meant to be equal. Homi Wadia would later recall how at ten every morning, just like in a school, a bell would ring and there would be a roll call. In general, a kind of egalitarianism prevailed and the actor not required in a shoot might bring food for everyone else or, the actress, temporarily unemployed, instead of retreating to her secluded room, would help hang curtains for the backdrop, or even repair costumes. In the style of good paternalistic employers, the Wadias provided free medical care for their employees. Such paternalism could lead to dependency and in August 1938, when Imperial Studios closed down, some thirty employees, former criminal offenders, who hadn't left the grounds for over seven years "out of fear of the law", just did not know what to do. So they camped outside the shut gates of the studio for days, hoping it would open, and they would not have to face the outside world again. The Wadias, however, by all accounts created a happy family, even if Nadia by her colour and her inability to speak the local language, was a bit apart.

Homi Wadia would later say, "Miss Nadia was a white lady, after all, and everyone in the studio felt out of their element when asked to work with her as a stunt actress. Back then she was still very reserved, very quiet, and a far cry from messing around like a buddy with those of us who had been in the team longer."

But this was about to change when the Wadias decided to make *Hunterwali*. It came about partly through accident. The Wadias were busy in another extravagant melodrama when, in December 1934, the leading lady fell ill and production had to be stopped. The Wadias already had the screenplay for a stunt film with Nadia ready and JBH, worried about the waste of studio time, was keen to get this much smaller, cheaper production going. Homi required a lot of convincing as he was not sure the blonde lead was capable.

The Wadias had tried to make Nadia Indian. Struggling to fit a large blonde woman into an Indian film, JBH suggested to Nadia that she take the screen name of 'Nanda Devi' and wear a black wig with long pigtails. Nadia reacted with fury, "Look here, Mr. Wadia, I am willing to try anything once, but this is ridiculous. I am a white woman and I will look foolish with long black hair. And my name is very well-known all over India as Nadia. I refuse to change my name. It has been chosen by an Armenian fortune-teller and it has brought me good luck. And besides, I am not Devi! Nadia even rhymes with Wadia!"

JBH was an admirer of Hollywood and Douglas Fairbanks, in particular. JBH was his host when he visited Bombay, secured the Indian rights to his *Mark of Zorro*, and now he had a script which included elements of this film and *The Perils of Pauline*. The stunt movie story transplanted Douglas Fairbanks' version to a mythical Indian kingdom, except that the palace looked neither opulent nor very regal. The ace in the Wadia pack was Nadia.

Nadia was to be trained by Meherjibhai Tarapore in Hindi; the script required her to appear in some palace scenes in a sari and to speak Hindi, but the centre-piece of the movie was the stunts and fighting scenes, including a fight with some bodyguards on a rooftop and then a leap from the roof. The feeling at Wadia Movietone was that Nadia was being asked to do things that would test their experienced stuntmen, Boman Shroff and Ustad Haqu, let alone this rather large blonde.

Homi decided to start shooting with the scene where Nadia was required to jump from the roof. As other employees gathered in fear and trepidation to see this shoot, Nadia coolly asked Homi, "I've heard I am to jump from a roof? Which one is it then?" When Homi pointed it out, Nadia said, "Okay."

Not long before, an experienced Wadia stuntman had almost drowned, having miscalculated a jump from a freight ship. In general, scrapes, dislocated joints, and often more severe injuries, were part of the daily fare. As the *mahurat* ceremony was performed Nadia was the only one unconcerned; everyone else was worried, particularly the other stunt people, who were dressed in police uniforms. But the shooting seemed to go perfectly, scene after scene was shot showing Nadia masked and fighting and Nadia dispatching the bandits from the roof until it came for her to jump. Homi was nervous and had asked Mr. Dhunbhoora to be on hand. He was regarded as an experienced 'bone-setter.' Nadia was required to leap on to a thin mattress. The jump seemed fine, the cameraman said 'okay', Homi shouted 'Cut!' but Nadia was motionless. Everyone ran to her, fearing the worst. Then Nadia opened her eyes and let out a loud laugh. Fear turned to wonder and everyone broke into applause. At the end of the day's shooting, Homi held a meeting in his office for the entire staff and christened Nadia 'Fearless Nadia', the name by which she was to be known for the rest of her film career; it was also a name that was used to publicise this movie, and the others that Nadia made.

As the filming progressed, Homi grew more confident about Nadia and asked her to be more daring. One day, Nadia was asked to lift up one of her stuntmen and carry him around; this would soon became a standard routine in the Fearless Nadia films.

There was a hiccough when Nadia got injured and needed rest and her mother warned her about her stunts but Nadia brushed aside her concerns. Soon Nadia's stunt abilities so enthused the Wadias they invested more money, introducing songs and scenes despite the fact that Billimoria, their business partner, was not convinced. He warned, "An Indian woman doing all that fighting—the public may not like it; we must sell the picture." His worries seemed well-founded when no cinema wanted to show *Hunterwali;* the idea of Indian men being beaten by a blonde woman at a time when India was fighting for her freedom from rule by white men, seemed far removed from the cinema they had got used to. The film had taken six months to make, a long time by the standards of the time, cost more than Rs. 80,000 and now faced the nightmarish prospect that it might never be seen by anybody. In the end, the Wadias decided to screen *Hunterwali* themselves. The Super Cinema on Grant Road, an area of Bombay where many Parsis lived, which was famous for Parsi food, and which is also not far from the city's red light district, was chosen.

In order to make sure Nadia did not come over as an alien, the film had a written title: "Brave Indian girl who sacrificed royal luxuries in the cause of her people and country." The advertisements in the film magazines showed a drawing of Nadia, sitting on a rearing horse, whip in hand. Beneath it, the slogan, "A spectacular thriller, the first of its kind in India."

The movie premiered in June 1935, the start of the monsoon season in Bombay, and appropriately heavy rain pelted down that evening as the cinema-goers hurried into the Super Cinema.

The Wadias waited apprehensively.

Nadia was there with Margaret and Bobby. "I was so nervous that my whole body was trembling. I spent the whole time looking around, trying to gauge the reactions on the faces of the audience. Mummy had to hold my left hand, Bobby the right. My first appearance was in the second reel, fifteen minutes into the film, and when my voice was heard, I heard the public gasping for breath. They were stunned by the performance. In the third reel, I swear I'll avenge my father's abduction and free him from the clutches of the evil minister. Then I crack the whip and say: 'From this day forth, call me Hunterwali! At this point, the audience went wild. They just couldn't stop whistling and applauding."

That night the cinema had been sold out. Now the Wadias knew it would be sold out for many more days and weeks. The objective was the coveted Silver Jubilee, twenty-five weeks of continuous showing; this was reached and it proved one of the big box office hits of the decade. Soon, other Indians were making the most of her success and unofficial Nadia whips, belts, matchboxes and playing cards were selling on the streets and her famous yell 'hey-y-y' became a catch phrase.

Nadia's monthly wage was increased and the Wadias began to build a new ensemble around their star, searching for bodybuilders with acting talent and trained animal stars. For subsequent movies, the Wadias added a new, even more appealing, touch. This showed Nadia carrying a man on her shoulders, riding the length of a train, and over the next five years, until 1940, Homi Wadia directed six Nadia films— *Hunterwali, Pahadi Kanya, Miss Fronier Mail, Lutaru Lalna, Punjab Mail* and *Diamond Queen*. The films, almost a movie a year, featured the great trains of the Raj: *Miss Frontier Mail* in 1936 was followed three years later by *Punjab Mail* in 1939. Indian audiences loved them, and loved her all the more when they learnt that she did not use a double, the first Indian actress not to do so, but did the stunts herself.

Nadia's male counterpart was the Parsi actor, John Cawas, who had won the 1930 All India Body Building Contest and had once carried a Chevrolet car with four passengers on his bare back. He was billed as India's Tarzan.

In 1941, came *Bombaiwali* (Woman from Bombay), and in 1942, *Jungle Princess*, for which a forty-foot jungle model, to show a storm in the jungle, was built and there were also high-speed car chases. In 1942, there was *Hunterwali ki Beti* (Daughter of Hunterwali), re-introducing the old, whip-cracking Nadia. The success of this movie, after a few bleak ones, was crucial and convinced Homi that cheap stunt movies, with Nadia, was the answer.

But, by this time, the two brothers were increasingly drifting apart. JBH had always been much more political; he had left the Congress to join the Radical Democratic Party founded by M.N. Roy, who had been a founder of the Indian Communist Party, and even advised the Chinese Communist Party in the 1920s, before renouncing Marxism. In essence JBH wanted to make socially more relevant films, while Homi wanted to stick to stunt movies. But these were not the only differences between the brothers. During the war, with an acute shortage of raw stock, they set up Basant Pictures to try and get more raw film and they did make some movies together. But in 1943, they finally split up and JBH eventually sold Wadia Movietone to V. Shantaram, while Homi continued to make stunt movies with Nadia until her retirement in 1956.

But how did the Wadias make a success of movies that were anti-British allegories, but featured a blonde woman who claimed British descent? Rosie Thomas, who interviewed Nadia for an essay about her says that, while from the start Nadia's ethnicity was an issue for the Wadias, and Indianising her was a project, one of the tricks the Wadias used was to refer to her as the '*Bombaiwali*' (The Woman from Bombay), which put great emphasis on the city's cosmopolitan sophistication and modernity, something the citizens of the city were, and still are, very proud of.

Thomas writes:

> Her western look was undeniably part of her exotic appeal and the Wadias were involved in a careful calculation. Billing her as India's Pearl White she could attract all the glamour of the Pearl White brand and exoticism of 'white men' (memsahib, as the white woman is known in India), whilst simultaneously constructing an all-Indian Nadia. Played cleverly, they could have it both ways, conflating two traditions: the Hollywood stunt queen (and by implication, the whole Hollywood stunt genre—her persona referred as much to Fairbanks as to White), and the legendary Indian warrior woman. Through these, a cosmopolitan modern femininity could be forged.

So successfully did the Wadias package Nadia, always fighting for the good cause, always fighting for justice, that for the Indian audiences, and in particular those that flocked to her movies, her whiteness did not matter. The Wadias were also shrewd enough to recognise that while the Indians were in the middle of their epic fight against the British, their nationalism was not xenophobic, so there was no great anti-white feeling, just a desire to be free and govern themselves.

Also, Indian leaders have often recruited white women to their cause, including Gandhi with Mirabhen, the daughter of a British admiral. If a white woman was ready to throw in her lot with India, as Nadia clearly was, she was acceptable. Her blondeness did not matter. She, like Robin Hood, avenged the poor, laughingly beat up her enemies, rode like the devil, and swung on chandeliers through the living-rooms of the rich, sporting tight-fitting shorts.

The Indian writer, Girish Karnad, who grew up in the 1940s, has testified to the hold Nadia had on audiences, particularly young men:

> The single most memorable sound of my childhood is the clarion call of 'Hey-y-y' as Fearless Nadia, regal upon her horse, her hand raised defiantly in the air, rode down upon the bad guys. To us school kids of the mid-forties, Nadia meant courage, strength, idealism.

Dorothee Wenner quotes another fan saying:

> We were forced to keep ourselves under control everywhere: at work, in the family, faced with our superiors, on the street; there was nowhere where we could give full rein to our emotions—apart from the cinema. There, we could shout and laugh and cry without being invasive or embarrassing. Everyone did it. And this is the reason why the Nadia films were so popular, because no other film managed to draw us in as much. Come the end of the film, we were completely drained and exhausted but, at the same time, there was a magnificent relief, a catharsis.

Off the screen, Nadia and Homi had become lovers, probably after her third or fourth film, which itself would have made a great script for a movie. For many years this love was kept hidden and, even when revealed, spun to make the story sound better to Indian ears. A marriage between an Indian and a Brit, even one like Nadia, who would be considered very low class by the ruling Brits, was difficult. For a start, Homi's Parsi family would not have cared for it. Homi, a very shy, private, man who preferred to stay in the shadow of his brother, was also something of a Mummy's boy and it was Nadia who took the initiative in their affair although, when it finally emerged, having long been Bombay gossip, Indian film magazines were given an official version which was at odds with the truth. Nadia described it as a love-at-first-sight relationship, claiming Homi had fallen in love with her when he looked at her through the lens of the camera for the first time. She had flashed just the briefest of smiles and it had happened. However it happened, the two of them had found one another by the end of the 1930s. Homi knew that marriage to her would not make Nadia a Parsi, nor would their children be Parsis, as the only way you can be a Parsi is by being born to parents both of whom are Parsis. In the end, a beach house near Juhu, one of Bombay's great beaches, provided a home for the lovers. "There," says Wenner, "beneath the palm trees, and looking out to the sea, they exchanged garlands of flowers and, in effect, became man and wife, although a formal ceremony took years."

It also took years for Nadia to get much recognition from the historians of the cinema. In her film heyday, the name Fearless Nadia on billboards had drawn crowds to the cinema in Beirut, Athens, Nairobi and Cape Town. But this star of Wadia Movietone did not get much space in Indian newspapers and was almost completely forgotten. She was rediscovered in the 1980's by Behroze Gandhy and Rosie Thomas who interviewed her. They wrote an essay describing her as a radical feminist actress and wondered how a blonde with European features succeeded in becoming a celebrated stunt queen in popular Indian cinema. At the Berlin Film Festival of 1993, a documentary was screened 'Fearless Nadia—The Huntenvali Story'. After the screening, it transpired that the director was the great-nephew of Fearless Nadia, Riyad Wadia, who had dug deep into the family archive to create a wonderful memorial to his great-aunt. In the audience was German film-maker Dorothee Wenner who, like the rest of the audience, was both dumbfounded and enthused to learn about Nadia.

A biography of Nadia in German followed; this was later translated into English and gave impetus to the idea, first articulated by Thomas and Gandhy, that Nadia was a radical feminist long before the word had been invented. Wenner had become part of a Nadia revival. Thomas's essay on Nadia was published in a Bollywood anthology in 2003. Nadia was now seen as something of a feminist icon. Those who hold to this view make much of her speech in *Diamond Queen* in the very first scene when, after beating a man who complains she has insulted his manhood, she says, "Hey, mister, don't think today's women are so weak they'll submit to the brutality of men. If India is to be free, women must be given their freedom…if you try and stop them, you'll face the consequences".

When I met Wenner in Berlin she made the point that Nadia's impact was, probably, more on the men than on the women:

> Her impact was more on the male audience. Remember, at that time few women were allowed to see the Nadia films. Maybe attitudes changed; but, for women, I am not so sure. She had a major impact on the self-esteem of men, in a weird way. She was opposite (in the British Colonial way) to the Indian way (which is supposed to be weak, feminine). Here she was powerful, would laugh at her enemies, and also had a strong physique. So this was an interesting model of esteem for the male. She was doing things that the Indian male could not normally do, politically. So, through Nadia, they were living vicariously. JBH was very clear about that. He didn't market the film as educational, but marketed it in a way so that it escaped the censors. JBH was a lawyer, knew what he was doing…put a lot of powerful messages in the movie to educate the villagers. For example, a dog barking, symbolised a British soldier. The British did not notice because it was a way of daily life. The Indians understood what he was saying.

If Nadia was the most remarkable female star of this period, she was by no means the only white woman actress in Bollywood. There were many such actresses to be seen, particularly in the studios of Bombay. In Ardeshir Irani's studio, where Prithviraj started, there was Ermeline, a Jewish actress, who was a big enough star to select her own leading man. On Prithviraj's third day, as she inspected the line of extras where Prithviraj was standing, she was much impressed by his good looks and selected him as the male lead opposite her in *Cinema Girl*, providing Prithviraj with his start in movies.

There were others, such as the actress Camilla, initially a rival of Nadia, and who became a friend, and whose background was Russian, Jewish, Armenian, and Anglo-Indian. Camilla, and her sister, Ramilla, were known for their beautiful complexion as the two peaches. Unlike Nadia, they kept away from stunt movies and made more social movies. But, while this was more acceptable to the Indian upper classes, it was the Nadia style stunt movies that made more money, always an important factor in money-conscious India.

A decade after Nadia, another star of exotic background emerged with a similar sounding name, Nadira. As we have seen in the early years of films, actresses like Sulochana, the Anglo-Indian Ruby Meyers in real life, were paid more than any other male actor, let alone a female one. And this desire to have white-skinned female stars would, a decade later, provide an incredible début for nineteen-year old Farah Ezekiel, a Jew of Iraqi origin whose grandparents had migrated to Calcutta. As Ezekiel would later tell the story, it came about because her rich grandmother fell in love with a baker and the couple eloped to Calcutta to escape the wrath of the grandmother's rich family who disapproved of her choice of husband. Ezekiel's arrival in Bombay was in the tradition of many Iraqi-Jews who had migrated to Bombay and become prominent in business there. The most famous of them were the Sassoons, who had become one of the most prominent businessmen of Bombay and whose present-day memorial is the Sassoon Docks in the city. David Sassoon had come rather quietly to the city in 1833, but Ezekiel arrived with a bang in Bollywood from Calcutta in 1952. Not yet twenty, and taking the screen name Nadira, she made a spectacular début as heroine in Mehboob Khan's *Aan*. *Aan* did not quite fulfil Khan's dreams and after that Nadira did not often play heroines; sometimes, as in *Shree 420*, a path-breaking movie of the 1950s, she played the bad woman but, even then, she mimed a song which became very famous. Her *Shree 420* song, *"Mud mud ke na dekh mud mud ke..."* remains a classic. She eventually appeared in sixty films but her bad woman role in *Shree 420* did typecast her and after that she was always the other woman and never played the heroine again.

Later still, in the 70s, she became what Bollywood calls a character actor, meaning mother, aunt, or older woman, and did it so well that in the 1975 *Julie*, playing the leading lady's Anglo-Indian mother, she won the award for "Best

Supporting Actress." The film was about love between a Hindu boy and an Anglo-Indian girl and the cultural differences between the two communities, which were then still quite a controversial subject for a film-maker to tackle. Nadira must have felt this was somewhat ironic for she never found true love and led a lonely life; her two brothers had migrated to the United States and Israel respectively, and she lived alone in her south Bombay flat, where the mahogany door advertised both her screen name and her real name, and where her constant companion was her maid, Shobha. Every year on December 5, her birthday, she celebrated by serving biryani and cakes to the children from the neighbourhood.

Unlike Nadia, Nadira life's became a sort of caricature of her screen roles and in Bollywood she became famous as one of the few film personalities who had an excellent library, books ranging through the works of Shakespeare, Adolf Hitler, Vivekananda, World War II, Judaism and Philosophy, which friends and neighbours used to borrow from time to time.

Nadira died in 2006, at the age of seventy-four, having suffered many illnesses, such as a liver disorder, due to her heavy drinking. In her last interview, shortly before her death, she came over as a reclusive lady with many secrets whom life had passed by. "I don't know if I really miss having a family because I have never really known family life. I have been alone for too long to miss being with someone."

That could hardly be said of the female Bollywood star of the 40s, who has left the most haunting legacy and provoked more "ifs" than any other actor or actress. This was Nur Jehan (the name has also been spelt Noor Jahan). Her career in Bollywood lasted just five years. She left India at the age of twenty-one, never to return except as a visitor shortly before her death. But, by this time, she had made so many films (sixty-nine), and sung so many songs (127), that she was a colossus of the screen, despite her youth and her career, and ignited a debate that lingers on to this day: had she stayed, could she have changed Bollywood? Nur Jehan could both sing and act, and, while she was, incomparably, the greater singer, so long as she was in India, Bollywood was no different from Hollywood; not all actors or actresses sang but, if a song was required, then they had to. The big if—had she stayed—is would Bollywood have continued like Hollywood—and other cinemas—in having actors and actresses who were required both to act and sing? The Bollywood divorce that followed Nur Jehan's departure was so total that this break between acting and singing is even greater than Kipling's divide between east and west and, today, nearly sixty years later, there is no question of the twain ever meeting. The debate, like all such "ifs", can never be resolved, but the fact that it is debated at all shows Nur Jehan's influence, and her story is like one of those tales which, had it been made into a Bollywood movie, would have been rejected as just too fantastic.

Born in Kasur on Saturday, 21 September 1926, to Madad Ali and Fateh Bibi, she was named Allah Wasai, the youngest in a family of thirteen. Of her seven brothers, three ended up in mental institutions. From a very early age, it was clear Nur Jehan had to look after the financial needs of her large family which included many who were not her immediate family. Many years later, when she was already quite old, she lamented, "People ask me why I don't stop working. Well, how can I? If I don't work, who is going to take care of all these people?" She appears to have made her first film when she was four although, like many things in her life, we cannot be certain. She herself liked to make her age something of a mystery and once, when asked about it, said, "People often wonder how old I am. Let me tell you. In terms of experience of life and men, I have always been a hundred years old."

Writers of the sub-continent have spent much time debating the facts of Nur Jehan's life and this is still the subject of lively internet discussion. Nur Jehan, for instance, claimed that she was a mother at fifteen, when she was probably a little bit older (sixteen and a half or seventeen, perhaps), having married Syed Shaukat Hussain Rizvi, who directed her in her first sound film *Khandan* in 1942. She was no more than a child herself; too young to understand, as she would later confess but, in film terms, already a veteran, having made twelve silent films, and with a career that went back to around 1930, when she appeared in the silent movie, *Hind ke Tare*, made by Calcutta's Indian Pictures.

Khandan, whose musical score was by Ghulam Haider, advertised her voice to a nationwide audience, a voice that would afterwards be consistently described as "her nightingale voice," and which had long been a feature of music halls of Lahore and the smaller towns of Punjab.

There is a charming story of one of Nur Jehan's early songs. It is Lahore, some time in the 1930s, followers of a local *Pir* (a Muslim holy man), have arranged a special evening of devotional music in his honour. Among those singing for him that day is a little girl. The Pir asks her to sing something in Punjabi. She launches into a Punjabi folk song, a line of which had a reference to the kite of this land of five rivers touching the skies. As she sings the words, the Pir appears to go into a trance. When she finishes, he rises, puts his hand on the girl's head and prophesies, "Go forth, little girl; your kite will one day touch the skies." At some stage in her singing career, Nur Jehan discovered a recipe that she felt was essential to maintain her voice: Although the conventional wisdom was that sour and oily things are bad for the throat, Nur Jehan loved pickles dipped in oil and she would eat enormous quantities of pickles before she sang, then she would drink iced water, believing that it sharpened the throat. Without such preparation, she would refuse to go anywhere near a microphone.

Khalid Hasan, who knew her well, describes the extraordinary film world of the 30s and 40s, as Nur Jehan was making her mark.

Rizvi, whom she married after a turbulent love affair in Lahore and Bombay, and divorced some years after they came to Pakistan after independence, recalled the first time he set eyes on her. His account of his life with her, *Noor Jahan ki Kahani Meri Zubani,* has not even one nice thing to say about her, including her voice and its undimmed magic, despite the passage of time. He wrote that she was no more than eight or nine. This was in Calcutta. He was film editor at a movie studio owned by Rai Bahadur Seth Dalsukh Karnani, a colourful and eccentric character who, despite his years, always had an eye out for a pretty girl, of whom there was hardly a shortage in his world. He would address all men in his Gujarati accent as "shand" or bull, while all women were "devi," even those he fired from their jobs. Once, he asked the manager of the Corinthian Theatre, a man by the name of Naseer, to go to the Punjab and come back with some girls. The man came back with fifteen to twenty of them, among whom were the Nur Jehan sisters, the two older ones, Eiden and Haider Bandi, and the eight-year old future queen of the Indian cinema. These girls were collectively called "Punjab Mail." One of the girls, Rashida, who was related to Nur Jehan, was installed as the Rai Bahadur's mistress. When Rizvi was asked to come to Lahore to direct *Khandan* in 1942, Nur Jehan, who with her sisters was in a dance party which performed from town to town, was in Amritsar. He was to choose a heroine for the new movie which was being produced by Dalsukh Pancholi. He recalls that through the help of S.P. Singha, who was vice-chancellor of the Punjab University, several girls were sent over for audition but he did not like any of them. He wanted his heroine to look no more than fifteen or sixteen on the screen, which was Nur Jehan's age at the time. He decided that it was she whom he wanted. She was sent for but he did not tell her that she was going to play the lead. That was when their affair began, which ended in marriage against the wishes of her brothers who did not wish to lose her. One day, during the shooting, Rizvi said to Nur Jehan by way of a joke, "What sort of oil do you use on your hair? It smells awful." He says the moment the words left his mouth, she burst out crying and just would not stop. As a result of this incident, the shooting remained interrupted for five or six days.

Khandan launched Nur Jehan so spectacularly that she was now in constant demand, not only by Punjabi film-makers in Lahore but also in Bombay. By 1947, she had made fifty-five movies in Bombay, in addition to eight in Calcutta, five in Lahore and one in Rangoon.

Manto, who knew her well, has described how fanatical some of Nur Jehan's fans could be. A barber in Lahore was prepared to do anything to prove he was a true fan:

He would sing her songs all day long and never tire of talking about her. Someone said to him, "Do you really love Nur Jehan?" "Without doubt" the barber replied sincerely. "If you really love her can you do what the legendary Punjabi lover

Mahiwal did for his beloved Sohni? He cut a piece of his flesh from his thigh to prove his love," the man said. The barber gave him his sharp cut-throat razor and said, "You can take a piece of flesh from any part of my body." His friend was a strange character because he slashed away a large chunk of flesh from his arm and ran away while the barber fainted after providing proof of his love. When the great lover regained consciousness in Mayo Hospital, Lahore, the first words that came to his lips were "Nur Jehan."

Both Manto and Nur Jehan would leave India for Pakistan in 1947 but while Manto, the intellectual who had no great affinity with the idea of having a Muslim state called Pakistan, left Bombay with great regret, never ceasing to miss it, Nur Jehan, always very religious, did so with gusto. When India fought Pakistan in wars she would often arrive at the studios of the state radio quite unannounced to sing patriotic songs to show her devotion to the state she had pledged herself to. But when it came to choosing her favourite song she chose one she had sung back when India was a united sub-continent. Nur Jehan was always reluctant to choose a song as her favourite. "They are like my children. How can I differentiate between them?" she said but, when Khalid Hasan insisted, she thought long and hard and replied it was *Badnam mohabat kaun kare* from *Dost*. "It was," says Hasan, "her favourite because it was composed by that finicky perfectionist, Sajjad," who, she added, "never made a *seedhi* or straight tune."

Manto found nothing appealing in her acting; what appealed to him was her singing. "To me there was just one thing about her which was phenomenal—her voice. After Saigal, she was the only singer who impressed me. Her voice was like pure crystal."

In this regard he could not have been more against contemporary opinion, which hailed her both as a great actress and a great singer, with her acting considered provocative—a ticking bombshell. In 1947, Nur Jehan played opposite Dilip Kumar, who was still making his mark in films such as *Jugnu,* of which *FilmIndia* said, "he (Dilip Kumar) tries to do his bit but he doesn't match well with Nur Jehan." The magazine found the film "dirty, disgusting, vulgar" and led a campaign to have it banned; this happened in October 1948, although the ban was lifted a few months later. *Jugnu* was to be Nur Jehan's last film in India, a movie which saw a new male play-back singer emerge in Mohammed Rafi. It went unnoticed then, but would acquire much significance later.

Nur Jehan's departure from India also meant another young female singer called Lata Mangeshkar, who was the same age as Nur Jehan and had arrived in Bombay at about the same time, found the singing stage invitingly open and seized her chance with great aplomb. Curiously, in *Anmol Ghadi*, a huge Nur Jehan hit, Nur's screen name had been Lata.

Manto does not believe the real Lata would have stood a chance had Nur Jehan remained in India, but her rise was part of the remaking of Bollywood that followed partition and the emergence of a free nation. Interestingly, Lata and Nur Jehan remained friends and years later they would often burn up the telephone lines between Bombay and Karachi, singing to each other.

Part III

Minting Film Gold in Bombay

9

Searching for the Right Masala

India's moment of freedom on August 15, 1947, has been described as bitter-sweet. The bitterness came from the fact that the country was partitioned, which saw an unofficial exchange of population between the two countries of India and Pakistan of between ten and fifteen million in about two months, with a million people slaughtered, and many more millions of divided families and ruined lives.

The state of Pakistan that was created was, itself, the most curious of states. It was created in the name of Islam, as Pakistani-Muslim leaders claimed that Muslims could not live together with Hindus in a state where they would be a minority. Yet the man who masterminded this remarkable twentieth century coup, Mohammed Ali Jinnah was, probably, the most westernised, secular politician of the sub-continent. He drank, he could not do without his peg of whisky every evening, ate pork and could barely speak Urdu, which was soon the national language of Pakistan. Also, Pakistan was literally two states, its western half bordering Afghanistan on the sub-continent's north-west borders, divided by 1,000 miles of Indian territory before you could get to east Pakistan on the eastern seaboard of the sub-continent, the former eastern half of Bengal.

This world of sunshine and shadow, joy mingled with great grief, was reflected in the film industry, which saw both wrenching separation but also great opportunities and further scope for Bombay to consolidate itself as the unrivalled centre of the Indian film world.

The partition of the country dealt a death blow to the industry in Lahore, capital of undivided Punjab. Lahore was essentially a Hindu and Sikh city but, now in Pakistan, it saw an exodus of its talent to Bombay. Pran Krishen Sikand, who had started his movie career in Lahore at the Dalsukh Pancholi's Lahore studios, taking the screen name Pran, had played the romantic lead opposite Nur Jehan in *Khandaan*. Now, as independence drew closer he took to carrying a knife. A few days before 15 August, he sent his family to India, following himself soon after and never returned to Lahore. On August 14, 1947 he was in Bombay looking for work.

There were many other film refugees from Lahore. They included fellow-actor Om Prakash, B.R. Chopra, the man not afraid to make Ashok Kumar re-take a shot, the actress Kamini Kaushal and also Wali Mohammed Wali who, back in 1940, had lured a reluctant Pran to the movies, giving him his first role in one of the many Punjabi films made by Pancholi. He was now in Bombay, having set up an office at Famous Studios near the racecourse at Mahalaxmi.

Bombay was a natural port of call for all of them.

Pran, for instance, born in Delhi, was fluent in Urdu, the language he was most comfortable with, and also Hindi. Although a Punjabi, when he had made his first film, *Yamla Jat,* in Lahore he could not speak Punjabi like a native and Wali had hired a diction master to perfect his accent. Now, at twenty-seven, he had no desire to learn a new regional language, which is what it would mean if he had chosen to go anywhere else. The idea did not even enter his head, nor did it of the many now being forced to seek a new film world. For them, Bombay was already there and it was only a question of finding a space.

The arrival of the film immigrants was to transform the city more dramatically than at any time in its previous 270 years. Ever since Gerald Aungier, the founding father of Bombay, had developed it, the city had physically progressed little beyond the southern and central parts of the seven islands that made it up. In the four decades since the start of the film industry, the people who worked in it lived either in south or central Bombay: stars, such as Suraiya and Nargis lived along Marine Drive, Ashok Kumar lived in a huge house on the sea face at Worli, Prithviraj lived in Matunga in central Bombay where other film folks like Sitara Devi and Chandramohan also lived. Until 1947, Manto, socialising with film people, rarely ventured beyond Shivaji Park in central Bombay.

The new crowd pushed the boundaries of the city further north and east, out to what a few years previously had been fairly desolate countryside. For the first time it began to give Bombay a feel of Hollywood in that film people now began to live in a previously largely uninhabited part of the town and which they could call their own. By the end of the 50s, Pali Hill in Bandra, which until then had been considered the outer limits of Bombay, was becoming Bombay's Beverly Hills and even being called that. Pran, who had started life in Bombay by staying at the Taj—he had been forced to move to cheaper hotels as he initially struggled to find work—soon had enough work to buy a flat in Union Park in Pali Hill surrounded by neighbours who were either directors, actors or in the film music business. Others, like Raj Kapoor, moved out even further to Chembur but this, in Bombay of the 1950s, was considered the outer edge of darkness and, as a child growing up in Bombay, whenever we drove past Bandra on to Chembur from our base in south Bombay we felt we were venturing into very virgin territory. For miles the road stretched out past fields and villages with not a human habitation to be seen. It is a sign of how much Bombay has grown that today the urban city, in the usual higgledy-piggledy chaotic way that Indian cities develop, has claimed it and it would be difficult to imagine the wilderness it was at the start of the 1950s.

Yet, if this indicated prosperity and the power of films, it had come against a background of very conflicting messages from the Government, if not at times downright hostility to the medium.

Back in 1927, when the Cinematograph Committee had asked Gandhi to complete its questionnaire, he had refused, saying he had never been to the cinema. "But even to an outsider the evil it has and is doing is patent. The good, if it has done any at all, remains to be proved," he said.

After that, many attempts had been made to get Gandhi to change his mind and in 1939, K.A. Abbas had written to Gandhi asking him to reconsider his view that the cinema was as much an evil as gambling, horse-racing and playing the stock market. "Give this little toy of ours, the cinema, which is not so useless as it looks, a little of your attention and bless it with a smile of toleration." But Gandhi refused to do that; as far as he was concerned, it was one of the modern Western evils that needed to be eradicated.

Nehru, who believed in modern Western progress, and could be expected to be different, did not have an ideological bias against the cinema as Gandhi did. But he did not think Indian cinema was very good. In 1939, Nehru in his message to the Indian Motion Picture Congress, criticised the industry for concentrating on entertainment and producing low quality films "I hope that the industry will consider now in terms of meeting standards and of aiming at producing high-class films which have educational and social values."

Independence did not change Nehru. As Benegal puts it:

> None of our national leaders cared for films, not even Nehru. Our pre-independent national leaders always saw popular Indian films as culturally wanting. They thought they were culturally not good enough, not artistic enough, and did not help in the evolution and development of culture. They always thought it was a very inferior kind of work. This attitude also infected the urban upper and middle-classes.

But, although independent India had no truck with Gandhi's back to pre-industrial age ideas, the one Gandhian idea that was implemented with great vigour was prohibition. There were strict state laws about it, this being a state subject, and in Bombay Morarji Desai, initially the local home minister, then chief minister, was a Gandhian who believed in drinking, not alcohol every morning, but a sip of his own urine. He enforced prohibition rigorously and only those who got a permit, which was given on health grounds, certified by the doctor and approved by the Collector of Customs, could legally drink. The result was the Bombay film world, where everybody drank, found itself pushed into a sort of ghetto, having to organise its own private parties where drink was available but which the hosts had to make sure did not cause any problems with the police.

A Bollywood director described to me how the film world changed in the years after independence:

> Film stars lived in Pali Hill and did their own thing. For you to be noticed on the social scene it was important that you were not part of the film scene. People belonging to films were seen as not important; you really did not want to mix with them. Clubs would say no to stars as members. Clubs like Willingdon, or Bombay Gymkhana would never allow film stars. This attitude by clubs lasted for many years until quite recently. Even clubs like the Otters Club, a relatively new club, only opened about fifteen or eighteen years ago. Feroze Khan, an actor and producer applied to be a member. They said they did not want film actors. But then he applied again. He was called for an interview. He is a very funny man. He said I have acted in forty films so that will tell you I am not an actor. In the 1950s, whenever there was help needed—flood relief, like when the Chinese war, or Pakistan war was on—films stars were wheeled out. Then film stars would go on lorries with huge sheets spread out in front of them and people would give them money for flood relief or other charities. Bombay was then a small town. Bandra was the edge of Bombay. Beyond Bandra was no man's land, wild country. And the industry was never mainstream in the way it has now become.

The hostility of the politicians to films resulted in the most curious phenomenon. Films which were actually made to highlight the Indian freedom struggle were banned as if the censors thought the British were still ruling India. Hemen Gupta's *Bhuli Nai*, which means 'I have not forgotten', made in 1948, centred on the partition of Bengal in 1905 and was about a secret organisation that seeks to use violence to end British rule. The censor felt it was too violent and banned it. Gupta's next film, *Forty Two*, made the following year, also ran into problems. It was based on a real incident in Midnapore, during the 1942 Quit India movement, which had seen police shoot unarmed protestors outside a police station. But, then, faced by protests, they were forced to surrender the station. Eventually, the area was bombed by British planes to retake the station. One scene showed how a man, whose daughter had been raped, was killed by being dragged behind a lorry. The Commissioner of Police, who was also the censor, banned the film in Bengal as not suitable.

Some banning orders on films suggested the censor might have got out of bed on the wrong side that day. So, in 1949, *Matlabi* was "rejected," as the censor put it, because it was a "sloppy, stunt movie." Interestingly, the Indian censors now began to display an intense Victorian prudery, totally impervious to the fact that this was the land that had given the world the Kama Sutra and had some of the most erotic sculptures on display in ancient rocks and caves. This was very noticeable in their attitude to any display of intimacy between men and women.

Before independence, the British censors were keen to make sure the white woman's exalted status was not compromised in the eyes of the natives but they had no objections to natives kissing each other. Kissing scenes were common, went on for minutes and Sulochana featured in several very erotic embraces with Dinshaw Billimoria in *Anarkali* and *Heer Ranjah*. Homi Wadia even got Nadia in a near-nude bathing scene in *Hunterwali* past the censors. But, now the censors drew the line at kissing. The moment a man or a woman got close enough to kiss, the film-maker, aware lips could not meet, would suddenly introduce some object like a tree or a bush and the lovers usually burst into song. The song they mimed could often be very suggestive, even erotic, but their lips could not meet. Bollywood was forced by the censors to find a new style to convey physical feeling between lovers.

The federal nature of India also made life difficult for Bollywood. Entertainment tax levied on films was levied by the state and some states levied tax as high as 75% on ticket sales. There were restrictions on where a cinema should be built and Hindi films suffered most as they fell in no man's land. They could not expect regional patronage as they were all-India films and there was no question of support from the Indian federal Government. While state Governments in the different regions promoted films in their own languages, a Hindi film was seen as a rival and state Governments were inclined to tax it heavily.

The fact that the Indian film industry was becoming globally important did not make any impression. Even before 1947, India was the third largest film production country in the world and the film industry was the fifth largest industry in the country. During the war, production had declined but, as soon as it ended, more film stock was available and as wartime restrictions were lifted production increased. From ninety-nine films in 1945, it more than doubled to 200 by 1946 and by 1950 it would reach 250 and make India the second biggest film-producing country in the world, only Hollywood produced more. This, given it was a third-world country, mired in poverty, was remarkable.

For two years after independence, the film industry tried to persuade the Government to listen to its demands. When all that failed on June 30, 1949, the various industry associations, showing a unity which was rare, organised the All India Cinema Protest Day and all cinema houses closed for the day.

The response was predictable. A film enquiry committee was set up, headed by S.K. Patil, the Tammany style boss of Congress politics in Bombay. It included Sircar and Shantaram as its members and, as in 1927, it heard evidence, went round the country, and a year and a half later, produced its report. This showed the country had 3,250 cinema houses, sixty studios and made around 250 films a year. The capital invested in films were Rs. 410 million which included Rs. 90 million in working capital; 600 million people went to the cinema every year, which suggested many people saw many more than one movie a year, producing an income of Rs. 200 million. But, while this made Indian movies second to Hollywood in terms of film production, the committee was very critical of the way the film industry was run: its organisation, its financing, "choice and handling of themes, the availability of talent and trained personnel, professional organisation and conduct and the supply of goods and services". In that sense the industry had appeared to have moved little since 1927 when the predecessor of this committee had castigated Indian films for being "generally crude in comparison with Western pictures".

This was, of course, one reason why Indian intellectuals shunned Hindi films and, significantly, why the Patil committee noted how Indian intellectuals were still apathetic to the industry.

Like its predecessor, this report made some very sensible recommendations. This included that a fixed proportion of the entertainment tax be used to set up a Film Finance Corporation to provide cheap finance, and for a school to train actors and technicians. But like all reports, it gathered dust for nearly ten years before some of the recommendations, like the Film Finance Corporation, began to be implemented. As always in India, change came, but slowly.

The Government could claim that it had more things than films to worry about. India had become a free nation with awesome problems. In a country of nearly 400 million people only 18% were literate, the average life expectancy was twenty-six years and there were a million refugees, as well as enormous food shortages.

The politicians were also seeking to create a nation and, in a certain sense, India had as great a task of nation-building as the United States did, as it moved from thirteen colonies on independence from Britain in 1776 to the fifty states today. True, India did not have to acquire land as the expanding American republic did but, in 1947, it did have to integrate the 565 princely states covering more than a third of the Indian landmass and two thirds of its population who had treaty arrangements with the British. All of them on August 15 1947, had the option of joining either India or Pakistan or going independent. The integration of these states into the modern republic of India was the work of Sardar Vallabhai Patel, the tough, no-nonsense Gujarati politician who ran Gandhi's political machine, and became deputy Prime Minister in Nehru's first Indian Cabinet. He bullied these princes into becoming part of India, giving up their princely states in return for a privy purse. When the old ruler created problems, the new India solved the situation with the sort of show of force, as in Hyderabad in 1948, that the Raj would have approved: send in the Indian army.

Shyam Benegal's early upbringing is a perfect illustration of how curious British rule in India was:

> My father, who was a nationalist, had a warrant for his arrest in British India.
> So he came to Hyderabad to live under the Nizam. No warrant of British India

was enforceable in the princely states, not even, I think, a death warrant. But we went to school in British India in the cantonment, Secunderabad, where British troops were stationed. School was British, home was Princely India. We made the journey every day. You could see the difference. The British cantonment was more orderly, more organised. My father had started off by sending his children to a Gurukul, a very Indian school but, then, seeing the education they were receiving, he changed his mind and sent us all to a convent school. He was a photographer, who had a studio and also had a 16 mm movie camera and, as his children were born—I was sixth out of ten children—he would shoot home movies of the children. I grew up with these movies. He would hang a huge sheet in the sitting room and these movies would be projected. But we would also go to the cinema in the cantonment, which was next to the club and the tennis court, and we would see movies sitting in the projectionist's room or standing next to the tennis court. This is where I saw most of the movies during childhood.

There was violence in the Indian nation-making, although not on the scale of the United States where the Americans slaughtered five million of their native Indian population in creating their country, and then fought a civil war to preserve it. The stories of these killings would be spun by Hollywood into Westerns: goodies versus baddies films, cowboys versus Indians. It could be said that the violence of partition was a sort of Indian civil war, but Bollywood did not tackle that subject. There were films like *Chinnamool* in 1950 by cameraman turned director, Nemai Ghosh, about the migration of millions of Hindus from former east Bengal to west Bengal but we had to wait until 1973, when M.S. Sathyu, in his directorial début, made *Garam Hawa* (Hot Wind), finally dealing with the trauma of partition. This showed a Muslim in Agra who, despite losing his family, his daughter's suicide, and his fellow-Muslims leaving for Pakistan, chose to stay on in India. It is widely considered to be the best film to deal with the issues of partition.

V.S. Naipaul has called what the Indians have done since independence "A million mutinies," but what made the process even more complicated was that in 1947, India did not have too many symbols that could be embraced by all Indians.

The British state in India had the appearance of a state but it lacked many of the essentials of a state. So, while a common criminal law was set up for British India in the middle of the nineteenth century, even this, as the Benegal example shows, did not extend to the princely states, and the British never made any moves to change, let alone modernise, the personal law of the Indians. The Hindus, Muslims, and the other Indian communities, conducted their marriages, inheritance, etc., according to their ancient customs and religious beliefs. The result was that Hindus and Muslims could take more than one wife, with Barua having two, and Shantaram three. Hindu law did change, causing, as we shall see,

Nargis' problems, but Muslim personal law was never changed; if anything, it lagged behind personal law in orthodox Muslim countries, and remains one of the most controversial issues in the country.

Although the British had created the railways and the armed forces, both great achievements of the Raj, they had to be reshaped to fit the independent nation. Only two institutions created during British rule were truly all India in scope: cricket and films.

The problem for films was to find a formula that would work. How difficult this was can be seen that in 1947, nearly 70% of the producers were newcomers: 157 out of 214. But by the end of 1948, only twenty-five of them were still in business; many of the others, who had fallen by the wayside, had not even completed their pictures.

Unlike Hollywood, Indians could not even have a single narrative to tell the story of how they won freedom. Bimal Roy had made a film about Subhas Bose's Indian National Army (INA) formed with Indian soldiers who had been captured by the Axis powers. Their mission was to fight for India's freedom. But Nehru had denounced Bose, saying if he came with his Japanese-backed army to India, he would fight him.

Bimal Roy's film about Bose's army was called *Pahela Aadmi*. The title 'The First Man' suggested a reverential treatment for Bose. In 1946, Shantaram decided to tackle the other side of the story with *Dr Kotnis Ki Amar Kahani* (The Immortal story of Dr Kotnis). This was based on the real life story of Dwarkanath Kotnis, who had led the Indian medical team to China to help the Chinese resist Japanese aggression, a mission that Nehru had sponsored and which had seen Kotnis serve in Mao's Eight Route Army. But, as he was there, Bose, in alliance with the Japanese, was telling the Chinese this was a new Japan they should make peace with. The film did not deal with such Indian contradictions, making it instead into a love story where Kotnis falls in love and marries a Chinese nurse, Ching Lan, played by Jayashree, before dying in an ambush.

However, when Shantaram wrote to the Congress leaders asking for endorsement, they rebuffed him, with Gandhi's secretary saying, "Don't harass the Mahatma with requests for blessings for such work." With Nehru now Prime Minister, Shantaram thought that, as he had sent Kotnis to China, he would like to be present at its inaugural screening in Delhi. Nehru declined, feeling Shanataram was trying to exploit his name for commercial gain. Nehru did have a point. Shantaram, while taken with the story, based on a novel by Abbas and V.P. Sathe, had also made the film because that was the only way he could get some more of the rationed film stock. He had started making it in 1944 and passed it off as a War Effort film. It was shown in London, with Shantaram spending some time trying to have it shown in America. Although the film was a success in India, its difficulties with politicians showed the problems of bringing the complex story of the country onto the screen.

The film-makers' answer to this problem of constructing a narrative of India was to opt for what is now called the Bollywood masala film, where every conceivable cinematic spice was put in one pot and stirred, making a mix quite unique. In the process, the film-makers of Bollywood created a new cinematic world, very different to Hollywood.

Benegal says:

> We have a different tradition of cinema compared to the Western tradition. The genres that Hollywood has were never created. The West broke up everything. They said this is drama, this is comedy. Hollywood created different genres: thrillers, supernatural films, caper movies, social films, comedies and tragedies. Because we have such a diverse audience we want to cater to different kinds of taste. And in order to do that we had to keep a common denominator, so you have to put in a little of everything so it attracts diverse kinds of people. Our films have everything. We created an all-encompassing genre. The same story will have comic sequences, will have tragic sequences, melodrama, music, song, and dance. I suppose it came because the artistic tradition in theatre, or any of our performing arts, have been of that kind. Look at our performing arts. Who were the performers? They were itinerants. They moved from place to place. And, naturally, not each place would want the same performance. So they had to have a good variety in their acts. To cater for a wide range of interests and sensibilities you had to create a form that would be suitable for everyone. So that is how our dramatic form developed. Popular cinema followed that tradition. The situations are typical, the situations more or less the same but they make the audience cry, they make the audience laugh, they make the audience enjoy the song, make their feet tap to the dances, all those kinds of things. The same film has to have everything in it. That's traditional, much like our food, because otherwise we don't feel satisfied, either with our food, or our entertainment.

Benegal's reference to food is shrewd. A proper Indian meal is an amazingly free-wheeling experience compared with the tightly structured Western cuisine. In the West, meals are a linear progression, moving in a certain stately order: from small starters to larger main courses and then desserts, with each course very distinctive and totally different to the previous one. Indian meals have no such neat, linear progression of starter, main course and pudding. On the Indian dining-table, one course follows another in no particular order and some Indians even begin their meal with puddings, or eat them in between mouthfuls of savoury. The Indian Thali, one of the classic meals of India, is a vivid example of how unstructured an Indian meal can be. All the various dishes, including sweets, are put in little pots with various kinds of food and arranged circularly round the edge of a stainless steel plate. Watch an Indian eat and he might dip into any of the pots or all of them, including the pot containing the sweets. Indians say this is a joyous symphony of diverse tastes, colours and flavours in one mouthful.

And so Bollywood now started making films which had action, violence, a wronged mother, a lost son, a foiled rape attempt, a successful rape attempt, a sub-plot involving a dastardly criminal and a maid—who may or may not be a lost daughter—and the whole thing interspersed with lots of songs. In a Hollywood musical, to which Bollywood films have been mistakenly compared, the songs arise from the story and move the story forward. In Bollywood, the start of the song meant presenting vaudeville on screen, with a chance to show extravagant costumes and scenery; these often bore no relation to the narrative, and nearly always meant the location of the movie suddenly changed, often without any explanation, from a crowded street scene in Bombay, to lush mountains and wonderful streams of water. In the 1950s, it was Kashmir that provided the exotic location, then it became the ski slopes of Switzerland or, in more recent times, Scotland, or even New Zealand (the sudden popularity of Scotland and New Zealand has to do with tax concessions offered to Indian film-makers).

The divorce from Hollywood had been coming for a long time. Benegal dates the moment from 1931 and the arrival of sound:

> During the silent era of Indian cinema, our films used to look like every other film made everywhere else in the world. But the moment sound came, we suddenly went back to our theatrical traditional form. That moment was in 1931, when our first sound film was made (*Alam Ara*), which had something like thirty songs. After that sixteen or seventeen songs became the norm, and most films from then on used to have those number of songs because music was an essential part of Indian cinema.

The 40s further fortified this process. However, through the 30s and 40s, the Hindi film industry maintained one Hollywood tradition, that of literature being the source for films. Films were based on novels by authors such as Tagore, Sarat Chandra Chatterjee and Hindi's greatest writer, Premchand, all of whom had novels turned into films.

Here is Benegal again:

> All the great American writers wrote for Hollywood, whether it was people like Hemmingway or Fitzgerald. It happened in India in the 1930s. We had Premchand, who wrote a couple of films. He wrote a film called *Mazdoor* (Worker). It was a huge failure in 1934. He got so cheesed off, he died soon after. Amrit Lal Nagar, a very fine Hindi writer, worked in films. In the 30's, a lot of very good Hindi writers, some good Urdu writers, worked for the cinema. Saadat Hasan Manto, the finest short story writer in Urdu, used to work as a writer in Bombay Talkies. He went to Pakistan in 1947 and died of drink. Others gave up, disillusioned by what they

saw, much in the fashion of what happened to writers who went to Hollywood. Because, you see, film business and writing are two completely different things. And the markets are so different. The same person who would read a book, would he see a film? That's open to question. I don't know if it actually happens or not.

But, while the writer may have migrated from Hollywood, the idea that a film must be based on a book, or some already existing literary product, continued. In India, however, there was a total divorce in the way Bollywood and Hollywood started making a movie. Hollywood still relied on the novel. In contrast, Bollywood went back to the oral story telling age, with a story being told orally to a high profile star. If he liked what he heard, then the movie went ahead. The story was never written down and no full bound pre-shooting script was ever produced. Script-writers worked on sets as the film was being shot, and actors and actresses were given the lines to read literally minutes before the scene was shot, with the star actor able to modify the script while shooting or even modify the script of others in the film. Benegal dates the full emergence of this style in the 1960s, rather than in the 1950s.

Back in 1938, a few years before he died, Tagore had said, in one of his classical comments, Indian cinema had not found its own voice and, until it finds it's own voice and its own aesthetic, it is in such a state of infancy that it's simply a pneumatic art. Now, a few years into independent India, Bollywood was about to find its most authentic, representative voice, although it was not quite the voice that Tagore had in mind.

The man who would help find it—Raj Kapoor—was a man who was more than an actor, director, writer, even song-writer, or producer. In truth, he was Bollywood's first and last showman. Between 1935 and 1990, he acted in over seventy films and, during that time, no other Bollywood personality came close to matching him, let alone expressing the flamboyance and extravagance that marked his approach to cinema and to life. It would be easy to debunk his films: they lacked the depth of Satyajit Ray, the subtlety of Guru Dutt, or the searing honesty of Bimal Roy. They were the ultimate expression of the art form Bollywood was now devising as its very own. The story lines in the films were often very simple and told with a minimum of fuss; but, they combined high-voltage melodrama and toe-tapping songs, and were so well spiced for every taste that they have lasted remarkably well, sixty years after they were first screened.

Years later, these films would be called the first of Bollywood's masala entertainments (the word had not been employed when Raj Kapoor made his first movie, but it is apt). What is more, they were so successful that Raj Kapoor had found movie spices that appealed not only to Indians but to many millions beyond India, in a swathe of countries stretching through the Middle-East, eastern Europe and north Africa. He was the first Indian to became a film superstar, whose popularity in his heyday was greater than that of the Hollywood stars of his day. He would not have a match until Amitabh Bachchan emerged nearly three decades later. But even Bachchan, for all his superstar status, has not combined the many roles Raj Kapoor played or has even attempted to do so. Bachchan's 'angry young man' did define a new style of Bollywood films but Raj Kapoor's 'tramp' remains the abiding image of Bollywood. But unlike the very literate Bachchan, Raj Kapoor did not even pass his matriculation examination, and a matriculate failure in India is shorthand for saying a man is truly illiterate and well below the salt.

10

The Great Indian Showman

Raj Kapoor was undoubtedly the most complex man Indian cinema has produced—a man who fell in love with his leading ladies, one of whom not only inspired his studio but financed some of his early films. He always dressed his leading ladies in white, as a symbol of his love. For a Hindu, and Raj Kapoor was a devout Hindu, white was the colour of mourning, and the colour widows wore at the moment of their husband's death.

The eldest son of Prithviraj and Ramsarni Kapoor, Raj Kapoor was a Pathan, born in Peshawar on December 14, 1924, to parents who were quite young. Prithviraj was eighteen, and his wife was sixteen. Raj had such blue eyes and such white skin that often, while walking home from school, he would be mistaken for a white boy and taken away to a restaurant and fed by whites, while his darker brother, Shammi, would sit outside the restaurant watching his older brother gulp down the food. With father, Prithviraj, pursuing a career on both the stage and the screen and constantly on the move, the Kapoors led a nomadic life and so Raj was often in and out of schools in various parts of the country. Early in life he suffered the sort of tragedy that might well have scarred him. Raj was about six when his four-year-old brother, Bindi, ate rat poison and died, while a second brother, Devi, also died a fortnight later, probably from pneumonia. Raj had to fetch his father, as Bindi lay dying. He would never stop mourning his brothers. This may explain why, throughout his childhood, he craved food and was therefore rather plump. He had less than fond memories of his childhood. "My childhood memories" he would later recall, "are pitted with indelible scars of experience. I was a fatty. Every sort of practical joke was played on me. Apart from some vivid patches of happiness, my childhood days were quite miserable."

And it was in order to protect himself that he assumed the role of a comedian:

I soon picked up the most natural defence mechanism—the one used by all the great jokers of the world. I learnt that the more one resisted being a target, the more one suffered. So, instead, I put on the mask of a joker by reacting as though I thoroughly enjoyed being made the butt of practical jokes. Indeed, I even took this a step further by inventing jokes against myself, which would make my colleagues laugh. You see, I was seeking that which every schoolboy seeks—the love, affection and esteem of others. I wanted to be liked.

There was little affection from his father with whom he had a very complicated relationship. Prithviraj was already the great actor of Indian stage and screen by the time Raj grew up, a man who, both in looks and achievements, towered over his son: tall, broad-shouldered and with enviable good looks, and a wonderful voice, that was made for the stage and which was his métier. Raj Kapoor kept away from the stage because he feared being seen as his father's son, whereas in films he could be his own man, although he did learn some of the elements of stagecraft, camerawork and lighting while working at Prithvi Theatres, which was set up by his father.

Raj had acted as a child in the movies and was only eleven when he made his first film, *Inquilab,* in 1935, where the stars were his father and Durga Khote. This was followed by a Debaki Bose film, *After the Earthquake.* Prithviraj was very worried that his son might suffer the same fate that Jackie Coogan, a Hollywood child actor, did. Prithviraj believed that his son should get no favours but learn the hard way. While he recognised his son might be a success, he also feared he might fail dreadfully. Not only had Raj failed to matriculate, he had failed to get into the cadet corps and also the navy. Prithviraj was none too pleased when Raj, having failed his matriculation, and struggling with Latin, told his father that he would rather learn from "the university of life", which meant going into films to produce, direct, and act.

As we have seen, Raj got a break in films with Kidar Sharma in 1947. It was Prithviraj who had persuaded his friend, Kidar, to take on his son. The story goes that the day Raj Kapoor started to work for the studio he waited outside his father's house. His father was about drive to work but insisted that his son take the bus. It was his way of starting him at the bottom.

However, on the set of the film Kidar Sharma was making, there was the first of many Raj Kapoor moments, which would change his life dramatically. Sharma had started him, as he said he would, right at the bottom, third assistant and clapper boy. Sharma was filming *Vish Kanya.* But as Sharma recalls, before giving the clap for the shot, Raj would always comb his hair and pose in front of the camera and only then give the clap. That day, Sharma wanted to take a close-up as the sun was going down and had told Raj not to comb his hair for, if the sunset was missed, it would mean having to make a forty to fifty mile return journey to the same location the next day. But Raj just carried on, and this time for good measure, caught the hero's beard in the clapperboard and it came off. Sharma lost his temper and slapped Raj Kapoor in front of the whole unit.

Afterwards, Sharma felt wretched over his loss of temper and spent a sleepless night worrying about it. Raj was, after all, his friend's son and he was working for free. The next morning Sharma called Raj into his office. It is said that the marks of the slap could still be seen on Raj's skin, although this may be retrospective imagination. What is undeniable, however, is that Sharma gave him a cheque for Rs5000 and signed him up as the hero of his next venture, *Neel Kamal*, which also introduced Madhubala to Hindi cinema. Three other films followed: *Chittor Vijay, Dil Ki Rani* and *Jail Yatra*. But all this was a prelude to what Raj Kapoor really wanted to do—to make films in his own way and under his own banner. As he later put it, "The money I got from acting I saved and that is how I became a producer, director and an actor all in one at the start of my career. My own company, R.K. Films, was thus born in the year 1947."

R.K. Films was first set up with an office at Famous Studios, and here Raj would produce, direct and act in his first film, *Aag. Aag* means fire and the 1948 story describes a theatre producer and three women all in flashback, and was based on his father's experiences. Some critics have seen this as a film which displayed the anger inside Raj Kapoor, but it is a beginner's film: the narrative is weak, although the love scenes show touches of the master to come. His mother had doubted his ability to make a movie without money, saying "You can't fry pakoras in spit," and Raj Kapoor had to mortgage everything, including his car, to make the film. He even borrowed money from his former servant to pay for tea and food for his unit. When he tried to get the film released, distributors were not interested. One of them even fell asleep during the screening. But he woke up to say he never looked at a film and always backed the man, and pressed a one rupee silver coin in Raj Kapoor's hands. The film ran for sixteen weeks and Raj Kapoor now began to plan the film that he felt would truly launch his career.

This was, *Barsaat,* released in 1949. He seemed to name his films after elements, as this one meant 'rain.' It proved a great hit and brought together what may be called the 'Raj Kapoor film clan.' These were the music composers Shankar and Jaikshen, the lyricists Shailendra and Hasrat Jaipuri, cinematographer Radhu Karmakar, art director M.R. Achrekar, the playback singers Lata Mangeshkar and Mukesh, who sang the songs Raj Kapoor mimed to in the movies, and above all his leading lady, Nargis.

If the story was fairly banal, the songs sung by Lata in the film made the movie such a success—songs such as '*Mujhe kisi se pyar*', '*Jiya bekarar hai*', and '*Hawa mein udta jaaye*'—and the role of Nargis was even more crucial. Nargis had acted with him in *Aag,* but now she became the very fabric of Raj Kapoor films both on screen and off screen as his lover. The emblem of R.K. Films seemed to symbolise that. Raj Kapoor would play the violin while the heroine, Nargis, would run into his arms. The shot would be frozen, with the hero holding the violin in one hand and the lady in the other, conveying a double theme of music and love that was now to become the trademark of all his films.

The story of Nargis and Raj Kapoor is one that, if offered at a Bollywood storytelling session, would probably have been rejected. Nargis had been a star long before Raj Kapoor combed his hair once too often. Nargis was introduced to cinema at the age of five, and was known as Baby Rani in the 1936 film, *Naachwali*. Her first lead role came at the age of fourteen in 1943, in *Taqdeer*, a comedy directed by Mehboob Khan. Born Fatima Rashid in 1929 to a Hindu father, Mohan Babu, and a Muslim mother, Jaddanbai, Nargis had been brought up as a Muslim. If Raj Kapoor had to come to terms with Prithviraj, then Nargis was ruled by her mother who always called her 'Baby', using the English term, although her mother tongue was Urdu. In her world, Jaddanbai was almost as great a figure as Prithviraj, having been a well-known actress, singer, composer and even a director herself. Jaddanbai established a production company, Sangeet Films, in 1936.

Raj Kapoor was spurred by wanting to prove to his father that he would become a success without the help of his father. Jaddanbai wanted to make Nargis a star, so that Jaddanbai's old age would be secure. Manto, who knew Jaddanbai well, writes, "Nargis could only have become an actress, given the fact of her birth. Jaddanbai was getting on and though she had two sons, her entire concentration was on Baby Nargis, a plain-looking girl who could not sing."

This was the Bombay film world of the 1940s, when the inability to sing was a major disadvantage for any actor or actress, but particularly an actress. Nur Jehan was beginning to make her mark and there was Suriya, who could both sing and act. Born in Lahore she, like Nargis, had made her début as a child star when just twelve years of age. The following year, in 1942, when she did the playback for Mehtaab in *Sharda,* under the music director Naushad's direction, she was so short that she had to stand on a stool to reach the microphone. However, by the time Nargis emerged, Suraiya was in her prime, having been launched as a singing star in the Bombay Talkies film, *Humaari Baat,* in 1943 and then starring in several films opposite K.L. Saigal. By 1948-49, Suraiya was the highest paid female star of her time. At this stage she was generating the sort of hysteria comparable only to Rajesh Khanna in the late 1960s and early 1970s. Shop owners would close their shops to see her films on the first day of their release; crowds would throng outside her residence at Marine Drive in Bombay just to get a glimpse of her, and the actor, Dharmendra, recalls going to see the film *Dillagi,* which was released in 1949, some forty times! Suraiya seemed to have everything: not just a fine singing voice but also the finer rudiments of acting, and her performances on the screen expertly integrated gesture, music and speech. Between Nargis and Suraiya there was intense hatred, with the fight being led by their mothers on both sides.

Manto describes a meeting Jaddanbai had organised when she wanted Ashok Kumar to take the lead part in one of her productions. Manto had been taken along to the meeting by Ashok Kumar for moral support against the mother and daughter combination. The talk was about money, big money, says Manto: "Each paisa was carefully discussed and accounted for. Nargis was pretty businesslike. She seemed to suggest, 'Look Ashok, I agree that you are a polished actor and famous but I cannot be undermined.You will have to concede that I can be your equal in acting. Off and on the woman in her would come to life as if she was telling Ashok, 'I know there are thousands of girls who are in love with you but, I, too, have thousands of admirers and if you don't believe me ask anyone; maybe you, too, will become my admirer one of these days."

Suraiya, being the leading actress, came into the conversation and when her name came up Jaddanbai, says Manto:

....pulled a long face and started saying nasty things about her family, pulling her down as if she was doing it out of a sense of duty. She said that Suraiya's voice was bad, she could not hold a note, she had no music training, that her teeth were bad and so on. I am sure that, had someone gone to Suraiya's home she would have witnessed the same kind of surgery being performed on Nargis and Jaddanbai.The woman Suraiya called grandmother, who was actually her mother, would have taken a drag on her *huqqua* (a long- stemmed Indian pipe) and told even nastier stories about Jaddanbai and Nargis. I know that whenever Nargis's name came up, Suriaya's mother would look disgusted and compare her face to a rotting papaya.

But it was Suraiya whose film career was soon rotting. By 1951, Suraiya could hardly get a role. Her great voice was no longer the asset it had been. By then, playback singing had been so entrenched that an actress who could also sing, counted for nothing. In fact, there was no further need for them. She faded away and while there were some attempts at comeback, by the late 50s she was very much yesterday's woman and spent the last forty years of her life in reclusive retirement, living alone in her apartment on Bombay's Marine Drive, not far from where Nargis had lived, with only the sea as her constant companion. She died in 2004.

Jaddanbai had played her cards superbly and long before the doors finally shut on Suraiya's flat, Nargis was established as the foremost heroine of the era. Even before Raj Kapoor came knocking at her door, she had starred opposite Dilip Kumar in films like *Mela, Jogan, Babul,* and *Deedar,* as a *femme fatale,* condemned by her beauty. When Manto had first seen her as a child of eleven or twelve, he remarked that, "she was a thin-legged girl with an unattractive, oblong face and two unlit eyes." By now, she had filled out as a woman and she was, he writes, "simple and playful and was always blowing her nose as if she had a perennial cold—this was used in the movie *Barsaat* as an endearing habit. Her wan face indicated that she had acting talent. She was in the habit of talking with her lips slightly joined. Her smile was self-conscious and was carefully cultivated. One could say that she would use these mannerisms as raw a material to forge her acting style."

She had done so with dramatic effect in another film released the same year as *Barsaat* Mehboob Khan's *Andaz*, where she was the female lead opposite

Dilip Kumar and Raj Kapoor. It was in this film that she displayed on screen something that had not been seen before—the modern Indian woman.

Very like the real life meeting with Ashok Kumar, where she combined an understanding of the movie business and the know-how to project her femininity, in this film she played a modern young woman who dresses in western style clothes and who runs her father's business empire. She played a headstrong, free-spirited child of a millionaire, who also had friendships with the opposite sex. For Indian audiences, the woman Nargis played was amazingly modern yet, in the end, reassuringly traditional.

The film shows her married to Raj Kapoor, but also friendly with Dilip Kumar, a man who had once rescued her and who now looks after her business. Kapoor suspects her of being unfaithful and Nargis shoots Dilip Kumar to prove her fidelity. In jail, she tells Kapoor that it was a mistake to be so modern and hopes her daughter will not follow her example. In the film, Nargis manages to go beyond the usual roles given to Indian women at that stage and convey the plight of a woman torn between two men, which was a daring new subject in Indian movies. The film shows Nargis responding to both men's love, as she is obviously more than just friends with Dilip Kumar. In fact, when Dilip Kumar declares his love for her on her wedding day, her reaction is not of shock but one that only confirms her suspicions.

It was a new role for the Indian cinema and defined Nargis's image for the decade to come. This was an Indian woman who could also be western—not afraid to wear sharp elegant western clothes, both sporting and casual. The two men in her life are also seen wearing suits. This is at a time when western dress, particularly for a woman, was synonymous with being morally loose and corrupt. Nargis, however, had the ability to carry it off and in Raj Kapoor's *Awara* she was the first Bollywood actress to wear a bathing suit. Instead of causing a scandal, she produced quite a stir.

Manto had been right to predict that Nargis would use her mannerisms to break away from the theatrical approach of acting. She used her hand gestures very well: the 'palm to forehead' swoon, a finger to the edge of a smiling mouth, to indicate coyness, and a fist against the temple to indicate anxiety. Indian actresses before her had used expansive, often hammy, gestures to convey emotion. Nargis used simple, effective and natural gestures.

It is a measure of how important actresses still were in that era, and in particular Nargis, that she was paid more than twice as much as Raj Kapoor and even more than Dilip Kumar, receiving Rs. 35,000 to Dilip Kumar's Rs. 25,000 and Raj Kapoor's Rs. 15,000.

So, when Raj Kapoor came calling on Nargis at her flat, quite unannounced (he had come to see Jaddanbai), he could be dismissed quite contemptuously by Nargis. "A fat blue-eyed pinkie has visited me," she told her friend, Lettitia. Kapoor was, on the other hand, awestruck. He later recalled, "She had been frying pakodas when I rang the bell. And when she opened the door she accidentally brushed her hand with *basean* (a yellowish paste) on it to cover her hair." Raj Kapoor was so overwhelmed that he rushed back to the studio and asked for Nargis to be written into the script. He would never forget the scene. More than a quarter century later in 1973, with Nargis long out of Raj Kapoor's life and a new sensation, Dimple Kapadia, being introduced in the teen hit *Bobby*, there was a scene in which Raj, played by Raj Kapoor's son Rishi Kapoor, goes to Bobby's house and she answers the door casually dressed, her hair dishevelled.

In *Aag,* Jaddanbai had insisted that Nargis, with already eight films behind her, be given a higher billing than the two other actresses, Kamini Kaushal and Nigal Sultana. Although she had agreed to a fee of Rs. 10,000 Nargis' brother saw to it that this was increased to Rs. 40,000. During *Aag,* Nargis noticed that "pinkie", as she called Raj was getting quite fresh. By the time *Barsaat* was made, she was more than happy for him to be fresh and the relationship would develop into a love affair. Madhu Jain, in *The Kapoors,* a history of the family, compares this love affair to that between Spencer Tracy and Katherine Hepburn. Tracy, a Catholic, could not divorce his wife. Kapoor who had had an arranged marriage just four months before he met Nargis, could also not leave his wife, although during his career his wife often did leave him but always came back. Nor did Raj Kapoor pursue the option that Barua, Shantaram and later Dharmendra did, of taking a second wife.

Raj Kapoor would later say, "Nargis was my inspiration, *meri sphoortti* (my energy). Women have always meant a lot in my life, but Nargis meant more than anybody else. I used to always tell her: Krishna is my wife and she is the mother of my children. I want you to be the mother of my films."

Visitors who came to his studio saw them behave as a couple might, Nargis cutting mangoes for him, Nargis clipping his nails.

Jaddanbai had an inkling of the love blossoming and initially tried to stop the affair. Raj Kapoor wanted to shoot scenes in Kashmir, as it became increasingly popular with the Bombay film world. But Jaddanbai said 'no,' and the shooting had to be done in Mahabaleshwar, a small hill station near Bombay.

But clearly, Jaddanbai could not stop her daughter getting in deeper and in *Barsaat,* as Raj Kapoor ran out of money, it was Nargis who provided the funds, even selling her gold bangles to fund the film, which was symbolically a huge act for an Indian woman. Nargis even acted in other films to raise money for R.K. Productions. Jain, who calls it a post-independence Bombay love story, says, "She was a partner alongside him at the helm of R.K. Films for much of their golden years together. Nargis was Raj Kapoor's friend, muse, partner at work, actress, lover, and his love." In an interview Nargis gave *Filmfare,* in 1954, she would say that her ideas had been bottled up before she met Raj Kapoor. He released them and she found that she had "the same views and ideas, the same outlook on all subjects."

By now the inequalities between the two, so evident at the start of their relationship, had disappeared both materially and intellectually. There had been a great contrast in wealth when they had first met. Nargis could demand high fees, while Raj was paid Rs. 201 a month by his father, a rupee more than what Bombay Talkies paid him. Nargis was educated in a convent and read complex novels. Raj Kapoor never read much beyond Archie comics, which he loved. The relationship kept evolving from the start and by the time *Awara* was released in 1951, which would take Raj Kapoor, Nargis and Bollywood, to a new level, it was clear Raj Kapoor was as great a star as Nargis, if not greater.

In 1950, Raj Kapoor expanded R.K. Films into a fully-fledged studio, opening R.K. Studios at Chembur, about two and a half miles from his home. In the Bombay of the 1950s, this was a remote rural place, far from its centre in south Bombay and the very outskirts of the city.

Raj Kapoor had admired many a Hollywood director. He was taken by the way Orson Wells used light and shade in *Citizen Kane*. His early films, *Aag, Barsaat* and *Awara* were very much influenced by Vittorio De Sica in *Miracle in Milan* and *Bicycle Thief*, and by Roberto Rossellini and Cesare Zavattini, the pioneers of the neo-realism movement. Kapoor was taken by the scene in *Bicycle Thief*, where the boy piddles and the father waits on the side of the road with his bicycle. In 1952, the year after *Awara* was released, an international film festival was held in Bombay and some of these film-makers came to Bombay. Kapoor had a long chat with Zavattini, who had written the screenplay for De Sica. He also spoke for many hours to Frank Capra, whose work, *It Happened one Night* and *Mr Smith Goes to Washington,* had much impressed him. Kapoor was so affected by Frank Capra that he would later admit that Capra had changed his art, infusing it with the optimism that he saw in Capra's *It Happened One Night.* "In many of my films, it is the common man, the underdog, who ultimately manages to get the best deal from life." These film-makers, in particular the Italians, also told Kapoor one other thing—to go and shoot outdoors. 'The light is so wonderful here in India, why shoot inside the studio.' Years later, this was also advice Shyam Benegal, who has always preferred to shoot outside, would heed. Raj would draw much inspiration from the Italian neo-realistic school.

However, one man who towered over all for Kapoor, and who was his mentor for *Awara,* and all his other films, was Charlie Chaplin. Dev Anand described how he and Kapoor went to see Chaplin in Montreux. As Oona played on the piano, they talked for three hours, with Raj sitting on the ground in Chaplin's backyard, almost literally at his feet. They had come by bus and, as they boarded the bus to leave, Anand says, "Raj kept looking back at the receding figure of Chaplin, which got smaller and smaller. Raj raised his hand and shouted, 'Hey, little fellow, bye, bye. We love you.'"

Kapoor, who had seen all the Chaplin movies: *City Lights, Modern Times, Gold Rush*, and *Limelight,* would later say, "What inspired me in his work was the little man and when I began my career then I saw the little man all around in our country—the downtrodden, the man beaten for no fault of his own. What drew me to Chaplin's films were Chaplin himself; the hobo, the bum, the common man. I was not drawn to him so much because of his get-up but because of the simplicity—of the little man and his human emotions. How he enjoyed life, even though he was so poor. There was so much of Chaplin that affected me, the thought process behind all of his beliefs. I think his hobo was one of the greatest characters ever conceived."

The very title *Awara*—vagabond, tramp—had strong echoes of Chaplin, as did the character Raju, which Kapoor played in a very Indian version, with his trousers rolled up, wearing torn shoes, and a trilby, which he doffed at everyone who passed by. Raj moved his lips as Mukesh sang '*Awara Hoon*: I have no home, no family, but I sing the song of your love, I am the victim of destiny and of your love'. And the whole nation sang with him.

Kapoor saw the film as representing the innocence of the Republic, born just a year before the film was released, and learning to cope with a difficult world. Kapoor would later say:

> *Awara* came at a time when films were of a totally different nature. We still had remnants of British imperial dominance and we wanted a new social order. I tried to create a balance between entertainment and what I had to say to the people. *Awara* had everything. It has the theme of class distinction. It had the greatest juvenile romantic story wrapped in the poverty that the post-independence era had inherited. It bloomed like a lotus in the mud and it went to people as something they had never seen before. Could this ever happen to a young man in such circumstances? With a song on his lips and a flower, he went through all the ordeals that socio-economic disruptions could bring about. The change that people wanted they saw in the sprit of the young man, who was the vagabond, the '*awara*.'

But, in the true traditions of the masala that Kapoor was fashioning, the story was told in flashback from an initial court-room scene. The first shot was of the Bombay High Court in a film which works at a myriad of levels. The wife of a judge played by Leela Chitnis, is abducted and she is rescued but on her return, the judge discovers she is pregnant and egged on by his sister-in-law suspects the child is not his but one of the abductors and throws her out of the house. The child born is Raju, who does not know who his father is. The judge never marries but soon looks after a young woman, played by Nargis, as his adopted daughter. It turns out later that she has been a childhood sweetheart of Raju and that her father was a friend of the judge. At one stage, the judge meets the child Raju, although they do not who the other is.

Raju grows up to be a vagabond who meets the man who had abducted his mother. He had done so in revenge against the judge, who had condemned him.

The judge is a great believer in nature, in the hereditary principle that a man born to thieves must become a thief. Now the thief watches as Raju grows up, taking growing pleasure from the fact that a judge's son has become a vagabond.

In the end, it all comes right as the character played by Nargis, who is a lawyer and a modern educated Indian woman, defends Raju in front of his father and in effect puts the judge in the dock.

Told this way, the story sounds horrendously complicated but Raj Kapoor interspersed the narrative with songs in all sorts of situation and borrowed from all cultures. There were songs on boats, songs in a vice den, songs using gypsy music, songs using Latin American music, and trumpets, oboes, casatanets and folk songs from various parts of India. There was also a much talked about nine-minute song sequence '*Ghar aaya mera pardesi*', which was shot on thirteen sets and remains a landmark in terms of set designing. Kapoor was the quintessential showman.

The film also conveyed Kapoor's attitude towards women and love, where the man demanded complete and unconditional submission from the woman; what critics called the 'caveman concept of love.' Kapoor admitted that this, and his other films, were a hodge-podge of everything. But, justifying it, he said, "I am not making films for drawing-room conversation. I am making films to entertain the millions of this country. So I have my music, I have my romanticism, beautiful script and everybody is happy and God is great."

It was the Marxist writer, Khwaja Ahmad Abbas, who had written the original *Awara* story which was adopted for the screen by himself and V.P. Sathe. Herein lay a paradox and a very sharp contrast with Hollywood. When Abbas proposed the idea to Raj Kapoor, Hollywood was in the middle of its McCarthy inspired witch-hunt against communism, which would see many of the leading lights of Hollywood leave and which created a scare that took it some time to recover from.

Yet in India, no such anti-Communist feeling developed, though, if anything, the Indian National Congress, the party that had won freedom and ruled, could have had every reason to target Communists. During the war, following Hitler's attack on the Soviet Union, the Indian Communists who had originally opposed the war as an 'imperialist war', now declared it was a 'people's war', taking the Soviet line and supporting the British rulers against the Congress. When Gandhi launched The Quit India Movement in 1942, the Communists helped the British put it down. Men like Subhas Bose, who had joined the Axis powers, were denounced as traitors, and ruthlessly vilified in the Communist press as German and Japanese puppets. One of Bose's main agents in India, the Communist Bhagat Ram Talwar, who was already supplying information to the Russians, went over to the British and spied for them as well, setting up a unique record in the war of having spied for the Italians, the Germans, as well as the Russians and the British.

After the war, the Communists were among the first of the Indian parties outside the Muslim League to support the idea of Pakistan and, in 1946, launched an armed revolt in Telangana. The initial revolt was against the rule of the Nizam, but after India won independence the revolt continued with the Communists saying that the independent Indian Government of Nehru was a Government of "national betrayal" and Telangana would be the Indian Yenan, where Mao had launched his Communist uprising. It was not until 1950, after Stalin had met the Indian Communist leaders in Moscow, that this armed struggle was abandoned. The campaign much upset Nehru but there was no edict banning the Communists. The Communists took part in the 1952 elections, and came second although a long way behind Congress. And as far as Bollywood was concerned, the Communists had nothing to fear. The IPTA flourished and Abbas, and men like him, had a free rein.

One reason for this was that in the Bombay film world the main concern was not so much communism, but communalism—the clashes between Hindus and Muslims and, in this regard, the Communists were in the vanguard of the movement to make sure that religion did not play a divisive role and secularism ruled in the film world. In 1948, Kapoor had marched in a procession organised by his father and others, on Gandhi's birthday, to preach communal harmony. Kapoor was no ideologue. His brother, Shashi Kapoor, has described him as being very conservative, very Hindu, but wanting to be on the right side. The right side in India in the 1950s was the left.

It is interesting to observe the impact that the release of the film made, particularly abroad. The film was released in 1951, by which time the anti-Communist McCarthy witch-hunt was at its height, having started in 1947, and forcing people like Joseph Losey to flee Hollywood for London where he made films under the name of Joseph Walton. In 1952, Elia Kazan who had been a Communist, gave names to the House Un-American Activities Committee.

Yet in India the Communists, advised by Stalin, had given up their armed struggle and Nehru was rebuffing American overtures to draw India into the anti-Communist world. Back in 1949, Nehru, on a visit to America, had been offered all the financial assistance he wanted for India but this would mean playing the American tune in the fight against communism. This included refusing to recognise China, where Mao had just won. America maintained the fiction that Taiwan represented all of China for another twenty-two years. Nehru refused and the divide between India and America was cemented when in 1952, the election of Dwight Eisenhower as President brought John Foster Dulles as Secretary of State, who proclaimed that "those who did not side with America in the fight against communism were enemies of freedom". Nehru's non-aligned stance became very suspect and in 1953 India refused an alliance with America. America soon made Pakistan its military ally in the region, and despite the fact that over the years military dictators ruled Pakistan, America supported Pakistan with arms against democratic India.

Nehru, who shared some of the upper-class English views about America, which reflected his own English upbringing, wrote, "I dislike more and more the exchange of persons between America and India. The fewer persons that go from India to America or that come from the United States to India, the better." And to a cabinet colleague he said, "We have had enough of American cultural values."

One of the great American values was materialism and this distrust of materialism was very marked in *Awara,* and in all of Kapoor's other films. When Raju first went to the house of Raghunath, he said, "Such a big house and it belongs to a judge," implying criticism of indecent wealth. Such an attitude would also mark other film-makers of the period. V.P. Sathe's comments to Gyatri Chatterjee implied that *Awara* showed the Marxist undertone of the film. "First, there was the old order, i.e. the feudal order; then the new order, i.e. the capitalist order. We wanted there to be a third one, and Raj Kapoor was to represent this new order."

Abbas and Sathe also worked in very clever references to the position of the Communists, although the word was never used or explicitly stated and went unnoticed. When Raju first meets the man, the dacoit who abducted his mother, he speaks to him in English and then apologises. Raju, who by this time has already been jailed, says "Dada, I'd met a political in the prison, so thought of learning some English from him." It is clear that four years after independence this would not be Indians fighting the British but were Communists jailed for their violent activities against the free Indian Government; the survivors of the ill-fated Telengana movement. As one critic put it, "Abbas was the ideological guide and Raj the faithful choreographer of dreams."

Awara was not only a hit in India but a movie that now travelled the world— Turkey, Iran, the Arabic world, and Eastern Europe—creating box office records. Millions across the globe joined Indians in singing Mukesh's song of the *Awara.* But, in the United Sates, where Raj Kapoor and Nargis went as part of an Indian film delegation, invited by the US State Department for an eight city tour, the film made no impression. That visit threw a fascinating light on how the two biggest cinema industries interacted. Raj Kapoor and Nargis are seen holding hands with President Harry Truman. The leading lights of the American motion picture industry met them and exchanged handshakes, and token gifts were given on such occasions. Ronald Regan, then president of the Actors Guild, escorted Kapoor to a college football game between Rice University of Texas and the University of California. The visitors were introduced with a card reproducing the flower of India and were addressed in Hindi, but nobody sang *Main Awara Hoon.* That came in the Soviet Union two years after this American visit and was an indication of both the impact of Kapoor's film and the changing political situation. Stalin had died in 1953 – the old dictator had never cared for India – and now, with the Soviet Union loosening up, *Awara* caused a sensation. Abbas's *Dharti Ka Lal,* made in 1946, which dealt with the events of the Bengal famine, had been shown in Moscow but created no particular stir. *Awara* was different. Eric Barnouw and S. Krishnaswamy in their *The Indian Film* describe what happened.

The Soviet Union is said to have made a massive distribution of *Awara,* dubbed into a number of its languages. Prints were even flown in to the Soviet Expeditions near the North Pole. The Soviet distribution began in 1954, after Raj Kapoor, Nargis, Abbas and the others had visited Moscow as members of a film delegation. On a return visit to the USSR two years later, Raj Kapoor and Nargis were astonished to find themselves well-known film personalities. Bands played *Awara Hun* at airports. *Awara* is reported to have been a favourite film of Mao Tse Tong.

A Soviet film which won the Golden Peacock award in the Delhi Film Festival, *Farewell Green Summer,* had some footage of the film. And one Russian who never forgot Raj Kapoor was Boris Yeltsin, who would say "I was in love with Raj Kapoor and I remember him even today."

So extensive was the *Awara* influence that even Alexander Solzhenitsyn's *Cancer Ward* had a reference to it, with the character Zoya described as being much taken by the film: "Suddenly, she flung out her arms, snapped the fingers of both hands, her whole body writhing to the urge of the popular song she began singing from a recent Indian film. *A-va-rai-ya-ya! A-va-rai-ya-a-a!*"

Oleg, who she sung to, was not amused, "No, don't. Not that song. Zoya, please," Zoya explains it is from *The Tramp.* "Haven't you seen it?" she asks. "Yes I have. Isn't it a wonderful movie? I saw it twice." Zoya had actually seen it four times but when she told Oleg that the "tramp's life was rather like yours", Oleg was not amused and made bitter criticism of the Raj Kapoor character in the film, and all that he represented, calling him " a typical grafter, a hood".

Oleg's view of the Kapoor character may or may not be valid, but that the film could find such echoes shows Raj Kapoor's ability to appeal beyond his own culture to many other cultures, and also to represent what the Indians call "the common man". Kapoor liked to keep in touch with the common man, a much-used Indian phrase, striking up friendships with ordinary workers in restaurants near his studio which, in hierarchical India, was quite revolutionary.

Kapoor would later say this film was his "little contribution to the USSR-India friendship" and it marked a remarkable honeymoon between the world's biggest democracy and the world's most entrenched dictatorship. Pankaj Mishra has written how even as late as the 1980s, this Indo-Soviet friendship blossomed and the Indian intellectual class certainly shunned America and saw the Soviet Union as the ideal society. The scales have fallen since the collapse of the Berlin Wall in 1989, but there remained a strain in the Indo-US relationship which only began to be modified with the increasing migration of middle-class Indians to America, and the creation of the well-off Indian Diaspora there.

By the time Raj Kapoor was being feted in Moscow, he was on his way to making the film which Satyajit Ray considered his best, *Shri 420.* The title itself was a Raj Kapoor joke. 420 is the number of the penal code which deals with petty crime and to call someone a "420" in India is shorthand for "a cheat", if at times in jest. Raj Kapoor plays a character again called Raju, again the tramp but this time a tramp who is educated, who is dazzled by money and wealth but, then, brought back to the ways of the real, poor, people by Nargis. 420 got so associated with Raj Kapoor that in later years even his employees at R.K. Studio called him "a 420".

This film also displayed his nationalism in songs like '*Mera joota hai Japani*' where, starting with his Japanese shoes, he shows how he is wearing everything made abroad except for his heart, which remains Indian.

There is a photograph of Nargis and Raj Kapoor taken in Russia where Raj Kapoor is in a suit, about to light a cigarette. Nargis is in a white sari and the pair appear to be a couple. Indeed, in Russia, Nargis was known as Mrs Raj Kapoor. However, the success in Moscow would also mark the beginning of the end of their relationship, with Nargis realising he would never marry her. By this time, almost five years had passed since Nargis had thought she and Raj would get married.

Marriage ideas had started way back on New Year's Eve, 1949. *Barsaat*, having been a huge success, Raj and Nargis had gone to a temple and Raj had tied the mangalsutra round her neck (a sacred black thread, the Hindu equivalent of the wedding ring). Nargis's biographer described how a deliriously happy Nargis rang Letticia, her friend, and screamed, "I'm in love with that man!" Letticia would later say, "I'll never forget that beautiful unearthly laughter. It lasted twenty minutes. She was so deliriously happy."

Later, she would persuade Letticia to accompany her to Morarji Desai, Bombay's Home Minister. Letticia described what happened to Bunny Reuben:

> We both went to Congress House. Nargis was very nervous. There was this huge table and Morarjibhai was seated behind it, looking very stern and serious. 'What is it?' he asked. Nargis was tongue-tied and I said. "Sir, she wants to talk about something important to you." Suddenly the tongue-tied Nargis blurted it out, 'Sir, I want to marry Raj Kapoor." Morajibhai put his pen down and said, "What! Don't you know the law? How dare you! Don't you dare come and ask me this again! Now both of you—please go."
>
> And we were unceremoniously bundled out of the office.

Reuben does not give the date of this story. But it must have taken place some time in 1955, after the Hindu Marriage Act banning polygamy amongst Hindus had become law. Of course, had Raj Kapoor decided to convert to Nargis's religion then he could have taken her as his second wife, but that thought did not appear to have entered his head.

Kapoor had always used his family in his movies. In *Awara,* the judge was played by Prithviraj, the young Raj by his brother, Shashi, and the little boy shown in the title sequence, was Rishi, his own boy. In *Shri 420,* his children played an even more significant part. In the famous scene where he and Nargis sing a song while sharing an umbrella as it pours down in Bombay, three children, all dressed in raincoats and gumboots, walk past. Raj Kapoor had arranged for them to miss school in order to take the shot. They got to keep the raincoats and gumboots as presents and he would later tell a friend that the three little Kapoors would be the children he and Nargis could have had. For good measure, the children were taken to lunch at Nanking, then one of Bombay's most select Chinese restaurants and a big treat as Chinese restaurants are very popular in India. The children were accompanied by their father, and the woman who could not be their mother.

Between 1948 and 1956, Raj Kapoor and Nargis made sixteen films together, including their last, *Chori Chori*. Nargis played major roles in all these films. In this time, Nargis had refused all films opposite Dilip Kumar, the other actor with whom she had made a successful team, and also the female lead in *Aan* offered by her mentor, Mehboob Khan. Although her roles in the Kapoor films were always strong and noteworthy—the hard-nosed lawyer in *Awara* who defends her vagabond lover in a predominantly male courtroom, and the teacher in *Shri 420*, who acts as the wayward hero's conscience keeper, by the middle 1950s Nargis was being told by her brothers, and a coterie around them, that Raj Kapoor had used her to became a star.

The Raj-Nargis relationship was framed by Raj Kapoor's own sexual upbringing and strong memories of childhood, which never left him. Awareness of sex had come early to Raj Kapoor and in a curious way. Once, when quite young, his family had returned to the village in Lyallpur, where his father was born. "An earthen oven was always kept lit in the centre of the village and women roasted channa on the fire. I remember having gone to buy channa, wearing a shirt and nothing under it. The woman at the oven had an odd smile on her face and said, "You don't have to pay for the channa; just raise your shirt and make a bowl out of it. I did, and stood like that, and she laughed her head off, looking at me. I was totally innocent. Years later when this memory came back to me and I understood the trick she must have been up to, it disturbed me a great deal. For some time in my life channa itself became a sex object." Kapoor later used this memory to construct a scene in his film, *Bobby*, made in 1973.

But, there were also other compulsions which some have argued are part of the Indian male psyche. There is a scene in *Awara* where Nargis is seen in a swimsuit, much too daring for Indian audiences. The character Raj Kapoor plays in the film upsets her and she calls him "a junglee", meaning a person from the jungle and Raj Kapoor slaps her repeatedly. Rita, the name of the character played by Nargis, falls to her knees and asks his forgiveness. Indian film historians have debated long and hard about what this means, with Gayatri Chatterjee, in her book *Awara*, suggesting it represented the Indian male desire to get women to go down on their knees to plead for protection and upkeep, and for love.

During their first visit to Moscow, Raj Kapoor and Nargis had behaved like a couple. Dev Anand was part of that delegation. Later, Anand recalled that, "Kapoor and Nargis were in the same room. Whenever we went anywhere they would play *Awara Hoon* on the piano. Sometimes, he would drink too much and had to be pulled out of the bedroom; we would all be waiting for him, and then Nargis would rush off and try to bring him down."

But, on a return visit to Moscow, and perhaps convinced by her brothers, Nargis felt marginalised. This time, while Raj Kapoor was treated like a pop star, girls mobbing him, his shirts being torn, Nargis decided to suddenly leave Moscow and return to India.

Back in India there followed what Raj Kapoor would later term, "betrayals". The most dramatic moment came in 1955 while they were in Madras, shooting *Chori Chori*, a film for a south Indian producer and a remake of *It Happened One Night*. They were due to go to a party when Raj Kapoor spotted a paper in Nargis's hand. Nargis claimed it was nothing and tore it up. Raj Kapoor later retrieved it and it was a marriage proposal from a producer. He put the letter together, framed it and it formed an incident in the film he would make a decade later, *Sangam*.

This was followed by yet another "betrayal". Kapoor had received the rights for *Phagun,* a story by Rajinder Singh Bedi, where Nargis would have to play an older woman. She refused the role, saying it would spoil her image but, unknown to Raj Kapoor, she had been approached by Mehboob Khan to play in *Mother India*, where during the film she would grow from a young to a much older woman.

The parting was very like a Raj Kapoor script. Nargis had already signed up for *Mother India*. The shooting had started in Billimoria, the ancestral village of Mehboob Khan. Raj Kapoor heard about this and also rumours of a romance between her and Sunil Dutt, who was playing her son in the film. Unable to bear it any longer, one night he drove to Letticia's house but she knew nothing as Nargis had kept her in the dark. Then Nargis returned from Billimoria and the two women drove out to R.K. Studios. According to Bunny Reuben, while Nargis still did not say anything, Raj Kapoor told Letticia, "See, you wouldn't tell me but it's written all over her face." Nargis still refused to put Raj Kapoor out of his misery and the two women drove back to south Bombay in silence. In the car, Letticia said, "Can't you stop the rumours?" "What can I do?" asked Nargis. "If it's there, it is there." "But you cannot go back to R.K. Studios?" "No, I am not going back to R.K. Studios."

But while Nargis did not return, her driver did. Nargis had her own room at the studio and there she had left personal things. Twenty years later, in 1974, Raj Kapoor would tell Suresh Koli, then chief editor of Sterling Publishers, that the driver said "Baby has asked for her *heel ke* sandals (high heel sandals). I said 'le jaiye'—take it. The driver came again, this time for *baaja* (harmonica). I then realised it was all over." Heels, *baaja*, and Sunil Dutt who was six feet tall. Raj Kapoor, much shorter, had to bow to a taller, younger man and soon after the shooting of *Mother India* finished, Nargis and Sunil Dutt were married.

The greatest romance in Bollywood—in all of Indian cinema—had ended. Raj Kapoor would go on for another thirty years, making films and becoming a legend, and the film that Nargis had secretly gone off to make would became the greatest ever film of India cinema, Bollywood's *Gone with the Wind*.

And since sentiment always pays such a big part in Indian life there is, perhaps appropriately, an on-screen sentimental scene to indicate when this remarkable cinematic and personal relationship ended. It was the last scene of *Jaagte Raho,* a 1956 film, in which Raj Kapoor plays a thirsty man searching for a drink of water during a hot Calcutta night. In the last scene Nargis makes a symbolic guest appearance and offers him water. She had not wanted to play the part and this scene has been accepted as her screen farewell. Needless to say, the film flopped, with the audience now aware that the pair were no longer together, unable to believe that they could be lovers on screen.

Interestingly, while the movie was being made Nargis was quite in command at R.K. Studios. Nargis ,who was always somewhat bossy at the studio, behaving as if she was a surrogate director, certainly acted as a director in the making of this film and gave instructions to the lighting people.

Her break with Kapoor came because clearly she wanted to take charge of her life and she now had the opportunity to do so. Raj Kapoor, after weeping copiously and also getting very drunk, found other heroines to try and replace Nargis. He dressed them in white and found them in the south, starting the tradition of the southern belle in Bollywood. In Moscow, Padmini, a southern actress nursed him after Nargis left and he had caught a cold, and soon there were other southern actresses at R.K. Studios.

Although *Jaagte Raho* had failed with Indian audiences, it did win Raj Kapoor a major international honour at the Karlovy Vary Film Festival. But this would have a consequence for Raj Kapoor, producing a breach with another great Indian film-maker.

While Raj Kapoor was becoming the first Bollywood superstar and reaching out to millions around the world, there was another Indian who would make an even greater impact on the world of cinema, what many would call the real cinema, as opposed to the tinsel town of Bollywood. That was Satyajit Ray. Now these great men of Indian cinema fell out badly. As it happened, the quarrel took place outside India, when both were being feted for their movies.

Benegal takes up the story:

> The Bombay film industry always thought that Ray was not doing right by India. Raj Kapoor and he had a big spat once. Raj Kapoor's film, *Jaagte Raho,* was directed by Shambhu Mitra, a famous Bengali theatre director who had the same stature as Ray in cinema. It won Raj Kapoor an award in the 1964 Karolvy Vary film festival, the same year that *Aparajito* won the Golden Lion in Venice. They met up at some

meeting where both were being felicitated. So Ray said it was a great recognition for Bengali cinema.

Raj Kapoor said, "Why Bengali, are you not an Indian? Why do you say you are a Bengali film-maker?"

Ray said, "I am a Bengali film-maker."

Raj Kapoor said, "Why can't you say you are an Indian film-maker? For god's sake." That was the spat. At that time, young Indians were encouraged to say that you were an Indian, not Bengali or Maharastrian or any other region.

Nargis later said in Parliament that Ray was peddling poverty: *Pather Panchali*, Ray's first film, which made his world-wide reputation, was presenting India in a poor light.

The two men represented not only very different cinematic traditions, but also very different ways of looking at life, and what it meant to be Indian. Ray was the last great product of the Bengali renaissance that in the nineteenth century, seeking to assimilate the best of British influence, had sought to revitalise a dying Indian culture. Bengal had led the national movement both for renewal and then freedom from the British. As a child, Ray would have been told "What Bengal thinks today, India thinks tomorrow." But, by 1947, after a decade of suffering and the partition of Bengal, Sardar Patel could mock Bengal, saying, "Bengal knows only how to cry." Raj Kapoor did not think that but he reflected a very different Indian culture, where to be identified as a regional person was not a badge of honour, but a sign of lack of patriotism and proof that the person was not really Indian.

The divide between these great men of Indian cinema would never be bridged.

11

Bollywood's Classic Era

In 1957, Mehboob Khan released *Mother India*, and in 1960, Karimuddin Asif released *Mughal-e Azam*. Before and during this period there were other films made by some of Bollywood's greatest directors—those films were and remain classics—but these two films in many ways are the two most important films of what is often called the "golden era of Bollywood".

The two films could not be more different on first inspection. *Mother India* was made by a man who was barely literate, and whose production company had the logo of a hammer and sickle on which the first letter of his own name was imposed, although the accompanying audio message spoke of the eternal power of God. The film was very much an on-message film for the India of the 1950s. As we have seen, it was a story of the terrible suffering of Indian peasants exemplified by a stoic mother who ends up killing her beloved son.

Three years later, *Mughal-e Azam* took us back to the sixteenth century and the court of the Mughal Emperor Akbar. While it was historically dubious, more a historical costume drama, the setting was opulent and the film itself was quite breathtaking to watch, with the songs having echoed down through the decades.

Yet in many ways, both films were similar. There was the similarity in that both directors were Muslims although, interestingly, Mehboob Khan was more often known by his first name and, with time, Asif's first name, Karimuddin, was almost entirely forgotten, and he was known only as Asif. But the religious similarity was rather a simple one, and hardly exceptional for Bollywood. By this time, Bollywood had long created an India that was very different to the real India outside. Here, none of the bitterness and divide between the two great religious communities, that only a decade earlier had led to the partition of the land, applied. In the India of Bollywood, Hindus fell in love with Muslims and even married them and it was quite common for Muslim actors and actresses to play Hindu characters. In the film, *Ram Rajya*, the only film Gandhi was supposed to have seen, which tells the story of the great Hindu god Ram, who had come to earth as the perfect human being, it was a Muslim who played Ram, while a Hindu played the demon Ravana who wanted to destroy him. In that sense, *Mughal-e Azam* was only noteworthy for being the only film where Dilip Kumar played a Muslim in a film. In all his other film roles, which numbered more than sixty-five, Kumar who was brought up as a devout Muslim, which he remained all his life, always played Hindu roles. Dilip Kumar himself was part of this cinematic religious reversal when in a 1981 film, *Kranti,* he played the Hindu while Shatrughan Sinha, who later became a politician, joining the BJP, a staunch Hindu party, played the Muslim.

But what made these two movies outstanding, were the messages they sent and the way that they finally came to the screen illustrating how, through the 1950s and early 1960s, the Bollywood that we know now was in its genesis. These two films were both telling the story of India, one projecting the new India that was being built from its feudal, oppressive past, while the other drew on the past to sustain a more tolerant India. *Mother India* was about the future of India. 1957 was a time when India was in the middle of its second five-year plan, which was very much a copy of the Soviet style of planning. But this planning also came combined with a Western-styled democracy. In 1957, the country also held its second general election.

Mehboob's film was overladen with symbols of modern India—Nehru's India. Indeed, the very first scene in the film shows men wearing the clothing that signified the uniform of Nehru's Congress party, escorting the mother to inaugurate the arrival of an irrigation canal in the village; just the sort of progress Nehru was seeking to make as India, finally, took the road towards industrialisation. The story is told in flashback, as the mother recalls her terrible past, but the film ends in hope, as much-needed water finally comes to the village.

Mughal-e Azam was a tragic love story between a prince and a dancing girl and a fight with his father over this, the father being the Mughal Emperor who not only married a Hindu wife but allowed her to perform her Hindi rituals in the harem. It was the son of this Hindu wife who succeeded him on the Mughal throne of India.

The other major common note for both films was that they were a long time in the making, which showed the problems of film-making in India. Mehboob may have been one of the great directors of India but he made the film against the background of the star system, taking over from the previous studio system. Both films were heavily influenced by one of the greatest stars of Bollywood—Dilip Kumar. In Asif's film, he played the lead role of Prince Salim, the rebellious prince, while in *Mother India* he could have played the lead role of the rebellious son, Birju but, in the end, did not. Despite this, he influenced the making of the film. The result was that both films, *Mughal-e Azam* more than *Mother India,* had a changing cast list, changes which kept being made before the final version was settled.

The making of *Mughal-e Azam* was an Indian version of *Waiting for Godot*. My childhood growing up in the Bombay of the 1950s and 1960s was dominated by the stories of how *Mughal-e Azam* was constantly being made. Every year, starting around 1951, we were told Asif's picture would emerge. It finally did in 1960, after Asif had been tormented by rivals who got in earlier. Seven years before he finally completed his movie, and as Asif struggled to find the money and replace actors who had died, or were no longer star material, he was mortified to find a movie with exactly the same storyline. What was worse, the movie had very catchy songs that became big hits. By the time Asif finally released his movie, it was twenty years after he had first conceived it and with a cast so totally different, that the man who was to be his first hero was long dead.

Mehboob Khan did not take quite that long to make *Mother India* although, like Asif, he had conceived of the idea for the movie nearly twenty years before the final print was ready and he had even had a trial run of the theme in an earlier version, some eight years before. But, in a sense, *Mother India* was the movie Mehboob Khan was destined to make ever since he was a child, growing up in a little village. Barely able to read, he was lured by movies and by Bombay itself.

Mehboob Ramzan Khan was born in a poor Muslim family in Billimoria. So little is known of his childhood that Gayatri Chatterjee, who wrote a book about *Mother India,* with the active help of his family, could not give us his birth date. She merely mentions that he was "born in the first decade of the twentieth century." Wikipedia, the internet encyclopaedia, says he was born in 1907, but does not mention the precise date. Billimoria then was part of the princely state of Baroda and Mehboob's father, who had been in the army of that princely state, was rather better known in his village as 'the ghode-nal Khan,' the man who fixed horseshoes. The family was very religious. Mehboob's middle name meant 'prayer' in Urdu, and Mehboob said his prayers five times a day, as a devout Muslim is required to do. He was also, as is the custom, married off at an early age to a girl called Fatima, and eventually produced a son.

Mehboob could not have had much of a formal education in the village. He could just about read in his mother tongue, Gujarati, but was helped by a guard who worked on the railway line between Baroda and Bombay to travel to the big city. In his early years, he appears to have slept on the benches outside Grant Road station. The story of villagers coming to Bombay looking for gold – the city is known as 'the city of gold' – is an old one and one that resonates to this day. In the case of Mehboob, there was not only work but glory to be found, although it would take time.

Curiously, in his first film, he did find a vat, not of gold, but of wood, where he was hidden as a thief in the 1927 *Alibaba and the Forty Thieves,* a silent film made by Ardeshir Irani's Imperial Film. Much later, after he had achieved success, he would wonder how he contributed to the film, as he was hidden in the vat.

1 Dadasaheb Phalke, the father of Indian cinema, who was inspired to make films on Indian mythological stories after seeing a movie of Christ. His first film *Raja Harishchandra* was made three years before D.W. Griffiths's *The Birth of a Nation*.

2 *Alam Ara*, India's first talkie made in Bombay in 1931 by Ardeshir Irani who just managed to beat competition from the Madans in Calcutta, the first step in the eventual domination by Bombay of India's film industry.

3   Devika Rani and Ashok Kumar, the first great on-screen couple of Indian cinema in the 1936 film *Achhut Kanya*, a Bombay Talkies production. A Hollywood style studio set up by Devika and her husband Himansu, it introduced many of the stars who would dominate Bollywood for decades.

4   Three of the biggest names in Bollywood. Dilip Kumar gazing across at Raj Kapoor, behind whom stands Nargis, in Mehboob Khan's *Andaaz*, the only film in which all three acted together. All had complicated private lives. Kapoor was more of a filmmaker, Kumar much more the pure actor.

5 Dev Anand (seated) with Geeta Bali in *Baazi*. Anand, Raj Kapoor and Dilip Kumar were the Big Three who dominated Bollywood for almost four decades. *Baazi*, an urban crime thriller made in 1951 by Navketan (Anand's own company), saw him became a great star and the film marked the directorial debut of Guru Dutt, one of Bollywood's great directors.

6 Nargis and Raj Kapoor in *Awara*, the film that saw Kapoor emerge as the great Indian showman in which he acted, directed and produced. The film for the first time put Bollywood on the world stage and its songs were sung from Russia and Eastern Europe to the Middle East and North Africa. The film was also a testament to the love between Raj and Nargis, although with Raj married this ended in tragedy.

7 Amitabh Bachchan created a new genre in the 1973 *Zanjeer*, playing the angry young man seeking justice. The above scene is from *Deewar* which followed the success of *Zanjeer*. The film came after years of failure but proved such a success that this shy man became the greatest star Bollywood has ever produced eclipsing Raj Kapoor.

8 Amitabh Bachchan riding a bike while Dharmendra sits on his shoulder. Classic male bonding in the 1975 *Sholay* which is one of the most successful Bollywood films ever made and created a new genre, the curry western imitating many of the features of the spaghetti western.

9 Opposite above: Aamir Khan in *Lagaan*, the story of how Indian villagers learnt to play cricket and 'defeat' their British masters. This was the first film to make it in the West, crossing a frontier that until then had proved such a barrier. Khan played the lead actor but also produced the movie, managing a cast of Indians and Britons, one of whom wrote a book on the film.

10 Salman Khan and Madhuri Dixit in *Hum Apke Hain Kaun*. Salman Khan is the bad boy of Bollywood, being prosecuted for a 2002 case where, allegedly driving while drunk, he killed some street sleepers. He has also been sentenced to prison for shooting an endangered species. Madhuri Dixit, the wholesome beauty, was the lead actress of the 1980s and early 1990s, then got married but returned to resume her dominance.

11 Shyam Benegal, a cousin of Guru Dutt, is the director who took Bollywood to a new level and who sought to make Satyajit Ray-style films in Bollywood. His films have always had a narrative and the remarkable ability to convey his points in a compelling fashion. He has discovered actors and actresses and shown great courage in tackling subjects the rest of Bollywood will not touch.

12 K.L. Saigal leaning over Kanan Devi in *Street Singer*, a film of the vanished era when Indian actors and actresses could both sing and act. Ironically it was Saigal, whose voice charmed a nation and produced many imitators, who started the unique Bollywood phenomenon of actors and actresses miming to songs sung by others.

13 Rajesh Khanna was the first Bollywood super star who dominated the early 1970s before he was swept aside by the Bachchan phenomenon. Here he is at his height with Sharmila Tagore in *Aradhana*. She, a member of the Tagore family, exemplified the Bengali school of acting. She later married Nawab of Pataudi, the Indian cricket captain. Their son is now in films.

14 Dilip Kumar and Nadira in Mehboob Khan's *Aan*, the first attempt at bringing colour to Indian films. Kumar was already a big name but Nadira was an unknown Jewish girl, Farah Ezekiel, then only 20, whose upfront style was much liked by Mehboob. But just as the film did not work so she did not become a great actress, although she continued for years in character roles.

15 Zeenat Aman was one of the new breed of actresses to emerge in the 1970s, more willing to display flesh. This 1978 film made by Raj Kapoor *Satyam Shivam Sundaram* had Kapoor boasting that a movie which showed Zeenat's boobs would do well. The movie did however create a rift between Kapoor and Lata Mangeshkar, the singer who sang most of the songs in his films.

16 Hrithik Roshan was born with two thumbs on his right hand and was very skinny but, helped by his great friend Salman Khan, he developed his body. Promoted by his father Rakesh Roshan, a well established producer, he then made it into films. His first role was a 13 year old with his father in *Bhagwan Dada*. Fame came when in 2000 his father made *Kaho Na...Pyaar Hai*.

However, he never forgot the experience. Eleven years later, now a director, when he himself had made *Alibaba,* he returned to the studio and shot the first scene of the movie there.

In the years between 1927 and 1940, Mehboob tried hard to make it as an actor but did not get a part in Irani's *Alam Ara,* which considerably upset him. Transferring to Sagar, he did play the lead in *The Romantic Hero* made in 1931 but, according to Chatterjee, the death of his father, which made him the breadwinner, forced him into directing.

His directorial début came in 1935, with *Al Hilal Judgement of Allah,* inspired by Cecil B. DeMille's 1932 *Sign of the Cross.* The DeMille film was set in Nero's time, with Charles Laughton playing an implicitly gay Nero and had the DeMille formula of sex, violence and spectacle presented in the guise of culture and morality. Mehboob, catering to Indian taste, did not have much sex in the film. DeMille had shown Claudete Colbert bathing up to her nipples in milk. Instead, Mehboob had a Roman Emperor, Caesar, attack a Muslim ruler and suffer defeat. The many battle scenes and natural catastrophes depicted proved quite popular. It was shot by Faredoon Irani, who became a Mehboob regular and photographed every film that followed. Irani and he would fall out socially, but their work was never interrupted.

The film also featured Sitara Devi, the Kathak dancer, who hailed from Nepal. Manto describes her as, "a woman who is born once in a hundred years" not so much a woman, but a typhoon, who swept many men along, including Mehboob. The film involved shooting outdoors in Hyderabad, and Manto writes, "Mehboob would offer his prayers with the greatest devotion and make love to her with the same single-minded enthusiasm." Sitara went through various lovers, including Nazir, the uncle of K. Asif, and then Asif himself.

It was in 1937, having made two other films, *Manmohan* in 936, inspired by Barua's *Devdas,* and *Jagirdar* in 1937, that Mehboob first got the idea of *Mother India.* It was inspired by seeing the film, *The Good Earth,* based on a novel by Pearl Buck, then a widely-read American writer who had won the Nobel Prize for literature. Mehboob, says Chatterjee, was diverted by his friend Babubhai Mehta who, unlike Mehboob, was a well-read man. Mehta told Mehboob to consider another Buck novel, *The Mother,* which dealt with the life of a Chinese woman. But, before he turned to that subject, Mehboob indicated his growing social awareness and political leanings in the 1939 film, *Ek hi Raasta,* a significant title as it meant "the only road". It was about a war veteran who, trying to cope with the effects of war, is charged with killing a rapist and is brought to trial. At the trial he raises questions about a system that made him a war hero yet condemns him for killing a criminal.

By the time Sagar had collapsed, Mehboob was part of National Studios, set up by some Sagar people and backed by the Tatas. The Tatas by now were one of India's biggest business houses, founded by the man who, having been turned away from Watsons, in the early days of the cinema, decided to open the Taj Mahal Hotel. It was for National that Mehboob made *Aurat* (Woman), in 1940. In any discussion of Mehboob, *Aurat* is seen as the seminal movie and is clearly a forerunner for *Mother India*. It highlighted a peasant's love for his land.

This was a story of a young woman who starts life full of hope and dreams but ends up old and care-worn, having survived flood, famine, starvation and a wayward son, whom she shoots to protect the honour of the village. *Mother India* was to be a very similar story and many critics are of the opinion that *Aurat* was much more realistic and had an earthiness that *Mother India* lacked.

Aurat was also to have a devastating effect on Mehboob's personal life. As with his first film, he again fell in love with *Aurat's* leading lady, Sardar Akthar, but with more long-term consequences. She had given an intuitive performance in the film which was much praised and, of course, she was very unlike his first wife, Fatima. Her sister was married to Kardar, a fellow director at Sagar, which meant that, by marrying her, Mehboob became part of the small incestuous world of Bombay films. Akthar was a woman who could be by his side as he tried to become the Cecil DeMille of India, his great ambition. In later years, she would accompany him on his foreign travels. By this time, Fatima had produced three sons and three daughters but Mehboob was not planning to divorce his wife as in those days polygamy was permissible for men of all religions in India. Mehboob, as a Muslim, had also the support of his religion, which allowed him four wives. It is an interesting paradox of Mehboob's life that while in his films, such as *Aurat* and *Mother India,* he liked portraying strong women who had to come to the rescue of weak men to protect their family, in his personal life he could play the strong man who dominated the weaker sex.

This, however, did not go down well with Faredoon Irani who was outraged. In the Indian way of working, Irani was now very much part of Mehboob's family and he refused to talk to Mehboob but continued working with him. When he had to say something during shooting, he spoke to others, who then spoke to Mehboob. How long this quarrel lasted is not clear, for two years later, in 1943, Mehboob started Mehboob Productions, with Irani becoming the director of the company.

Irani and Mehboob always had a combustible relationship. In 1949, when Mehboob signed Dilip Kumar for *Andaz,* Irani watched quietly as Dilip Kumar came to the studio on the first day for costume fittings. Then, as Mehboob later recalled, Irani, "asked innocently 'Who is this monkey?' and was aghast when told he was my choice for a leading role in *Andaz*."

This must be balanced against the fact that Mehboob himself had been dismissive of Dilip Kumar when he heard he had been chosen for the film *Milan,* the film that kick-started Dilip Kumar's career, after a disastrous launch. Mehboob chided Hiten Chowdhury, the director, for taking him on saying, "You should have taken a name star. This lad doesn't impress me."

Before Mehboob set out on his own, he produced two more films for National: *Bahen* in 1941, which was about a brother's obsessive love for his little sister, and *Roti* in 1942, where Mehboob showed the first real signs of his growing belief that capitalism could not work and that real people could only be found in villages. Set in a fictional land where there is no money and people barter things, Mehboob contrasted city people who only valued money, against tribes who lived by barter. In the end, the rich city type, played by the actor Chandramohan, is shown dying in the desert. His car is full of gold ingots but he dies of thirst representing the classic, perhaps clichéd argument, that for all the gold in the world, it does not help you get water in the desert.

Soon Chandramohan was to provide a link with Asif and *Mughal-e Azam*. Although only thirty-seven, he was then one of the rising stars of the screen and his portrayal in this and other films was so effective that three years later, in 1945, as Asif first began to think of making *Mughal-e Azam* he signed up Chandramohan to play Emperor Akbar. According to Naushad, Asif also signed up "Nargis, Sapau & Mubarak in the lead roles; the film was being financed by Shiraz Ali Hakim and was being shot in black and white at the Bombay Talkies." As we shall see, it was the first of many twists and turns in the *Mughal-e Azam* saga.

A year after *Roti,* Mehboob Productions was up and running; the hammer and sickle had been chosen for the company's emblem although Mehboob never joined the Communist Party. The initial offerings were not remarkable, except for the 1946 *Anmol Ghadi,* which had three singing stars together—Surendra, Nur Jehan and Suraiya—proving how important it still was for actors and actresses to sing. The film was also notable for the partnership between music composers, Naushad and Mehboob. He, like Faredoon behind the camera, was now to become a constant of Mehboob's films.

Naushad had to work just as hard as Mehboob to establish himself. Born Naushad Ali in Lucknow, where he was heavily influenced by Indian classical music, his early years in Bombay had been similar to Mehboob, scrounging for work and even spending some nights sleeping on the city's pavements. Years later, when one of his films premiered at a Bombay cinema, his fellow Bollywood stars were surprised to find him weeping. He explained he had slept on the pavement opposite the cinema when he first came to the city.

He worked as a pianist in composer Mushtaq Hussain's orchestra and got his chance to emerge as a music director when the classical musician, Zhande Khan, found it distasteful to compose light tunes. While working with Zhande Khan, Naushad impressed a Russian director by composing a simple light tune, which was beyond Zhande Khan, and was promoted to the position of music director. Through the early 1940s, he began to compose music for films but it was his music for *Rattan,* in 1944, that would stamp him as one of the great music directors of his generation. After *Rattan,* Naushad could charge as much as

Rs. 25,000 per film, huge money in India in the 1940s, and the songs from the movie would be endlessly copied in films such as *Devdas,* a decade later. They proved such a success that the disc royalties from *Rattan* would eventually bring in more money than the entire film.

Naushad had worked for Kardar so, working for Mehboob, was keeping it in the family, although their partnership began on rocky terms. As Naushad later recalled to Raju Bharatan:

> When I recorded my first song for Mehboob's *Anmol Ghadi*, he asked Noorjehan [her name can also be spelt as Nur Jehan and is spelt in that fashion in Pakistan] to change a note here, a stress there—he was the boss. The next day I purposely went onto the sets as the song was picturised. Mehboob welcomed me saying, 'Look! your song's being taken.' 'May I see it through the camera?' I asked. I peered through and, greatly daring, asked him to move this table left, that chair right. Mehboob caught me by the ear and said, 'Who do think you are? Scram! this is not your job. Your job is music; direction is my job.' I said that was the very admission I wanted from him—that his job was direction, not music! Mehboob's answer was shown by his never again entering my music room and I did all his films unfettered.

Their partnership, however, was threatened by partition when Mehboob was drawn to making his home in Pakistan. Several had gone, including Rizvi, his wife, Nur Jehan and, with Pakistan advertised as a land created for Muslims, it must have looked very alluring. Mehboob and his brother-in-law, Kardar, with their respective wives, headed across the border. We do not know why it did not work out. Mehboob's biographer, Bunny Reuben, says, "After a while, both Mehboob Khan and A.R. Kardar returned quietly. For reasons best known to themselves, they preferred to remain on the side of the border where they had been born." Perhaps they had a premonition. Most of the Muslims who went to the new state vanished without trace, with the exception of Nur Jehan. Mehboob returned to find his studio had been declared evacuee property. This happened the moment Mehboob left India. But, with the help of Baburao Patel, who owned the influential magazine *FilmIndia*, Mehboob managed to get it back. Patel lived next door to the ICS official who was the Custodian of Evacuee Property. Later Mehboob, with Patel's contacts with people in high places, also converted the land around the studio from residential to commercial use, allowing for further development.

The effect of partition in some ways had a more devastating effect on Asif and his plans to make *Mughal-e Azam*. Asif, fourteen years younger than Mehboob, had just made his first film when partition came. Like Mehboob, he was a migrant to Bombay, having arrived some time in the early 1940s. But, unlike Mehboob, he had connections—his uncle Nazir was well-established in Bombay as an actor. Keen as Asif was to make it into films, Nazir was not, and initially set him up with a tailoring shop. But Asif, calling himself "a ladies tailor", was soon keener on the ladies, rather than making dresses for them, with the result that Nazir closed the shop down and introduced him to films. What Nazir was soon to realise was that his nephew's roving eye extended to his own mistress, Sitara, although to be fair this was more a case of Sitara targeting Asif; as Manto puts it, "she fed on young men like Asif". Although she had taken up with Nazir after his previous mistress, the Jewish actress, Yasmin, had left, she had never believed in one lover at a time and, even before Asif, was carrying on affairs with a fair bit of the Bombay film world, including Mehboob. For good measure, she was also married to a hapless Mr Desai.

Soon, in a tale that would have made an ideal movie, she was double-crossing Nazir with his nephew. Manto says the uncle even caught them "*flagrante delicto*." At one stage, Asif suddenly disappeared from Bombay to Delhi where he was rumoured to have married Sitara in a Muslim ceremony and converted her to Islam with a new name, Begum K. Asif. But, when Manto asked Asif, having met Asif and Sitara at the Bombay racecourse, he replied, "What ceremony? What marriage?"

But whether he got married or not, in Delhi he found the money to venture into movies, after having secured financing from a Hindu businessman called Lala Jagat Narayan. This was to lead to his first film, directing *Phool* for producer Seth Shiraz Ali Hakim, who ran the famous Cine Laboratories. It is not clear who wrote the story but Manto has a brilliant description of Asif narrating the story to him:

> I had never heard him tell a story and it was quite an experience. He rolled up the sleeves of his silk shirt, loosened his belt, pulled up his legs and assumed the classic posture of a yogi. 'Now listen to the story. It is called *Phool*. What do you think of the name?' 'It is good,' I replied. 'Thank you, I will narrate it scene by scene...' he said. Then he began to speak in his typical manner. I do not know who was the author but Asif was playing all the characters, raising his voice, moving around all the time. Now he would be on the sofa, the next minute his back would be against the wall, then he would push his legs against it and his upper torso would be on the floor. At times, he would jump from the sofa on to the floor, only to climb onto a chair in the next minute. Then he would stand up straight, looking like a leader asking for votes in an election. It was a long story, like the intestine of the devil, as the expression goes. After he finished his narration we were silent for a few minutes. 'What do you think about it?' Asif asked. 'It is trash,' I replied.

Manto, who had been paid a fee of Rs. 500 to listen to the narration, suggested changes which were accepted and Manto identifies this as one of the great qualities in Asif. An intelligent man, with a great deal of self-confidence, he did not, as a director surround himself with a small coterie but "invited a cross-section of people to advise him, never hesitating to accept a good suggestion or idea."

It was after *Phool* that Asif began to think of making *Mughal-e Azam,* although it was not yet called by that name. There had been an Urdu drama called *Anarkali,* about the doomed love affair between Salim, the son of Akbar, and a dancer called Anarkali. There is no historical basis to this story, but Imitiaz Ali Taj, back in the 1920s, had written a plausible story, and there had even been a silent movie made in 1928. Asif got him involved, and also got Kamal Amrohi to write the script. Not happy with the script, he asked Manto for advice and everything seemed to go well. Then two things intervened. Chandramohan died, which meant Asif had to look for a new Akbar.

More crucially, following partition, Shiraz Ali Hakim felt he might not be welcomed in India. Some time before partition, at a public meeting, he had felicitated Jinnah and, as Jinnah was now being demonised in India, he decided Pakistan was safer. He sold his studios and Asif's first *Mughal-e Azam* project came to a shuddering halt. Interestingly, while his uncle Nazir left for Pakistan, Asif did not, and opted for India, while planning for a resumption of *Mughal-e Azam.*

Meanwhile, Mehboob had retuned to India, determined to at last become the great director he believed he was destined to be. In 1949, he produced and directed *Andaz.* The film is notable for all sorts of cinematic firsts in Bollywood. For the first time, Naushad was joined by Lata Mangeshkar; Lata sang for Nargis, while Mukesh sang for the men (although Dilip Kumar, who could sing, did sing many years later in the film, *Musafir,* but insisted he be accompanied by Lata). With Saigal dead and Nur Jehan in Pakistan, the era of actors and actresses who had to sing was gone and from now on it was all playback singing. And, for the first and only time, Nargis, Dilip Kumar and Raj Kapoor appeared together on the screen.

The film, as we have seen, is the classic love triangle and stamped Mehboob as one of the great directors of India. The film so dazzled Indians that Lord Meghnad Desai, who wrote a biography of Dilip Kumar, says he saw it in excess of fifteen times. Desai recalls the film being released in the newly-constructed, air-conditioned Liberty cinema of south Bombay, making the first dent in the social apartheid where only English language films were watched in such comfort, while Hindi ones were more often shown in rat-infested cinemas. It ran for twenty-eight weeks, collecting seven lakhs, Rs. 700,000, a colossal sum of money in 1949 India. Sanjit Narwekar, a film-maker and historian has described it, "as a dark moralistic tale of what happens when the permissiveness of a western lifestyle is allowed to impinge on what is considered to be Indian culture". It also had what would be a recurring Mehboob theme of a woman shooting a man she held dear.

Andaz cemented the close relationship between Mehboob and Dilip Kumar. The two men certainly had need for each other. The film had been marked by personal tragedies for Mehboob, Dilip Kumar and also Nargis. Mehboob lost his mother a week before the film opened, delaying the première, while his younger brother died in a motorcycle accident. Nargis lost Jaddanbai, and thugs in Worli attacked Dilip Kumar.

The greater menace that faced Dilip Kumar was that, having been bestowed with the title of the Tragedian, the man who always played the jilted lover, and more often than not died by the end of the film, he now found real life frighteningly similar to the roles he played on the screen. In the year leading up to *Andaz,* he had acted in four films with Uma Kashyap, who took the screen name of Kamini Kaushal. If Durga Khote was the first well-brought-up Indian girl to go into films, then Uma Kashyap was still in a small minority of such girls. Her late father had been a *Rai Bahadur,* a title the British gave to prominent Indians who collaborated with them. He had been President of the Indian Science Congress and she herself had come third in her BA examination. But her life had been touched by tragedy. Following the death of her sister in a car accident, she had married her brother-in-law, largely to look after her sister's two children. But then came the movies with Dilip Kumar and the two fell hopelessly in love.

Publicly, this love was never declared. It could not be. *FilmIndia's* reviews of the films spoke in a coded language, which made it clear to readers that they were lovers on the screen and off.

Interestingly, Sitara Devi, who knew about love, or at least affairs, was a witness to this love. She would later tell a journalist that once, while travelling on the Bombay train, she saw the couple together. When she asked where they were going, Dilip Kumar replied, "We aren't going anywhere." It seemed that in order to get some time together they just travelled up and down the Bombay trains, something stars of the late 1940s could do, but which would be unthinkable today. Some time later, Dilip Kumar came to Sitara's house and shut himself in her bedroom. An hour later, he emerged to reveal red eyes and a swollen face which indicated he had been crying. It marked the moment when the affair was over and Kumar would later call this his "hour of crisis". It could have been a very tragic hour as well.

While Kaushal was shooting a film called *Pugree,* in which Dilip Kumar was not involved, he kept visiting Kaushal on the set. One day, Kamini Kaushal's brother, a military man, arrived on the set dressed in his uniform, with a pistol in his belt. He warned he would shoot Dilip Kumar if he did not end the affair. Kumar is alleged to have hidden in the ladies' cloakroom to escape his wrath.

One of Dilip Kumar's biographers says the incident actually took place on the set of *Aarzoo,* the last film the pair made together, which had started with Kamini telling friends that she wanted to leave her husband and marry Dilip Kumar, but ended with the pair hardly talking to each other. The film, not surprisingly, proved a disaster. However, in 1963, the story of this doomed love was itself made into a movie, *Gumrah.* The director, B.R. Chopra, even asked Dilip Kumar to act in it but he declined, although the film proved a great success.

If Dilip Kumar had personal problems then Mehboob, now becoming something of a mentor to him, had professional ones. Abbas and Sathe had approached him with the idea of *Awara,* but Mehboob could not make up his mind and they went to Raj Kapoor, who instantly bought the rights. Reuben, who is a biographer of Mehboob, Dilip Kumar and Raj Kapoor, says this increased what was already developing into a major Bollywood rivalry. This made Mehboob decide that he would do something that nobody had achieved before in Bollywood: a spectacular Technicolor picture which was to be called *Aan.* Mehboob, having met DeMille in Hollywood and lapped up the praise DeMille lavished on him, wanted to bring colour to India.

India at this stage was well behind Hollywood in colour films. There were no colour laboratories; film-makers had to go to London, and Mehboob decided to use 16mm Kodachrome and then have the film blown up into 35mm Technicolour. He also decided to shoot in Hindi, Tamil and English, although the English version was later abandoned.

Mehboob had originally cast Nargis in the lead role opposite Kumar, and she was involved in the early shooting but, with *Awara* also being shot she, to his fury, withdrew and he vowed never to employ her again. His fury was all the greater as he felt he had given Nargis her first break in a film (*Taqdeer,* in 1943). He drafted in Farah Ezekiel, the last of the Jewish actresses, to play a major role in a Bollywood film. Dilip Kumar did not take to her and thought her impudent, but Mehboob shrewdly saw in this impudence an actress who was not afraid of acting, "She is neither impudent, nor audacious; she is just unafraid of the camera," Khan told Kumar. Khan had chosen this feisty and boisterous women mostly for her glowing skin, sharp features and European looks as he wanted to dub *Aan* into English as well. He was to send the film to Cecil DeMille, who wrote back a polite letter calling it "an important piece of work, which showed the tremendous potential of Indian motion pictures for securing world markets".

Philip Lutgendorf, Professor of Film at the University of Iowa, has described *Aan* as set in a fictional kingdom which looks like a cross between Rajasthan and mad King Ludwig's Bavaria, "an over-the-top operatic fairytale that looks at times like Disney animation come to life, though Disney would not have dared the out-front eroticism and fashion and footwear fetishism that permeated Mehboob's *mis-en-scène*".

It made it to London as *The Savage Princes,* and in Paris as *Mangala, Fille des Indes.* There was appreciation, and although one critic felt, "it goes aan and aan and aan," the film did put Bollywood on the world cinematic map. The BBC even interviewed Dilip Kumar, which was rare for Bollywood actors then. But the making of the film took a lot out of Mehboob Khan and his team. A scene would involve endless takes because of the different language versions and the entire film took 450 shooting days and, having started in 1949, it was released only in 1952. And while it was a hit, it also nearly made Mehboob Khan broke.

The London première of *Aan* had seen Dilip Kumar accompanying Mehboob Khan there. The film had displayed another side of Dilip Kumar, not many in Bollywood had suspected he possessed. Before *Aan,* Dilip Kumar was identified with playing tragic lovers. In *Aan* he played the swashbuckling Errol Flyn character who could ride horses, have sword fights and did not die in the final scene. Dilip Kumar had come to London with his mind full of thoughts of his next film and in London he began to talk to some film-makers and other British experts about a budget for *Mughal-e Azam.*

On June 13, 1952, *Filmfare* reported:

Dilip Kumar has invested most of his money in property and pictures and is producing another film now in association with K. Asif. "I can see my dream come true!" he says. When asked, "What dream?" he answers: "Oh, once when I was a boy, I dreamt that there was a big pavilion lined by Romans and there was a big carpet in the middle and I was walking on it, flanked by guards in resplendent uniforms. I was wearing a flowing robe and everything glittered around me. And then, at the end of the passage, an old man garlanded me!"

The movie was not named but it was clear Asif was back on the trail of his Holy Grail and, by this time, he had not only got close to Dilip Kumar but, with Shiraz Ali Hakim no longer there, had settled on Dilip Kumar to play Prince Salim. Asif had also recast the film. With Chandramohan dead, Prithiviraj was signed up to play Emperor Akar; various other cast changes were made and only Durga Khote remained from the original 1945 cast, still playing Akbar's Hindu wife, Jodabai. Asif also hired Mohan Studios at Andheri, then the edge of darkness as far as most people in Bombay were concerned, being far from the south Bombay centre. Here, he began constructing a huge set as he planned this to be the sort of extravaganza Bollywood had never seen. The set was soon the hive of activity with carpenters, labourers, masons, and even tailors present.

But Asif faced one major problem. Who would play Anarkali, the female lead opposite Dilip Kumar?

Asif might have thought of casting Nargis but, in 1950, while Dilip Kumar was filming *Hulchul,* an Asif production—although it was being directed by his assistant, S.K. Ojha—there had been a major falling-out between Dilip Kumar and Nargis. Like all Asif productions, it took a long time to make. The film originally started before India's independence, was only released in 1951, and Dilip Kumar was more than a mere actor in it. He was in effect producing it and determining how it was shot, how the scenes looked, and how intimate his scenes with Nargis were. Nargis's brother objected to the time taken to make it. Nargis soon fell ill but, after she returned to complete the film, her brother argued about the way Dilip Kumar wanted some of the more intimate scenes shot, and she was never to play opposite Dilip Kumar again. Asif had to find another heroine.

In what was an extraordinary move in Bollywood, Asif actually advertised for actresses to apply for the lead female role. On February 8 1952, an advertisement appeared in *Screen,* the weekly trade paper, asking girls between sixteen and twenty-two to apply. Five were selected but it was clear none of them was suitable. The result was that Nutan, then making her mark, was selected.

Filmfare reported:

> Nutan was initially selected to play the role of Anarkali in K. Asif's *Mughal-e Azam.* Asif and Dilip Kumar went on a countrywide search and interviewed hundreds of candidates for the role—and not one came up to their expectations! Finally, they have selected Nutan, who will definitely be a misfit (says a reader), in a role which calls for grace and histrionic ability. Madhubala would have been a better choice.

On May 2 1952, *Screen* was still saying it would be Nutan. But it was not to be. She declined and soon the production hit fresh problems. With Asif running out of money, work at Mohan Studios came to a halt, and Bollywood assumed Asif's film would never come.

This was certainly the reaction of Kamal Amrohi, who had written the script for Asif. He decided to sell the script to a company called Filmkar, run by two brothers, Makhanlal and Rajendra Jain, who also asked him to direct the film.

Quite independently of this Sasadhar Mukherjee, of Filmistan, also announced the making of a film called *Anarkali* and, unlike Asif, he not only had a hero, Pradeep Kumar, to play Prince Salim, but a heroine, Bina Rai, to play Anarkali, in addition to a music director, a lyricist and, of course, he would, himself, direct. For Dilip Kumar, these were friends setting up rival films. Mukherjee was something of a mentor and Filmkar was the company which had made *Deedar,* in which Dilip Kumar had starred with Ashok Kumar and Nargis. The film had been directed by another mentor, Nitin Bose, who had advised him to develop the naturalistic, soft-spoken style that was his hallmark. It was during the shooting of this film that the infamous "Dilip Kumar bites Ashok Kumar" incident took place. Ashok Kumar, unhappy at how the scenes were going, landed a few punches on Dilip, who bit his hand. When Ashok protested to Nitin, the director asked Dilip, "How could you bite a senior actor like that?" Dilip Kumar replied, "Why did he punch me? Am I not younger than him?" The incident, however, did not affect the friendship between the two actors.

Asif realised he faced major problems with these two rival films. Furious as he was, he could do nothing about the Mukherjee film. He was determined not to let Amrohi get away with it. Amrohi had written the script for his film, and he had been paid for it, making the script the copyright of Asif, and he enforced his rights. Filmkar was forced to cancel its plans. Mukherjee went ahead and produced a film that was well-received but even more than the story, it was the songs sung by Lata Mangeshkar that proved a great hit, the toe-tapping songs that

Indian audiences love. Asif, meanwhile could only stamp his feet at frustration as he once again started on the search for a heroine for his movie.

This was the cue for Madhubala to enter as Anarkali. And here, as with so much in Bollywood, real life mimicked screen life. Madhubala had come a long way since her début with Ashok Kumar. She was now a beautiful young woman, who had played opposite Dilip Kumar and had also fallen in love with him.

Madhubala could have been in Dilip Kumar's very first film but received the summons for it from Devika Rani too late. The pair had started making a movie together back in 1949, but it had never been completed. They finally got their act together in *Tarana,* in 1951. A story of romance, it featured the usual quota of coincidences and villains, with Madhubala playing an unlettered village girl who is the love of an English doctor, played by Dilip Kumar. By this time, both were ready for love off the screen. Kumar had got Kamini Kaushal out of his system and Madhubala, still only seventeen, was yearning for it.

On the first day of the shooting, she got her make-up woman to take a rose to Dilip Kumar's dressing-room. It bore the message: "if you want me, please order this rose; if not, send it back". Dilip Kumar eagerly accepted, and one of Bollywood's most dramatic love stories began. It was so potent that it ended up in court and had more drama than anything seen on the screen.

There can be little doubt that Dilip Kumar persuaded Asif that Madhubala must play Anarkali in his film. The problem for Asif was Madhubala's father, Attaullah Khan. This was like a replay of a Victorian suitor seeking the permission of a father for his daughter's hand. Attaullah Khan specified that his daughter would not do any night shooting, no visitors were to be allowed on the sets, she would have sight of the full script with dialogue for the shooting in advance, and no last minute changes of the kind Bollywood loved. At one stage, Asif got so angry he walked out but Madhubala, keen to be with the love of her life, called him to one side and, outside her father's hearing, said, "Be sure I'm playing Anarkali in your film, Asif Sahab. Don't worry about anything that Abba says. I guarantee you unconditional obedience and full support on this film."

Attaullah probably insisted on the conditions because he was aware that his daughter had fallen for Dilip Kumar. In theory, the romance between the two, even the marriage which Madhubala so desired, should have been no problem. Both were single, both Muslims, indeed Pathans, and it seems at first even Attaullah and Dilip got on.

It was common for Dilip Kumar to come to his house and pick up Madhubala in his car and drive off for an evening out. At this stage, according to Reuben, Dilip Kumar was not her lover but he was merely acting as the good friend of Premnath with whom Madhubala had acted in films like *Badal,* and to whom she had also sent a rose and who had also responded. Premnath, in the 1950s, was seen as the Indian Douglas Fairbanks, and Dilip and Premnath were bosom friends. They had acted together in *Aan* and he would often be sitting crouched in the back seat, as Dilip Kumar and Madubhala were bidding goodbye to Attaullah and driving off into the Bombay sunset. Premnath only emerged once he knew they were out of sight of Attaullah. Attaullah would certainly have objected to Premnath, as he was a Hindu. This situation may have continued for some time but then the friendship between Dilip and Premnath abruptly ended when Premnath decided to make a film called *Dilip—The Donkey.* Premnath tried to mollify Dilip by saying Dilip should be pleased as he, Premnath, would play the donkey. But that is not how Dilip saw it. Premnath, who was the brother-in-law of Raj Kapoor, being his wife's brother would, in one of those Bollywood's ironies, eventually marry the woman who first portrayed Anarkali on film, Bina Rai.

The Dilip Kumar-Madhubala romance was clearly blossoming by the early 1950s, certainly after *Tarana.* Unlike with Kamini Kaushal, the two stars did not have to journey up and down on Bombay trains. There was now more money in Bollywood and, in any case, trains were overcrowded. Dilip Kumar would visit her on sets when she was acting in films in which he was not; they would meet in cars, in each other's make-up rooms or, sometimes, in the houses of common friends, like Sushila Rani.

The film, *Amar,* which Mehboob Khan made, starring both of them, provided more opportunities for such meetings. By this time, Dilip Kumar was making sure Madhubala was in as many of his films as conceivably possible and every time an opportunity arose he pushed her name forward. Mehboob had begun shooting the film with another lead actress, Meena Kumari, but she left after a disagreement between Mehboob and her husband, Kamal Amrohi. This allowed Dilip Kumar to persuade Mehboob to replace her with Madhubala. In the film, Dilip Kumar rapes a woman (Nimmi) who, fleeing from a villain, had taken shelter with him. The cowardly hero now refuses to come forward and allows the woman to suffer the consequences of the rape. When his fiancée, Madhubala, finds out what has happened, she stands up for the girl and the hero eventually marries her. But, if the film helped their romance, it did nothing for Mehboob. Although he considered this story his favourite film, it flopped as audiences, used to heroes who were strong and dominant, refused to accept a weak and negative one. This was followed by two other failures, but all this did not deter Mehboob. He was determined to make *Mother India* and by this time, was busy working on the idea.

In October 1952, he wrote to the Joint Chief Controller of Imports, requesting an import permit for raw film which would make 180 prints. This was nearly three times the usual amount sanctioned, and long negotiations ensued. Mehboob also brought to India Sabu Dastogir, who had played *The Elephant Boy* in the 1935 film, directed by Robert Flaherty, and put him up at Bombay's Ambassador Hotel, a posh hotel, paying him Rs. 5,000 a month. At this stage, Mehboob had not called the film *Mother India.* Indeed, when he performed the *Muharat* ceremony for it, he titled it: *This Land is Mine.*

Mehboob was clearly working on various ideas as to how to make the movie and this included having long talks with Dilip Kumar, whom he saw as playing Birju, the rebellious son of Radha, the character played by Nargis. Their friendship was now so strong that he even interceded with Baburao Patel, who had always been critical of Dilip Kumar's acting, to write something positive about the star. But, as Dilip Kumar made more demands suggesting how Birju could be the central character, and also about the shooting of the film, Mehboob distanced himself from the actor. Their relationship was also affected by the fact that Mehboob did nothing to help Dilip Kumar over his brother, Nasir Khan. He had gone to Pakistan but, like many of Bollywood's Muslim immigrants, failed to do much there and returned to Bombay looking for work. Dilip Kumar wanted him to play the lead in *Aawaz,* directed by one of Mehboob's scriptwriters, Zia Sarhady. But he had already cast someone else in that role. Mehboob did not want to intervene in the creative process and this marked the end of the partnership between Mehboob and Dilip Kumar. Their personal friendship did not cease and some years later Mehboob would suggest how Dilip Kumar could play a crucial scene in what would prove a landmark film.

The role of Birju went to Sunil Dutt who, although he had made his début in films, was still working in the Bombay bus depot while doing some broadcasting assignments for Radio Ceylon.

Dastogir soon flew back to Los Angeles and Mehboob now decided to reinstate the old title, *Mother India.* This, however, was fraught with difficulties. In Government eyes, the title *Mother India* raised the spectre of Mayo's book, *Mother India,* and Mehboob Khan had to write letters reassuring the Government that far from denigrating India, the movie was intended to be an answer to Mayo. At that time, many politicians were convinced that movies were bad for the country. In June 1954, 13,000 housewives had presented a petition to Nehru saying the cinema was a threat to "the moral health of the country" and was "a major factor in incitement to crime and general unsettlement of society". This was taken up eagerly by some politicians who tabled a motion in the Indian Parliament to ban "undesirable films".

One of the most vociferous anti-cinema politicians was K.M. Munishi, a very right-wing member of the Congress party who was about to join the Swantra Party, espousing a capitalist line of development, as opposed to Nehru's socialism. Although he had written for films, and also acted as a lawyer for film companies, he and his wife, Leelavati, launched an anti-cinema campaign, holding public meetings backing the housewives' line. In 1956, as Mehboob was busy shooting *Mother India,* Leelavati would complain to Prvithiraj about Dilip Kumar's hairstyle. He had a mop of hair which fell over his eyes, *zulfay,* as it is called in Urdu. For his fans it was much celebrated and in 1954, when he led a procession of stars to collect money for flood relief, the sheets holding the money donated were found to contain, in addition to the many thousands of rupee notes, quite a few combs. Leelavati told Prithviraj that Dilip Kumar's hair-style was having "adverse effects" on the country's youth to which Prithviraj replied that an actor's hairstyle was not relevant. He, himself, had not been to a barber since 1941, but trimmed his own hair, so what did that make him?

The view that films and everything associated with films was bad had sympathisers in the Government. The Minister of Information and Broadcasting, Dr B.V. Keskar, who disliked both cricket and films and was the great Indian kill-joy, said film songs only appealed to "raw and immature people like children and adolescents". Following his orders All India Radio first cut down on songs and, then, for a time banned them. All it succeeded in doing was making a foreign radio station very rich. Radio Ceylon launched a Hindi service, broadcasting Hindi film music, earning millions of rupees in advertising revenue, all of it coming from India and made stars of various Indians, including Sunil Dutt. This must be unique in cinema history: that a Government deliberately tried to damage its own national industry and helped that of another country. But such stupidity can be all too common in India.

Mehboob also had to live with the censor's scissors. One dialogue, where the rapacious village money-lender taunts Nargis, was considered too cruel; another, where after a flood villagers are seen approaching the landlord but he refuses to help, much too provocative. Mehboob fought hard against some of the deletions and the film carried a mark showing the director had objected.

Like Asif, Mehboob also had his battles over copyright. National, for whom he had made *Aurat* back in 1940, filed a court action alleging breach of copyright and Mehboob replied that what National owned was *Aurat's* first production rights, not permanent ownership, and the case was settled out of court. Mehboob did use the old *Aurat* script, written by Vajahat Mirza, but got Ali Raza to revise it. Others joined in scriptwriting sessions, but it was largely the work of Mirza and Raza, although just before the film was released Mirza, a doyen among the scriptwriters objected to having his name associated with Raza, who was much more junior to him, an indication of the hierarchical nature of Indian society. Raza graciously asked Mehboob to remove his name but Mehboob would not oblige. All this delayed Mehboob's film, although not on the scale of Asif's, but it provided enough time for Nargis to play in a movie by I.S. Johar, called *Miss India,* which was finished and released by March 1957, several months before *Mother India.*

Mehboob was able to get the principal actors Nargis and Raj Kumar—who played Nargis's husband—to learn farming methods, such as how to use a plough, sowing, reaping, and cotton-picking. Mehboob was keen to bring as much realism as he could and, according to Chatterjee, the first shots of the films were taken by Irani back in September 1955 in Uttar Pradesh, which had experienced flooding. Irani travelled there soon after the floods. Later, actual villages near Billimoria were used and villagers were paid, although the publicity material for the film made the villagers appear keen to help with the film with no mention of money being involved. Rather than using film extras as dancers, villagers were used for rural dancing sequences shown in the film. The many village scenes in the film have influences of both the American film-maker, King Vidor, and also Soviet influences. India, as part of its five-year plan, was then in the middle of its co-operative farming plan, persuading farmers to come together in large farms, in order to curb the power of the landlords.

The colour for the film had caused many problems and Mehboob, aware that time was passing, finally decided to shoot in Gevacolour and then process in Technicolor, with Irani travelling to the London offices of Technicolour for this purpose. Mehboob wanted to release the film on August 15 1957, to emphasise its nationalist credentials but did not manage that, although the publicity campaign of the film was launched on Radio Ceylon. Mehboob was well aware that no Indian film buff missed the station's acclaimed programme, *Binaca Geetmala*, a programme of film songs sponsored by Binaca, a popular toothpaste brand in the country.

The film was finally premiered on October 25 1957 at Liberty, where Mehboob had an arrangement with the owners for exhibiting his films. Mehboob need not have worried about its success for soon there was such high demand that a vigorous black market started. Two days earlier, Mehboob had visited the holy shrine of Aulia Chishti in Ajmer to seek blessings. Mehboob was the sort of secular man Nehru wanted Indians to be. Although he was privately religious, he never brought religion into his films.

Before the première, Mehboob had cultivated Nehru and had written to him asking for his blessing for the film. His letter to Nehru was fawning in the extreme saying that, "No function in our country is complete without your dynamic personality." If Nehru liked the picture and gave him a certificate, then he offered to frame the certificate "as an heirloom in my humble family." This was part of his desire to make sure the film received public support from the Government, which could also be useful in getting some relief from the punitive entertainment tax local Governments imposed on films. High Government officials and ministers had been present at the première. Soon the film was being viewed in Rashtrapati Bhavan, the Viceregal Palace, now the home of Indian Presidents. At the viewing was Rajendra Prasad, the President, along with Nehru, and his daughter Indira. In various parts of the country, other politicians also saw the film. In Calcutta, Nehru's lover, Padmaja Naidu, who was then Governor of West Bengal, saw it with the Congress Chief Minister of the State, B.C. Roy. In Bombay, Morarji Desai, by now Chief Minister of Bombay, came to the première. He even agreed to Mehboob's request to exempt it from entertainment tax in the state of Bombay. Nehru's views on the film are not known but Indira wrote a note to Nargis saying, "The film is drawing very good reviews. Everyone has praised your acting. The same cannot be said of the others."

Mehboob had sold rights only to those distributors who paid in advance. In Delhi, Indira Films paid Rs. 400,000. However, Mehboob, fearful of piracy, took great care when sending the prints around the country. His men accompanied them, sat in the theatre while the film was being shown, and collected the prints afterwards. Also, nobody was allowed to screen the film in the morning or for early matinée shows. It was only shown at three, six or nine p.m. – prime viewing times for movies in India then.

Mehboob was keen for its release abroad and had been selling the foreign distributions rights since 1954, but the film had to be shortened to two hours. Its success in countries where *Awara* had been a hit was, perhaps, to be expected. Countries such as Greece, Spain, and Russia loved the movie, but countries like Poland, Czechoslovakia and much of Eastern Europe also saw it and liked it as well. So did Brazil, Peru, Bolivia and Ecuador, and the Arab countries, and many parts of Africa.

Years later, Brian Larkins, in *Bollywood Comes to Nigeria,* would write, "It's a Friday night in Kano, northern Nigeria and *Mother India* is playing at Marhaba cinema. Outside, scalpers are hurriedly selling the last tickets to 2,000 people lucky enough to buy seats in this open cinema on the edge of Africa's Shield Desert."

The West, or at least parts of it, also liked it. It was shown in Paris in June 1958, where it was well-received, with one producer/director saying, "This man is the world's greatest film-maker today." But in London's Rialto, where a 95-minute version was shown, it was not a success nor was it taken around the country. In New York, *The Monthly Film Bulletin* dismissed it as a "rag bag pantomime."

It was not actually shown in the United States until 1959, despite the fact that it was one of the five nominations for the 1958 Oscars in the Academy's Foreign Film Awards category. Although this was a great honour, this also caused problems. There was no English subtitled version of *Mother India,* in stark contrast to the other four nominations. This could only be done in London and Mehboob had run out of foreign exchange which, by this time, was very scarce in India. Also, the prints had developed scratches and the Academy wanted a pristine print. Technicolour came to the rescue and a subtitled pristine print was provided.

Mehboob, his wife Sardar, and Nargis, decided to go to Los Angeles for the Oscars. The problem was foreign exchange. India was now in the grip of a severe foreign exchange shortage. In 1947, India had come to freedom with large sterling balances built up during the war as a result of goods and services supplied to Britain. But they had long been spent and, so bad was the foreign exchange situation, that Indians seeking to travel abroad had to fill a Form P for travel, authorised by the Reserve Bank of India, and were allowed only £3 for a trip, just enough the joke went for a peg of whisky on the Air India flight. $75 had been sanctioned for each of the three and Mehboob wrote a pleading letter to Nehru:

Our picture (by "our" I mean picture belongs to our great country) has been selected as one of the five best pictures. You know I am pure swadeshi [the Gandhian term meaning a lover of Indian goods and ideas] producer without any English education, and I badly need the help and support of our nation's representatives in America. Like other international producers, I should be able to show that our Government is also backing me. Otherwise, I will look small and lonely.

Chatterjee says this letter reflects that India was still in a feudal state, a letter a villager might write to a village elder, and it indicates how Mehboob, while a movie moghul in his studio, could "bend and be child-like before another figure of authority." But it worked and $1,200 was sanctioned for each of the three. It was certainly enough for Mehboob to hold a press conference after the ceremony, where he looked far from small and lonely.

Unfortunately, the press conference was not a victory conference. *Mother India* had been beaten by Fellini's, *Nights of Cabiria,* by one vote. But in India, it was showered with awards, including 'Best Picture' at the *Filmfare* Awards. *Filmfare,* having taken over from Mehboob's friend, Patel's *FilmIndia,* as the country's leading film magazine, and its awards being the country's Oscars. Mehboob got the Award for Direction, Irani for Cinematography and for Best Sound, while Nargis got the Best Actress Award. She also got a similar award at the Karlovy Vary Film Festival in then Czechoslovakia.

Mehboob, though, had suffered a heart attack in Los Angeles on 26 March and it was some months, and a stay in London, before he recovered. But in the cinematic sense, he never did recover and never completed another film like *Mother India,* although there was a *Son of India* (a movie that is considered to be his worst). He had plans to make a film on the life of Habba Khatoon, the sixteenth century poetess and queen of Kashmir. But before this came to anything, he died.

He died on May 28 1964, the day after Nehru died, a death for Indians of my generation comparable to that of John F. Kennedy for Americans in the 1960s. A few months before his death, Mehboob received the *Padmashri,* the awards India had started after independence to replace the discarded British honours and which Nargis had received back in 1958, just months after the release of *Mother India.* Like Nehru's death, which marked the end of an era in Indian politics, Mehboob's passing brought the curtain down on a certain kind of Indian film-making.

If Mehboob made nothing worthwhile after *Mother India,* then this also effectively marked the end of Nargis in films, as she would only make one more. The year after *Mother India* was released, Nargis had married Sunil Dutt, in a romance that stunned Bollywood, not just because of the son marrying the actress who played his mother in a film, but also because it was a Hindu-Muslim marriage. However, the way Sunil Dutt would later present it, he was drawn to her because he thought she would be good for his family—just the sort of sentiments *Mother India* was promoting:

Actually, I saw her first at a première. She had a luminous aura, a rare beauty of goodness that shone through. It was as if she was from another world and beyond reach. Her generosity and kindness was something I discovered later when she took my ailing sister and had her operated upon quietly, even though I didn't know her very well. I always knew that the woman who would become my wife had to be someone who would be able to take care of my younger brother and sister, and keep my mother happy. I realised soon after that she was the woman for me. One day, I finally decided that the time had come to tell Nargisji how I felt about her and I finally gathered enough courage to tell her on a drive back home. She didn't say anything, but a couple of days later she told my sister to tell me her answer was yes.

Mother India would leave many legacies. But one legacy profoundly affected how Bollywood actually made films. *Mother India* was the last film to be shot with sync sound, meaning the sound was recorded on location during shooting. After that, the lines the actors and actresses spoke as the film was shot became irrelevant, as this was not recorded. Instead, some time after the shoot, they would come to a studio and record their dialogues, what became known as dubbed sound. Mehboob thought it was soulless, but other Indian directors felt it helped them overcome the problems of the noise the cameras made and gave them a better quality of sound. This would affect the working conditions in Indian sets. Those working there, aware that the sounds being recorded were not going to be used, continued to make a racket while the film was shot, in contrast to the silent studios of the West. This did not change for more than forty years until Aamir Khan made *Lagaan* and reintroduced sync sound. Suddenly, Indian actors, actresses and technicians had to learn to be quiet when the director said, 'Action!'

The days of shooting with Mehboob had returned. And what was Asif doing while Mehboob was finally screening *Mother India?*

12

Asif's Godot Finally Arrives

In 1957, Asif was still in the throes of making the film when complications arose, not so much with the film but between Dilip Kumar and Madhubala, which would result in an extraordinary court case.

B.R. Chopra, the young man who Ashok Kumar had taken such a liking to, was looking for an idea for a film when the writer, Akhtar Mirza, narrated a story. After the deal was done, and a down-payment was made, Mirza said he had another story idea which he much preferred. Would Chopra listen to it? This may seem very odd behaviour but it was standard for Bollywood, and the reason was that Mirza knew this second story had been rejected by many directors, including Mehboob. Now having received a deal, he thought this second idea was worth a try with Chopra. It worked and Chopra was much taken by it, more than the original idea which he had bought. The story was about a fight between man and machine, with the man triumphant in the end.

Chopra immediately thought this would be an ideal film for Dilip Kumar and Madhubala. The result was the film *Naya Daur*, where Dilip Kumar played a villager who has a *tonga* (a horse carriage) which he races against a bus, and wins.

Everything seemed to be going fine until it came to location shooting. The film was set in and around Bhopal, and Chopra planned to shoot it in a village called Budhni, around 150 miles from the city.

But when he went to Madhbubala's father to seek permission, he flatly refused. Attaullah was no longer the indulgent father who had waved Dilip and Madhubala away in their car for a drive around Bombay. Bunny Reuben says the friendship turned to enmity when Attaullah Khan, who also fancied making films, wanted to cast Dilip Kumar and Madhubala in a film. Kumar rejected it, as he did not like mixing business with personal relations. He also made it clear that he did not want anything to do with his father-in-law-to-be once they were married, and that Madhubala would no longer be allowed to act, once she was his wife. For Attaullah, given that Madhubala was his source of money, this was a terrible prospect to behold.

Chopra decided that in that case, he would do without her. Dilip Kumar was already involved in another film with Vyjayanthimala, and Chopra signed her up. What is more, he took full page ads in all the trade papers showing Madhubala's name crossed out, and Vyjayanthimala's name inserted. Madhubala retaliated by placing adverts showing all the films she was working in and with *Naya Daur* crossed out.

But this was not enough for Attaullah. He was so outraged that he filed a case against Chopra alleging he had sacked Madhubala on flimsy grounds and there was no need for shooting outside Bombay, as all the locations required could easily be found in the city. Chopra counter-sued in a criminal case against Madhubala, asking for his signing-fee back.

Nothing like this had ever been seen in Bombay. As the hearing opened, crowds lined the street around the Magistrate's Court in Girgaum. The Magistrate, R.S. Parekh, heard some remarkable evidence, including the first public acknowledgement of the romance between Dilip Kumar and Madhubala. It ended with Dilip Kumar's dramatic statement, "I love this woman and I shall love her till my dying day." Bollywood was electrified. In a world where there were any number of rumoured romances and affairs, no one had ever made such a statement, and in open court at that.

In the end, Chopra emerged victorious. The judge, on seeing the film, was convinced location shooting was necessary but Chopra, generously, did not pursue Attaullah for the money, although Ataullah did some time later have the cheek to approach Chopra and ask him to direct a story idea he had.

The case, it would seem, marked the moment when Dilip Kumar's love for Madhubala turned sour, although Madhubala never stopped loving him and soon after, when Bunny Reuben went to interview her, braving the Alsatian dogs that guarded the Attaullah house, she told him she still carried a torch for him. But, when this declaration was carried back to Dilip Kumar, he snorted, "What bloody torch!"

Asif could not have been pleased that his two principal players were now more foes than lovers. And this at a time when he was still not sure the film could be completed. He would often come to Dilip Kumar for advice and on one occasion turned up during the shooting of *Naya Daur*. He had secured the backing of Shapoorji Pallonji, the Parsi construction baron, who Hakim had introduced him to before leaving for Pakistan, and who was also a great admirer of Dilip Kumar. But this was a rocky relationship. His more consuming worry was what to do with Attaullah, when the close-up scenes between Dilip Kumar and Madhubala were to be shot.

In the film, Prince Salim wore a feather, and the scenes would be as intimate as anything ever seen on the Indian screen till then. In one scene, as Madhubala lies prostrate on the floor, Dilip Kumar leans over in an unmistakable erotic suggestion and caresses Madhubala's face with an ostrich feather. Asif was terrified that old Attalluah would create such a real-life scene while the cinematic one was being shot, that he would never be able to complete the scene. So Asif told his publicist, Taraknath Gandhi, that during the shooting of that scene, and during similar such scenes between Dilip Kumar and Madhubala, he had a very simple task: to keep Attaullah engaged. He liked playing rummy and liked winning. "Your job from today," said Asif, "as well as for the next few days, is to play rummy with Khan Saheb, and lose! Go on losing, do you understand? You must keep him happy until my work is done."

Taraknath played his cards beautifully, lost a lot of money, Attaullah did not leave the card table, and Asif filmed some of the most magical love scenes ever seen on the Indian screen.

Dilip Kumar continued to promote the film often persuading actors to take roles in it. The actor, Ajit, who played a secondary role as the chivalrous Rajput Duijan Singh, had initially refused the part. But, as he later recalled, "my friend Dilip Kumar persuaded me to accept it. He assured me that the significance of the role will not be lost in the grandeur of the film. I know now that Dilip was absolutely right."

On June 20, 1958, *Filmfare* reported, "*Mughal-e Azam*, the Dilip Kumar-Madhubala film, which went on the floor in 1952, is at last nearing completion. Last month, director K. Asif shot a number of battle scenes on location in Madhya Bharat and Rajasthan."

Asif knew the film made no historical sense. There was no Anarkali and there were other inaccuracies. While Akbar had Hindu wives, and the real Salim's mother was a Hindu, she was not the Jodabai of the film who is portrayed as the daughter of a major Rajput king. In real life, the Hindu mother of Salim was the daughter of Raja Bhagara Mal, a very minor royalty, and she was not called Jodabai. That was the name of the Hindu wife of Salim, who produced his son and became Shah Jahan, the creator of the Taj Mahal. And, while Salim did rebel against his father, Akbar, it was not over a dancing girl but due to the Mughal politics of the day.

But Asif was also very aware that Indians did not care for authentic history, but for costume dramas, where history was just a peg on which to hang a story. There had been Bollywood film-makers who had tried proper historical films and failed. Shorab Modi was a warning to all film-makers who tried to attract Indian audiences with anything like authentic history. Back in 1941 – long before Asif had met Sitara Devi, or conceived of *Mughal-e Azam* – at his studio, Minerva Movietone, Modi, had made *Sikandar*—his historical film about Alexander and his encounter with the Indian King Porus (Sikander being the name for Alexander in the East). Modi was such a stickler for history that he even had the actual weight of Sikander estimated, and required his actors to strip down to their underwear every day and weigh themselves to make sure they were near that weight. Prithviraj played Sikander, but the film caused problems with the

British censors as they did not like the scene of Alexander's soldiers' mutiny and feared it might give their Indian soldiers ideas. It was therefore banned in some areas of the country. The movie announced Prithviraj as a great actor and was well-received by critics. But it proved a commercial failure. In 1953, Modi made what is considered his greatest film, *Rani of Jhansi*, about the rebel queen who, in 1857, defied the British. It cost Rs. 9 million and was such a failure it bankrupted Modi, and his studio. Asif had no desire to follow that route. Modi, however, was to figure in *Mughal-e Azam* in a curious way, as we shall see.

For Asif , choosing Prithviraj to play Akbar was easy, although he realised he must treat him with care. Prithviraj was in reality a great stage actor. Geoffrey Kendal, whose daughter, Jennifer, married Shashi during the shooting of the film (with Asif providing a Dakota to fly Prithviraj to the wedding), called him a "throw back to the old-time English actor-manager relationship".

But, by the time he came to make *Mughal-e Azam,* Prithviraj was old and kept forgetting his lines and, for one scene, there were nineteen takes. Asif would, before shooting a scene, send a man to the great actor's dressing- room, only to be told, "Prithviraj was ready, but Akbar was not." There were occasions when the old actor and the director clashed which once led Prithviraj to say to Asif, "Nobody has ever talked to me like that." But he still had the old actor's desire to experience what he was presenting. In the film there was a scene where, as Akbar, he had to walk over burning sand. Asif offered him slippers and to shoot the scene in such a way it would not show, but he refused the slippers and insisted the shot be done with him walking on bare feet.

In one scene, portraying the clash between father and son, Akbar and Salim, Prithviraj is seen with his back to the audience. Madhu Jain writes:

> Apparently, when he requested Asif to film that particular scene without showing his face, the cynics tittered that the elder thespian feared he would not be able to maintain the histrionics of the younger actor and fellow-Pathan, Dilip Kumar. Prithiviraj incarnated the old theatrical school of acting, whereas Dilip Kumar, with his quiet voice and understated acting, was clearly a creature of the cinema…Others claimed Kapoor could do more with his back than Dilip Kumar could with his face.

The critical view is that Prithviraj won the scene with the way he clenched and unclenched his hands. Certainly, at the première of the film, more attention was paid to Prithviraj than to Dilip Kumar. After the première of *Mughal-e Azam, Filmfare* concentrated a great deal on Prithviraj saying, "As the title role player, Prithviraj Kapoor was one of the few basking in the glory of the moment. He had worked hard and earnestly. Back in 1952, on his very first shooting day for the picture, he reported for work with his feet swollen and painful with varicose ulcers. After getting his feet with difficulty into the shoes prescribed by the producer the pain,when he tried to walk, made him all but scream. Yet, he went on with the day's work. On another occasion, during the shooting of an outdoor scene on a baking summer day, he walked barefoot on the scalding sands of Rajasthan. And he walked erect through the picture wearing armour so heavy that it once frightened away a hulking 'extra,' who was chosen as a double for Prithviraj in a scene."

Asif's great ability, as with Prithviraj, was to pick talent and he did so splendidly with his recruitment of Naushad as the film's music director. Years later Naushad would recall:

> K. Asif was a dreamer. He would often dream and talk of making a grand film one day. My friendship with him went back to the days when I was simply Naushad and not Naushad, the musician. We (Asif saab and me) had a common friend Nazie (the actor), and we would often while away the time over umpteen cups of chai. I was working on the music for one of Mehboob's films when Asif approached me to compose the music for his film. I was in my house, bent over the harmonium, fiddling with some tunes when suddenly I heard a loud thud. I looked up and saw bundles of notes lying on my harmonium. I counted them. They were Rs. 50,000 in all. Asif towered above me, blowing smoke from his cigarette. Very nonchalantly, he told me he wanted me to compose the music for *Mughal-e Azam!* I was trembling with rage and threw the notes back at him and asked him to give the money to some musician who did not work without an advance. My servant heard me yell and told my wife that the room was filled with fluttering notes. She rushed down to see the miracle! I've never worked for money. My only aim was and is to smell the soil of India in my music.

Naushad says he worked for the film without money, and this helped in his relationship with Pallonji which, given Asif's way of working, was quite the most dramatic. The businessman just could not get a budget for the film from Asif and the more Asif refused, the more terrified the financier became until he asked Naushad to convince Asif to give him a budget. "But who was I to stop a dreamer?" says Naushad.

Naushad, however, often had to mediate between Asif and Shapoorji.

> For instance, shooting the war scene, according to Asif, required at least Rs. 300,000—a figure he arrived at after much persuasion from Shapoorji to give him a budget. But, by the time the set and cast was assembled, and the set was readied, some years had passed and consequently the budget shot up. Shapoorji was very upset. However, Asif had found a way to deal with him. He laid a bet with me that Shapoorji would not only give him Rs. 600,000 but, more importantly, give it with a smile! The idea was so far-fetched it was funny. The next day we gathered at a studio. Shapoorji was still cribbing and complaining. Asif had organised the screening of some war scene. The moment the screening was over, Shapoorji was not just smiling, he was happy, and sanctioned the money for the *Mughal-e Azam* war scene!

What had made Shapoorji smile, as Asif quickly explained to Naushad, was "Akbar is his favourite character from history and every time Shapoorji sees him on screen, it makes him extremely happy." Asif used Akbar every time Shapoorji refused money!

However, there was an occasion when Shapoorji completely lost his head. And this would come close to scuppering the making of the movie. It was over the Sheesh Mahal Asif built by special 'karigars' (workers) he had brought from Ferozabad, near Delhi. Shapoorji was horrified by the cost. He decided to take things in his own hands and approached Sohrab Modi to take over the directorship. Modi assured him that he would complete the film in three months and without overshooting the budget.

Asif was having trouble shooting the 'Sheesh Mahal' due to the reflecting mirrors and had been unable to come up with a solution, so far. Meanwhile, Shapoorji had told Naushad of his plan to take Modi to the set at Mohan Studio, to familiarise him with the film and the set.

Naushad cautioned Asif of the impending visit. So, when the duo reached the set, Shapoorji asked the spot boy to turn on the lights. Suddenly, Asif emerged and threatened to break anyone's legs who dared to enter his set. And he also promised to complete the shooting of the song in time.

As if to prove he could do it, Asif took some shots—a long shot, a mid-shot and a close-up—and sent them to the Technicolor lab in London. They loved the effect and so did Shapoorji. He told Naushad "Asif is so brilliant!" But, then, Asif shocked him by saying that he had fulfilled his promise of shooting the song, so now he could employ Modi! Naushad had again to step in to resolve that crisis.

Then, again, Asif wanted to use marble for the scene where Anarkali had to be buried alive. But Shapoorji was terrified, as Rs. 125,000 000 had been spent and he was being told that the film would not generate any money in the market. That crisis also blew over, but there were many others before the film could be completed.

Naushad always believed that "a reason why the film took so long in the making was that there was just not enough money for shooting continuously". In the end, the film took so long that the stars' contract had to be renewed nearly three times during its making.

The picture Naushad has painted of Asif is of a man who truly valued his art, rather than money. When Shapoorji approached him to broker a deal with Dilip Kumar for a profit-sharing partnership in the film *Ganga Jamuna*, a film that he also financed, he readily did so. In order to show his gratitude, Shapoorji gave him Rs. 50,000 but Asif was so livid that he refused to take the money. The anger may have been partly due to the fact that Asif had proved the money man wrong on *Mughal-e Azam*. He had sold the film to all distributors throughout the country for Rs. 1,500,000—and that without showing them the film! Shapoorji got back his entire investment, even before the film was released! Naushad says, "While Shapoorji's family is still reaping the profits from the film, K. Asif had earned nothing at all." According to Naushad, Asif was given a paltry salary from Shapoorji. "A generous man, he would give away most of his salary to anyone in need. He was a simple man and would only sleep on a mat."

Asif, however, knew how to use money to lure unlikely artists and this was brilliantly demonstrated in his recruitment of Ustad Bade Ghulam Ali Khan for two songs Naushad wanted him to sing in the film. The moment Naushad mentioned his name, Asif readily agreed, and it proved a sensation.

Ustad Bade Ghulam Ali Khan was one of the finest representatives of the Hindustani music tradition in the twentieth century and, even as early as 1944, was considered the uncrowned king of Hindustani music, with some people going so far as to refer to him as the Tansen of the twentieth century. Having lived at various times in Lahore, Mumbai, Kolkata and Hyderabad, he returned to his home in Pakistan, but came back to India some time afterwards. When Asif approached him, it was not long after he had become an Indian citizen. However, classic musicians like him shunned film music which they thought was beneath them.

Asif and Naushad visited the home of the great man, who was known as Khan Saab. Naushad recalls:

> Khan Saab loved eating, and the more people, the merrier. We arrived in time for a meal. On seeing us, he asked us for the reason for our visit. I explained the reason. But he refused point blank, as he found singing in films very frivolous. "Naushad saab," he said, "three minutes was not enough for anybody to sing, especially people like me who need at least half and hour to clear my throat."

At this point Asif, who was watching the proceedings, spoke. "Only you will sing those songs in my film. It will only be you," he said. Khan saab was very angry and asked Naushad about the "gustaakh" (sinner). Naushad introduced Asif to Khan saab and said he was the director of the film. Ali Khan had heard of the making of *Mughal-e Azam* but thought little of it and would not budge, and nor would Asif. Finally, Naushad took Khan saab aside and tried to convince him. But to no avail. He told him that if he refused to sing, he would fall in the eyes of the director. Khan saab came up with a plan that would help Naushad keep his respect. He would, he told Naushad, ask so much money that Asif just would not be able to afford him. Khan saab returned to the room and told Asif that he would sing but he would charge Rs. 25,000 per song, expecting Asif to say this was an impossible sum for a couple of songs.

To everybody's surprise, Asif not only agreed but also immediately produced Rs10,000 in cash and gave it to Khan saab. At the time most singers were paid round Rs. 300 for a song.

Later, Bade Ghulam Ali would say that another reason why he agreed was not merely the money, but he feared for his life. As the great man had kept saying

'No', Asif, a nervous man at the best of times, had started smoking cigarettes, cupping them in his fingers in his characteristic fashion. As the smoke rose from the fingers, Khan saab got so frightened that this lunatic, whom he had never met before, would set his house on fire, he agreed he would sing just to get him out of the house. The visitors were not offered any food or even tea, the sort of discourtesy that is unforgivable in India, and hurriedly ushered out.

Recording the romantic song proved to be another feat in itself. Bade Ghulam Ali Khan just failed to understand that it was a romantic song and that it needed a soft tune and tone. The argument between Naushad and him continued all day. Finally, Naushad summoned Asif, who arranged for the editing of the romantic scene between Dilip Kumar and Madhubala overnight, and showed the film to Khan saab.

Khan saab eventually understood the nuances of the scene and was very impressed by the beauty of Madhubala. But, then, he decided that he would sing along with the film and Naushad had to arrange for the recording accordingly. Khan saab got so carried away that he sang continuously all day, till an exasperated Naushad asked his assistant to stop recording. Undeterred, Khan saab continued to sing late into the night. "It took me nearly four days to edit the song. But it was worth it," says Naushad.

Indians finally got to see Asif's *Godot* on August 5, 1960. The film was premiered at Bombay's Maratha Mandir. The cinema gleamed under dozens of floodlights; it was the convergence point of streams of cars, of humming, pushing waves of people, who exuded excitement that this movie, which they had been told was being made for a decade, had finally been completed. Raj Kapoor had flown back to Bombay only a few hours previously from Czechoslovakia. Shammi Kapoor, who had been away on a tour of the Far East, had also timed his return to be present at the premiere. And, as the crowds converged on the cinema, the first thing they noticed was a huge portrait at the front of the theatre—of a tall, well-built, imperious-looking man, dressed in Royal Mughal robes. That was Prithviraj Kapoor. It had taken 500 shooting days, twenty years from when it was first conceived, and Rs 15 million to produce.

Asif had planned the publicity well, with what contemporary newspapers describe as a promotional pre-release extravaganza on a national scale. Journalists were flown from all over the country to Bombay and were put up at the Taj Mahal Hotel for some days, previous to the première.

Filmfare reported on August 26, 1960:

During the last fortnight K. Asif, creator & director of *Mughal-e Azam*, dominated the Indian film scene with the most sensational release of his mammoth, long-awaited film simultaneously at 150 cinema houses throughout India. The film created records in several respects. In one week alone it collected Rs. 1 lakh (Rs. 100,000) by way of advance bookings. Eight days before the release of the film, about sixty film critics of important daily newspapers and periodicals from all parts of the country were flown to Bombay and taken to the Sheesh Mahal.

Sheesh Mahal, for several years, continued to remain the centre of attraction at the Mohan Studios. Built by artisans from Ferozabad, after the shooting the set was covered with a huge tarpaulin and was only shown to a select few people. It attracted the attention of a rich Arab, who wanted to buy the Sheesh Mahal and take it to his country, but Asif refused the offer, wanting to use the set for his next film '*Taj Mahal*'. But this was never even started and he died before finishing the film of the story of Laila and Majnu, entitled '*Love & God*' which he had begun after *Mughal-e Azam*. Asif only made three films in his life but, if he had done nothing but *Mughal-e Azam*, he would deserve a chapter in Bollywood history. Garga is absolutely right when he writes, "There is no denying Asif's considerable cinematic talents…The best of *Mughal-e Azam* has never been surpassed".

The film was originally released in black and white, apart from one colour scene where Madhubala performs a song and dance routine with the words of the song sung by Lata Mangeshkar. This was a defiant song of love which Akbar, with Salim sitting next to him, listens in increasing rage. Asif re-shot this, considered the greatest scene in the film, in colour later.

If Akbar's cinematic rage was about his heir falling in love with a dancing girl then there was a real life rage about the movie by the Pakistani authorities, as Jimmy Mehta was to realise to his cost.

Jimmy Mehta was Pallonji's son-in-law, a Davis Cup player and on the executive committee of CCI, who later died in the Air India crash of 1978. However, some time before that, he was on a visit to London. The British Airways flight from Bombay in those days went via Karachi to Cairo and then to London, and just before he left, his father-in-law suggested he stop in Karachi and meet Zulfikar Bhutto, then foreign minister of Pakistan. Jimmy and Zulfi were great friends, a friendship dating from before partition.

"Why not visit him? He is the foreign minister. You know we would love to release *Mughal-e Azam* in Pakistan; maybe he can help." Jimmy agreed and rang his friend.

"Zulfi, this is Jimmy."

"Jimmy, how are you?"

"I am coming to Karachi; my plane will be there for two hours at Karachi airport. You send me a car. I shall meet up with you and then catch the flight to London."

At Karachi, Bhutto was at the airport to meet his old friend and took him to his house. It was evening by then. He took him to a dark room, put the lights on and revealed a hidden bar, Pakistan being a Muslim country where drinking was frowned on. The two old friends drank whisky and reminisced about old times and mutual friends. Then Bhutto asked, "Jimmy, what have you come for?"

"Have you heard about *Mughal-e Azam?*"

"Yes."

"My father–in-law was the producer. If this film is released in this country, then the two countries will come close."

What happened next was out of some horror movie. Jimmy would later tell Raj Singh, "I could not believe it. His eyes became red. He banged the glass table so hard I do not know how he did not break it. He said, 'Not for a thousand years can these two countries become one. I shall catch you by the throat for making such a suggestion'. He made a move towards me. I thought if he caught me he would kill me. I started running. It was dark. I ran through several rooms. I did not know where I was running. Ultimately, I came to the verandah, jumped into the car and left. I was never so relieved to see the airport."

In April 2006, forty-six years after Asif had finally finished his epic, Pakistan lifted its ban on the movie, with a première in Lahore. *Taj Mahal*, the film Asif wanted to make, but which a new generation of Bollywood film-makers had made in 2005, was also screened. The decision was part of what was described as a "confidence-building measure" between the two countries. The general ban on Bollywood movies remained but Pakistan's authorities, in justifying the temporary lifting of the ban, said that neither film had "un-Islamic values" and that both dealt with an era when the sub-continent's Muslims were in the ascendant.

How Asif would have laughed at those comments!

Part IV

A Laugh, a Song
and a Tear

13

The Explosion of the Bombay Film Song

On April 14, 1944, huge explosions rocked Bombay's docks. The immediate fear was this was Japanese bombing. It turned out that a fire had broken out in a ship loaded with cotton, timber, and ammunition, lying in the Bombay docks but, such was the force of the fire, it gave the impression of a bombing raid. This was the only damage the city suffered during the war, killing 500, injuring 2,000, and destroying large amounts of shipping, food and stores.

On that day, as Bombay got to grips with the devastation, a 14-year-old girl arrived in the city for the first time. Many years later the girl, now a very famous and rich woman, would recall, "I arrived in Bombay on April 14, 1944. On that day, there was a big blast in the Bombay docks. I was staying at Girgaum. There, I was down with malaria. I was taken care of by Mrs Pendse, a neighbour."

The woman who wrote that was Lata Mangeshkar. By the time she came to write her autobiography, she had caused an even greater explosion in Bollywood, although of an infinitely more welcome kind. Its effects are still felt in Indian cinema and, in many ways, define the very special world that is Bollywood.

There is nothing in Hollywood or, indeed, in the history of world cinema, to compare with Mangeshkar for the simple reason there is nothing like the genre of playback singing that forms the bedrock of Bollywood. But even within Bollywood's playback singing world, which has produced a number of male and female stars of quite exceptional quality, Mangeshkar remains an astounding phenomenon. Post-1947, and the end of the era when actors and actresses also sang, would see a number of talented male playback singers emerge, all seeking to copy Saigal. This would include the big three male singers who dominated the industry between 1950 and 1980: Mohammed Rafi, Mukesh, and Talat Mehmood. Kishore Kumar, another brilliant talent, was much more than a mere singer. But Lata was almost on her own among the women and her only competitor was her own sister, Asha, four years her junior. Lata's dominance of the Binaca Geet Mala chart list emphasises this. From 1953 to 1980, over a thirty-seven year period, eleven singers shared the top of the chart position. Of these eleven, seven were males, four females. Lata, on her own or as part of a duo with a male singer, had ten hit songs; Asha, her nearest female competitor, had four. As Indians say, only one Lata. Lata remains without a peer and defines the very distinctive style of Bollywood cinema. In 1986, when *India Today* carried out a survey to find who deserved a Padma Bhushan (a high honour awarded by the state) for Art and Culture, the readers put Lata first, before Raj Kapoor, Amitabh Bachchan, the writer R.K. Narayan, the dancer Mrinalini Sarabhai, the singer Bhimsen Joshi and the painter, M.F. Hussain. She was later to win the award, and many others, including India's highest, the Bharat Ratna in 2001.

The Lata who arrived in Bombay on the day of that explosion, could not have imagined the success she would have one day nor, even, that she would be a singer for, at that time, she was an actress as well. Indeed, she had acted in more films than she had sung songs. She had come to Bombay for work, work she desperately needed to keep herself and her family of six (three sisters and a brother all younger than her and her mother) alive. Two years earlier, at the age of twelve, she had become the breadwinner when her father, Dinanath Mangeshkar, died.

The story of Lata is the classic Indian Bollywood story of the daughter who never marries, achieves huge success but always dedicates everything to the dead father.

There is a story told of when Lata was nine. One morning Dinanath, an Indian classical music singer, was teaching some students to sing. He told them, "I shall have my bath and come back but you go on singing." As he was having his bath Lata came in and told the students, "That is not the way Baba told you to sing; this is how he means you to sing." She then proceeded to demonstrate. Dinanath rushed out of the bath, barely covering himself with his bath towel, and told his wife, "She is exceptional; and she will make my name. You will forget me. You will remember me only as Lata Mangeshkar's father."

Perhaps the story has been embellished in the endless retelling but Lata, and her sister, Asha, always observe their father's birth anniversary. In her Puja room, she has the portrait of her father and, when she funded a hospital in Pune, it was named Dinanath, the daughter paying homage to the father who taught her, but never lived to see her make the family name a "legend", the English word Indians use to describe her.

The Mangeshkars had not always been poor and their history has been quite colourful, reflecting the history of India. There was a suggestion that they should not be called Mangeshkar at all. The forefathers of the Mangeshkars came from Somnath, where they were *devdasi* (temple musicians and dancers) at the temple, which was then the richest in India. Its wealth attracted the Muslim ruler, Mohammed of Ghazni, whose annual winter habit was to plunder India. He invaded the country every year for sixteen years at the beginning of the eleventh century. The story goes that, after the sacking of the temple, and its wonderful treasures, by Mohammed,

Lata's ancestors fled Somnath for the south and settled in Goa, in a place called Mangesh, where there is a temple of Mangeshi, Shiva's temple. Here they once again resumed their service as *devdasis*. This is how the family got the name Mangeshkar. There is, however, some evidence that the surname should have been Abhishekar. Dinanath was an illegitimate child and there is an Abhisheki family in Mangesh, with whom Lata and her family have always maintained an excellent relationship, Jitendra Abhisheki having been a classical singer of repute.

Lata has always been cagey about her antecedents and, in her autobiography, written in Marathi, her native language, there is no reference to all this.

The illegitimate Dinanath had to struggle at first but succeeded in training as a classical singer and establishing himself in some style. The family moved to Indore, where Lata was born, Dinanath having married a Gujerati lady called Shevanti. Dinanath sang for the princely Holkar family and this was to introduce Lata to some of India's greatest cricketers, including C.K. Nayaudu, India's first Test captain. She developed a consuming interest in the game and a companionship with Raj Singh, a former player and now a leading administrator of the game in India.

Lata has never married and, although Bollywood gossip has long been that she and Raj Singh are all but man and wife, Raj Singh has always denied such rumours saying their close friendship is purely platonic. He tells a charming story of her interest in cricket:

> I may know the legend but I am not a musical man. Our friendship was not based on music. In fact, she was more into cricket than I was into music. C.K. Nayudu used to come to their house and Vijay Hazare (another Indian cricketing great) came regularly. She has a picture of Don Bradman (arguably the greatest ever cricketer), which is signed, "To Lata, from Don." She was given this when she helped an Australian. When asked what he could do to repay her, she said she would like to have Bradman's picture. She also had a book signed by Keith Miller (another great cricketer). Miller wrote in the book, 'To Lata' and then was told to write the word "Ji" (the suffix Indians use as a term of great respect), so he added "Ji" separately, thinking it was a separate name.

Dinanath was not only an accomplished classical singer, but had a touring drama company, which produced Marathi plays all over the state. He even produced a film and, for a time after Lata's birth, was well off, if not rich. It is not exactly clear how the slide began but it seems drink had a major part to play, both in his decline in fortune, and his health. In April 1942, at just 44, he died. His death had a devastating effect on the family—from having been fairly well off they were now paupers and Lata, not yet 13, became the breadwinner.

Like many of that era in Bollywood, Lata had not gone to school. One story has it that she went to school for one day but, when reprimanded by her teachers for singing, she left in a huff. In fact, she probably did attend school for a little longer than that, but for no more than a year or two. By the time her father died, she was already quite an experienced performer. Indeed, a month before his death, she sang for the Marathi film *Kiti Hasaal* (How Much Can you Make me Laugh). Dinanath did not like that much as, like many Indian classical musicians, he held film music in contempt, but was too ill to intervene. By this time, Lata had taken part in plays, and won a nationwide competition held by Dalsukh Pancholi to mark the success of his film, *Khazanchi*, the music for which was composed by Pancholi's fellow-citizen from Lahore, Master Ghulam Haider. He had introduced the Punjabi dholak and drums in the film and followed this with success in *Khandaan*, where Nur Jehan made her début. These two films of the early forties became trendsetters. Haider made a careful note of the young girl's talent. Her early singing had come from listening to her maternal grandmother's music. Its rhythm was shaped by the grinding of wheat and the Gujarat Garba dancing. Lata also loved listening to Saigal and Nur Jehan but, above all, there was Dinanath tutoring and nurturing what was clearly a very great, inherited talent. Lata's autobiography is full of memories of her father—how he would wake her early for *riaaz* (classical music practice) and get her to practise on the tanpura, the stringed drone instrument used in Indian classical music.

Lata and her family were saved from destitution by a certain Mr Vinayak. He had no surname because he was illegitimate and was known as Master Vinayak, an accomplished comic actor. Later, he would become better known as the father of actress Baby Nanda. He ran Prafull Pictures and, on the death of his friend, Dinanath, he promised to look after his family and took them to Kholapur. It was while Lata was in Kholapur that she acted in three Marathi films for Prafull Pictures: *Majha Baal* (the whole Mangeshkar family Lata, Asha, her sisters and brother sang in this film), followed by *Chimukla Sansar*, and *Gajabhau*. It was in this film that she also sang her first Hindi song. Lata hated acting and in her autobiography says, "I never liked to act in movies. I had a great passion for music. But money had to be earned because I was poor."

Vinayak was paying her Rs. 80 a month, which was not much to maintain a family of six and, in 1945, Bhalji Pendharkar, doyen of the Marathi film industry, offered her Rs. 300. But Vinayak persuaded her to stick with him. He brought her back to Bombay in 1945. For a time she lived in Kumud Villas in Shivaji Park, a couple of miles from Nur Jehan. It was a year later, after having moved house several times, that she gave up acting and concentrated on singing, her first song in a Hindi movie being in *Badi Maa* (the Big Mother), in which Nur Jehan played the heroine.

It was to take one further turn of the wheel of fortune before Lata truly found herself. Vinayak died in 1947, and things looked bleak. But, then, Ghulam Haider, who had not forgotten her, took her to Filmistan to record a trial duet with another singer. Sasadhar Mukherjee, in awe of Nur Jehan, as almost everyone was then, was less than impressed. "Her voice is too thin," he said, rejecting her as the playback singer for Kamini Kaushal. Haider retorted, "Let me foretell today that this kid will very soon put to shame everyone else, including Nur Jehan." Haider backed his judgement by using her in *Majboor* and then persuaded his friend, Naushad, to use her in *Andaz*.

Her singing in *Andaz* was a seminal moment in her career. It was on the sets of *Andaz* that Raj Kapoor heard her sing and decided he must have her voice for his film, *Barsaat*. Soon, other composers like Khemchand Prakash, composing for Kamal Amrohi's *Mahal,* followed. It had been six years since she had arrived in Bombay on the day of the explosions; now she was ready to explode herself.

In fact, Lata Mangeshkar had timed her arrival in Bombay brilliantly. The Bombay film song was just taking off. Songs had been part of Indian films since the days of the talkies, reflecting the enormous part music, song and dance play in Indian daily life. Early films borrowed from Indian theatre and music directors transplanted music and dance from stage to screen. But the war years had given rise to a very new phenomenon—the Bombay film song—something which had never existed in India before.

Bhaskar Chandavarkar expertly analysed in *The Tradition of Music in Indian Cinema* how the Bombay film song became the template, not only for film music but also for music in India. He dates its emergence from 1944, soon after Lata first arrived in the city, making Bombay the song centre of India. From that moment nobody could hope to record any song that did not have harmony, an assortment of voices with varied melodies and a large, colourful orchestra, which symbolised the power of a music director. If Bengali composers like Anil Biswas, Salil Chowdhury, the Burmans, both father and son, would play a huge part in the development of the Bombay film song, then Indians from all over the country also contributed. Raj Kapoor's composers, Shankar and Jaikishen, are a classic illustration. They were actually two individuals: Shankar Raghuvanshini, a Punjabi, born in Madhya Pradesh in central India, but raised in Andhra in the south, and a fluent Telugu speaker, and Jaikishen Panchal, a Gujarati who, like many, had migrated to Bombay. So had O.P. Nayyar, who was born in Lahore, and Madan Mohan, who was born in Baghdad, where his grandfather was Rai Bahader Chunilal, a colleague of Himansu Rai and, later, Ashok Kumar.

According to Chandavarkar, the Bombay song was fast-paced, often higher in pitch, used more musical instruments and was better organised in musical composition than most other songs. Each song lasted three minutes and twenty seconds and could be put on a 78rpm disc and, if necessary, recorded on both sides. Like Indian food, the Bombay song had everything in the Indian musical lexicon: ragas and semi-classical thumris of Northern India, and folk songs from all over India. Saigal had used the Urdu '*ghazal*' form, a light semi-classical Indian song form originating in Persia. It was, and remains, hugely popular in North India and Pakistan. Although the ghazal was heavily influenced by Muslim culture, it was also popular with Hindus, showing how the two communities produced a common musical culture. The Bombay film song took this even further as it synthesised a variety of musical elements, including bhajans, quawwalis, and Latin American and Western ones, to create an essentially Bollywood genre.

Earlier male singers, who were more linear, were displaced, helped by the fact that Saigal died in 1947. The music demanded more delicate voices, and singers such as Pankaj Mullick, K.C. Dey, and Pahari Sanyal, all Bengalis, incidentally, were overtaken by Rafi, Mukesh, Manna Dey, and Talat Mehmood. The post-1947 films often incorporated the word *naya* (new) in their titles to indicate the new, free country that had emerged. Their characters sang while riding bicycles and horses, and driving cars. This was all indicative of the new fast pace of Bombay, stamping itself as the cosmopolitan New York of India.

Films such as *Kismet* and *Rattan* also helped shape the Bombay song. *Kismet* made Anil Biswas into one of the more remarkable composers of Bollywood. Born in Barisal, then East Bengal, just before the First World War, he was a revolutionary and was often jailed by the British. He worked with the great Bengali poet, Kazi Nazrul Islam. He moved to Bombay where he demonstrated his innovative use of trumpets, saxophone, piano, and even the sounds made by trains, to make music that appealed across the castes and classes of India.

He had worked on the songs of *Basant,* helping his brother-in-law, Pannalal Ghosh. He showed a mastery of beat, using it to introduce a slow and unfolding melody, which flowed into all sorts of exciting passages. Biswas could create emotion without being sentimental. One could trace Bhatiali (folk song of East Bengal) roots in many of his melodies. The rhythms of his songs were Bengali-inspired yet, through his imaginative use of the orchestra, he avoided the folksy, laid-back, mood.

The story goes that, once he was driving with a song writer in Bombay. The song writer made an unscheduled stop to visit someone for a few minutes. He gave Biswas a piece of paper with a lyric of a song he had written, hoping he would think about a tune for it. When he returned, he found Biswas had composed the tune, and he sang the song to the accompaniment of the steering wheel as a percussion instrument.

Naushad, like Ghulam Haider, used the dholak but mixed it with a double bass and tabla. He brought in a vibraphone and set it up next to a sarangi, brought in folk tunes from his native Uttar Pradesh, hired new lyric writers and exploited the chorus in his songs. Naushad understood the needs of the post-war Indian audience, which wanted modernity and freshness—something sweet and simple.

However, in order to create the Bombay song these composers, mostly schooled in Indian classical music, were rewriting the musical history that had existed for centuries and was so very different from Western music.

The music that Hollywood used in its films was a progression of the Western musical traditions which had lasted for well over five hundred years by the time cinema arrived. This included great musical composers, who also wrote for both ballet and opera. There were huge musical differences between Mozart, Beethoven, Tchaikovsky and Wagner but they all composed operas, ballets, and symphonies in the classical tradition of European music. A Western musical performance generally had an orchestra and a score, which provided a record of the performance and which could even be sold. The great musical composers of the West had left behind a treasure trove of music which the cinema drew upon. So, Western films incorporated classics, such as Beethoven's *Moonlight Sonata* and Tchaikovsky suites, to accompany the romantic scenes shown on the screen.

Things could not be more different in India. For a start, Indian classical musicians looked down upon the music of the theatre, which formed the basis of early Indian films.

And, at that stage, India's classical music was in very poor shape. Much of this was raga music, presented through khayal songs, written and composed centuries earlier, but sung in a sort of Hindi dialect that was understood by only a few. It could be argued that this is true of Western opera but there, words can be separated from the music. In India, this was just not on. There was a strong religious background to classical Indian music, and a kriti in the South, or a khayal in the North, were taught and learned by musicians with devotional fervour. There were *gharanas* (schools) of singers for whom the unfolding of the raga had hardly any independent existence outside of the khayal *bandish* (handed-down composition of both melody and words). This also meant that independent instrumental music was ruled out. Instruments imitated voices. Indian orchestra in the Western sense did not exist.

There was, of course, folk music, but in the early days of film there were not many links between an urban-based cinema and the largely rural folk music, often confined to small communities who had little awareness of the wider world. The continental nature of India meant the folk songs of Bengal did not reach those of Punjab in the north or Madras in the south.

From the beginning, cinema forced Indian musicians to change. Even in the days of the silent movies, when musicians played in halls, they had learnt to adjust. The duration and tempo of the ghazal on the harmonium had to suit the film the musician was accompanying. This in itself was a highly rebellious act since a classically trained Indian musician would have learnt from his *ustad* (guru) that nothing could deviate from the mehfil which had been created—a performance meant for the élite few. Cinema was challenging that.

But this began to change as the twentieth century dawned. Indian classical music changed when Vishnu Narayan Bhatkhande and Vishnu Digambar Paluskar started the renaissance of north Indian classical music in the first decades of the twentieth century. The invention of the gramophone, and its arrival in rural India, like television nearly eighty years later, revolutionised both rural life and Indian music. For the first time, Indian classical music had an existence outside the performance on the stage or in the concert hall, in the darbars of rajas, nawabs and zamindars. The gramophone made music a highly saleable commodity. Classical records began to be produced and ragas and songs had to be restricted to fit onto one side of the disc. And, for the first time in Indian musical history, a musician performed without an audience being present. The gramophone, or phonograph, as it was called, could be heard by millions across the sub-continent, cutting through the rigid musical caste barriers that had previously existed. This was what the Bollywood film was trying to do, and the Bombay film song was an essential part of this armoury. The requirement here was for a short song that would appeal as much to northern as southern India; where people might know little of the Hindi language the film was made in—their mother tongue being Bengali, Punjabi, Tamil, or Telugu—but could tap their toes to the music.

In the classical Indian musical tradition, the audience plays a part, unlike in Western classical music. Indian classical music performances are like a continuous dialogue with the audience. A performance of classical Western music takes place in front of an audience but the audience has to be silent until it is over. It is conceivable it could even take place without one. Not so in India.

As opposed to the Western conductor and his orchestra following the written music in front of them, in an Indian classical music performance an individual might sing, compose and be his own orchestra. Unless, and until, he takes great pleasure in his own art, he is not going to keep the audience entranced. This makes Indian music very individualistic, while the Western one is more collective, following a score and based on team-work, led by the conductor. During the performance, there is no scope for individual variation, no scope for intuition as the music is being played. The audience goes to listen to a particular composition knowing what to expect.

The Indian tradition had created teachers—gurus and ustads—not composers. Ustads, for example, created *bandishes* or compositions that taught a student the principles of a raga which, in turn, would continue to be cultivated and refined as the *bandishes* were handed down to the next generation. A performer like Ravi Shankar does not perform with an orchestra. He has disciples and, as he performs, he is giving them lessons on how to perform in public. Of course, before the performance he has tutored them and made sure they are ready for such a public display. During the performance, his disciples on sitar will respond to him and he will go on teaching them in public. No conductor in Western music would ever conceive of such an idea. This means that, as opposed to the organised collective face a Western classical music performance represents, Indian music is intuitive, individualistic, and also very anarchic.

This is best seen when there are duets in Indian classical music which can result in one musician throwing a challenge to the other. Something like a musical fencing match, with each in turn taking inspiration from the other, and also seeing the other's performance as a challenge. Watch the two brothers

Nazakat Ali Khan and Salamat Ali Khan perform classical music. They sing together. As one sings, the other responds and takes the note further, then he waits for his brother to come back, and so it goes on.

Unlike Western musical pieces, which often end in a crescendo, Indian music is circular, performing an *avartan* (a circular return). In an *avartan* you start from one point. You take the whole *taan* (a rhythmic combination of notes of a particular scale called a *raga*), and then you complete the circle and arrive at the same point again. Indian classical music has three parts in the presentation. Slow tempo 'alap,' where the *raga* (scale) is introduced. In instrumental presentation, this is done without *tabla* accompaniment. Then, a medium tempo composition (called Jodh in instrumental presentation), which is performed with *tabla* and *tans*, is mostly used here. Lastly, a fast tempo composition (*Jhala*, in case of instruments) where the *raga* is presented at a very fast speed. The last section can be called a 'crescendo', but the theme is always to come back to the 'central point' of the scale. From alap to the end of the presentation it could go on for an hour or more. The basic core of Indian classical music is that you say you are in the circle.

Classical Indian music also has its *gharana*s (schools), with each gharna having its own tradition. So, there is the Gwalior *gharana*, Kirana *gharana*, Jaipur *gharana*, Agra *gharana*, Mawati *gharana*, and Maihar *gharana*, which is Ravi Shankar's *gharana*. The differences are in presentation. There is one *raga*, Yaman, sung by practically every *gharana*. It has got its own framework but that framework is slightly different with each *gharana*. Classical Indian music enthusiasts would immediately recognise the different *gharanas*. The singer has only to start for the audience to say, "He is from Gwalior *gharana*," for instance, signifying a tradition that has come down the generations and was a fusion of Hindu and Muslim musical traditions.

With classical Indian music not having a concept of notation, it was film songs with many hundreds being sung every year that forced Indians to note music down, since it was impossible to remember every tune. A musical piece also had to be planned and composed—it could not depend on inspiration or impromptu improvisation.

The fusion of the popular and the classical with Western music was the result of India's greatest literary figure, Rabindranath Tagore, who was well versed in Western and Indian music, and even took to singing. In 1900, he had sung Bankim Chandra's *Vande Mataram* for a recording. In 1920, his voice was recorded on 78rpm records. Tagore's songs created a new genre which is called Rabindra Sangeet, the music of Rabindranath Tagore, and were a source of inspiration for many singers, such as Pankaj Mullick and K.C. Dey. They fused Bengali folk songs with the use of instruments like the piano and the organ. So, from the beginning of sound in films, the music showed the Bengali influence along with the theatrical Nautanki style derived from Parsi theatre, and Hindustani music, brought in from Maharashtra, and the early stage plays. Film music also broke down the rigid barrier between classical and popular music. Ravi Shankar directed music for *Neecha Nagar* and *Dharti Ke Lal*. Ali Akbar Kan, the sarod maestro, made music for *Andhian* and other films. Nikhil Bannerjee, Halim Jaffer Khan, Ram Narain, Vilayat Khan, Bismillah Khan and Shanta Prasad all helped to create melodious songs for film. They joined all sorts of musicians, some from hotel bands and restaurants, others from the army and even folk-artists, as film music directors looked for new sounds for their orchestras.

In Indian classical music such mixing would have been like an untouchable dining with the upper castes in the worst days of the Hindu caste system.

Indian musicians were also raiding the world for musical instruments. India had already shown how eclectic it could be in adapting to musical instruments from far and wide. The harmonium, now considered an Indian instrument, and practically forgotten in the West, was brought to India by the Jesuits in the seventeenth century. Pannalal Ghosh, who later left films, was a virtuoso flautist. Sajjad Hussein, an eccentric and hot-tempered but gifted composer, made much use of the mandolin, which originated in Italy. It could easily pass as an eastern instrument and Hussein's lead was followed by others. The introduction of sound did see one Western instrument fall by the wayside. The clarinet had been brought by British army bands and used for music in cinema halls showing silent movies. The music for the Prabhat emblem, a melody in *Raga Bhupali*, was played in E flat on a high- pitched clarinet while, on the screen, a slim, young girl arched backwards as she blew on the traditional Maharashtrian *shing* (horn). But it could not make the transition to Indian sound.

The Hawaiian guitar, which closely resembled the *vichitra veena* of the north, and *gottuvadyam* of the south was, probably, the first electric instrument in the film orchestra. A small microphone, the size of a rupee coin, could be attached to the belly of the guitar. This was called the contact mike. The amplified sound was loud, clear and sustained. Everything that a human voice could do, could be melodically reproduced by the electric guitar. Various composers and singers used it and Sachin Dev Burman, another Bengali from east Bengal, who had been trained in classical music, but was also familiar with folk music, used the electric guitar in his earlier songs. Burman also brought the east Bengal style of singing where what Bengalis called the *thakha* (push) was employed when singing to give the impression the singer was literally performing a thrusting motion as he sang. The piano accordion came to India after the Second World War and in *Awara*, Shankar-Jaikishen used it for the song *Awara Hoon* that became known around the world. The accordion worked a lot like the harmonium and, being a portable reed/wind instrument, street performers often strapped their harmoniums around their neck. The accordion would become a popular instrument in film songs, with many composers using it. Claviolin, an instrument that had a keyboard and sounded like a violin and which has been converted into an electric organ, also came after the Second World War. It was used by Kalyanji Veerji Shah for the songs in the film *Nagin*, one of many films where the song remained in memory far longer than the film. His use of the instrument was extremely clever to help simulate the sound of a snake-charmer's pipe, a German invention reproducing something uniquely Indian.

The Indians also used castanets, rattles, bells and drums—they have many kinds of drums (which keep the timing and rhythmic cycles of their music). All drums played with vocal and instrumental music are played with the hands. The *tabla* is most common of them. Martial and folk event drums are played by sticks, for example, the *dholok*. As Bhaskar Chandavarkar says, the list of instruments was endless and represented every continent on earth. Foreign instruments and their unique sounds were combined with traditional Indian sounds. It was this blending that created unique harmonies which became an integral part of Indian music and contributed to the great Bombay film song we know today.

One composer who could combine many elements was Salil Chowdhury who, like many Bengalis of his generation, having seen suffering during the Bengal famine, was a man of the left and as part of the IPTA composed songs for the Communist party. Many years later he would say, "…the primary emotion that burned deep inside me was one of fierce protest. I railed against the torment and cruelty that was killing humanity little by little." Called to Bombay by Bimal Roy, where he provided music for *Do Bigha Zameen,* he went on to establish the reputation of a music man who knew how to combine various elements, both Indian and Western. Lata, in a rare, fulsome passage in her memoirs, would say:

> Salil-da had something different in his composition. He had a wonderful ear for folk music. He had a wonderful ear for Mozart, Beethoven, Bach and he had made good use of it in his songs. In one song in *Chaaya*, 'Itna Na Mujse Pyaar Bada', he has used everything of Mozart, Beethoven and Bach.

Salil Chowdhury, who also wrote the screen play for films like *Do Bigha Zameen,* impressed Lata with the care he took during the recording of songs, making sure he was in the recording booth, not in the singing area.

Lata's praise of Salil Chowdhury was not just fawning. He has the distinction of getting Dilip Kumar to sing and, in effect, become his own playback singer. Kumar, like all Indian actors, did not sing but had been influenced by classical music, studied the sitar and the violin but also wanted to make sure about the songs that singers were recording for him. He would attend recording sessions. During the making of Bimal Roy's *Madhumati,* where Chowdhury was the music director, he was watching the recording of a song and started humming the tune. Although at that moment Chowdhury became irritated and asked him to stop, he was struck by the fact that Kumar was quite melodious. So perhaps he could sing? There was no scope for that in *Madhumati*.

However, Dilip Kumar was also playing the lead role in the film, *Musafir,* which was being made by Bimal Roy's chief assistant, Hrishikesh Mukherjee. Dilip

Kumar had played a major part in getting Mukherjee to make the film. Kumar had always been impressed with Mukherjee's editing and one day suggested he should direct his own films. But Mukherjee was not sure anyone would finance it. Dilip Kumar offered to listen to the story he wanted to make and went to his house, where Mukherjee was a paying guest. Kumar found a room with names, dates and graffiti scribbled on the walls. Mukherjee narrating the story said the film would be about three couples who had all lived in the same room. Kumar liked the story and agreed to act, irrespective of how much Mukherjee might pay. With Kumar on board, Mukherjee now had a saleable idea.

The role required Dilip Kumar to play his usual tragic character, but it also involved him playing the violin at one stage. Salil Chowdhury, who was the music director, suggested to Hrishikesh Mukherjee that Kumar might also sing. They both went to his Pali Hill home to put the idea to him. Initially he refused, "Humming a tune is different but, rendering it as a singer, requires aptitude and skill." However, Chowdhury was persistent and Kumar agreed. Chowdhury arranged a song session to test his new protégé and advised him to "sing the tunes with an open voice, the same way in which he was humming at the time of the *Mahdumati* song recording." Kumar was so nervous that he hummed the first few lines with his eyes closed. Chowdhury then summoned the lyricist, Shailendra, and got him to compose the words to match the tune. The song had been planned as a solo but Kumar was so nervous that he wanted an orchestra or a chorus. Chowdhury could sense Kumar's anxiety and got Shailendra to shorten the song. Chowdhury ruled out a chorus or orchestra, as he felt this would make Kumar even more worried. Instead, he suggested that Lata should sing a duet with Dilip. There followed a number of rehearsals which boosted Dilip Kumar's confidence and the final recording session went smoothly. Chowdhury would later consider this a highlight of his musical directorship to "become the only musical director to record a song with the voice of Dilip Kumar."

There is a photograph showing Lata Mangeshkar and Dilip Kumar sharing a mike as the song is recorded, a photo which must be unique in the annals of Bollywood—the voice legend meeting the love legend, albeit in one brief song.

Lata's own musical upbringing shows the mixture of musical influences by no means uncommon in Bollywood. Following her father's advice, she learned from Indian classical musicians, deepening her knowledge of ragas. She particularly liked musicians such as Bade Ghulam Ali Khan, who was equally proficient in Indian classical music, as well as thumbri and ghazal. After Dilip Kumar suggested that her Urdu accent was less than perfect, she worked on it and, later, also learned Bengali and sang Bengali songs, impressing even the finicky Bengalis, who can be very possessive about their language which they consider the sweetest in the world. She also took to Western music although not Western classical. In her autobiography, she says:

I don't like opera singing. But I like Bing Crosby. The Western singer I like most is Nat King Cole because he had that wonderful, husky voice, that would identify him with the audience immediately. I never had the chance of meeting Nat King Cole; he was dead before I went to America.

In the 1960s, as the Beatles emerged, Lata Mangeshkar became a fan:

People say the Beatles are a fad. But I don't think so. They have their own style. There is no country in the world where the Beatles are not imitated. They have taken many things from different parts of the world and they have created their own style. If you listen to the Beatles properly, you get a feel of old Roman music. Sometimes, you get a feel of Indian music, sometimes you get a feel of Assamese folk songs. On the face value you may feel it is a bad thing but, no, there is inner soul to the Beatles' music. Moreover, they are more experimental. The Beatles took lessons on sitar from Ravi Shankar and they impart that sitar into their music. That is their greatness.

By now, the Bombay film song had become the Indian song, with a song for every situation—romance, laughter, sadness, cabarets, eroticism—important in a country where the censor did not allow kissing on the screen. And, in the process, the singers became India's pop stars. Radio Ceylon's Bianca Geet Mala, which broadcast Hindi film songs, became the nation's Top of the Pops. The songs lived on long after the films had been forgotten and Indian movie-goers had made it clear that a film without song was not worth going to.

It is interesting to contrast this with Hollywood. The theme tune of *Pretty Woman* is the Roy Orbison song composed quite independently of the film, but used brilliantly to shape the message of the film. In Bollywood, on the other hand, the songs were created for the films but then acquired a life of their own. The singers, led by Lata, became pop stars with their own fan clubs and devotees.

Mukesh Chand Mathur, known as Mukesh, the singing voice of Raj Kapoor, for instance, had fans ranging from the great Indian cricketer, Bhagwat Chandrashekar, to the former Pakistan Prime Minister, Benazir Bhutto—Chandra listened to Mukesh's music during that dramatic day in August 1971 when he bowled India to her first ever victory in a cricket Test on English soil and a tape of Mukesh always accompanied Benazir on her car rides while Prime Minister.

Through the 1950s, actors, music composers and lyricists formed very distinct groups in Bollywood. Raj Kapoor always used Shankar-Jaikishen and lyricists Shailendra, a very committed socialist, and Hasrat Jaipuri. Dilip Kumar worked with Naushad and lyricist Shakeel Badayuni, while Dev Anand's composer was often S.D. Burman and lyricist Sahir Ludhianvi. Not that there was no crossover. In Bimal Roy's *Devdas*, in 1956, Dilip Kumar played the lead, S.D. Burman provided the music and Sahir Ludhianvi, the lyrics. But, generally, the groups stuck together, aware they were working to a formula and the trick was to repeat the formula every time.

Over the years, the popularity of various composers would change and in 1975, for instance, out of eighty-nine films made in Bombay, forty-four had scores by only three composing teams: Laxmikant-Pyarelal, Kalyanji-Anandji, and R.D. Burman.

With song had also come dance, adapting Bharat Natyam, the dance the *devdasis*, Lata's ancestors, performed. Back in 1948, Uday Shankar had made an attempt to represent the complete dance film, *Kalpana*, in an effort to rehabilitate the classical dance. But, outside Bengal, it failed although it had inspired Vasan to make *Chandralekha*.

But in 1955, Shantaram took the dance theme to make his first Technicolor film, just two years before Mehboob got his onto the screen. He had a number of failures just before that and, at that very moment, was temporarily working in the Government's Films Division, producing a film on the folk dances of India. Shantaram decided to have an abundance of dance with what his son admits was a paper-thin story and just "an excuse to unleash an extravaganza of exquisite song and dance sequences." Shantaram wanted all the colours to be done in India but the result did not please the critics. The costumes for the dancers clashed with the background and his fountains, producing multi-coloured water, one critic said, "blinded the senses." But he knew his Indian audience. *Jhanak Jhanak Payal Baaje* (Jingle, Jingle, Sound the anklet Bells), was the first Hindi film to be shown at Metro in Bombay (now Mumbai), which used to be a haven for Hollywood films. It ran in one theatre for 104 weeks and was voted the best picture in the *Filmfare* Awards. It also won him the President's Gold Medal.

Interestingly, Shantaram had turned down Vyjayanthimala as the leading lady, instead going with Sandhya who, in his previous film, *Teen Batti Chaar Raasta*, had agreed to darken-up to play a dark-coloured girl, and to illustrate the colour prejudice of Indians. But she was always much more of a dancer and soon became yet another of Raj Kapoor's heroines, combining Bharat Natyam dance steps, with Khatak dance and Bhangra, a Punjabi folk dance, in the film *New Delhi*. There were other films which showed cabaret dancing where Western, mainly Anglo-Indian, dancers like Cuckoo and Helen achieved stardom in their own right. Cabaret dancing, however, portrayed women as vamps or victims.

Another form of dancing was used as part of the courtesan film genre, and was well-established and respected in ancient India. This dancing prevailed in all the royal courts of India but, as the legend of Anarkali shows, it was also considered not much above the position of a prostitute and would never be admitted to high society, or gain wide social acceptance. Yet courtesan films were very influential in the careers of some famous actresses, including Meena Kumari, Vyjayanthimala, Sharmila Tagore and Rekha, whose *Umrao Jaan Ada*, made in 1981, told the story of a thirty-year-old abducted and sold to a brothel. It is considered the quintessential courtesan film of Bollywood. Rekha portrays a woman who becomes an accomplished poet and singer. The sets are lavish, the music enchanting, and Rekha quite stunning. This was Muzaffar Ali's second film and continued to show his interest in the past. The setting was the independent kingdom of Audh, before it was annexed by the British East India Company. But, like *Jhanak, Jhanak*, while the critics panned it, the cinema-goers loved it.

Films about courtesans and dancing were not new. In 1971, Kamal Amrohi had made *Pakeezah*, which was also set in Lucknow, where Meena Kumari played the courtesan, seeking love and not finding it. Amrohi, her husband in real life, was then estranged from her. Meena Kumari was dying, and the film, full of heartbreak, seemed to be reflecting her life. Meena Kumari was so ill that she could not perform all the intricate mujra dances the film required. To be fair, she was not that much of a dancer and there had to be a sort of playback dancing sequence where the dance for the climactic song, sung by Lata, was actually performed by Padma Khan, pretending to be Meena Kumari. A veil hid her face.

The film, with a beautiful score by Ghulam Mohammed, revealed the perfectionist in Amrohi. He had started making it in 1959, shades of *Mughal-e Azam* here, leasing an Anomorphic lens which was attached to a 35mm camera. The film was sent to be processed in London but Amrohi said it was out of focus. Twice it was sent back. Finally, says his son, a committee in the US found it to be out of focus by 1/100 of a second, "So impressed was twentieth Century that they gifted my father the lens."

The film was to show the power of Bollywood, cutting across even the bitter political divide of the sub-continent. This was demonstrated in 1973 in Simla when Indira Gandhi and Zulikar Ali Bhutto, the Pakistani Prime Minister, met to sign the Simla Accords. This followed the 1971 Bangladesh war when India had defeated Pakistan in battle and helped create Bangladesh. During the protracted negotiations in Simla, Bhutto and his entourage required a screening of *Pakeezah*, and this was arranged. Bhutto may very nearly have killed Jimmy Mehta for suggesting *Mughal-e Azam* be shown in Pakistan but *Pakeezah*, with its tale of the old, dying Mughal world appealed to him.

Lata sang for both Vyjayanthimala and Meena Kumari and the contrasts she sees in them are interesting. For Meena Kumari, widely considered one of Bollywood's great actresses, she has nothing but admiration in her memoirs. Vyjayanthimala is treated very differently.

Meena Kumari was one of three heroines of whose acting she says she had to take notice and sing accordingly. The other two were Nargis and Nutan who, according to Lata, could emote as well as Meena Kumari. Nutan had an ear for music and could sing, unlike Nargis or Meena Kumari, neither of whom had a singing voice:

> Whenever I used to sing for Meena Kumari, naturally I used to go into that particular role. She was known as the tragedy queen. All her songs were very sad songs and I like sad songs.

Yet, on Vyjayanthimala, Lata could not be more damning of her ability to act:

> She did not have good pronunciation as far as Hindi and Urdu were concerned. She used to portray herself as more sexy than she was in various dance sequences.

Vyjayanthimala was certainly not like Nargis, the first Raj Kapoor actress Lata sang for, and of whom she says:

> She had the uncanny art of knowing the meaning of song, how to project on screen and how to act. Whenever I used to sing for Nargis, I had to take care of everything that was happening on screen. When I sang for her for the first time in *Andaaz, tod diya dil mera* (my heart is broken), and Nargis was going to project it onto the screen, I had to take care that my singing matched her acting. Again, I sang a song for her in Raj Kapoor's *Aah Arre Raja ki ayegi barat*. The hero is down with TB. And she knows about it; he is neglecting her, he is not taking notice of her, he is going to die and still she sings *Raja ki ayegi barat*. There, I really gave justice to that particular song and, equally, justice was given by Nargis in her acting.

Was her less-than-enthusiastic endorsement of Vyjayanthimala because she did not entirely approve of how Raj Kapoor handled Lata, and the resulting split this provoked between Kapoor and Mangeshkar?

Kapoor's *Barsaat* had given Lata an all-Indian profile and there was now a wonderful chemistry between film-maker and singer. After she had recorded the songs in *Barsaat* she, along with Raj Kapoor and others, had sat on the pavement outside R.K. Studios, wondering how it would fare. For *Awara,* where she sang from nine in the evening until dawn the next day, she joined Kapoor, Shankar and Jaikishen to eat at what was called an Irani restaurant (a restaurant run by immigrants from Iran). Lata, like Raj Kapoor's actresses, only wore white saris with coloured borders, and Raju Bharatan, one of her biographers, says, "Lata in white was, for Raj, a replica of Nargis in white; somewhere the voice and vision merged."

Was there perhaps a suggestion of love here? Madhu Jain talks of a special relationship but whether this was love, it is hard to say. What is much more certain is that the feeling she had for another composer, who was not part of the Kapoor film circuit but, according to Bhau Marathe, who witnessed the events at close hand, was the love Lata has never spoken about. This was the composer, C. Ramchandra.

C. Ramchandra was a Brahmin from Maharashtra, whose antecedents are shrouded in mystery. It is not certain where he was born but he had his basic training in classical music in Pune and then, Nagpur. At birth, he was Ramchandra Narhar Chitalkar and had sung in films under that name, as well as various others. But, on becoming a composer, he did what is more usual for an actor or actress. He decided to take the name, C. Ramchandra, neatly reversing his given names. Today, he is virtually a forgotten name, except to writers of Bollywood film music, yet he was one of the four pillars of the melody school that developed in the 1950s, the others being Anil Biswas, Madan Mohan and Roshan Lal Nagrath, who was known just by his first name. Chandravarkar, and others, who have written about the Bombay film songs, have no doubt about C. Ramchandra's place. He could adapt anything from Natya Sangeet to Latin American music, could add appropriate Indian ornamentation to Western or Latin pieces and make the song instantly Indian.

Bhau Marathe knew him well. He lived next door to him and was part of his family. He has no doubt that he made Lata the singer she is, and was also the great love of her life:

> C. Ramchandra was a wonderful music composer. He could judge the quality of the voice, the tonal quality. He made Lata by bringing her out from the shadow of Nur Jehan. When Lata came to playback singing, she was under the great influence of Nur Jehan. She, herself, says she was imitating Nur Jehan. He told her: "You have your own style of singing. You have got your own identity. You are Lata Mangeshkar." This emerged in *Anarkali*. Sasadhar Mukherjee, still not convinced of Lata's abilities, was insisting on Geeta Dutt, as playback singer for *Anarkali*. Sri Ramchandra put his foot down. He said: "Only Lata will sing for *Anarkali*." It was in this film that Lata sang Ramchandra's *Ye Zindagi usi ki hai* (This Life is for Him), a love song of total surrender. No second compromise. It was one of the best songs he had composed and, in *Anarkali,* she found her identity as Lata Mangeshkar and escaped the shadow of Nur Jehan.

What fascinated Ramchandra about Lata was that she had what he called a blotting-paper memory. This meant she could absorb songs in a fraction of a second. This was particularly important in those days as a song was recorded live; there was none of the modern pre-mixing of sound. Today, a recording session for a song means a pre-mixed sound track, with the singer singing on top of this soundtrack. In those days, all the musicians including the composer, had to be present in the studio as the song was recorded, and the singers sang with a live orchestra. If something went wrong, the whole song had to be sung again. It was common to take four or five hours to record one song. Once, a song sung by Talat Mehmood for Sajjad Hussain had to have thirty-five takes. Lata, with her blotting-paper memory, was a godsend for C. Ramchandra. Over time, the sheer growth of film songs forced Indian musical directors to write down musical compositions, something alien to the Indian musical tradition.

Unfortunately, C. Ramchandra lost the diary in which he had written a dozen or so tunes for Lata to sing, giving both the words and the notations.

The bond between Lata and C. Ramchandra grew and Marathe says:

She wanted to marry him. He did not want to marry her. He was already married, although he did not have children. This was in 1960. I, myself, was 11 years old. I spent my childhood at C. Ramchandra's place near Shivaji Park in central Mumbai. I have seen their relationship myself with my own eyes. I have a vivid memory of him showing Lata how he wanted a song to be sung. The complete orchestra is sitting in front of them. She stopped singing with C. Ramchandra from 1960. They might have had differences of opinion, I do not know. But she suddenly stopped and she told everyone I am not going to sing with C. Ramchandra. The year following C. Ramchandra's parting with Lata, no producer came to him. That was the real downfall of C. Ramchandra. She does not mention him in her book. She never even utters the name. She has sung in programmes in India, as well as abroad, nearly three to four songs of his but not a word has been mentioned who the composer was. That to me indicates the feud. It was only many years later when she was interviewed at the age of seventy-five on Star World that she uttered the word C. Ramchandra. She said he was a good composer; a very talented person, who would compose ten tunes for one song.

In contrast to this virtual silence on C. Ramchandra, in her memoir Mangeshkar lavished praise on two other composers. Anil Biswas also helped her emerge from of the shadow of Nur Jehan, and taught her how to control her breathing. Salil Chowdhury also hugely impressed Lata with his eclecticism and his ability to compose songs that mixed Bengali folk songs with Western classical music.

In his autobiography, C. Ramchandra does not mention Lata but mentions a woman called Sita, whose story reads very like Lata's.

Was this perhaps Lata's ability to be ruthless with people who had crossed her? Manek Premchand, in *Yesterday's Melodies, Today's Memories*, which has short biographies of the significant composers and musical directors of Bollywood going back to the start of sound, contrasts the public Lata, endlessly praised as the legend, with the private one, who is distrusted and feared:

Over the decades, there have been strong rumours of Lata using subtle, but powerful, methods to scuttle the careers of many singers... Also, after a few years of success, Lata became the only singer consistently to arrive last for recordings. Only when everyone was present could she be called by telephone for the recording. Of course, she was known to cancel recordings at the very last minute, much more than many other singers, entailing losses for producers... So how, and why, did people allow her to get away with it? It was simple: because of her voice... Producers laughed all the way to the bank. Composers and writers of songs valued this perfect link—her vocals—in their creative chain. Actresses became successful because of her voice; musicians got work. And the public got to hear a divine voice, often singing beautiful melodies, many of them unforgettable in our lifetimes.

Premchand's book is homage to the singers and composers of Bollywood but, while acknowledging the greatness of Lata, his essay on her is also the bleakest, and he concludes that there are two Latas: the public one that enchants and the private one that appals.

The stories against her are, of course, familiar stories of the prima donna. Maria Callas did much worse and Lata may be forgiven for travelling first-class while her entourage travelled at the back of the bus.

In a sense, the criticism of Lata Mangeshkar is due the fact that she has always had a shrewd sense of her own worth and has not been bashful in making the most of it. In a country where the culture is not to ask for money up front, Lata has been an exception. Before Lata, the norm was for singers to be paid a flat fee. But these songs would then be released by a music company and sold in their millions. Lata demanded that the music companies should pay a royalty. This led to a fight with Raj Kapoor about royalties which lasted for almost a decade. Lata started by demanding 5%, and then settled for 2.5%, a target she eventually achieved when Kapoor made the film *Bobby* in 1973.

But then you could argue she knew her worth. Look at her impact on Raj Kapoor's films.

Kapoor, post-Nargis, had first Padmini, and then another south Indian, Vyjayanthimala, as his lady in white, playing in movies that were more sexually charged than during the Nargis era. *Jis Desh Mein Ganga Behti Hai* featured Padmini as a voluptuous bandit princess, and Kapoor as the simpleton, reformist hero. This film, backed by Lata's songs, was a success, as was *Sangam* in 1964 where Raj Kapoor, again with Vyjayanthimala, now gave Indian audiences, most of whom would never leave India, a glimpse of London, Paris, Venice and Switzerland. The story was banal—two friends and the girl they grew up with. The settings were exotic but it was the songs that were arresting.

Lata was clearly realising her worth. And not having received her final payment for *Sangam*, she did not sing for *Mera Nam Joker* in 1970, where Abbas wrote what was in effect Raj Kapoor's life story through the guise of a clown. It took four hours and fifteen minutes, Raj Kapoor even bringing the entire Russian circus, and a ballerina from the Bolshoi, for the film but, despite all this, it was a disastrous failure. Whether this was solely due to the lack of Lata is hard to say but it clearly played a part. It would be too much to say that Lata made Kapoor's films but she was a very important part of them. She did return for *Bobby* in 1973, but there was again a problem for *Satyam Shivam Sundaram* in 1978. As her biographer, Raju Bharatan, said, she did turn up for the recording of the last song but did not sing it. She sat outside in her white Ambassador car while Kapoor, with folded arms, waited for her. She then drove off. "The look on Lata's visage as she thus took off was one of score-settling triumph."

There was probably more than money involved. She had been less than pleased that the idea for this film, which she had discussed with Kapoor, and which had an anthem of the body and the soul. Kapoor and she had spoken about making a film about a girl with a beautiful voice and an ugly body. The result, which featured Zeenat Aman with the concentration on her beauty and breasts, did not go down well with Lata who, says Bharatan, "did not like the body beauty theme. She expected the fusion of emotion and vision, and got fusion of vision and passion."

Whatever the reason for the differences, Lata Mangeshkar had finally determined the worth of the singer.

This explains why many in Bollywood, while acknowledging the greatness of Lata, also fear and distrust her. They contrast her with her contemporaries, like Mohammed Rafi, who are praised for their generosity and their willingness, at least on Rafi's part, to sing for producers who could not pay. Rafi and Lata fell out about royalties, with Rafi arguing that the singer should be satisfied with a one-off payment. He was also not happy when the Guinness Book of Records listed Lata as having sung the most ever songs in the world: 30,000 recordings. Rafi wrote to Guinness saying he had started earlier than her, was of better physique than the small petite Lata, and must have sung more. As it happens, when this dispute was resolved in 1989, it emerged that the real winner was neither, but Lata's sister, Asha, who by 1989, had in fact sung a mere 7,500 songs!

However, to present Lata as some hugely money-conscious figure would be to fall for an Indian trick. Raj Singh describes her life in 1959, when they first met and when, after almost nine years at the top of her profession, having topped the Binaca Geetmala charts and won the inaugural 1958 *Filmfare* best female play-back singer award, she was not rich enough to afford a proper dining table. When she entertained friends they had to eat on the floor.

> I arrived in Bombay in August, 1959. The city was awash with rain. I had by then played the Ranji Trophy making my début in 1956. I desperately wanted to play cricket. I knew Swapan Sardesai, a wicket keeper. I told him I can't survive without playing cricket. He said, 'I know the Mangeshkar family very well. Her brother has some problems with his leg and if you want to play tennis ball cricket, I will take you.' I told him. I don't care if he is Mangeshkar or Sangeshkar, I have to play cricket, any cricket, cricket with a tennis ball or a rubber ball. He took me to Lata's building at Walkeshwar, Walkeshwar House on the hill, which is dominated on the top by Raj Bhavan, where the Governor of Bombay resided. So I went and I played in the courtyard behind the building. We played cricket with a tennis ball. Her brother, Hridayanth, was nice to me. She was not at home. She had gone for a recording. She used to go for recordings from nine in the morning to nine at night, at least. I was taken up and given a cup of tea. I drank my first cup of tea. I could not say no. I ate paw paw. It was a very ordinary two-bedroomed flat. Most of them used to sleep on the floor in the drawing-room: Lata, Meena, Asha and Hryidanath and

their widowed mother. They are still together. They said 'come again tomorrow'. That was an invitation I was not going to refuse. I was dying of rain in Bombay. The next day she was there. The first time I met her. She was very nice. As I was leaving, she said, 'Aaap kaise aaye?' (How did you get here?) I said, 'By taxi.' She said, 'Take my car' and called the driver. She came right down and saw me off.

After four or five days she called me and my brother-in-law for the Sarat Purnima (coconut festival). I had dinner at her place. The dining-room was too small. Dinner was in her bedroom and we sat down on the ground. That is how I came to know her. Then I went to recordings.

All this makes Lata very much an enigma for Indians and is further underlined by her relationship with her sister. Asha could not be more different. At fourteen, she was married to a Ganpat Bhosle, and produced three children, but it proved an impossible marriage. Bhosle, realising the worth of his wife's voice, set out to exploit her. Her daughter, Varsha, has spoken of her childhood memories of a terrible father and how she "erased my father from my memory." Asha did something very daring for an Indian woman of that time—she walked out. However she did not divorce her husband and she only remarried after his death. Her second husband was Rahul Dev Burman. In the intervening years she had been involved with O.P. Nayyar, a married man, in a romance that was much talked about in Bollywood but could not lead to marriage.

The association with Nayyar had one interesting aspect. During the 1950s and 1960s, Nayyar was the only major music composer in Bollywood who never used Lata. It is possible that this was because Asha had, from the beginning, set out to be different from her sister. Lata sang the songs with greater gravitas, the more soulful songs, while Asha sang the more ebullient ones, the cabaret and mujra numbers. As Premchand puts it, "Asha became identified with the supporting actress or vamp and Lata with the goody-goody heroine."

Asha also made it clear that she never set out to imitate her sister or to be a duplicate. She had no desire to be the second choice if Lata was not available. She set out to create her own style. This began to emerge from 1957 in films like *Paying Guest, Tumsa Nahin Dekha, Howrah Bridge* and *Naya Daur,* her first playback song having been a decade earlier in 1947. It was in *Howrah Bridge,* made in 1957, that Nayyar gave her tracks with plenty of oomph in them to make her sound very distinct from Lata's. Occasionally, the two singers sang together in the same film. Both *Teesri Kasam* and *Do Badan,* with Rehman playing the leading role, had one song by Lata and also a song by Asha, and it is possible to distinguish the style of the two sisters. It proved Asha's point that she survived honourably as Asha Bhosle, not just as Lata's younger sister.

Asha has continued to be the more extrovert of the two sisters, often appearing on the many television channels now available, and counting Michael Jackson as one of her friends.

The contrasting styles of the two sisters had fed Bollywood gossip that the sisters do not get along. But they live on the same floor in a building in Bombay's prestigious Peddar Road, and Asha flatly denies any rift, "There can be none like *Didi* (the term of respect used for older sister). I love her songs, her voice, her style. See when I am ill, Didi is at my side and *vice versa*. When we meet, we don't discuss music at all but she's four years older and I give her the respect due to her. I touch her feet and sometimes even press her feet at night because she likes that."

As for rivalry about who is the greater, she had always denied the sisters had any rivalry. In sheer numbers though, Asha is ahead of her sister.

The 1980s marked the end of what may be called the golden era of the Bombay film song. The dominance Lata had exercised, and her virtual monopoly with Asha, came to an end. This decade also saw the three leading male singers either die or retire.

Mukesh, who had migrated to Bombay from Delhi, and who had been weaned away from his infatuation with Saigal by Anil Biswas, had died of a sudden heart attack in 1976 while he was touring America. By common consent of the three great male singers, what Indians call his *soor* (tune), was not quite pukka.

Four years later, Mohammed Rafi, who had an almost perfect education in music, having trained under classical Indian musicians, including Barkat Ali Khan – the younger brother of Bade Ghulam Ali Khan – developing a very manly, but still very captivating voice, like Mukesh's, died suddenly of a heart attack. Naushad recalls how the day he died it rained in Bombay but, despite this, his funeral created mass hysteria and the graveyard in Juhu was besieged by mourning crowds.

Talat Mehmood who was born in Lucknow, had studied music and, like Mukesh, considered Saigal his great god. Anil Biswas again weaned him away from Saigal, encouraging him to develop his own style, with a distinguished voice. After the failure of the film *Jahan Ara,* Madan Mohan having chosen him to sing in the film despite the producer wanting Rafi, he quit singing. Almost a decade later, in June 1990, he would tell the journalist, Meera Khurana, that he had given up singing because music had changed in Indian films. "There was a radical change in film music. Romance went out, violence came in. Melody gave in to western pop. You can't sing about grace and beauty in a discotheque. I couldn't cope with the change in the trend of music; the change was sudden, very sudden. I felt completely disoriented."

The era of the Bombay film song was ending.

Lata, however, still carries on although she is not quite as dominant now; nobody can match the power and influence she has exercised, and continues to, exercise.

Raj Singh tells the story of a recording of a song from *Mughal-e Azam,* which sums up this remarkable singer.

The song was *Raat itni matvali Subha ka Alam Khya Hoga*. I went with her to Mehboob Studios: eighty-piece orchestra, forty violins. We used to go to Naushad's place for rehearsal. He lived in Bandra.

Naushad said, 'Lataji are you ready?'

Lata: 'Can we rehearse once more?'

So he accompanied her on the harmonium.

Then he said 'I have composed the song. You put the four moons on it. I cannot put the four moons.' (What he meant was the finesse Lata put into her singing.)

Lata said, 'Are you ready?'

Naushad said 'I am ready. Come to the mike.'

She went to a cabin.

After a few seconds she stopped.

Naushad said, 'What happened?'

'Naushad Sahib, the boy with a blue shirt who is playing the violin. He is not keeping to the tune and he is making me go out of tune.'

Naushad said, 'You are not out of tune.'

Lata said, 'If I am not yet out of tune, I will be. Please stop him.'

Naushad: 'This is a bit early in the morning for you. An hour before you came, I did a rehearsal and nobody was out of tune. Don't worry about this.'

Lata said, 'Since you want me to sing, I shall sing again.'

She sang again and she stopped.

Naushad said, 'There is no problem.'

She sang again and stopped.

Lata said, 'Naushad Sahib, I am telling you it is a very easy thing. I shall go away, get someone else to do the song.'

Naushad: 'What are you saying? I have been composing this song for two years. There is neither in heaven or hell a singer like you. What are you doing?'

Lata: 'You are not accepting my word'.

Naushad: 'I shall hear the orchestra again.'

He listened to the orchestra.

He got up and put his hands on the score and said, 'It is not for nothing people call you Saraswathi?' He then called out, 'Boy leave the violin and sit down.'

There were forty violins and she could still say that one boy was out of tune.

She was very obstinate. She would have left.

14

Laughter and Tears

It is a truism to say that Bollywood has never made a true comic film. In Hollywood, the genre is well-established and the list of comedy films runs into several pages. But, even in Subhas K. Jha's *The Essential Guide to Bollywood*, which has a foreword by Amitabh Bachchan, and which makes a determined attempt to list Bollywood movies by genre from 1950 onwards, the section on comedy is one of the thinnest, with just seventeen films in fifty years, eight of which date from 1980. Many may question whether the films listed are real comedies, in the sense of a film having a comic denouement, such as in *Gentlemen Prefer Blondes*, rather than ones with more comic situations than most other Hindi films. The fact is, Bollywood does not do full-length comedy films but all its movies have some comic sequences, even the most tragic ones.

Benegal has argued that one reason for this was due to the fact that Hindi cinema had to create a film that would cater to all the language groups right across the country:

> Take American comedy: that is essentially New York comedy, which is very Yiddish comedy. It came because of the Ashkenazy Jews who had come from Eastern Europe. This comedy of the Jewish people eventually became the American national comedy. You got that sort of thing in regional cinemas in India. There are characters in Ray's films, such as *Middle Man,* or the Bengali actor, Bhanu Bannerjee, who are great comic characters; there are no characters like that in Hindi movies. In that sense, regional cinema like Bengal cinema, had greater depth. Their comic actions were central to the story. The comedy would emerge from the setting of the story. That could only happen in the regional cinema. There is a certain cultural specificity to comedy which Hindi cinema could not bring out. With Hindi cinema you have to appeal to a pan-national audience. And if you are going to a pan-national audience then you cannot have cultural specificity of any kind. As Hindi cinema developed in the absence of cultural specificity, the films had to create a never-never land.

In this never-never land, comedy played a curious part. Every Hindi film, of whatever type, had to have a comic role for an actor who did nothing but essentially 'bit' comic roles. This may explain why nearly all the great comedians of Bollywood had very foreign-sounding names, one of the best-loved named after the Johnny Walker brand of Scotch. A large proportion of them were also Muslims, although this may have been just a coincidence.

It has been argued that having a small comic role in every film was in keeping with Indian tradition. Bharata, in his *Natyashastra*, the foundational treatise on Indian dance, drama and poetry, written in the golden age of Hindus around AD 500, specified that *hasya* (laughter) was one of the eight rasas. A *vidushak* (comedian) was always part of the Indian stage. But ancient Sanskrit drama never had a full-blown comedy, just as it never had Greek-style tragedy. So it has been with Bollywood films.

Sanjit Narwekar, in *Eeena Meena Deeka, The Story of the Hindi Film Comedy*, has summarised it rather well:

> …because comedy is often one of the many elements of a Hindi film, the concentration has always been on the gag-related comedy in which a kind of visual (and often verbal ad-libbing) routine developed between the hero and his comic sidekick (all through the 1950s and 1960s) or two comedians who are woven in the story for comic relief, and generally have a separate track unrelated to the main story (often a pair of servants). Much of Hindi screen comedy—from Noor Mohammed Charlie to Johnny Walker to Johnny Lever—is based on the development of the cinematic gags which are actually very short stories within the framework of the main story, usually with some dramatic climax—the "punch-line." It is the performance of the gag that often makes it funny, rather than the story itself.

The comic situation in Bollywood can depend on mistaken identity or in a character telling a lie, which leads to all sorts of situations or comedies based on fads and foibles of the middle-class. But, as Narwekar says, "There are very few examples of comedies of characters in Hindi cinema, primarily because most Hindi films use comedians as stereotypes rather than etching special characters for them." Bollywood has not been helped by the fact that while Indians, contrary to their perceived image, have a sense of humour, and can laugh at themselves, when it comes to film, as in writing, they like serious work. For a person to be considered a good actor, he had to be serious; to prove his sincerity. Comedy is regarded as frivolous and those who wanted to be taken as serious actors could not dabble in it.

Bollywood audiences liked to see the same stock characters play comic roles in films, just as they found it hard to accept that an actor like Pran, who early in the 1950s had established himself as a villain, could play anything other than a villain. Bollywood greats did occasionally play comic roles, but this was a rarity.

So much so that, when in 1967 Dilip Kumar played his one and only comic role in *Ram Aur Shyam,* it created a sensation.

Dilip Kumar was then going through a mid-life change. In the previous decade, he had tried to get away from being typecast as the tragic lover. This had so got him down that he had consulted two psychiatrists in London, one of them D.W.S.D. Nicol, who also counted George VI and Anthony Eden as his patients. There had been further psychoanalysis in Bombay with Dr Ramanlal Patel. All this had made him take on different roles, and the year before he made his comic movie, he finally married the actress Saira Banu, who was almost twenty years his junior.

The film was a remake of a remake. A Tamil film, *Enga Veetu Pillai,* had been based on *The Prince and the Pauper. Ram aur Shyam* was the Hindi version of the Tamil film made, appropriately, by the south Indian producer, Nagi Reddy. Dilip Kumar played a double role: Ram, the serious character, and his long-lost twin, Shyam, the buffoon, with a lot of the action in the movie in the great tradition of slapstick revolving round mistaken identity. The film proved to be one of the biggest hits of Bollywood and Kumar's role has been the model for other Bollywood films, such as *Seeta aur Geeta, Chalbaaz* and *Kishen Kanhaiya.*

Interestingly, in Hollywood's slim selection of comedies Kumar's wife, Saira Banu, was to feature in a film released the following year, *Padosan,* which many consider the funniest Bollywood movie of the last fifty years.

A decade after *Ram aur Shyam,* Sanjeev Kumar, another serious actor, who will always be famous for playing the angry police chief seeking revenge on gangsters in *Sholay,* played a married man with a roving eye in convincing comic style in *Pati Patni Aur Wo.*

But these are exceptions. In Bollywood, actors who want to be taken seriously, just do not do comedy. Dhirendranath Ganguly's *Bilet Pherat,* as we have seen, was an early Indian comedy and after that several actors emerged who took to comedy, but they remained bit players. None of them was taken seriously as an actor.

In the heyday of Ranjit Studios, there were several comedians who were compared to Hollywood's classics. There was even an Indian Laurel and Hardy. The fat Manohar Janadhan Dikshit—his film name was Dixit – who, weighing 220lbs, modelled himself on Hardy, and the slim Nazir Mohammed Ghory, who was the Indian Laurel. They acted until 1947, when Ghory left for Pakistan. Two years later Dixit died of a heart attack.

In many ways, the most engaging pre-independence comic actor was V.H. Desai, a law graduate, whose first love was acting. Desai had a wonderful, natural comic touch; his problem was he could never remember his lines. Manto, who devoted an entire chapter to him, calling him God's clown, has a hilarious description of the shooting of *Eight Days,* a film that Ashok Kumar was producing. It required Desai to say to the heroine, "Neela Devi, you don't have a thing to worry about. I have also drunk the water of Peshawar." But Desai, unable to remember the lines, would say "Neela Devi, you don't have a thing to worry about. I have also drunk the urine of Peshawar." In Urdu, the word for urine, *peeshap,* is quite close to Peshawar and Desai, a nervous actor, got them confused. In the endless retakes he made other mistakes, once saying, "Neela Devi, you do not have a thing to Peshwar about. I have also drunk your water," causing the actress playing Neela Devi to collapse with laugher. Either in this, or another film, Desai's record for a single shot was seventy-five takes. Manto, who saw him make four films, says he wasted thousands of feet of film.

But directors knew he could make audiences laugh and, as Franz Osten told him, "Mr Desai, the problem is that the audience likes you. The moment you appear on the screen, they start laughing. Had that not been the case I would have lifted you myself and chucked you out today."

His last role was in the film, *Andaz,* where Mehboob cast him as Professor Devdas Dharamdas Trivedi, alias DDT, then a popular pesticide in India, who spoke at breakneck speed. The year after the film was released, Desai was dead of a heart attack.

If Raj Kapoor saw Charlie Chalpin as his mentor there was, through the 1930s and 1940s, a comic actor who was actually known as Charlie. Noor Mohammed Charlie got his nickname, Charlie, after he starred in a 1929 film, *The Indian Charlie* which, for some curious reason, was not released until 1933. After that he made between five and seven films a year. In 1943, he played Nargis's father in her first film, *Taqdeer,* where Nargis had to visit her screen father in jail. The scene was not meant to be funny, but serious and tense, however Charlie was so funny that Nargis was reduced to helpless laughter. A furious Mehboob scolded her and Nargis then burst into tears and, as she later recalled, "Mehboob, having got the mood he wanted, quickly shot the scene."

Charlie went on to direct his own movie *Dhandhora*, and there followed other movies but in 1947 he migrated to Pakistan ending a remarkable comic career. But as Narwekar says, "Charlie has left long shadows on the Indian film scene. Every comedian, beginning with Johnny Walker, has been in some way or other influenced by him."

Johnny Walker, in many ways, was the classic comedian of Bollywood who for over a decade until the mid-1960s defined comic acting in Bollywood. But what makes Johnny Walker unique is that he did his best work for the man who was, and remains, the very epitome of the tragic movie-maker, whose movies were about sadness, decline and sorrow. The Guru Dutt-Johnny Walker coupling in Bollywood is one of the more remarkable episodes of Indian cinema, where the man of tragedy inspired the comic actor to produce some of his best comic moments. It is a pairing that could only have happened in Bollywood.

Like the best of stories, it happened quite by chance. Badruddin Jamaluddin Qazi, for that was his real name, was doing his usual clowning on a Bombay bus. Born in Indore in 1924, he had moved with his family to Bombay, when the textile mill his father worked for closed. Life was hard, five of his siblings died and Qazi did various jobs, including selling vegetables, ice-cream and then, finally, worked on the buses. His hero was Noor Mohammed 'Charlie' and he desperately wanted to act in films but was aware that his intensely-religious family would not stand for it.

Then came the moment on the bus when, unknown to him, one of the passengers was Balraj Sahni, an actor of acute sensitivity and also a script-writer. He had been scripting a film for Guru Dutt called *Baazi* and, on seeing Qazi's uncanny ability to hold the attention of his passengers with improvised speeches, he decided to take a bet. It is said that Sahni instructed him to barge into offices of Navketan, the production company set up by Dev Anan and his older brother Chetan Anand, where Guru Dutt, Dev Anand and Chetan Anand were working. His routine as a drunkard impressed everyone especially when, after the performance, he was back to his sober self. So, despite the fact that *Baazi* was nearly complete and Guru Dutt did not want another character, a role was developed for him in the film.

His impersonation of the drunk also gave him his nickname, Johnny Walker being a very valuable and much sought-after Scotch in Bombay. This despite the fact that by 1951 Bombay was in the grip of total prohibition and drinking was only allowed either at home or in special permit rooms. In any case, as a Muslim, Qazi would not drink. Qazi had, in fact, acted in a few films before then, as many as twenty according to one count, but it was *Baazi,* and as Johnny Walker, that he achieved fame, developing a characteristic style as the hero's comic side-kick. He made the most of his pencil-thin moustache, facial grimaces and nasal drawl and soon built up a fan base where audiences were drawn to any movie with him in to listen to his squeaky voice and the faces he pulled—his smile reached his ears when happy, and mouth drooped low when he sulked.

Although, like Qazi, an immigrant to Bombay, Guru Dutt's career had followed a very different path. A year younger than Qazi (he was born on July 9, 1925), Guru Dutt had travelled up and down India as a child, accompanying his mother, Vasanthi Padukone: from Bangalore to Calcutta, from there to Mangalore, and then to Ahmedabad and finally back to Calcutta. These journeys were necessary due to her unhappy marriage to a husband who constantly changed jobs. Shivshankar Padukone went from being a headmaster in a village school near Mangalore, to a bank official in Banglore, then manager of a printing press in Mangalore and, finally, an administrative clerk at the Burmah Shell Company in Calcutta, where he stayed for almost thirty years. Calcutta exposed Guru Dutt to Bengali jatras—rural theatres—and he would be glued to performances held in the open space next to their house in Bhowanipur. Then, on coming home he would act out what he had seen. B.B. Benegal, an uncle who, as commercial artist, designed and painted cinema hoardings, was also a great influence. Young

Guru had a talent for dance and composed a snake-dance round a theme from one of Benegal's paintings. But the family's finances meant there were few opportunities to exploit his art. When he had just turned sixteen and passed his matriculation, he had to give up studies and work as a telephone operator in a factory for Rs. 40 a month. Hearing that Uday Shankar was in town, he gave an audition of the snake-dance and impressed the maestro but could not afford to go to Almora, where Uday Shankar had set up an academy. It was Benegal who intervened to make it possible. As part of the Uday Shankar academy, Guru Dutt toured India, visiting Hyderabad, where a young Shyam Benegal watched his cousin perform. However, as foreign funds dried up during the Second World War, Uday Shankar had to close the academy and Dutt joined his family in Bombay. It was here, in 1944, again with the help of Benegal, that Dutt was given an introduction to Prabhat where, as we have seen, he met Dev Anand and the two made a pact about the future.

Soon after he was back in Bombay, where he found it difficult to eke out a living as a writer with his short stories being rejected by *The Illustrated Weekly of India*, then the leading Indian magazine. He did, however, write a script called *Kashmakash*, which he put in a drawer, hoping to make something of it in the future.

Although Dutt did work as an assistant director to Amiya Chakravarty and, later, Gyan Mukherjee, he was so frustrated that he thought of opening a bookshop when Dev Anand kept his end of the bargain. He had set up Navketan and asked Guru Dutt to direct Navketan's second production, *Baazi*. The success of the film established Guru Dutt as a director. He could now even think of luxuries and immediately bought a ceiling-fan for the family home in Matunga, this being June when the heat in Bombay is awful.

Like other film-makers, the movie also established what became known as the Guru Dutt team: lyricist Sahir Ludhianvi, music director Sachin Dev Burman and camera assistant V.K. Murthy, who worked as a cameraman on all his films. Some of these films are still seen as providing lessons to modern Indian film-makers and Murthy is considered to be one of the greatest cinematographers in the history of Bollywood. During the making of this film, Guru Dutt met singer Geeta Roy. They married in 1953 and she herself had a distinguished career as a singer in many of her husband's films.

Nasreen Munni Kabir, whose biography on Guru Dutt brought many facts about him into the public domain including his relationship with Johnny Walker, has Walker recalling how he interacted with Dutt:

> He used to tell me—Here's your scene, your dialogue. If you can do better, go ahead. In every rehearsal I would come up with something new. Guru Dutt used to love that. He used to look at everyone on the sets and see if the light boys, the cameraman, the assistants were laughing at my dialogues. Guru Dutt then had an assistant write down whatever I said in the rehearsals. That's how we worked.

Johnny Walker was now a regular of Guru Dutt films. He was in the 1952 film, *Jaal*, where Dev Anand was the male lead, and Geeta Bali shone as the leading lady.

Guru Dutt was acclaimed for the way he picturised the songs and his outdoor locations. This was one of his many contributions to film making in Bollywood. Like all Bollywood movie-makers, Guru Dutt knew there could be no movie without songs. But Hindi movies were not like Western musicals—the songs could introduce a totally unreal element to the unfolding of the narrative. And, because Bollywood needed songs, the art of movie making had not developed beyond this. Guru Dutt changed the very concept of how songs were filmed. The song became, not something detached, but very much a part of the film and its narrative. It was not a sort of commercial break but actually took the story forward. In most other films audiences could get up and wander out during a song. They would miss the lush scenery and some wonderful music but the story line would remain the same. Not with Guru Dutt's films. So the song sung by Kalu, the taxi driver in *Aar Paar*, is set in a garage, Rustam the masseur in *Pyaasa*, probably his greatest film, solicits customers in plain, realistic dialogue rather than flowery language. The song matched the settings and the mood of the film.

In his early years, Dutt made crime thrillers but, after the failure of *Baaz,* a costume drama set on the high seas, which was panned by critics and hated by the masses, he decided to make different kinds of movies. He also decided to give Johnny Walker a song—it was unusual for a comedian to have one, although Johnny Walker's hero, Charlie, did have songs picturised on him. It worked very well in *Aar Paar*, which was made in 1954. Rafi sang for Johnny Walker, with Rafi changing his singing voice to try and fit the comic personality Johnny Walker was portraying. This worked so well that many got the impression that it was Johnny Walker who was really singing.

This was vividly demonstrated in *Mrs and Mrs 55* where, in one scene, Johnny Walker had to compliment Guru Dutt while he rendered a song. Narwekar says, "He does such a perfect mime job that the song seems incomplete without his presence." This film is the nearest Guru Dutt came to making a comedy. With a new dialogue writer in Abrar Alvi, the film had an engaging repartee which was genuinely witty and introduced a new idiom for dialogue in Hindi films. It also broke away from the stylised, almost theatrical, dialogue many a Hindi film had favoured. Dutt had made this film and the previous one with his own production company. Many of the themes of the Dutt films first emerged here: technical virtuosity in elegant camera movements, the play of light and shadows, creative use of close-ups and tracking shots and Dutt's poetic style. By now, of course, Johnny Walker and Dutt were not just colleagues but firm friends who would often going fishing together or even on hunting expeditions.

Johnny Walker was also in huge demand and, in 1955, he had twelve other films released. Until the end of the decade, he averaged around ten films a year, and worked in other films besides those with Guru Dutt—with B.R. Chopra in *Naya Daur* in 1957, and with Bimal Roy, *Madhumati,* in 1958. It had also become mandatory to have a song for him which often would be the highlight of the film. (*Main Bombay ka Babu,* in the former, and *Jungle Mein Mor Naacha,* in the latter, are remembered and hummed even today). Besides these, he starred in a series of films as a comic hero, often opposite Shyama: *Chhoomantar* in 1956, and *Shrimati 420*, also the same year and then, in 1957, *Johnny Walker* and in 1958, *Mr. Qartoon, MA*.

The next two Guru Dutt films, *Pyaasa* in 1957, and *Kaagaz Ke Phool* in 1959, made Guru Dutt a legend of Bollywood, making his reputation as master film-maker in all aspects: script, performance, music, and cinematography. They represent the best of Bollywood and have acquired a cult status. They are now seen as films that, through camera work never before seen in Bollywood, liberated Hindi cinema from its theatrical moorings. They showed how far Dutt had come from *Baazi* and his growing mastery of the medium.

His two greatest films were autobiographical notes: *Pyaasa*, based on the story he had written a decade ago, is of a rejected and scorned poet who becomes a cult figure and is mistakenly believed to have died in an accident. *Kaagaz Ke Phool* is about a film-maker who dies a lonely and forgotten man.

Pyaasa also saw him introduce a new actress who defined a woman with a very different background coming into movies. She, also, had a devastating effect on his personal life. Until the 1940s, no woman from a respectable family would act, Durga Khote and Devika Rani being the exceptions. From the late 1940s, daughters of actresses of previous generations, who had been well-educated, like Nargis, broke through. Now there was Waheeda Rehman, born into a traditional Muslim family in Hyderabad, and trained in Bharatnatyam. She would later tell a journalist how, by the time she came, girls from respectable families were entering films. "I was lucky to have been given the opportunity to build up an image of dignity." She did it so well that she is now seen as the embodiment of classic Muslim beauty, with a truly transcendental appeal.

She had been acting in films for a year, albeit Telugu films: *Jaisimha* in 1955, followed by *Rojulu Marayi,* the same year, and was a huge, regional success when Guru Dutt spotted her and brought her to Bombay. He cast her as the vamp in his 1956 film, *C.I.D,.* directed by his protégé, Raj Khosla. The song, *Kahin Pe Nigahein Kahin Pe Nishana,* as she tries to seduce the villain and allow the hero to escape, reveals her extraordinary facial mobility and dancer's grace. But it was in *Pyaasa,* playing the proverbial prostitute with the heart of gold, that she made her mark as an actress of note. Nadira, in an interview with *Cine Blitz* (December 2005), rubbished the idea that Waheda Rehman could act, "Please, what's the matter with you? She is just very lucky with the kind of films that came to her. There's a lot of difference between being a good actress and being plain lucky." But Nadira was just about to die and she was being bitchy about almost all her contemporaries. Nargis was dismissed as "a big bully" and Meena Kumari as a woman who was always threatening to die but didn't have the guts to do so and, also, an actress who "was a big cheat as far as acting was concerned. She knew which angle of her face suited the camera best, how much glycerine she would need for a shot." Nadira called Meena Kumari "*Chor number 11*" (thief number 11).

The more acceptable view of Rehman was that she blended nuances of love, desire and despair in a film which Dutt and his assistants had planned with meticulous attention to detail. Rehman's role as prostitute had been conceived when, one night in Bombay, Abrar Alvi (Dutt's scriptwriter) and a friend had visited the city's red light district. "I got talking to a girl who called herself Gulabo and I managed to get her pathetic story out of her. As I left, she thanked me in broken voice saying it was the first time that she had been treated with respect, in a place where she heard only abuses and gaalis (swear words). I used her exact words in the film."

There is a dramatic scene in the movie where Waheeda follows Guru Dutt up the stairs to the terrace to the strains of *Aaj Sajan Mohe Ang Laga Lo*. By now she had also got involved with Guru Dutt. And it was ironic that his wife Geeta Dutt's voice was used on Waheeda Rehman, the actress, as she 'sang' sweet nothings to Guru Dutt.

Unfortunately for Guru Dutt, *Kaagaz Ke Phool,* for all its artistic success, was a box office disaster. He decided he would no longer direct. As a director he did not have the self-confidence of Mehboob or Asif—he would keep asking his assistant to tell him where he had gone wrong with a shot. Now he gave the directorial credit to Alvi while he acted in the lead role for his 1964 film, *Sahib Bibi Aur Ghulam,* based on Bimal Mitra's novel and revolving round the lonely daughter-in-law of a nineteenth century feudal family, played by Meena Kumari. It is still seen as a Bollywood benchmark of brilliant scripting and hypnotic cinematography.

But it could not bring him out of the conviction he had formed since the failure of *Kaagaz Ke Phool:* that Bollywood had no place for him. It did not help that his personal life was disintegrating. His marriage had broken up, he had got involved with Waheeda Rehman, and her success in films other than his own, tore them apart personally, and professionally. Waheeda Rehman completed *Sahib Bibi Aur Ghulam* under some strain. Guru Dutt, in trying to cope with an unhappy and tense domestic situation, started drinking and smoking heavily. During the final days of the shooting of *Sahib Bibi Aur Ghulam* he had become increasingly depressed. He took an overdose of sleeping pills and slipped into a coma. It did not help that, despite the rave reviews it got in India, where it won the President's Silver Medal, the film had a very indifferent reception at the Berlin Film Festival in 1963. Waheeda and he broke up after that. Guru Dutt could never really get over her and on October 10 1964, he killed himself.

1964 also marked the moment when Johnny Walker's film career took a dive from which it never recovered. In 1965, he even had to contend with a man called Johnny Whiskey paying comic roles. Johnny Walker continued working regularly right up to the late 1970s, and sporadically into the 1980s, with a small cameo in the Kamal Hassan's, *Chachi 420*. This was Bollywood's remake of *Mrs Doubtfire* and displayed the new comedians such as Paresh Rawal, a comedian of a very different kind. But of Johnny Walker's later work, perhaps his only memorable role was in Hrishikesh Mukherjee's, *Anand* in 1970.

Johnny Walker would explain his decline in terms of morality saying, "It is very easy to make people laugh by using vulgarity and double-meaning dialogue. But that is not genuine comedy; that is not the comedy you can enjoy with your entire family."

Was this, perhaps, a dig at the comedian who took over from Johnny Walker in the mid 1960s earning the title the King of Comedy: Mehmood? Certainly in his heyday, Mehmood made films which were considered by critics to be in bad taste, with vulgar jokes, and Narwekar refers to films like *Do Phool,* made in 1973, and *Kunwara Baap* in 1974, as examples, with the latter film having a eunuch song which was felt to be in rather bad taste.

Yet, ironically, it was Johnny Walker and Guru Dutt who gave Mehmood his start in film and launched him on the high road that would make him a comedy king.

Unlike Walker or Guru Dutt, Mehmood was not an outsider. He was born into films and came from the milieu of the Bombay film world. He was the son of actor/dancer Mumtaz Ali and later married the sister of Meena Kumari. Although born in Byculla, in central Bombay in 1932, his interest in films was aroused when his father moved to Malad, near Bombay Talkies.

He would often go the studio, entertaining actors and actresses with his ability to mime. In 1943, he played the young Ashok Kumar in *Kismet* but had little interest in acting as a career and, as a young man, did various jobs, selling poultry products, teaching table-tennis to Meena Kumari and being a chauffeur for, among others, director P.L. Santoshi. When Santoshi's son, Rajkumar, made his own comedy, *Andaz Apna Apna*, he wrote in a special part for Mehmood, not as a chauffeur but as a producer of sleazy films.

Mehmood had small parts in various films, including Roy's *Do Bigha Zameen* but his first major role came thanks to Johnny Walker who introduced him to Guru Dutt and he got the part of a murderer in *C.I.D.* In *Pyaasa,* he played one of Dutt's screen brothers.

Mehmood's first big moment came in the 1958 film, *Parvarish,* playing the brother of the hero Raj Kapoor during the filming for which Raj Kapoor was supposed to have given him a hard time. He got his revenge twenty years later in 1971 when Randhir Kapoor made the Kapoor's three-generation family saga, *Kal, Aaj aur Kal*, with Prithvi, Raj and Randhir Kapoor. Mehmood produced a spoof film called *Humjoli,* where he played grandfather, father and son and, as he said later, "I copied Papaji's [Prithviraj's] heavy baritone, Raj Kapoor's voice and his stiff hand and Dabbo's [Randhir's nickname] vigorous shaking of the head." The Mehmood film proved a great success, while the Kapoor one failed.

Mehmood's great gift had always been his ability as a mimic. As a child he did so well that stars like Premanth and Nutan would summon him to entertain them. And he remembered mannerisms. So, as a young man having watched Tolaram Jalan of Filmistan and his style of talking, his habit of saying, "The whole thing is that," he used it with great effect in the film, *Sabse Bada Rupiya.*

Mehmood not only copied others' mannerisms, he also copied from other films. Many of his best, most vivid comedy movements were actually taken from Tamil films featuring the comedian Nagesh. Three of Mehmood's most successful films, *Pyar Kiye Jaa, Main Sundar Hoon* and *Bombay to Goa,* were based on Nagesh's Tamil hits with *Bombay to Goa* having been called *Madras to Pondicherry* in the Tamil version. Both films were based on the idea of a bus journey from a part of India formerly controlled by the British to a part formerly under another European power, Pondicherry having been French, and Goa Portuguese. *Bombay to Goa,* as we shall see, also served as a Bollywood footnote in the role it played in the career of one of Bollywood's greatest actors.

Parvraish gave Mehmood his first good notices and three years later came the first film which stamped him as the great comedian of Bollywood. This was *Sasural.* Both *Paravarish* and *Sasural* were films that were full of tears and anguish but Bollywood audiences also liked laughter to cope with the tears and Mehmood provided buckets full. *Sasural,* which means in-laws, also paired him with actress Shuba Khote. Their zany combination was so successful that they went on to become a "comedy pair" in many hit films thereafter—hits like *Love in Tokyo* and *Ziddi.* Later, Aruna Irani replaced Khote in the comedy team. Unlike Khote Irani had ambitions to be a leading lady, not just a comic actress , so she let Mehmood set the pace.

Mehmood also teamed up with another comedian, I.S. Johar, who was much more than a comedian. He wrote and directed as well and was one of the few Bollywood actors who played in Hollywood movies including *Lawrence of Arabia* and *Death on the Nile.* He was, says Narweker, at his best "delivering dry sardonic dialogue tinged with cynicism and accompanied by a raised eyebrow." He had come into comedy quite by accident. In the 1949 film, *Ek Thi Ladkhi,* as he performed a walk-on role, which was to chase the heroine's boat, he shot so far ahead of the boat that the director and the cameraman fell about laughing and decided he was a natural comedian. The man who had financed the film could not stop laughing as well when he saw the rushes.

They teamed up in what was advertised as "India's first feature-length comedy"—*Namasteji.* This was followed by movies incorporating their names in the film's titles—*Johar Mehmood in Goa,* where Johar played the cynic and Mehmood, the musical humorist, and was followed by *Johar Mehmood in Hong*

Kong. There was also *Gumnam,* which was based on Agatha Christie's *Ten Little Niggers.* This was a great success but not so the Hong Kong versions of their Johar Mehmood film.

By the late 1960s, Mehmood had far surpassed Johnnny Walker and, in an industry where success was judged by money, he was said to be paid more highly than some of the lesser heroes of Bollywood. This bred resentment and insecurity in Bollywood acting circles and Mehmood's comedy began to come undone. He was accused by many of downgrading the quality of comedy in Hindi films, in particular when he tried to play comic south Indian characters.

India, like all countries, makes jokes of certain of their countrymen. The Americans have "Polak" jokes about people with Polish origins, the English joke about the Irish, the Irish have "Kerry" man jokes. In India the jokes are about Sardars, as the Sikhs are called. But this had rarely translated into movies, Bollywood being aware it had to appeal across many divides. But Mehmood started making jokes about south Indians, including the "lungi uthake" jokes. This referred to the lungi, the cloth that the south Indians wear to cover their bottoms and which he would lift in a provocative fashion. In Bombay then the south Indian run Udipi restaurants serving south Indian food—the Indian version of fast food, McDonalds having not yet come to the country—were much in the spotlight. This was the time when a Bombay cartoonist called Bal Thackeray was forming a political party aimed at expelling the south Indian migrants from the city. His party would grow more vicious and fascist and end up targeting Muslims, Mehmood's own community, but that came much later.

Long before that Mehmood, partly as a result of the criticism, decided to concentrate on his own production house, which he had started in the early 1960s, his first production being *Chhote Nawab* in 1961. This had been followed by a suspense–comedy–thriller called *Bhoot Bangla*, in which Mehmood had taken the director's chair for the first time. His company's major success was *Padosan* which reunited Mehmood with Kishore Kumar.

Back in his Bombay talkies' days Mehmood had not only got to know Ashok Kumar but also his brother Kishore and the story goes that, with Kishore riding high, Mehmood approached him for a role in one of his movies. Kishore Kumar, knowing Mehmood's excellent sense of comedy, made a remark that became famous in Bollywood legend, "How can I give a chance to someone who will compete with me?" To this, Mehmood is supposed to have good-humouredly replied, "One day I will become a big film-maker and I will cast you in a role in my film!"

Padosan was the result and many consider it to be Bollywood's most enduring comedy film and Kishore Kumar Bollywood's lost comic genius.

As Benegal says, "He was not a bit player. The others could be used as bit players. He was the central character. He was a comic hero. He was one of the few comic heroes we created at that time, the nearest we have had to a Walter Mathau or Jack Lemmon."

Kishore Kumar elevated the comedian from being a side kick in the movies to a major star but could not convert Bollywood comedy into Hollywood – style comedy. He might have done so if he had not been so reluctant a comedian. In some ways the tragedy for Bollywood was that Kishore Kumar could act, sing, compose, direct and acting was the least of his ambitions. He had always wanted to be a singer with Saigal being his hero although he also used to imitate Ashok or "Dadamoni," as he called his older brother.

Ashok Kumar recalls that as a child Kishore Kumar had an awful voice, "As a child his voice was very shrill. His speech too, was not clear as he was often down with coughs and colds. But he was very fond of singing. It was more like screeching than singing." Ashok Kumar had given him a harmonium but when he sang his family dreaded it as it sounded like a bamboo being split, it made such a grating noise. But then around ten he had an accident when playing the fool in the kitchen (he remained a practical joker all his life). One of his toes was badly cut. With limited medical facilities available and no pain killers the child was in such agony, says Ashok, that he cried for twenty hours a day for almost a month. "Gradually the wound healed up. But one month's practice of crying suddenly cleared his voice and it became melodious."

Kishore Kumar was just eighteen when he came to Bombay to join Ashok Kumar. His older brother had no intention of encouraging him to become a singer. Instead he wanted him to become an actor and, after a few early films such as *Shikari* and *Shehnai* which went unnoticed, he made his mark with *Ziddi* which made Dev Anand's reputation. Ashok pushed him into the film when the actor due to play the gardener did not turn up, although Kishore was so frightened that he ran away and was only found two hours later. He also sang a song in the film *Marne ki Duayen Kyon Mangu* for Dev Anand, in the style of his great hero Saigal. And like his hero Kishore Kumar both acted and sang, although from the beginning he made it clear that he wanted to sing.

In both acting and singing Kishore was very different from his brother Ashok. While Ashok had no acting education but had been trained in classical singing, and had tried to learn from the acting of Hollywood stars, for Kishore, acting was instinctive. But he would amaze people by how easily he could convey both emotions and provoke laughter.

Ashok Kumar had been impressed with his brother's natural acting style and so had Phani Majumdar, the veteran director. He said, "I have heard some people not appreciating Kishore's gesticulations in acting. But I must say only he can manage whatever he does. No one else can get anywhere close to his acting style. Along with comedy he can play serious roles with great ease." H.S. Rawail, who directed him in his earlier films, said, "He was a comic par excellence. The best we have had. He had that musicality bred in his very marrow. So he could dance, he had that fantastic flair of gesture."

After a decade in which he acted in different films and was the voice of Dev Anand in many of his movies, he stamped himself as Bollywood's greatest comic talent in two films—*Bhagambhag* where he, and another comedian, Bhagwan, try and find an expensive coat, a search which leads to two women and all sorts of escapades. Two years later came *Chalti Ka Naam Gaadi* which is considered one of the best Bollywood comedies where all three Kumar brothers Ashok, Kishore and Anup feature along with Madhubala, whom Kishore eventually married. In the film the brothers run a garage, Madhubala has a car that needs to be repaired, the character Kishore plays falls in love with her and the comedy is about Kishore trying to meet Madhubala despite his brother, played by Ashok, who is a misogynist. However, in the nature of Bollywood comedy, it ended on a serious note but was appreciated for its many zany situations and rousing songs by Kishore Kumar.

Kishore, the actor, never stopped playing the fool on or off the set. Once he was required to drive along a certain path in and out of shot. He did so by driving right out of the studio and for another 30 miles. He then rang and said he had reached the outskirts of the city, just where the city ends and the road to the 'ghats,' (mountains) begins. When the director protested he said "You explained the shot but did not say at what spot I should stop."

This was Kishore Kumar's way of getting back at directors who he hated, "Directors are like school teachers. Do this. Do that. Do not do that. I dreaded them."

But much as he hated them, he has left us with a riveting picture of what it was like to be an actor in the Bollywood of the 1950s and 1960s. "There were so many films I was doing in those days that I had to run from one set to another, changing on the way. Imagine, me—my shirt falling off, my trousers falling off. Very often I would mix up my lines and look angry in a romantic scene or lovey dovey in the midst of a fierce battle. It was terrible and I hated it."

For Kishore Kumar acting was keeping him away from his only love—singing. "I only wanted to sing. But I was conned into acting. I tried virtually every trick possible to get out of it—I muffed my lines, pretended to be crazy, shaved my head off, played difficult, began yodelling in the midst of tragic scenes, told Meena Kumari what I was a supposed to tell Bina Rai in some other film—but they would not let me go."

However, in one film he did prove impossible and his extraordinary behaviour gave the chance to a man who would became the great big star of Bollywood of the early 1970s.

In 1970, Hrishikesh Mukherjee had chosen Kishore Kumar to pay the lead in his film *Anand*. The film was about a dying cancer patient. Kishore Kumar did not like the part but Mukherjee finally got him to accept and all the important dates were agreed. On the first day of the shooting Kishore Kumar turned up but one look at him and Mukherjee knew it would not do. He had shaved his hair off. Mukherjee then decided to offer the part to Rajesh Khanna, who the previous year had made the film *Aradhana* and was an up and coming actor. He walked away with the *Filmfare* award for best actor and for a few years became the biggest star Bollywood had ever known.

Kishore Kumar did not mind. For the next decade and a half Kishore Kumar sang some of his best songs for Rajesh Khanna and they formed a very successful partnership.

His advantage as singer was that he could picture how the song he was singing would look on the screen. Though, he was formally untrained, he assimilated various musical notes into a rhythmic sequence and once a beat was established, could depart from the established pattern and combine notes and words into new kinds of musical harmony.

And because he could both act and sing this gave him an edge over his contemporaries. So when he came to act, the ability to sing and dance that he could often bring to his acting style fazed his fellow actors. This was most evident in *Padosan* released in 1968, where he plays a music teacher who helps a naive young man get a musically inclined girl. The problem is the young man is tone deaf and the comedy centres round this. Kishore Kumar's part was not the lead but Mehmood and Sunil Dutt, who had bigger parts, were so worried by how well Kishore was acting that during the making of the film they rewrote their parts to make sure they were not completely obscured. Nevertheless, when the movie was released it was Kishore Kumar who stole the limelight.

That year, however, marked the end of his acting career and this was largely due to his chaotic personal life. If Kishore Kumar was the nearly great man of Bollywood on the screen, he was a disaster in his personal life. He had four wives. He divorced his first. He buried his second wife, the beautiful Madhubala. The marriage proved extremely difficult and saw Madhubala, still pining for Dilip, considerably distraught before she died. Kishore followed this with marriage to another actress, Yogita Bali, which lasted just about a month (because, it is said, he would not let her share his bathroom) and then married his fourth wife, Leena Chandavarkar, who was two years older than his son, Amit.

All this may be seen as part of his eccentricities. He put up a board outside his house saying 'THIS IS A LUNATIC ASYLUM'. He reportedly spoke to his trees in his backyard addressing each by a special name. It was not unknown for him to pretend he was not in, even telling visitors in a made up voice that he was not in while he was hiding behind the sofa, he did this even when Ashok Kumar came calling.

Kishore Kumar always had problems with money and the tax department. In the 1960s, his tax problems had forced him do B-films.

When the then journalist, now film producer, Pritish Nandy visited him he found some piles of badly kept files. Their conversation went as follows:

Nandy: What are those files?

KK: My income-tax records.

Nandy: Rat-eaten?

KK: We use them as pesticides. They are very effective. The rats die quite easily after biting into them.

Nandy: What do you show the tax people when they ask for the papers?

KK: The dead rats.

Nandy: I see.

KK: You like rats?

Nandy: Not particularly.

KK: Lots of people like them in other parts of the world.

Nandy: I guess so.

KK: Haute cuisine. Expensive too. Costs a lot of money.

Nandy: Yes?

KK: Good business, rats. One can make money from them if one is enterprising.

Not surprisingly the tax man raided his home.

Kishore never did lose his sense of fun and Asha Bhosle, with whom he sang many duets, has described how Kishore Kumar could cause chaos. As they were singing together, Kishore Kumar, singing with his eyes closed as he often did, tumbled over Asha. "I tumbled upon Bhola Shreshta and he in turn fell on the tabla player (the drummer). We had become human dominoes, until the entire orchestra was flat out. I was severely hurt on my nose. The tabla was destroyed beyond repair, and the accordion player had sprained his ankle. But Kishore acted as if nothing had happened. All of us were in tears holding our stomachs and laughing uproariously."

Kishore Kumar often came to recordings as if he was in the company of an invisible boy. Asha says, "This non-existent boy and Kishoreda (a term of respect) used to talk to each other continuously, at times cracking jokes and breaking into laughter…." Kishore Kumar would invite Asha Bhosle to join the conversation but she could never make anything of this.

If this suggests a touch of madness, then this is confirmed by the experience of H.S. Rawail. There are several versions of this story. One goes that Kishore had not come to a shoot and Rawail went to his home only to find he was pretending to be a dog with a chain round his neck, a plate of chappati near him with a bowl of water and a sign saying 'Do not disturb the dog'. When Rawail tried to get in on the act and held out his hand as you would to a dog, Kishore bit his hand and barked incessantly. The other version is he went to pay Kishore money and still got bitten with Kishore saying, "Did you not see the sign?"

His death had the sort of sadness touched with comedy. He had just taken a phone call from a music producer to sing some songs and discussed the price but instead of taking money had spoken about how many mangoes he would be

given. Then he settled down to watch *The River of No Return*. Upstairs his wife
Leena was having a massage. Suddenly Kishore Kumar came up and lay on the
bed, a bedroom where he had hung a photograph of his mother next to one of
Marlon Brando from the *Godfather*. From his breathing, his wife thought he might
be having a heart attack. She was about to call the doctor but Kishore intervened
to saying he was all right and, if she called a doctor, he would have a real heart
attack.

This turned out to be his last words. The doctor arrived but heart massage
proved useless and on October 13, 1986, Kishore Kumar died aged fifty-eight.
Bollywood had lost the man who could have been its greatest comedian but had
instead become a man almost impossible to classify.

Ten years before he died, Kishore Kumar had had an introduction to India's
political world which was far from funny, indeed frightening; Mrs Gandhi had
declared an emergency in June 1975. Kishore's biographer Kishore Valicha takes
up the story.

7

    In the same year, around December, an evening was organised in New Delhi,
at Sanjay Gandhi's instance, to publicise the six point programme Gandhi had
visualised for the country. Film stars and leading singers from the film industry in
Bombay were invited to attend. Almost all of them were present to speak through
the mike and to sing to a large audience in an open theatre.

    Kishore Kumar was not there. His absence was not only noticed but deeply missed by
the spectators who had gathered there in adoration of the glamorous celebrities. Kishore
had not responded and had simply not shown up. He seemed not to care.

    The consequence was severe and dreadful, though not unexpected. The broadcast
of Kishore Kumar's songs on the Government-run All-India Radio and on the
black and white television of those days was totally banned on the quasi-authority
of those who held the political reins in their hands. The official reason given was
that his songs were obscene. No song of Kishore was broadcast until the end of the
Emergency when Mrs Indira Gandhi lost the election. The punishment could not
have been more colossal.

By this time Mehmood's career was all but over and as the 1980s came to a
close he was reduced to playing second fiddle to a Marathi film comedian Dada
Kodkhe who was trying to break into Hindi films.

Mehmood does provide a link between Bollywood of the 1950s and the
world that has now developed. When Mehmood was his height in the 1970s,
a young man arrived in Bombay hoping to make it into films. The immigrant
had no place to stay so Mehmood's brother offered him a room in his house.
At that time, Mehmood was producing his comedy called *Bombay to Goa* where
Mehmood was playing a bus conductor. He needed a hero and decided to cast
the young man in that role. The young man was Amitabh Bachchan and this was

his first movie as a leading man.

Almost twenty years later Mehmood, who was not in the best of health but keen to revive his career, had one last crack at comedy. In 1996 he made *Dushman Duniya Ka*. Mehmood managed quite a cast list for this film and the young Mehmood, complete with toothbrush moustache and manic eye-rolls, was played by Shah Rukh Khan, who has never concealed his admiration for Mehmood. But despite his presence, and that of other big names, the film proved a flop.

Mehmood died in his sleep in July 2004, far from his beloved Bombay, in a hotel room in Pennsylvania, where he had gone for medical treatment.

Perhaps the sort of lonely end that comes to all comedians.

Part V

Anger and After

15

A Shy Man and his Use of Anger

On February 15, 1969, a gangly twenty-seven year old, uncommonly tall for an Indian, certainly for an Indian actor, arrived in Bombay determined to make it in movies and that very day he got his chance. That film flopped, but success could not be denied him; it came four years later with a movie that was seen as a landmark new film, and soon the star was to revolutionise Bollywood. That young man was Amitabh Bachchan. It is tempting and quite feasible to write the history of Bollywood since 1973, when Bachchan had his first hit with *Zanjeer*, with Bachchan as its central character. He emerged when the Big Three of the 50s were still going strong but, since 1973, there has only been one actor. Even today, at sixty-four years old, such is his domination of Bollywood that, when he decided to play the teacher of a deaf and dumb girl in the movie *Black*, in 2005, he not only produced a triumph, but a movie that charted new territory for both himself, and for Bollywood.

Shyam Benegal told me:

> There is not a figure remotely comparable, not just in Bollywood, but in no theatre or cinema business do you have an equivalent figure anywhere in the world. He is a bigger star than anybody today on the planet, anywhere in the world. As an actor, he is as respected as Olivier or Gielgud in Britain for the quality of his performance. No exaggeration. He is an exceptionally good actor. He was not trained. He is an unlikely person to become such a big star; nobody would have given him half a chance. You should have seen him when he first came to Bombay. Nobody could have believed that he would make such a big impact; that he would even make a star. There were a number of other actors when Amitabh Bachchan came to Bombay. Amitabh broke a barrier in the way no other actor has done, not even the Big Three. He filled a kind of vacuum. First of all he wasn't a romantic hero. He represented in many ways the oppressed. He came at a time when the early hope of independence had gone. People were threatening a lot of things and the ability of the Government to deal with issues was in doubt. In *Sholay*, he

dies. One of the main characters. In that sense it was a different role. In *Black* he is playing an older character. He is no longer playing a hero. He had retired. As a consequence he becomes as big if not a bigger star in his middle age. *Zanjeer* gave him a profile that became his public persona. That changed recently when he was the presenter of Kaun Banaga Crorepati [India's equivalent of 'Who wants to become a Millionaire?']. This gave yet another kind of characteristic which became much more satisfying to a much larger audience. If he was a superstar before KBC, he was a superstar for a section of the Indian audience that followed Indian cinema After KBC, he has became a national icon. That had not happened to him before. Nobody is bigger than him. He is much bigger than Sachin Tendulkar. Amitabh has a persona now which is so extraordinary. He can be seen as a role model for just about anybody and everybody. He has nothing in his personal life that you could consider not right or reprehensible in anyway whatsoever.

Even the Bofors scandal did not affect him. He was put through a great deal of embarrassment for no reason.

It is widely believed in Bollywood that Amitabh's going rate for movies is between three and five crores of rupees (Rs. 30 million ro Rs. 50 million). The norm for him is to be paid 10% or 20% on signing.

Khalid Mohammed in *To be or Not to be Amitabh Bachchan* has written:

> ...no other actor has been more unsmiling in cracking a joke, and no actor has conveyed solitariness with so little self-pity. No one else on the screen has looked at us, seated out there in the dark of the auditorium, so hard, so searchingly. It all sounds impossible. But come sunset or sunshine, the real impossibility is to think of cinema and our lives without him.

But tempting as it is to tell the Bollywood story of the last thirty years in terms of this public schoolboy, there were also others, actors, actresses and directors, who played a part in the making of the story. Above all, wider economic and political factors helped Bachchan achieve his dominance and become a figure that is unique, not only in Bollywood but in world cinema.

Bachchan announced himself in the movies the very year that India took a decisive and, as it has turned out, disastrous turn, which meant it was facing completely the opposite direction to most of the world and, in particular, to the Asian countries to the south and east of her. In the decade that followed these countries, often emerging from cruel dictatorships, shed their repressive governments, took to liberal capitalism and launched the tiger economies, whose growth rates stunned the world. In contrast, going down the socialist route, India was mired in what was called the Hindu rate of growth, never more than 3.5% a year, and it was only in 1991, facing a severe foreign exchange crisis and forced by the IMF, that Indians changed tack and rejoined the world. This has relevance to the Bachchan story, for the woman who took this decisive turning, Indira Gandhi, was a great family friend of the Bachchans; her daughter-in-law to be, an Italian girl called Sonia Maino, born near Turin, who became Sonia Gandhi, stayed with the Bachchans when she first arrived in India to get married to Indira's son, Rajiv. It may be a coincidence that 1969, the year of Bachchan's début in films, was also the year Indira Gandhi made her decisive turn in Indian politics, a few months after Bachchan's arrival in Bombay but, nevertheless, it is of some significance.

In July 1969, Indira Gandhi, then Prime Minister of India, announced the nationalisation of all the banks of the country. The move was presented as something essential to help the poor. The Indian poor certainly had reason to be unhappy and wonder what twenty years of freedom had brought. In 1966, there had been famine in Bihar and Maharashtra. In Kerala, there had been rice riots, and Mrs Gandhi had theatrically announced she would not eat rice till people in Kerala got rice. So acute was the food shortage that there were so-called "guest control orders" which meant nobody could hold a party serving food to more than fifty people. In parties where greater numbers were invited the custom was to serve just a thin slice of ice cream which, it was rumoured, was made with blotting paper. India, in the previous decade, had had two wars with its neighbours. In 1962, it had been badly mauled by China, in 1965, it had the better of a draw with Pakistan. Mrs Gandhi, who had come to power a year after that war, made populist noises which were later to be summed up in her campaign slogan "Remove Poverty". What really prompted the movement was her feeling she may lose power to the right-wing Congress bosses who went under the name of the syndicate, and controlled the party machine. They had put her in power, hoping she would be a pliable woman, a little doll, as they put it. But she was to prove a tiger, Mother Durga, the great Hindu goddess that slays demons, and her move in 1969 was the first of her counter-strikes against the syndicate. This would include proposing her own candidate as President of India, opposing her party's official nominee, and then on August 15, 1969, splitting the party that her father and Mahatma Gandhi (no relation of Indira) had spent a lifetime building. The party that was formed was named after her, a name that it still carries, while the old official Congress party vanished, as if it had never existed.

The India that Indira had taken over, after nearly two decades of rule by her father, Jawaharlal Nehru, was the most curious kind of country. It was a thriving democracy that could rightly claim to be the world's largest democracy, yet it had the most socialist legislation outside the Soviet Union. But that was on paper and the effect of this legislation was not Soviet-style communism but monopoly capitalism, what Indians called the permit-license Raj, in place of the old British Raj. To get anything done, licenses were required from bureaucrats, leading to much corruption, and it had also led to horrendous monopolies where a small group of private businesses could control vast sectors of the economy. So, as

Bachchan was making his first films, only two types of cars were available. One was the Ambassador, a car based on the old Morris Oxford and manufactured by the Birlas, the business group that had financed Mahatma Gandhi and done very well out of India's independence. The other car was a 1960s version of the Italian Fiat. Demand so outstripped supply that the waiting list for a Fiat was fourteen years, and for an Ambassador four years. The net result was that second-hand cars fetched vastly more money than the price of the car when new. There was also no television to speak of except for an experimental television station in Delhi and, while the written press was free and raucous, radio was tightly controlled by the Government through the Information and Broadcasting Ministry (the British-created war-time ministry that the Indians had carried on). The Government also required all cinema houses to show propaganda films before a movie could be screened. As likely as not, these propaganda films often had exhortations on Indians not to waste food. It was against this background of shortages and growing disillusionment that Bachchan, and the new style of movies, began to emerge in the 1970s.

Interestingly, the character Bachchan played in his first movie success, *Zanjeer,* to an extent reflected the political style Mrs Gandhi so successfully adopted in 1969. This was of a person who was part of the system but yet against it. Her dramatic decision in 1969 was made when she was very much the Indian establishment. During her father's reign, she had often been the companion of her widower father at many an official function, and on his various overseas trips. She had been Congress President, when she played a prominent part in removing the elected Communist Government of Kerala from power. Then, having been a Minister of Information and Broadcasting and thereby in charge of films, she became Prime Minister. But her moves against her party were presented as that of a little brave woman fighting the evil syndicate party bosses, helped by the fact that most of them looked fat and ugly, as party bosses tend to. One, Atulya Ghosh from Bengal, always wore dark glasses and another, Kamaraj, spoke no English or Hindi. In contrast Mrs Gandhi, always looking petite, could easily portray them as evil men who did not care for the people, and it was her concern for these poor masses which was forcing her to tear the party apart. Mrs Gandhi rode to victory and success, as the woman in power bucking the system until, undone by her son, Sanjay, and cronies in the party, she overreached herself with the Emergency, which was imposed two years after Bachchan's success in *Zanjeer.*

In the movie, *Zanjeer,* Bachchan played a cop who, as a child, had seen his parents murdered. He becomes a cop, then uses the services of a Pathan, who has often been in trouble with the police, and a street girl, to avenge himself on the killer. The film would set the pattern for many of Bachchan's movies that followed, and gave the films of the 1970s the convenient shorthand title of the decade of the angry young man. Bachchan was the brooding loner, with very little time for song and dance. He had no hesitation in taking the law into his own hands to ensure justice, which the system had failed to provide, was meted out to deserving criminals.

Bachchan's skill, says film-maker Govind Nihalani, was that his acting summed up the mood of the nation as, in an earlier generation, Raj Kapoor's movies had done:

> Any kind of image attributed to an actor, like the Angry Young Man, concerns not only that actor, but also the environment that prevails in that period of history in which people are functioning. If there is a certain anger in the minds of the people, against certain kinds of system or against some kind of Governmental policies or social norms, or taboos, and if somebody expresses it...if the actor is able to convey that anger effectively, then he's actually expressing the anger of the pent-up emotions of his own generation.

For a man who would be identified as the angry young man of the country, Amitabh Bachchan's background and upbringing can have done very little to foster the screen anger he displayed. As a young boy, he was very much the good boy that Subhas Bose had warned Indians not to be. However, reflecting the times, in, he was very nearly given the name of *Inquilab* (revolution), having been born on October 11, 1942, just as India was in the midst of the Quit India movement, the fourth and last of the great movements launched by Mahatma Gandhi to get India's freedom from British rule. The British put it down with remarkable severity and Amitabh's father, Harivanshrai Bachchan, wanted to call his son Inquilab, but accepted the poetess Sumitra Nandan Pant's suggestion of Amitabh, which comes from Amit and Abha; some friends still call him Amit, which means Everlasting Light. In many ways Amitabh Bachchan was born in what would become the Indian establishment soon after independence. His birthplace, Allahabad, was the home town of the Nehrus, and both his parents, his mother, Teji, and father, Harivanshrai, were dedicated nationalists. Amitabh considers himself very much an Allahbadi, a city with a strong mixture of Hindu and Muslim culture, and one that influenced the Nehrus so much that Nirad Chaudhuri would argue that Nehru was more influenced by Muslim than Hindu culture.

The Bachchans were also well connected to the rising Bollywood establishment. His family was very friendly with the Kapoors. Harivanshrai would go to Prithviraj's stage performances and then, at the backstage soirées, recite poems which Prithviraj liked. But when in 1969, Amitabh came to Bombay looking for work he did not make his way to R.K. Studios, preferring to try and make it without "pull" as the Indians put it.

Amitabh grew up in what he calls an ambience of East and West. His father, a poet, a writer and well-respected figure in Hindi literature, his mother, from what is called the Westernised Indian family (her father had been called to the bar in London); she was educated at a convent and had had an English nanny.

Amitabh was brought up strictly, which may explain why he was shy and had problems with simple tasks like entering a restaurant on his own. This shyness was to plague him in his early days as a struggling film actor. Once, he had to meet the actor Manoj Kumar for an assignment, and Kumar asked him to come to the Filmistan Studios where he was shooting at the time. Every day for a week, Bachchan went all the way to the studio, only to falter at the gates, unable to walk in, undone by shyness. Surprisingly, despite his superstar status, and after years in cinema and many live programmes, he still admits to being extremely shy and an introvert, a trait that is often mistaken for arrogance. Perhaps this diffidence may explain, why even in his conversations with Khalid Mohammed recorded in 2002, he would say, "I've always been a mediocre actor. Believe me, every film, every performance, is an effort. I could always have been more sensitive and brighter. We are steeped in mediocrity."

The family were not exactly rich: Bachchan senior earned Rs. 500 a month and they neither had a fridge nor a ceiling fan and, in the intense northern Indian summer heat, his mother would flood the floor with water to cool the room and place ice slabs before the rickety table-fan to cope with the afternoon heat.

The Bachchan recall is that there was never too much money, but the parents clearly directed the children to what they felt was wholesome entertainment. Amitabh's first movie love was Laurel and Hardy, and his first Hindi movie was Satyen Bose's 1954 film *Jagriti*, a film with strong nationalistic overtones about encouraging the young to think of India and its glories. Later, he would cherish Montgomery Clift's acting in *A Place in the Sun,* as well as Marlon Brando in almost every film of his, particularly *The Wild One;* he could not sleep for nights after he saw Charlie Chaplin's *Limelight*, with the music in the film haunting him for a long time. The family's friendship with the Nehru family meant Bachchan did have privileged access. He and his family would be invited to screenings of films at Rashtrapati Bhavan, the President's Palace, and here he saw Czech, Polish and Russian films, although their anti-war messages did not particularly grab him. He has always felt that the aim of the cinema was not to preach, but to entertain.

In 1956 Bachchan, after his early schooling in Allahabad, went to a boarding-school, Sherwood College, in the hill station of Nainital. This was a missionary school where a Rev. R.C. Llewellyn was the Principal. It may seem strange the Bachchans could afford boarding-school. But, by then, his father had changed his job and bettered himself. He had gone to England to do his PhD, sponsored by Nehru, only to find on returning to Allahabad University, where he was Professor of English, that they wanted to reduce his salary. In a huff, he resigned. Nehru found him a job as head of the Hindi division of the External Affairs Ministry (in independent India, Nehru, in addition to being Prime Minister, was also the Indian Foreign Minister). It meant that the family moved to Delhi, more money became available and Amitabh went to boarding-school.

At school, he showed a proficiency in the sciences and fared rather abysmally in the arts, so much so that he even thought of becoming a scientist. He was an active participant in dramatics, tutored by an Englishman, a Mr Berry. For his performance as the Mayor in Gogol's *Inspector General,* he won the Kendall Cup named after Geoffrey Kendall, father of Jennifer and Felicity, whose touring Shakespearean company was well-known in India, particularly at boarding-schools. Kendall, himself, presented the cup to Amitabh and Amitabh honed his talents further at Kirorimal College in Delhi through their theatre society, 'The Players'. Despite opting for the science stream, his academic performance at college was pretty mediocre and he only got a second class degree when he graduated in 1962. There then followed some years in Calcutta, working as a boxwallah, as they call those who worked for the managing agencies that the British had set up and which controlled a number of diverse companies.

It was hardly a glamorous start. He had not got a good degree and, as he would later, admit, "I had to take what I got and that was in the coal department of the agency house, Bird and Co. I was there for two years, before moving to the freight-broking firm, Blacker and Co." The salary was better, he had a car, a black Morris Minor, which then became a somewhat bigger, Standard Herald. His first pay packet was Rs. 480, out of which he had to pay Rs. 300 for his rent, sharing a room with eight in Russell Street, a main street in the centre of Calcutta. Bird provided free lunch, and dinner was often whatever he could get "from here and there" on the streets of Calcutta. "It was an ordinary run of the mill lifestyle, very mediocre."

But Calcutta did provide him more opportunities for amateur dramatics; Sartre, Arthur Miller, Tennessee Williams, Beckett, Shakespeare, Harold Pinter were all performed, with Bachchan acting as Nick in *Who's Afraid of Virginia Woolf,* and as Casio in *Othello.* His boss, David Gilani, thought his acting was of a very high standard.

However, Bachchan had to cope with the race prejudice that still lingered in Calcutta in the early 60s, a decade and a half after the British had left:

> There were two groups there. The Amateurs and the Calcutta Dramatic Society, which was a white, British group. The Amateurs was made up of Indians, mainly public-school guys. So, between the two groups, there was a racial colour discrimination. The Calcutta swimming club had barred Indians. Some of us were among the first to be accepted by the club. Later, of course, things improved. The discrimination subsided.

It was his brother, Ajitabh, who encouraged Bachchan's film ambitions and took pictures of him outside Calcutta's Victoria Memorial, sending them to the *Filmfare*-Madhuri talent contest. But nothing happened, and it seemed Amitabh's life would be a continual series of failures; after all, the man who has probably one of the best voices in Bollywood failed tests as an announcer for All India Radio, both in English and Hindi. The pictures, though, were to come in useful.

Like all those who want to make it in films, Bombay beckoned and, in the late 60s, Amitabh started coming to the city. Although he did not take advantage of the family's connections with the Kapoors, he did stay with friends of his father but, then, feeling he had overstayed his welcome, spent a night on a bench on Marine Drive. Then, like the best stories in life, through a lucky turn of the wheel of fortune, he finally got an opportunity to make it in the movies.

The photographs that Ajitabh had taken had done the rounds of Bollywood. Sunil Dutt had seen them, his wife Nargis had got to know Amitabh's mother and wanted to help, and B.R. Chopra had summoned him from Calcutta to have a screen test. But the problem always was he was a *Lambu*, a Hindi word which means tall and which can be used in a pejorative sense. He was just too tall to have any front line actress wanting to play opposite him. After one screen test, one producer suggested he take to writing. "You look like a writer and, since you are the son of a reputed poet, it should not be difficult for you." The advice to Amitabh was very clear: do not give up your day job, which was now quite a good one, earning Rs. 2,500 a month, a very good salary in India then, with a car and a flat, although he did find life in Calcutta insular.

When he was near despair, the photographs, through the help of an actress friend, Neena Singh, reached K.A. Abbas, director of *Saat Hindustani*. It helped that Abbas still held on to his radical ideas and was a different kind of film-maker. The film was a patriotic tale of six Indians joining their comrade in Goa to liberate it from Portuguese occupation, and Abbas was keen to "scramble up" the Indians. So he wanted a Muslim playing a Hindu bigot, a Bengali playing a Punjabi and Amitabh, because of his looks and his height, made Abbas instinctively feel that he looked the part of the poet he wanted, and a Muslim poet, at that. But even here, the actual part came to him when another actor, Tinnu Anand, who had taken the photographs to Abbas, dropped out to go to Calcutta to work with Satyajit Ray and become a director.

The film was a failure but there was one moment during the shooting that stood out, marking the actor to come.

The last scene saw the seven Indians of the title scrambling up a steep hill. They were all tied to each other by ropes, with Amitabh the last. He would not allow a stunt man to play him in the scene, which involved losing his footing over some loose rock and dangling over a waterfall before being pulled to safety by his comrades. "With a duplicate," recalled Abbas later, "I would have had to take a long shot. But, since it was him, I could zoom in and show the agony on the character's face." After the scene had been shot, Bachchan crawled up with scraped shins and, as he did so, all the technicians, who had all been drenched by the spray of the waterfall, burst out into applause.

But, if this showed his dedication to the craft he had just entered, off the screen he was still the well brought-up young public schoolboy. Like all Abbas films, this was a low budget film. The actors had been told to bring their own bedding and accommodation for the six week shooting in Goa was a large hall where all the actors spread out their bedding on the floor and slept. "Each one of us" says Abbas, "had our suitcases against the wall with the bedding spread alongside. Except Amitabh. Every night he would open the trunk (he had brought the biggest trunk Abbas had ever seen), take out his bedding, and pack it up in the morning."

He was still his mother's boy. When he met Madhu, then a leading Malayalam actor, on the sets, he introduced himself as Teji Bachchan's son. Madhu had met his mother when he was studying at the National School of Drama in Delhi and was a great admirer of his father's poetry. Madhu noticed he recited his father's verses all the time, a practice to which Madhu attributes the quality of Bachchan's voice. When, in *Shatranj Ke Khiladi,* Satyajit Ray wanted someone for the voice-over narration, he turned to Bachchan, and his baritone voice was heard in that film.

Despite the failure of the movie, Bachchan did start getting parts but none of them looked like making him a star, let alone a big star, and he had to take whatever roles he was offered. In a world where a man who aspires to be a hero never portrays unsympathetic characters in films, Bachchan had negative roles in *Gehri Chaal* and *Parwana.* In *Reshma Aur Shera,* which featured some stars of the future, like Vinod Khanna and Raakhee and where Sunil Dutt kept his promise to give him a film role, Bachchan ended up playing a mute.

Not that in 1969 Bollywood was looking for a star. The Big Three were aging but a young man had appeared who it seemed was certain to take over from Dilip Kumar, Dev Anand and Raj Kapoor.

Rajesh Khanna could not have been more different to Amitabh Bachchan. Shobhaa De has provided the most vivid pen portrait of the two men:

> Amitabh is a low-impact guy. You notice his voice, his eyes, and then the aura takes over. It's the aura of success that transforms the most ordinary of individuals into larger-than-life beings. Amitabh wears his very well. Or used to, till his career and image hit a downslide. Be that as it may, he's still a cut above Khanna...But then Khanna was not part of the Nehru-Gandhi coterie. He was only an inner city boy who had made good. Amitabh came as a package, with all his antecedents clearly marked on it. Well-spoken, well-read, urbane and suave, he was the sort of man who'd be comfortable in the world's saloons. Not Rajesh, with his innumerable hang-ups and self-doubts. Both men flopped in politics—Amitabh got out prematurely, while Rajesh hangs in there for want of a better career option. Rajesh is marked by a persecution complex that he doesn't bother to disguise, Amitabh by his studied silence. The one thing they have in common is their aloofness. Rajesh may be *kakaji* (uncle) to his hangers-on and Amitabh may gamely put up with fawning socialites

dying to be seen dancing with him in public, but nobody back-slaps these two or acts familiar with them. It is important for even fading superstars to maintain a distance, if the mystique is to be preserved.

Of course De was writing in 1998, when Amitabh seemed down and out, only to be reincarnated through television and then make it back into the movies.

Rajesh Khanna, born Jatin Khanna, was the adopted son of his parents and, after a stint in theatre, he won a talent contest, something Amitabh could not do. He made his film début in Chetan Anand's 1966 *Aakhri Khat*, a very different start to Bachchan, for Chetan Anand was a big name director from the very established Anand movie establishment, a far cry from making films with Abbas in Goa. In 1969, while Amitabh was going round Bombay with the pictures Ajitabh had taken, Khanna played a dual role, father and son, both air force pilots, in *Aradhana*. He cut a dashing figure in uniform and the mannerisms he displayed, crinkling his eyes and shaking his head, as he beckoned the heroine to him, made him the great romantic hero. The S.D. Burman songs also helped and the film was a huge hit. In December 1969, Khanna starred in another film, Raj Khosla's *Do Raaste*, and produced something Bollywood had never seen before. *Aradhana* was already running at the Opera House when *Do Raaste* opened at Roxy, across the road, and Bombay witnessed the remarkable phenomenon of two movies with the same star playing to packed houses and both having golden jubilee runs.

The Rajesh Khanna phenomenon was sweeping everyone in Bollywood off their feet and the hysteria he generated was unlike anything seen before or after. As hit followed hit, and women all over the country swooned over him, Rajesh Khanna admitted feeling 'next to God'. Five years later, in 1977, with Amitabh Bachchan well-established as the greatest hero Bollywood had ever seen, and Khanna's career in ruins, he was said to have gone out one evening onto his terrace in pouring rain and asked God whether his patience was being tested.

Bachchan knew he was in the shadow of this superstar and in 1970 he deliberately decided to play the doctor who looks after the dying cancer patient, Anand, played by Khanna in the film called *Anand*. Bachchan's motivation was that if he played off the super star he would get some attention. Mehmood, whose brother Anwar Ali had become a great friend—it was through him that Bachchan became a paying guest at the sprawling Mehmood home and got to know Mehmood, acting in *Bombay to Goa*—advised him, "Design your performance round Rajesh Khanna. Imagine him dying… it's an enormous thing…the nation will cry their hearts out for him." That, says Bachchan, is just what happened. "The very fact that I'd been teamed with Rajesh Khanna, the greatest idol, gave me a semblance of importance and respectability."

Bachchan would later recall, "Rajesh Khanna—the word superstar was coined for him—brought attention to me. Here was a brilliant story and script exceptionally handled by Hrishida. The film looked so real, it left millions

of Rajesh Khanna fans very emotionally disturbed." The last scene showed
Bachchan, the brooding, sensitive, doctor watching as Khanna, who had borne
his suffering with a smile and shown great spirit in adversity, dies. It helped that
the film was made by what may be called the Bimal Roy school of film-making;
both the director, Hrishikesh Mukherjee, who also wrote the story, and the writer
of the screen play, Gulzar, had been assistants of Roy, with the music composed
by Salil Chowdhury. During the making of this film, a bond developed between
Bachchan and Hrishikesh Mukherjee; Bachchan would come to revere the
director and recall with fondness how he had calmed him down when playing
the last scene where Khanna dies. The thought of performing in the scene had
made him so nervous that he was unable to perform till Mukherjee got him
to relax. It was with Mukherjee that Bachchan was to act in eight films, more
than with any other director. In the years ahead, Bachchan would be directed
by many others but Mukherjee was always the standard against whom he
measured them and some of the directors also invoked Mukherjee to define their
own contrasting styles when directing Bachchan. Bachchan would later say of
Mukherjee's directing:

> I've done my maximum number of films with Hrishida. It's never been a
> professional relationship with him, it's purely been a personal one. He'd scold Jaya
> and me on the sets, we'd sulk and then brighten up on being patted on the head.
> Outside the studio, he'd reprimand us, check us and we'd always obey him to the
> last word. Being a brilliant editor, his film would be already cut and synthesised in
> his mind even before he shot it. To be economical, he would often avoid shots of his
> artists into, and exiting, from a frame.

Bachchan's performance won him his first *Filmfare* Award for Best Supporting
Actor but, while critics finally took notice and were even complimentary, none
of them thought he would be anything other than a strong character actor, at
best a 1970s version of Balraj Sahni. But, at least this was a change from the
relentless bad notices Bikram Singh, film critic of *The Times of India,* gave him.
He, as Bachchan says, "always harped on my gaunt face and gawkiness". This
was Bachchan's first real success, where he had shown undoubted acting ability.
Mehmood's *Bombay to Goa* had been a box office success but that was more due
to the hilarious cameos in the film.

But, since like all commercial cinema Bollywood values box office more than
anything else, *Bombay to Goa* had been noticed and, when the following year
Prakash Mehra set out to make *Zanjeer,* he turned to Amitabh, although he was
fifth choice after Dev Anand, Raj Kumar, Dharmendra and Rajesh Khanna.
Dev Anand, Mehra's first choice, wanted the actor to be allowed to sing two or
three more songs, but Mehra had to tell him it was not that kind of character.
Then, bizarrely, he offered to produce and finance the film through Navketan

and get Mehra to direct, an offer that quite astounded Mehra. He had started the discussion offering the veteran a role only to find the veteran offering him a job. Mehra had an understanding with Dharmendra, but he could not fit it into his schedule, while Rajesh Khanna felt the character did not go with his romantic image. Pran, who was to play the Pathan, suggested Mehra go and see *Bombay to Goa* and, in particular, the young actor, Amitabh. So, with his two script-writers, Salim Khan and Javed Akhtar, known as Salim-Javed in the business, Mehra went to the movies to have a look at Amitabh. As it happens Pran, who does not like going to the movies, had not seen the film but relied on what his son had told him. The film had a fight scene and the moment Mehra saw it he screamed *Mil Gaya*, meaning "We have got it." While the rest of the audience in that hall turned to look at him in surprise, Mehra got up and walked out – he did not need to see the film till the end – and, as he did so, he told Javed, "We have found our hero."

But having got a hero, there was now a problem with the heroine.

Khanna's rejection meant Mumtaz turned it down. An actress from a good middle-class Muslim family, who made the most of her voluptuous figure and an alluring pout, she had starred with Khanna in several successful films and had been so successful that, in 1970, she won the Best Actress Award. With Khanna no longer the hero, she was not interested. But, fortunately for Amitabh, Jaya Bhaduri stepped in. Daughter of a Bengali writer, she had been a child actress and, as a thirteen year old she had acted in Ray's *Mahanagar*, and was one of the first to be trained at the recently set up Film Institute at Poona. The two of them had also acted in films together, although their first pairing in *Guddi*, which is when they first met, did not last long for, after a few shots, Amitabh was dropped for reasons that mystified Jaya. Perhaps it was because by then Amitabh's own schedule of making more than one film at a time meant he could not fit in with the demands of the film. By the time *Zanjeer* came along they were an item, although in a wholly Indian way. According to Jaya, this did not extend much beyond going to movies together, leaving before the end as by now they were sufficiently well-known to be recognised, but there was nothing in the nature of any Western-style dating, not even romantic, candle-lit dinners. Most of the time they spent together would be in the company of other friends and Amitabh would drive her round town in his Fiat and give her expensive sarees. The only problem was most of them were white, with a purple border, a colour Jaya hated but she wore them nevertheless so as not to upset him.

The making of the film was beset with problems. Pran, who played the Pathan, a villain who befriends the policeman as he seeks justice, was in many senses the central selling-point of the film, being the established star. But, on the first day of the shooting, he threatened to walk out when he discovered he had to sing a song. The song and the words had not been given to him in advance and, having been cast as the eternal villain of Bollywood for almost three decades, it was well-known in the industry that Pran Sahib, as he was called, did not do songs and dances, and all that running round trees. Mehra had to rush to Pran's house to plead with him, saying without him the film would not work as Amitabh as a hero was not a bankable box office proposition.

Pran having recommended Amitabh without ever seeing him act found him quite a greenhorn who had to be coached. They had a scene together in the police station where Amitabh had to kick a chair away from Pran, in a show of anger. Amitabh just could not demonstrate the necessary anger. He was close to Pran's son and, in the Indian fashion, called Pran uncle. Pran would tell his biographer, "I knew what was happening inside him. So I told him 'Don't think of me as your uncle. Think of me as the villain here. Forget the uncle and kick the chair. Only then could he do the scene well enough. He was so respectful."

Bollywood had sneered before the film was released. Mehra, a failed lyricist, had taken to directing and had just one halfway decent hit to his credit, but the writers Salim-Javed had no credentials to speak of. Salim was a wannabe actor who had had a couple of very small roles and an acting career that was going nowhere. Javed was busy ghost-writing dialogues for forgettable films. While *Zanjeer* was being made, Bachchan's *Bandhe Haath* was released and was a disaster; that meant he had thirteen flops, and the mood in the *Zanjeer* camp was so gloomy that Prakash Mehra, more to raise morale and get Bachchan out of his depression, announced his second production would be *Hera Pheri*, a comedy starring Bachchan with Vinod Khanna. But, on May 23 1973, when *Zanjeer* opened at Liberty Theatre in Mumbai, it went on to make film history. The film, quite unexpectedly, just took off.

If Bachchan was a failure before *Zanjeer,* after its release everything he did was a success. Of the seventy-odd films he starred in from 1973-1984, when he took a sabbatical from films to enter politics, only three failed to recover their costs. A 1984 survey showed that of the fifteen all-time top grossing films in Hindi cinema, 40%, starred Bachchan. Even those films considered flops at the time of their initial release, went on to become successful when re-released. In fact, some of his films made more money on re-releases than many a hit film starring other actors. On May 1, 1980, he made the cover of *India Today*. He was pictured in a red jacket against palm trees and the story was headlined: The One-Man Industry. The author Vir Sanghvi wrote:

> At any given time of the day over a *lakh* (100,000) people are watching him sing, dance, fight on the screen. Every year, over four crore people(100 million) watch this man battle the forces of evil. Each time he leaves home, investments worth Rs. 50 crore (500 million) ride on him. As French producer Alain Chamas, who tried to unsuccessfully sign him, said in exasperation, "Amitabh Bachchan is an industry."

However, while *Zanjeer* was being made, and before Bachchan had become a film industry on his own, he was involved in the movie that would define Bollywood for the modern era, the 1970s, and beyond. If *Mother India* and *Mughal-e Azam* were the iconic movies of the 1950s and early 1960s, then *Sholay* was to prove to be, arguably, the most memorable movie produced by Bollywood and which took Hindi cinema to a level it had never attained before.

As a film, it broke all box office records; the movie ran uninterruptedly for 286 weeks in Bombay's Minerva Theatre. At the fiftieth *Filmfare* awards it was recognised as the Best Film of fifty years, and voted the "Film of the Millennium" by BBC India and internet polls in 1999. It was also the highest grossing movie of all time in India, with collections of Rs. 2,134,500,000 – or US $50 million, a record that stood till 1994 when *Hum Aapke Hain Kaun* surpassed it. It is widely acknowledged by movie critics to be one of the best movies ever created by Bollywood and to be the most-watched movie, revolutionising Hindi film—making and bringing true professionalism to script-writing. It was the first Hindi (and possibly Indian) movie to have a stereophonic soundtrack. The director, Shekhar Kapur, has said, "There has never been a more defining film on the Indian screen. Indian film industry can be divided into *Sholay* BC and *Sholay* AD." The dialogue in the film is so well-known that some of its most dramatic lines are used in ordinary Indian conversation in much the way that dialogue from the first *Godfather* movie, which starred Marlon Brando, has been recycled in the West. The film has been used to sell everything from glucose biscuits to gripe water. A ticket black marketeer in Delhi made so much money he built a house from its profits; rickshaws in towns like Patna are named after Dhanno, the mare that featured in the film, and one actor who had a single line but a dramatic few moments being shown on screen as a man on a rock holding a gun, was waved through by a New York immigration officer who instantly recognised him. It took two years to make the movie and the actors and actresses who performed in it had their own particular agendas, providing a counter point to the story they were seeking to narrate, with one pair pursuing a love that was forbidden, another marrying during its film-making and a third, unable to find love, taking to drink and slowly wasting away.

The making of the film itself, and the various plots and counter plots between the performers, would itself have made an excellent movie and, many years later, Anupama Chopra would write one of the best books to emerge on the Indian cinema, *Sholay: The Making of a Classic*. The film, and those who made it, in many ways reflected all of contemporary Indian life.

The year *Sholay* was released was also the year another of Amitabh's films was released: *Deewar,* which, for all the commercial success of *Sholay,* hogged the honours at that year's *Filmfare* Awards. Two years later came *Amar Akbar Anthony* which became a great cult movie. The two directors Amitabh worked for on that film could not have been more different to Ramesh Sippy, the director of *Sholay*.

Deewar was directed by Yash Chopra who, by then, was no longer known as just the younger brother of B.R. Chopra. In fact, having lived in one family unit, the brothers had split in a messy convoluted dispute that defies simple analysis, as Chopra's biographer points out. *Amar Akbar Anthony* was by Manmohan Desai, who could not have been more different to Chopra.

Yash Chopra developed the reputation in Bollywood as the director who was reinventing himself every decade. Although Chopra would become known as the 'king of romantic films', he also made movies which could more accurately be classified as thrillers, or even high drama. Brought up since the age of thirteen by B.R, who was eighteen years his elder, Yash showed his style in the very first film that his brother B.R. gave him to direct, *Dhool Ka Phool*. This is the story of a woman betrayed by her lover and the fate of her illegitimate children. In *Dharmaputra*, Yash Chopra considered a Muslim child brought up in a Hindu household and who, unaware of his religion, becomes a Hindu fanatic. In *Ittefaq,* there was yet another development, a songless thriller involving a man accused of murdering his wife and a single woman who shelters him.

But it was *Deewar,* and the association with Amitabh Bachchan, that marked his most successful period. Bachchan may have established the brand of angry young man with *Zanjeer* but it really took off in *Deewar*. Like so many Bollywood films, the story drew much from *Mother India,* but then few films have not. However, even then it broke many of the unwritten, but long-established Bollywood rules.

It had only two songs, the '*qawwali*' and the title song; the hero turned out to be an anti-hero; there was no innocent virgin, just a very small role for the heroine and, therefore, little scope for any romance; the lost father died with no chance of the sort of final scene reunion Bollywood specialises in and the hero actually died at the hand of his own brother.

In *Mother India,* the mother kills the son; in *Deewar,* the bad son, Vijay, played by Bachchan, is killed by his brother Ravi, a policeman played by Shashi Kapoor. The climax involves a shoot-out with Vijay, dying in his mother's arms in front of a temple.

Bachchan's involvement in *Deewar* came in the traditional fashion. He was shooting another film when the script-writers, Salim-Javed, narrated the story. "We agreed that Yash Chopra would be best suited to direct it. Salim-Javed and I went over to meet Yashji at Girnar Apartments on Pali Hill, where he was then living."

Deewar for Bachchan was stark and hard-hitting: 'There were no duplicates in any shot, no fancy camerawork to highlight some of the rather stunning stunts, and no protective paraphernalia to safeguard us from injury. That didn't exist then. Stuntmen and artistes suffered in silence. Most of the excitement, however, used to take place behind the camera, where a very involved and animated Yash Chopra kept knocking down his assistant every time he shouted, 'Action!'

It was Manmohan Desai who himself narrated the story of *Amar Akbar Anthony* to Bachchan but, unlike *Deewar,* which instantly grabbed Bachchan, he could not believe in the film: 'When Manmohan Desai narrated the subject of *Amar Akbar Anthony* at the Mangal lawns one evening, I was flummoxed. I'd never seen or heard of a guy like Anthony. I laughed out loud, 'Man (as his friends called him), what kind of a movie are you hatching?' And he retorted, 'Look, as soon as it is released, people on the streets will call you Anthonybhai.' And he was so right. Throughout the making of AAA, it was a helluva fun ride. Whether I was handling that Lilliputian horse, Tonga, or sweeping the floors to get on with the next scene, it was all one combined effort. There was laughter, gaiety...a fantastically big cast...and 'Man' kept us all going. Even the most ridiculous moment was meticulously planned."

The story was the classic one of the cultural unity of India, despite its religious differences. A father in difficulties abandons his three sons. One of them, Amar, remains a Hindu; another, Akbar, becomes a Muslim, and the third played by Amitabh finds himself in a church and becomes Anthony. Abandoned children and their stories are a staple diet of Bollywood but nobody had done it quite this way, and with such symbolism. In the film, the family is shown splintering on August 15th, just as India did in 1947 and, for all their different religious upbringings, the movie emphasises that all Indians are brothers. The opening credits are accompanied by the song *'Khoon khoon hotaa haipaani nahin'* (Blood is blood, not water), and the message is the unity of the Indian nation, through the portrayal of a family reunited, after suffering dreadful loss and much sorrow.

But then Manmohan Desai was a trend-setter in the film industry. His films generally took place in the scenic outdoors, or they were stylised by the studios to look that way, where everyday life could carry on into fantasy. As Bachchan would later say, 'Manmohan Desai's films might be described as 'fanaticised' expressions of romantic idealism...love, honour, separation, vindication, and reunion were his abiding obsessions...while always containing the key element of wonderment... To know Manmohan Desai was to know a man of compassion.' In essence, he adopted the familiar Bollywood formula.

Of the twenty films that he directed in his career of twenty-nine years (between 1960 and 1988), thirteen were huge hits. From 1973-1981, he delivered box office successes, with Amitabh Bachchan at the centre of these films.

Manmohan Desai, whose name meant 'mind charmer', was a child of Bollywood but fashioned a life story just that bit different. When he married, it was something out of a Bollywood script. Jeevan Prabha Gandhi, a Marathi girl, was a woman who was living across the street from him and had smiled at him from the window. Although, in a technical sense, he was an immigrant, moving with his Gujarati family to the city at the age of four, he always saw the city as his home, and grew up with films. His father, Kikubhai Desai, was the owner of Paramount Studios where he produced thirty-two films between 1931 and

1941, mostly stunt films. Kikubhai died at the age of thirty-nine from a ruptured appendix, the irony being that there was no penicillin, which was discovered a month after his death. Kikubhai's death meant that the family was left with much debt. Kalavati, his mother, had to sell off the family's bungalow and cars to support her family, but fought to hold on to the studio which would provide a monthly income of Rs. 500 and where the family would live in its four rooms.

Manmohan had his early film experience when his brother started working for Homi Wadia. He went on to direct and, in 1960, he gave Manmohan, then aged twenty-four, a chance to direct with the film, *Chhalia*.

Manmohan rarely left anything to chance and, as Bachchan says, "The only thing that was spontaneously done in *Amar Akbar Anhony* was my drunken scene when he wasn't present on the sets. He'd left the scene to his assistants.....I told his assistants that I'd do the drunken scene based on my observations of someone who'd get punch-drunk on Calcutta's Park Street...after having two or three too many."

In many ways the most unexpected thing in his life was his death. On 1 March 1994, Manmohan Desai fell from the terrace of his Khetwadi home in central Bombay instantly killing him. He was fifty-seven years old. There has never been any explanation as to why he would have wanted to take his life.

16

The Great Indian Curry Western

Gopaldas Parmanand Sippy, a Hindu Sindhi, had migrated from Karachi, after partition, to Bombay with nothing but his wits. Noticing one lunch-time a long queue outside the restaurant he was eating in, he discovered that these were office-workers seeking food during their lunch-break. Clearly, there was need for a restaurant and he quickly hired premises, instantly mortgaged it to raise money, and opened a restaurant. He then moved into property and got hooked on films when he built a house for Nargis. He started producing movies in the 1950s but they were unmemorable, mostly B grade crime thrillers. By the 1970s, having made money and some more successful movies, he was very keen to make a multi-starrer, something nobody had dared venture into after Raj Kapoor's *Mera Naam Joker* had flopped, back in 1970.

By then his son, Ramesh, twenty-seven, who had been sent to the London School of Economics, had decided he would rather be in Bombay and came home ostensibly to study psychology, but really to work with his father in films.

He directed Rajesh Khanna in *Andaz* with some success and had a much bigger hit with *Seeta Aur Geeta*. It was shortly after this that he was presented with an idea by Salim-Javed for an intriguing film. The idea had done the rounds of Bollywood. It had been rejected by Manmohan Desai, then an up-and-coming director and, also, by Prakash Mehra, who was far too busy then with *Zanjeer*. The production company Mehra was working for had actually bought the idea but, at Salim-Javed's request, they released it, and they now brought it to the Sippys.

Both these writers were Muslims, although of a very unconventional kind. Salim, the son of a police officer in Indore, had been spotted at a wedding and hired as an actor on Rs. 400 a month. Javed, the son of a poet who was a member of the Communist party, was raised more on the Communist manifesto rather than the Quran, and his father is said to have recited the Communist manifesto to his son when he was still a child. Javed had come to Bombay hoping to work with Guru Dutt, but five days later Dutt killed himself, and since then he had existed on the margins of Bollywood. Salim had become a script-writer when a director, M. Sagar, unable to find one, had turned to Salim who was working as a clapper-boy for him. Soon Sagar also offered Javed a job and the partnership was formed. But while they toiled away, virtually unnoticed, both men were extremely ambitious and wanted the sort of credit script-writers in Hollywood got but which was unknown in Bollywood. In the Bollywood pecking order at that time, heroes were top of the pile, then came heroines, followed by directors and producers, with the script-writers treated in the same way that upper caste Hindus had always treated the untouchables: necessary but never to be allowed inside the tent. Salim-Javed wanted to change that.

They had already worked for father and son sippy, in *Seeta aur Geeta,* but did not like either the money or the publicity, or the lack of it. Their biggest grouse was their worth as script-writers was not recognised. Instead of their script-writing being acknowledged, the credits for script in that film was given to the Sippy story department. Just before they took the *Sholay* idea to the Sippys, Salim-Javed had told Abrar Alvi, Guru Dutt's script-writer, that script-writers would one day earn as much as stars. He had laughed, saying, "Have you taken leave of your senses?"

The idea they had for a story was about an army officer whose family gets massacred and decides to hire two junior officers who have been court-martialled, but who were really lovable rogues, to help him avenge himself on the killer. In March 1973, Ramesh Sippy started working with Salim-Javed on the script and it was quickly decided that an Army background would cause too many problems, with permission having to be sought from the military for filming, and there could be censorship headaches. Salim-Javed changed the army officer to a police officer seeking revenge. By then Ramesh Sippy knew who he would cast in the film although Amitabh Bachchan was not Sippy's first choice

Exactly two months before the Sippys began to work with Salim-Javed, they held a party at father Sippy's house on Altamount Road, high above the hills overlooking the sea at Marine Drive—the traditional haunt of the rich and the well-off of the city. *Seeta Aur Geeta* was a success and all of Bombay wanted to know what the Sippys would do next. That evening, many of the leading men and women of Bollywood gathered there to probe their intentions. As in the style of such Indian parties, there was plenty of liquor combined with light snacks, like pakoras and samosas—the real food would come much later, round about midnight. And now that prohibition had been relaxed, the liquor flowed freely and it was mostly whisky. The guests knew that since the Sippys were well-off, much of the booze would be genuine Scotch, not the foreign-made Indian liquor, meaning Indian whisky, which others served. By the time the food arrived it was well past midnight and this is when one of the main stars, who hoped to be in the Sippys next film, arrived.

The party was an occasion for actors and actresses to parade. The details of what the Sippys were planning were not known because the Sippys themselves did not know at this stage. The word was it would be an escapade-adventure film with many stars. Hema Malini, the lead actress of *Seeta Aur Geeta*, which had won her the *Filmfare* Best Actress Award, was there, as was her co-star, Dharmendra It was taken for granted that these two would be in the next Sippy film. But what about the third main star? The industry sources were sure that it had to be Shatrughan Sinha, then a leading actor in Bombay. It was the fight scene between him and Amitabh in *Bombay to Goa* that had made Prakash Mehra scream out in pleasure. But he was a much bigger star than Amitabh. He arrived at around midnight and the moment he did so Amitabh, who had arrived much earlier with a temperature of around 102° and a throbbing headache—for a time he had to lie down in the Sippy's bedroom—was edged out. Anupama Chopra describes the scene:

> He (Sinha) posed with Dharmendra and Hema Malini, smiling, and slowly edged Bachchan out of the frame. As onlookers toasted the team, spontaneous applause broke out. A distributor leaned towards Ramesh and whispered into his ear, 'Yeh hai app ki casting. Us lambujhi ka sochna bhi mat. (This is your cast. Do not even think of the tall guy). Ramesh only smiled.

Amitabh eventually secured the part because Ramesh was worried Sinha would be one big star too many; he already had two. Also, Amitabh had asked Dharmendra to help and, as Chopra says, "the lobbying worked." However, with the success of *Zanjeer* still five months away, it was touch and go whether Amitabh would make it.

Working in what Chopra describes as a dreary beige, twelve by twelve room in Sippy's office, with a semi-circular divan and a barred window, which overlooked a terracotta-red boundary wall, Salim-Javed and Ramesh formed a script-writing trio and in a month developed a story that heavily borrowed from foreign influences, such as Akira Kuosawa's *Seven Samurai, The Magnificent Seven, Butch Cassidy and the Sundance Kid* and Sergio Leon's spaghetti Westerns. But to these they added those touches that make Hindi cinema so distinctive. If this made it the first truly masala curry Western, it also carried the story forward with a plot much tauter than any previous Hindi film of this genre.

Salim worked many real persons into the script. The name of the bandit, Gabbar, came from a story told by his father, who was a real policeman, about a bandit with that name. Veeru and Jai, the two main characters, were names of his college friends; Thakur Baldev Singh, the police officer out to get the bandit, was the name of Salim's father-in-law, a Hindu who had opposed his daughter marrying Salim and did not speak to his son-in-law for seven years.

Like many Hindi scripts, it was originally written in Urdu by Javed and then translated into Hindi by an assistant. In the way Bollywood films are made, actors and actresses heard narration with Javed narrating and Salim butting in to elaborate or emphasise a point or a scene.

The story, which uses several flashbacks, starts with a police officer, now retired, called Thakur, played by Sanjeev Kumar, coming back to his place of work to recruit two small time crooks, Veeru and Jai, portrayed by Amitabh and Dharmendra He wants them to capture a dangerous bandit called Gabbar Singh. Then we are told in flashback how Thakur, while still a police officer, had captured Gabbar and put him behind bars. But he escapes and, travelling to Thakur's home village of Ramgarh, kills his entire family: sons, daughters-in-law, grandchildren—all except one daughter-in-law who, at that moment, happened to be away. Gabbar wreaks his havoc just before Thakur returns home. The scene which shows him entering his village, carrying presents for the family, only to find them butchered, is classic Bollywood pathos. He goes after Gabbar but Gabbar easily overpowers him and then, in another act of butchery, cuts his arms off. It is this armless officer who now seeks to avenge himself and while the men he recruits may be crooks, their hearts are in the right place.

But he warns them that they must not kill Gabbar. They must bring him back alive and Thakur will deliver justice to his nemesis himself. He wants a helpless Gabbar to be lying at his feet; the bandit may have hacked his arms off but it is he who is now made powerless by the power of Thakur's feet. The original script had Thakur, having had shoes fitted with nails, using them to crush Gabbar, hammering them into his body with such force that he ends up a bloody mess. He then breaks down and cries; he has won but he knows he cannot regain the world Gabbar has destroyed.

But the censors would not allow such a conclusion to the film. Their argument was that a film which showed a police officer, albeit a retired one, taking the law into his own hands was not morally acceptable. Ramesh Sippy was keen to fight them, insisting they had no right to tamper with his artistic conception, but he was convinced by his father that the economics of the film, if nothing else, meant they had to give in and reshoot the ending. So, just a month before the release, the cast had to be hurriedly reassembled, with Sanjeev Kumar summoned back from the Soviet Union. This time, the final scene showed that just as Thakur raised his lethal shoes to crush Gabbar, the horizon filled with policemen and, overcoming Thakur's protests, they took over saying that, as a police officer, he must know this was a matter for the police to handle. This made the ending contrived in the extreme and made little sense in the light of everything that had gone on for the previous four hours. As Chopra says, the censors had forced "an easy pabulum about the virtues of following the law" although somewhere the original ending is available, fuzzy, with poor sound quality, but chilling in its effect when it shows Sanjeev Kumar weeping after killing Gabbar. Ramesh Sippy had carefully crafted the violent scenes; very little bloodshed was actually shown, something rare in Bollywood even today. Even then the censors objected to some scenes, fearing it may become the norm for other Bollywood movie-makers to follow. Ramesh Sippy was inclined to reject the cuts but, in the end, with great reluctance, he accepted, as any delay in showing the film would have been financially ruinous.

The cuts the censor imposed were extremely irritating but they could not alter the fundamental way Ramesh Sippy crafted the film, and the way he had used very Indian themes to make this Indian spaghetti Western.

Sippy, borrowing from Leone, had used silence very effectively. After Gabbar and his bandits butcher Thakur's family and ride away, the only sound heard is that of the empty swing in the courtyard. Sippy also borrowed from both the *Seven Samurai* and *The Magnificent Seven* to introduce the villain Gabbar Singh. He makes us wait before we see him; he comes after several scenes have been shown and one song has already been sung. Even then, his face is not shown immediately. The sound of shoes clashing onto the rock signifies Gabbar's entrance. The camera shows his henchmen's terrified faces from the angle of Gabbar's shoes. Suspense is built up through several characters' hushed mentions of his name and we hear his very maniacal laugh that would not sound out of place in a mental asylum.

The characters were sharply delineated but, unlike so often in Hindi cinema, they were not caricatures, but believable. Veeru and Jai do make us believe they are friends, with Jai having a nice line in sarcasm, always making fun of Veeru, whose humour is both broad and rather childish. This is best shown through their romancing of the village women.

Veeru falls for the local, horse-carriage driver, Basanti, played by Hema Malini, and Jai starts to have romantic feelings for Thakur's widowed daughter-in-law, Radha played by Jaya Bhaduri. To add the necessary secular touch, there is a Muslim in the village, a very pious man who is the Imam and who is also blind. He suffers the death of his only son at the hands of Gabbar and his bandits, with Gabbar sending the body back as a warning to the villagers to get rid of Jai and Veeru. But, despite this, he supports the desire of Thakur to go after the bandits. In one scene Basanti, a devout Hindu, is shown leading the blind Muslim Imam to the mosque, something his murdered son used to do.

Sippy also used the film to comment on the divide between urban and rural India; between urban sophistication and rural naivety.

This is best brought out when Veeru, frustrated in seeking Basanti's love, threatens to kill himself. He does this theatrically, in a drunken stupor and, while villagers watch, he says in Hindi "Wohi kar raha hoon bhaiya jo Majnu ne Laila ke liye kiya tha, Ranjha ne Heer ke liye tha, Romeo ne Juliet ke liye tha... *Sooside* (he uses the English word suicide and what he is saying is, 'I am only doing what Majnu did for Laila, Ranjha did for Heer, Romeo for Juliet... *Suicide*)"

One villager turns to another and asks, "This word 'sooside'—what does he mean?" The other villager explains, "That is the word English people use when they want to die."

Here there are themes common to many Bollywood films. To the villagers of Ramgarh, the arrival of Jai and Veeru is both a threat and an opportunity. They represent change but hold out the promise of a happier and progressive future. Veeru and Jai emphasise their urban outlook by wearing denim jeans. At one stage. Basanti complains to Jai and Veeru, "*Tum shaherwale samajhte ho ke hum gaonwale ka akal hai hi nahin* (You city people think that we have no brains)." These two urban immigrants are shown as being opposed to traditionalism. Basanti's aunt refuses to allow her marriage to Veeru to go ahead because he lacks education, and does not have any great financial prospects. Ramgarh is a traditional Indian village where elders are respected, but Veeru's refusal to accept Basanti's guardian's final decision, marks him out as a rebel. Here, Sippy, clearly borrowing from the young rebellious character in both Kurosowa's *Seven Samurai* and *The Magnificent Seven,* had added a very Indian touch.

Whereas Veeru and Basanti's relationship is steeped in the traditional Bollywood style of loud fun and humour, Radha and Jai are united together through silence. When they meet they rarely speak to each other. Every evening, Jai sits outside the house playing his harmonica while watching Radha walk around the building, turning off the lamps in the house. After that, Radha goes into her room to listen to the sound of Jai's harmonica. Every light in the house is off but she does not turn the light off in her room. The light in her room indicates hope of a new beginning.

But this cannot be. Radha is a widow and in India, particularly in rural India, widows carry on living after their husband's death as if their life is over and are treated as outcastes, a barely-tolerated existence where they always seem to carry round with them the heavy sorrow of their husband's death. Jai dares to break this rule by asking for Thakur's permission to let Radha marry again. Sippy's film raises the question of breaking a taboo but ends with tradition maintained. In the final scene, with Jai and Veeru having done their job, and delivered Gabbar to Thakur, Jai dies and Radha is left behind in the village, waiting for the real death to deliver her from the death-like existence she has suffered ever since Gabbar butchered her husband. Ramgarh wants change, getting rid of the menace of Gabbar Singh; but will not stand for changing society's age-old rules. Veeru and Basanti do find happiness, but only by leaving the village.

It was part of the skill of Salim and Javed that they wrote lines for their characters which were both witty and struck such chords with the audiences that they became part of ordinary Indian conversation for decades to come. So Hema Malini's Basanti is shown as a chatter-box, who cannot stop talking but, at one stage, cuts someone off by saying, "*Kyunke mujhe befuzool baat karne ki aadat to hai nahin* (I am not one to engage in idle talk)."

While the musical score by R.D. Burman was considered masterful, particularly the concoction of operatic music during the opening train sequence when Jai and Veeru help Thakur fend off a group of hijackers, Salim–Javed's dialogue was so pithy that even Burman's musical numbers were overshadowed, an inversion of normal Bollywood cinema where audiences quickly forget the plot and the dialogue but, invariably, remember the songs. Even then, the song that Jai and Veru sing, "*Yeh Dosti Hum Nahin Todenge*"(This friendship of ours will never break) is a classic, made memorable by its filming. Amitabh is seen riding a motorbike with a sidecar, carrying Dharmendra, playing the harmonica, on his shoulders. Sippy had decided that this demonstrated male bonding but the shooting was so intricate that it took twenty-one days to shoot this song sequence.

The cinematic love between Veeru and Basanti and that between Jai and Radha was mirrored in real life, although in very different ways. Amitabh and Jaya Bhaduri got married just before shooting began. They had promised themselves a holiday in London if *Zanjeer* was a success but, since their parents would not allow them to go on holiday unmarried, they got married in a hurry and went off for Amitabh's first visit overseas. So, when shooting for *Sholay* began in October 1973, and the first scene to be shot was of Amitabh, as Jai, returning some keys to Jaya, as Radha, she was three months pregnant. Her pregnancy would cause problems that had to be delicately negotiated, such as Jaya suffering from morning sickness. She would grow quite plump as the film was shot, and as the film took two years to shoot, she delivered a child and remained plump, which hardly suited a character meant to play an emaciated widow.

If the love in the film between Veeru and Basanti was the standard stuff of romances as depicted in Bollywood films, the real life one between Dharmendra and Hema was far more complicated and like the making of *Sholay*, more like that of *Mughal-e Azam,* took years to resolve.

For a start, with Dharmendra married, and with no intention of leaving his wife, it was a love that dare not speak its name. What is more Hema had another suitor, Sanjeev Kumar, who was unmarried and had already proposed to her but had been turned down.

On becoming an actor, Sanjeev Kumar had changed his name from Haribhai Jariwala, the name reflecting his traditional Gujarati business milieu, with Jariwala meaning people whose business it is to produce garments of silver thread. The change was more to do with the fact that, ever since Ashok Kumar, and then Dilip Kumar, anybody in Bollywood who wanted to be a hero, as Haribhai Jariwala undoubtedly wanted to be, stood a much better chance if they had Kumar as a last name. But things did not quite work out like that for Jariwala. Although one of the few leading actors of that period who had come from the theatre, where he was a leading light of the Indian People's Theatre Association, such were his acting skills and his versatility that directors often preferred him to play character roles. In one film, *Naya Din, Navi Raat,* he played no less than nine roles. Over the years this would frustrate him and he once complained bitterly to A.K.Hangal, a legend of IPTA, who played the blind Imam in *Sholay*, about this. Hangal, who had lived his life in theatres, making only the occasional film (his biography—almost as an afterthought—listed the few films in which he had acted) commented tartly, "If you start with a hero's role, that's all you'll remain. You'll never become an actor." But as Sanjeev discovered, a hero in Bollywood can get other rewards; Dharmendra, who only played hero, got his woman; Sanjeev did not.

During the making of *Sholay*, he stayed in a different hotel to where Hema, Dharmendra, and many of the other stars of the film, stayed. Never far from his beloved Scotch, he drank late, ate even later, often at two or three in the morning, and slept in late. So, with shooting usually starting at seven in the morning, Ramesh Sippy made sure his scenes were never shot in the morning. A decade after the making of *Sholay,* he died, still a bachelor, while Hema had already become a mother for Dharmendra's second lot of children.

Hema Malini has never spoken of her relationship with Sanjeev Kumar, except to say that they were "too personal and complicated to be disclosed."

This could be a reference to the darker side of Sanjeev Kumar, in contrast to the image of him as polished urbane actor who never struck a wrong note. More than twenty years after the making of *Sholay*, Shobhaa De in *Selective Memory* wrote about her experiences with the star when she was editing the film magazine, *Stardust*. At an international film festival in Delhi, Shobhaa was invited to his suite for dinner and was disconcerted to find him drinking heavily. It got worse when she went to the bathroom. As she was washing her hands:

> I saw our host's face leering stupidly. I turned round calmly, expecting him to step aside and let me pass. He stood there like an obstinate ox, blocking my way, his voice of a grain-seller...a shopkeeper...his choice of words disgustingly crass...It was the degenerate nature of his voice that lingered long after I'd forgotten his exact words. If I'd had to hear that same voice from behind a screen, I'd have associated it with a man born on the wrong side of the tracks—an underprivileged, uneducated, frustrated labourer, not a refined, gifted actor, whose very presence on the screen spelt restraint and respectability. So much for illusion.

Sholay was to give a definite impetus to the romance between Hema Malini and Dharmendra At one stage during the making of the film Dharmendra, realising that the real star of the film would be Gabbar, which is how it turned out, suggested to Ramesh Sippy that he wanted to switch to playing him. Sippy said, "We can talk about it if you want but don't forget that even though he is central it is a character role...Besides, if we switch roles, then Sanjeev gets Hema Malini in the end." Dharmendra decided that it was too big a risk to take. "Veeru is good. I think I'll stick to playing Veeru."

Dharmendra, keen to develop his romance with Hema ,conceived of a simple but effective ploy. Chopra writes:

When he and Hema shot romantic sequences, he paid the light boys to make mistakes so he could embrace her again and again. Dharmendra and the light boys had a perfectly worked-out code language: when he pulled his ear, the light boys would make a mistake—mess up the trolley movement or make a reflector fall—but when he touched his nose they okayed the shot; the fee was Rs. 100 per retake. On a good day, the light boys returned from the day's shooting richer by Rs. 2,000.

The romance between Dharmendra and Hema was in the classic tradition started by Raj Kapoor, of the big, brawny northern Indian males seducing the southern beauty. Dharmendra, who was born Dharam Singh Deol in Phagwara in the Punjab, had been married at the age of nineteen; two years before he had given up his job, boring tubewells for the American Drilling Company, to seek the Bombay road to films that so many northern Indian males, starting with Dilip Kumar, Dev Anand and Sunil Dutt, had taken. Like them, in his early years he struggled to make a mark, his muscular frame being considered a handicap, with one producer saying he was looking for a hero, not a kabaadi player—kabaadi is the indigenous national sport of India. But women always found him appealing and, in the early 1960s, after he had starred in a few action films, a poll in India had voted him one of the five most handsome men in the world. It was his friendship with Meena Kumari which made him the talk of Bollywood gossip; the word was they were lovers, and marked a turning point in his career. Dharmendra himself would recall how in their first film together she pulled his ear and he blushed like a schoolgirl and when Meena Kumari asked what was wrong, he stammered, "Oh it is nothing, just blood circulating." But, by the time *Sholay* started, this awkward, beefy young man, who did not know how to react to women when he had first come to Bombay, had become one who knew the woman he wanted and was determined to get her.

Hema had a much more middle-class background than Dharmendra, a background that reflected her very southern upbringing and culture. Although Hema grew up in Delhi she was from the south, having been born in Thrichinapalli in south India. Her father worked as a regional director of an insurance company and her mother was a painter, who had also trained in classical Indian singing. But, like many southerners, she did not have a family name that matched that of her parents, as even today a southern name incorporates many elements including clan, village, and caste names. Hema's mother, for instance, is called Jaya Chakravarty. And, in the tradition of southern actresses like Vyjayanthimala and Rekha, she was a talented dancer, having been coached in classical Indian dancing. Producers had initially tried to call her Sujata, as they felt this would be more appropriate for somebody aspiring to be a great star. It was her mother who pushed her into acting, with her father being more uncomfortable, worried by the reaction of his work colleagues to having a daughter in films.

But, like all the southern actresses, she struggled with her Hindi; it had a very strong southern accent and this caused problems in *Sholay,* as she was required to speak a lot. Initially, she had not much liked her part, that of a women who rides a tonga, and had complained to Ramesh Sippy that for an actress of her standing she had a mere five and a half scenes. He frankly admitted to her that the film was about Sanjeev and Gabbar, but promised that her role would be interesting. However, when she found that even for the five and half scenes she would always be talking non-stop in Hindi she bristled, and it required a special session with Javed enacting her part before she relented. Even then she had to have special lessons on how to ride a tonga, which took some mastering.

Interestingly, Hema's mother, who was the crucial influence in her life, was initially pleased she was working with Dharmendra, as he was a married man and therefore considered safe.

Despite this, and also the fact that her mother who had pushed Hema into films, she would often accompany her to most of her early shootings just to make sure nothing happened to ruin her daughter's much-prized virtue. After that, Hema had many chaperons and over the years it changed from her mother to an aunt and then her father taking over to ensure nothing untoward happened. This could extend to making sure even who sat next to her in the car.

A year after *Sholay*, while shooting in Malta for Ramanand Sagar's *Charas,* her father, by now worried she would be abroad with Dharmendra for weeks on end, decided to accompany his daughter.

Hema would later tell her biographer:

> And since I was shooting with him (Dharmendra), my father insisted on coming along with me. Often, while driving to a location, there would be a shortage of cars and we would travel together. My father disapproved of this because it meant him (Dharmendra) spending time with me. As we would get into the car, my father would, in Tamil, warn me to sit in the corner while he'll sit beside me in the middle. Father made sure that he (Dharmendra) would not sit by my side in the car, But he (Dharmendra) was one up on my father. Through some excuse or the other he would at the last minute open my side of the door, push me in the middle and eventually sit beside me.

Such childish games between grown-ups is, of course, a revealing attitude of the control Indian parents try and exercise over their children. Father and son-in-law-to-be eventually got on, although there would be an amazing drama some years later which might have taxed even the ingenuity of Salim-Javed. This was when another actor, Jeetendra, who had played the male lead in many a movie with Hema and was also single, fell in love with her and made it clear he wanted to marry her. Hema's mother, who Hema calls Amma, exercising her privilege as the dominant influence in her life, now suggested this would be a good thing. And something like an arranged match was organised by the parents for these two grown-up heart-throbs of Bollywood. Jeetendra flew to Madras with his parents to the Malini home there and a wedding was quickly organised, with the registrar summoned to the house to witness the marriage. But before he could pronounce the couple man and wife, Dharmendra, who had been alerted by a Bombay newspaper, flew into Madras taking with him Jeetendra's long-standing girl-friend, Shobha Sippy. Hema's father, furious at seeing Dharmendra, shouted at him, "Why don't you get out of my daughter's life? You are a married man, you cannot marry my daughter."

Picture the scene. Hema and her family from the south, Dharmendra and Jeetendra from the north and all of them speaking in English, trying to maintain traditional Indian norms. Dharmendra, undaunted, took Hema to another room for a chat, which is said to have involved much sobbing, and Hema eventually emerged with red eyes and asked Jeetendra whether the wedding could not be postponed by a day or two. Jeetendra refused and, accompanied by his parents, stormed out.

When, many years later, Hema spoke about this bizarre episode, the way she recalled it is as if she had had an out-of-body experience over which she had no control:

> I did not propose to Jeetendra. His parents made the proposal to me. I was confused. It was the most unexpected thing that has ever happened to me. They came in the morning. By evening, Shobha had landed there and the matter ended there. But as far as the press was concerned, that is where the story began.

Hema clearly liked playing games with the men in her life for when Dharmendra declared his love for her while they were making a movie together, and asked how she felt for him, she said, "I will only marry the person I love." When he protested that was not an answer she said, "That is my answer."

Jeetendra remained a thorn in Dharmendra's side for almost half a decade after *Sholay.* He had already once stormed onto one set where Hema was in a film with Jeetendra, and dragged her to her make-up room for a lengthy tear-filled chat. Bollywood gossip was full of stories that Dharmendra had performed what is called a gandharva ceremony with Hema, where they exchange garlands proclaiming them man and wife. But, in 1977, two years after *Sholay,* when the film journalist Devyani Chaubal wrote about this, Dharmendra chased her, then assaulted her, and also M.S. Krishna and the film-maker Basu Bhattacharya. It would set a precedent for other stars in the future. But clearly this union was still not pukka, to use that lovely Indian word that the English translation of genuine does not quite convey.

In 1979, Dharmendra heard that in the film *Hum Tere Ashique Hain,* based on *My Fair Lady,* Hema had planted a kiss on Jeetendra's cheeks and also cried in the movie without the help of glycerine. He decided he had to act and, in May 1980, he married her. What kind of marriage they had is hard to say. Dharmendra's marriage became a political controversy in 2004 when he stood for parliament with opponents alleging he had become a Muslim in order to marry. *Outlook* magazine produced a *Nikahnama* (muslim marriage certificate) to that effect. Dharmendra told *Outlook,*

"This allegation is totally incorrect. I am not the kind of man who will change his religion to suit his interests." The controversy did nothing to prevent Dharmendra getting elected. When Hema Malini's authorised biography appeared in 2007 it was described as a ceremony performed "as per *Iyengar* traditions at Hema's bungalow in Juhu and attended by just the family including Dharmendra's late father". The book carries a picture of Hema garlanding Dharmendra. Shobhaa De has called it a "farcical marriage."

Conventional, certainly it is not. When her two daughters were born they had to be legally adopted by their biological father. De describes it as follows:

> She lives in her own house with her daughters and picks up all the bills. Her husband lives with his family in a sprawling bungalow that also houses his wife's sons (who have since made it to the movies). their wives and grandchildren. Hema leads a busy, productive life and looks perfectly content. There hasn't been even a whiff of scandal about any involvement with any other man in all these decades. She deals with her problems on her own, without resorting to cheap tactics like involving the press in her affairs. Her references to Dharamji are always affectionate, respectful and indulgent.

Over the years the couple have said little about their marriage. In 1991, when Hema finally broke her silence, it was only to speak in such elliptical terms that it is almost impossible to make out what she was saying. The burden of her speech was that this was a private matter about which no one had the right to know. Given that she was such a public figure who, during her acting career was projected as the great screen sex goddess and heart-throb of millions of Indian males, her answer was a revealing attitude Bollywood stars have to such issues.

The Sippys were not afraid to innovate in making their film. For *Sholay,* they decided to make it in 70mm. McKenna's Gold, which had recently come to India, was a 70mm movie and had done very well. But this would require importing new cameras and it was decided to shoot in 35mm, then blow it up for 70mm. Tests were done with the help of Ajit, one of Ramesh's brothers who lived in London, but since not many screens in India had the facilities for 70mm, it was decided to have two sets of negatives, one in 35mm and one in 70mm, so every shot was done twice.

It was perhaps in conceiving the bandit of the film, and the location for the shooting, that the Sippys were at their most innovative.

Bollywood's bandit movies had traditionally had a standard location. It was normally always shot in the Chambal Valley of central India. The Sippys decided to be different and they located the movie in Ramnagaram, an hour's drive from Bangalore, which had been selected by art director Ram Yedekar who, accompanied by a cook and driver, had driven hundreds of miles in south India to find the place. Bangalore then was not the capital of world outsourcing and computer technology as it has now become. It was a sleepy, colonial town with a couple of good hotels, and the Sippy's film caravan soon monopolised these during the shooting. One of them, Ashoka, had just opened and was considered the best in the town. The then demure, intensely conservative, southern city had seen nothing like it before.

With Gabbar, the Sippys had made an important decision, this being largely the work of father Sippy. Bollywood had a particular way of portraying villains. Many great stars of Bollywood had played villains, such as Dilip Kumar, but they were always shown as men who had taken to banditry because the world was unjust. So Dilip Kumar, in *Ganga Jamuna,* had been framed for murder and become a baddie as had Sunil Dutt and Vinod Khanna in their baddie roles in other films. But, says Chopra, "The Sippys wanted none of these easy clichés. Gabbar was amoral. He was the distilled essence of evil. He could never be reformed because he had no sense of right or wrong. And he wore army fatigues."

Sippy knew Gabbar, the bandit, would be a major figure and his original choice was Danny Denzongpa who, like Jaya Bhaduri, was a graduate of the Film Institute and at that time a much in demand actor. A native of Sikkim in eastern India, he had overcome the prejudice of colour and caste that his looks generated, being closer to the Nepalese with slanting eyes and other features common to the inhabitants of the eastern part of the sub-continent, making him very distinct from the facial characteristics of mainstream Indians. Despite this, he had became a major Indian actor. Dharmendra was not the only one who wanted to play Gabbar; Amitabh did and so did Sanjeev.

But then, with shooting just a month away, Denzongpa announced he could not fulfil his commitment. Like many a Bollywood actor, he had signed up for many movies: one of them, being a Bollywood version of *The Godfather,* involved shooting in Afghanistan at the same time as *Sholay.* It was impossible to change the Afghan shooting days.

The Sippys were faced with a horrendous problem which was again solved by chance. On the bandstand at Bandra, a suburb of Bombay, Salim met an actor he knew called Amjad Khan. His forte was the theatre; he was nervous but keen, growing his hair, blackening his teeth and even becoming religious (the day he flew to Bangalore for the shooting he would place the Quran on his head and pray). Amjad worked hard to make it as a film actor; he even took to sleeping in the army fatigues he had picked up in Bombay's Chor bazaar. This was a difficult time for him: his father was dying of cancer, his son was about to be born; his family fortunes depended on his being a success. But it was such hard going and he found the rhythms of the film camera so different to the stage that, at one point there was talk of replacing him. Salim-Javed having found him even suggested such a drastic course of action, but Ramesh Sippy would not hear of it. His judgement was to be proved right. Amjad Khan's Gabbar Singh was to prove an iconic Bollywood bandit although Amjad heard of plans to drop him and never forgave Salim-Javed.

His animosity against them increased when, at the editing stage, Salim-Javed, worried by Amjad's voice, suggested it be dubbed. His voice was raspy and sing-song, when villains of Bollywood were meant to look threatening and sound like thunder. Dubbing of voices is common in Bollywood but to dub a character would be shattering. Ramesh kept faith with Amjad and his voice would prove a great best-seller.

Some time after *Sholay* had become a huge hit, Amjad met Danny Denzongpa. They were driving in opposite directions near Juhu, a suburb of Bombay, famous for its beach and an area favoured by Bollywood stars. Danny, who had never met Amjad, flagged down his car, congratulated him and Amjad thanked him for making his moment in the sun possible. Danny, too, had reason to be grateful to Amjad. He was now such a big star that he could charge Rs 1.1 million for a movie and Danny, as the man who had turned it down, had hiked his previous rate of Rs. 600,000 to over a million.

Amjad also played a key role in one of the Sippys' major innovations: to hire foreign technicians for the action shots. Ramesh Sippy wanted the sophistication that Hollywood showed, but which Bollywood was just not capable of. Many of the action shots were exact copies of movies such as *Butch Cassidy and the Sundance Kid* and Ramesh did not want the Bollywood ones to look second-rate. Ramesh had originally hired two of Bollywood's best technicians for action movies: Azeem bhai (he only had a first name, Azeem—bhai means brother) and Mohammed Hussain. Hussain displayed a typically casual Bollywood attitude which was graphically illustrated when there was an accident while Hema's double, Reshma, was riding the tonga. The tonga skidded, Reshma fell and the wheel went over her and she fainted. Hussain carried on and, when told about the girl, said, "She's fainted, she hasn't died."

Ramesh, through his brother Ajit, brought in an English stunt director, Jim Allen. The English unit faced problems. They had to get used to the heat, and the song and dance routines and, while everybody spoke English, the English of some of the actors was very poor while that of others, like Dharmendra, was difficult to understand. But, above all, the major factor was the fact that stunts were being performed by people working with primitive equipment and at great personal peril to themselves.

Ramesh Sippy's decision to bring Jim Allen and his crew was a major decision. Hussein and Azeem bhai left and, for the first time in Bollywood since the days of Bombay Talkies four decades earlier, foreign technical help was being used. The English, called Angreez (the Hindi word for the English) brought gadgets and equipment Bollywood had not seen before: pads for shoulders, ankles, knees and elbows. They also taught the Bollywood stunt people new techniques on how to cushion falls or time jumps. There were, inevitably, cultural problems. The English were used to a more rigorous method of working. During one scene, where Dharmendra had to shoot with real bullets, he had got drunk sipping what looked like coconut water but which was laced with booze. The bullets he fired flew perilously close to Amitabh. It was Amjad, whose English was very good, who acted as go-between for the Indian action boys and the English, and helped defuse what might have been a difficult racial and cultural situation. In the end it worked well. Chopra says, "The Angreez thought *Paji* (a Punjabi term of respect for Dharmendra) was a world-class star, and he, like the other members of the *Sholay* team, acknowledged that the Englishmen had revolutionised Hindi film action, both in the way it looked and the way it was done."

But if the Sippys would prove themselves innovators, they also clung to many traditional ways of making films. So, as in all Bollywood films, additions were made as the film was being shot and through chance encounters. The film would take two years to make and during that time Ramesh Sippy and his wife Geeta, visited London. At his brother Ajit's place, Ramesh heard a Demis Roussos number. He fell in love with it and wanted to adapt it for the film. But this meant creating an artificial scene. This was conceived to be Gabbar, after a weapon-buying spree, coming back to his hideout in the ravines and relaxing in the evening by listening to gypsies playing a song and dance number. This was cliché Bollywood; the sequence did not take the story forward in any way but it enabled Sippy to introduce Helen, who always played the vamp in movies. Javed, who had worked hard on a taut script, did not like it and there were heated exchanges between script-writer and director but in the end he gave way and the song and dance Ramesh had been inspired to include, as a result of a chance encounter in London, proved a great hit.

The Sippys showed their most traditional touch in the way *Sholay*'s music was made. It took a great deal of work and it was the, by now traditional, Bollywood method of creating songs, dances and music. This was the work of R.D. Burman, son of S.D, and known as Pancham. He would sit through the story narration and song situation sessions, and create tunes to match the song sequences required. The tunes would come before the lyrics were written.

In some ways their most original idea for the music was in the distribution of it. The music was sold to Polydor, a company owned by Ramesh's father-in-law, and which wanted to break the HMV monopoly. Polydor paid Rs. 500,000, a colossal sum of money in those days, and a first for Bollywood. Polydor would later find that even more than the music, it was the record of the words spoken, particularly by Gabbar, that set sales standards that would take years to break. The financing of the film was more conventional. The Sippys had budgeted Rs 10m and distribution was the usual mix: some rights were sold to Rajshris, traditional distributors for the Sippys' rights. These were for Delhi and northern India, but the Bombay rights were kept by the Sippys.

The problem before the première was whether the 70mm prints would make it back from London. Chopra says a senior bureaucrat in the finance ministry had fallen out with the Sippys and was determined to be difficult. With so much of the post-production work being done abroad, the permit license Raj was in full swing and the Sippys had to get scores of permissions. The plan was to collect the 70mm print, have a show at the Odeon in Marble Arch, then fly back to India for a Bombay première scheduled for 14 August, with the film released nationwide on 15 August, Indian Independence Day. Ramesh invited the Indian High Commission for the London screening but, when the official said he had no such permission – he only had permission to collect the print and take it back to India – Ramesh sensed a rat and feared the High Commission may seize the film. He cancelled the screening and sure enough the High Commission staff arrived to seize the 70mm print. When Ramesh Sippy arrived back in Bombay, he was strip-searched and, on the day of the première, the film was still in customs.

Father Sippy engaged Rajni Patel, a prominent lawyer and close to Indira Gandhi. V.C.Shukla, Mrs Gandhi's Information and Broadcasting Minister, who was guest of honour at the première, intervened and the 70mm was released but not in time for the première, where Shukla and others saw the 35mm version.

The audience at the première did not seem to think the film was worth all the fuss. Nobody cheered; Burman thought they hated it. But Prakash Mehra realised its worth immediately and wondered why he had ever let this story slip through his fingers. The 70mm print arrived for a second showing the same night, and the première actually finished at 5 in the morning.

For some time it seemed Burman was right. The critics hated it. Bikram Singh, in *Filmfare,* called it, "imitation Western—neither here nor there." The Sippys toured Bombay. They found there were big crowds wanting to see the film, despite the fact that this being August and Bombay in the middle of its monsoon, but there was none of the rapturous approval that marked a hit. A crisis meeting was called at Amitabh's house and, according to Chopra, a different ending was discussed. Amitabh was now not the actor who Shatrughan Sinha had edged out back in January 1973. He was the star of *Zanjeer* and, also, *Deevar.* Should he die? Or, perhaps he should not die? For a few weeks everyone was convinced the film was a failure; crowds declined; the press was dismissive and Amitabh was convinced he was involved with a flop, having seen his career rise so dramatically since *Zanjeer.*

Then the tide began to turn, or the realisation dawned, how different *Sholay* was to any other films that had gone before. The owner of the Geeta cinema in *Worli* reassured Ramesh Sippy that he had the greatest of hits. "Why?" asked Ramesh. "Because," said the owner "sales of ice creams and soft drinks are down. By the interval, the audience are so stunned that they are not coming out of the theatre." That is when, says Chopra, "Ramesh understood why there was no reaction. People were overawed by what they were seeing. They needed time. Now, clearly, *Sholay* had found its audience." Ten weeks after its release, the film was declared a super-hit. *Sholay* would continue to find its audience for decades and father Sippy believes that over the years it has been seen by the equivalent of the entire Indian population.

By this time, it was four months since Mrs Gandhi had declared a state of emergency, in June 1975, following a judgement by the Allahabad High Court that, back in 1971, she had misused her official position to win the elections. For the first and only time since India's freedom, the country was not a democracy. Mrs Gandhi faced opposition demands to resign led by Jai Prakash Narain, an old-time politician and former colleague of her father, who had also launched a campaign to rid the country of corrupt politicians. Mrs Gandhi got so unnerved about possible loss of power that she imprisoned politicians, censored newspapers and suspended civil liberties and fundamental rights. Indians, who endlessly debate politics, suddenly found their newspapers were like Soviet papers, only repeating speeches by Mrs Gandhi. The then President of India, Zail Singh, said he would gladly "sweep the ground" that Indira Gandhi walked on. The nadir was reached when a now-forgotten Congress President called Dev Kant Barooah, said, "India is Indira and Indira is India. Who lives if Indira dies?"

This had an odd impact on *Sholay*. The film ran for three hours and twenty minutes. But, under the emergency, the last show had to end by 12 midnight and the Rajshris got worried in their territories in the north and asked the Sippys for a shorter version. But most of the country saw the fuller version and even the shorter version lasted only for a few weeks.

Yet, in many ways, the emergency helped *Sholay* in the sense that with Indians unable to talk about politics, and the papers unable to report politics in the way they had since 1947, films like *Sholay* filled the gap left behind by lack of normal political discourse. Papers moved from politics to what they called human interest stories. In Calcutta, in 1976, the murder of a housewife of a respectable family, suspected to be have been poisoned by her husband, although this was never proved, filled the pages of the papers. Even the prestigious *Statesman* which, in the past, would have disdained treating such murders at such length gave it front page prominence. For a change from Mrs Gandhi's speeches about the twenty-point programme, another populist gesture, or the even more appalling speeches of her henchmen and her son, Sanjay, this was at least diverting news. The emergency had many consequences, not least teaching Indians how important it was to value democracy, but it had also unexpected bonuses and helped change Indian life and Bollywood

17

Change in a Time of Darkness

Some time at the height of the emergency, the then Indian Minister of Information and Broadcasting, Vidya Charan Shukla, the man with power of life and death over Indian cinema, took a drive down Bombay's Marine Drive. Sitting in the back seat, on either side of him, was Burjor Karanjia, editor of *Filmfare,* whose annual awards are the Indian Oscars, and Shobhaa De, editor of *Stardust,* then a brash, provocative film magazine, a few years old. The editors of the two film magazines were part of a group that met at the city's Natraj Hotel, a prominent hotel on Marine Drive—it has since changed its name—to discuss how to deal with the emergency and diktats at the behest of Sanjay Gandhi. This required all articles to be submitted to the chief government censor before publication.

The magazine editors had thought of various ways of coping with this. One way was to stop writing about Bachchan in retaliation, as it was felt that being close to the Gandhis, and in particular Sanjay Gandhi, he was behind the censorship. There was also talk of trying to influence Shukla and, when he arrived in town, the film magazines decided to invite him to address them at their Natraj gathering. He was staying at Raj Bhavan, the home of the Governor of Maharashtra, and Karanjia and De had been sent to fetch him and escort him to the meeting. The drive to the meeting literally meant the great man would be coming down, as Raj Bhavan is at the top of the little hill that overlooks the bay.

De, in *Selective Memory,* provides a wonderfully sharp vignette of this drive down one of the loveliest roads in Bombay, that twists and turns as it hugs the sea at every bend, and the less than lovely atmosphere in the car:

> He'd glared at me malevolently after the introductions and snarled something unintelligible. In the car, as we cruised along Marine Drive, he turned to me abruptly, and announced 'We could hang you in a public square for what you are writing in *Stardust.*' . It wasn't a joke. I smiled uneasily and asked him to elaborate.

He turned his face, looked straight ahead and delivered a stern speech on social responsibility. B.K's expression was stiff and frozen. The fixed permanent smile I'd always associated with him had vanished. He looked visibly paler. We drove the rest of the way in stony silence. We got to the Natraj and Shukla strode out rudely and walked to the dais. He wasn't there to listen. There was no question of a dialogue. He thundered on about our irresponsible writing and warned us of worse strictures to follow. Devoid of charm, or even basic good manners, he was the face of the Emergency—autocratic, despotic, despicable. After he'd left, there was complete gloom. The directives were harsh and unrealistic. The chief censor had been instructed accordingly. His red pencil ran through 80 % of all submitted copy. Often, almost the entire issue had to be rewritten at the last minute.

The Emergency certainly affected Bachchan and his relationship with the press. Amitabh, who now says that the media has grown more compassionate towards him as he has grown older, recalls how he reacted:

> During the Emergency, a feeling arose in the film media that its imposition was my doing...because of my family's friendship with Mrs Indira Gandhi. Without cross-checking the facts, a ban was clamped on me. I wasn't to be written about and my photographs weren't to be printed in the film press. I felt this was wrong; that this was a form of misrepresentation. If the press had the liberty to ban me, I had the liberty to ban them. The ban lasted for nearly ten years till I went into politics. Since you're accountable in politics, I started talking to the media. I owed that to the electorate.

The film magazines survived the Emergency, as did Bollywood. No editor performed any heroics, none went to jail or was hanged. But then the editors of all the main Indian newspapers also did not challenge the Emergency in any way. The only exception in this docile press acceptance of the Emergency was the editor of, perhaps, one of the least known magazines, the editor of *The Eastern Economist,* who wrote some thunderous articles against Mrs Gandhi and only stopped when his staff, fearful the Government might seize the press and put them out of a job, pleaded with him to let up.

Yet, if the Indian media was easily cowed down during the Emergency, one of the most fascinating aspects of that time was that it came just as many things were bubbling away, which was to determine the course of Indian life for the decades ahead. Certain changes had started before the Emergency, others started during it; and the Emergency was a bit like the whole of India being put in a deep freeze compartment for two and a half years. Then, when it was defrosted, all sorts of things crawled out.

The start of *Stardust* was itself an example of this. It was launched in 1971 by a businessman called Nari Hira, who was then running an advertising agency and who felt India needed something in the style of *Photoplay* or *Screenplay*. For his first editor he got Shobhaa De, who proved an iconoclastic figure in the tradition of Baburao Patel.

Patel's *FilmIndia* had been started in the 1930s by the man who owned a printing press which produced all the posters and publicity for Shantaraman's *Prabhat*. Baburao was an unlikely man to produce the coruscating prose which was often so critical of the stars of the 30s and 40s. When Saadat Hasan Manto met him he could not believe that this "peasant" with small eyes embedded in a big face, with a large and bulbous nose, could produce "such elegant and finely-honed humour." All the more so as when Rao spoke, his accent turned out to be, Manto says, "atrocious; he sounded as if he was speaking English in Marathi, and Marathi in street-Bombayese. And, of course, before every full stop there was the ubiquitous *sala* (bastard)" Baburao even called his father, with whom he had no relationship, a "pucca sala," an absolute bastard.

His private life matched his language. He had a wife and a mistress, in addition to a secretary called Rita Carlyle who was, in Manto's words, "a strong-legged, bosomy, dark-complexioned Christian girl" who also shared his bed. His style, when at the office, was to behave like some boss in a B-movie. Baburao would summon Rita, ask her to turn round, smack her on her bottom and then say, "Get some paper and a pencil" in readiness for dictation.

By the time *Stardust* emerged, *FilmIndia* was old history. Baburao, after partition, became increasingly political and, after his daughter married a Muslim, he made his magazine a political one calling it *Mother India* and spewing anti-Muslim rants. The film magazines that took over the space vacated by *FilmIndia* were staid, decorous and almost Victorian, exemplified by *Filmfare*. Hira, a smart Sindhi businessman, realised there was a market for something different for the new Indians who had grown up in independent India and, in Shobhaa De, he had the ideal editor. Although she had no journalistic experience she was the supreme representative of what may be called Midnight's Children.

Born in 1948, she had a degree in psychology from St. Xavier's College, where I went to as well, had been a model by the age of seventeen, then by accident was hired by Nari Hira, first for his copywriting agency, and then for his new magazine. She was barely twenty-three years when she became editor, never having been a journalist before. The one big difference between her and Baburao was that while Baburao, despite being physically ugly, produced trenchant prose, Shobhaa's caustic prose was matched by great beauty. When, after some time as editor, she took her first trip abroad, the Belgian air hostess gushed, "You are the most beautiful woman I have ever seen in my whole life." And like most Indians of my generation and educational background, she hated Hindi films and the Hindi film world.

I was first made aware of this some time in the mid-70s, just after the Emergency had been lifted, when I went to interview Shobhaa. She was dismissive of the lives and loves of the Hindi film stars she chronicled. "I hardly ever see Indian films. I don't know film people, I don't even like them." She had a shrewd estimate of her public, "What our readers are interested in is who goes to bed with whom. Many of them are not sophisticated enough to understand what we write. They just cut out our colour blow-ups and worship them, or worse. I don't know. I don't even care."

Twenty years later, when she wrote *Selective Memory,* her views on Bollywood had not changed:

> Movie people are incapable of normal feelings—loyalty, friendship, caring. But they get pretty good at faking them. Wide-eyed young people, who walk into magazine offices, overwhelmed at the thought of meeting their idols, often fail to recognise the in-built manipulation of the system. Most movie stars are uncouth, coarse, small-minded egotists. People deal with them at their own peril. So long as you expect nothing from the association, your sanity is unthreatened. Those who dare to go beyond that invisible barrier, end up disillusioned and shattered.

In her ten years as editor of *Stardust,* Shobhaa herself never went to a film studio, attended a *mahurat,* or visited a star's home. She even turned down an invitation from Ray for a part in his film. "There was no question" she writes, "of getting sucked into something I wasn't attracted to in the first place."

Yet, when Bachchan had his problems, particularly his political problems, the person he turned to was Shobhaa De, and the great man drove all the way from his Juhu home to the De house in south Bombay to talk about it.

It is part of the sharp Shobhaa De style of observation that she noticed that Bachchan, on that visit, was happy to eat frozen samosas and, despite the fact that he drank three glasses of water and two cups of coffee, he didn't ask to use her bathroom.

From the beginning, Shobhaa De ruled out the corruption she says was then part of film journalism in Bollywood, "Most of the other publications had routinised the 'packet system': specified amounts of cash slipped into marked envelopes and passed on to reporters on a regular basis. Rs. 250 for a one-paragraph mention for a new film, and thousands for a well-timed cover." In that sense Bollywood had not moved much forward since the 1920s as the 1928 commission of inquiry had reported.

With a largely female staff but recruited, says De, from "good families," and with names like Uma Rao, Ingrid Albuquerque and Vanita Bakshi, representing the cosmopolitan mix of Bombay, the magazine set out to reflect the very different Bombay and, indeed, India, that had emerged by the 1970s. In the test piece of journalism that Nari Hira had set Shobhaa, before appointing her editor, she had written an imaginary piece on Shashi Kapoor, a star (he was not yet a full-blown star then, but on his way to one) who was different. He was no arriviste, like many of the other stars, being part of the royal family of Bollywood, the Kapoors, and younger brother of Raj and Shammi. And his wife was English: Jennifer, the daughter of Geoffrey Kendal and the sister of Felicity. This meant, as she herself told me once, that he kept away from the sort of gossip over affairs and the curious goings-on between Hema, Dharmendra and Jeetendra that was the staple diet of Bollywood.

The first issue, in October 1971, had a cover story entitled "Is Rajesh Khanna secretly married?" and was a story given to Nari Hira by the mother of Khanna's girl-friend, Anju Mahendroo, in the hope, probably, of getting Rajesh to wed her daughter. Back in 1966, Anju had made the front page of *The Times of India* by announcing her engagement to Gary Sobers, the captain of the visiting West Indies cricket team, an announcement that provoked wonder and lasted no more than the proverbial nine days.

She had lasted a lot longer as Rajesh Khanna's girl-friend and, although the article did not serve her mother's purpose (Khanna married Dimple Kapadia), the article was a lot different to the ones that film magazines then ran. What is more, with Shobhaa and others, who had all been educated in English-speaking schools, what Indians call English-medium schools, *Stardust* avoided the sort of "Marathi-English" for which Shobhaa, despite the fact that Marathi was her mother tongue, had such contempt, a view echoed by her colleagues.

By 1974, it had a rival in *Cine Blitz,* started by the brother of Burjor Karanjia, who edited *Blitz,* the current affairs weekly; both magazines found that the more they attacked the stars, the more the stars wanted them. Shobhaa had to appear in court now and again as some stars, unhappy about what was said, sued. The most famous was when Raj Kapoor sued them when *Stardust* called his 1978 film, *Satyam Shivam Sundaram, Satyam Shivam Boredom* but, given India's arcane laws, and even more creaky judicial system—the waiting list for cases run into years—these cases were never heard, only endlessly postponed. Shobhaa recounts how she would have to stand next to "underage prostitutes, seasoned pimps, pickpockets, even shackled men accused of murder," waiting for Nari Hira's lawyer to ask for an adjournment. After a few such adjournments the case would be forgotten. Even Raj Kapoor, after his film was a modest hit, forgot about his court case.

Stardust changed the face of film magazines, forcing others to respond and, a decade later, when Shobhaa De had left film journalism, *Cine Blitz* could trumpet their own great scoop discovering that Dilip Kumar, after spending a night with a woman from Hyderabad called Asma Begum, had married her, while remaining married to his first wife, Saira Banu, which he could do as a Muslim. For several issues it carried on its investigation, culminating in interviews with Dilip Kumar and discovery of romantic couplets written on the headed notepaper of the Sheriff of Bombay, which Dilip Kumar had been in 1979. He was later to divorce Asma, paying her Rs300,000, and it remains a chapter in his life which he does not like talking about.

The Emergency also saw the start of magazines like *India Today*, a clone of *Time*, which, for the first time, provided India with a national news magazine, important in a country which then did not have national newspapers. It helped that the mid-1970s was also to see what, in an article I wrote for *New Society* in 1977, I called Middle India:

> It is an India that has an embarrassingly high reserve of foreign exchange; it seriously contemplates the export of surplus grain, has discovered off-shore oil, exports machine tools to Czechoslovakia, and trekkers to England. It is where Mother Teresa is somebody you read about in the newspapers. It is constantly outraged that the West always spurns its generous overtures. It would be easy to mock Middle India. It would be possible to doubt it ever existed. Unlike Middle America, it has no distinct geographical area. It is distinct from the familiar stereotypes of opulent Maharajas and diseased Oxfam kids. Basically, it represents those who have reaped all the benefits from India's uneven post-independence, the ones who have never had it so good and are quite determined to enjoy it, whatever the West might say.

This was the period when Bombay was transformed. The Bombay in which I grew up, in the 1950s and 1960s, was the colonial city the British had left behind. The highest building in Bombay was seven storeys high, owned by Standard Vacuum Oil Company which we, as kids, would stand outside and gaze at in wonder. For us, tales of the Empire State building might well have been scripted by Jules Verne or H.G. Wells. But this began to change in the late 1960s and early 1970s. There was further reclamation of land from the sea round Back Bay and Nariman Point. As a child, I had played cricket on the beach at Back Bay. Now, high-rise buildings emerged as Bombay aped Manhattan and decided to go skywards. It was in one of these high-rise buildings that Shobhaa De lived and where, in the 1980s, Bachchan came visiting. Old colonial bungalows were demolished for such high-rise structures. The original plan had been to build a New Bombay in Vashi, which was on the mainland across the harbour from Chembur, where Raj Kapoor had built his studios. But things did not develop quite as planned. New Bombay did not replace old Bombay. What happened was that the land between the outskirts of the island city and the mainland which, when Himansu Rai had built his studio in Malad, was pretty desolate and rural, now began to be part of urban Bombay. But south Bombay remained the centre. And round this old island city centre, the area round the old Watsons Hotel, which had screened the first film to be seen in India, developed a five-star culture, with new hotels coming and an old hotel, the Taj, getting a modern foyer. This is where the movers and shakers of Bollywood, who lived in the growing suburbs, came to display themselves, or just to air their grievances.

It was in the Taj Mahal hotel foyer that the actress Zeenat Aman was publicly humiliated and abused by Sanjay Khan, who has been both an actor and director and who is part of the Khan Bollywood clan (his daughter is married to Hrithik Roshan, one of Bollywood's current idols). Khan, whose real name is Abbas, had designated Zeenat his wife "number two" giving, says Shobhaa De, "a false sense of respectability and security" before the public humiliation, which included a slap that permanently damaged an eye-lid. Shobhaa De has described it as "one of the most sordid and shocking incidents in the history of Bollywood. Had it occurred in today's times, it would have made it to the front page of our dailies. And Abbas would have been jailed for abuse and assault."

Such assaults were hardly unknown in Bollywood but, in the past, it did not happen in public view. Nor what followed. Shobhaa, who had herself in her modelling days been pictured with Zeenat, rang her and Zeenat suggested a drive. Soon she arrived in a chauffeur-driven Mercedes. Shobhaa noticed, "One of her eyes was shut, her face was swollen and black and blue bruises were visible on her bare arms." Zeenat had already drunk half a bottle of champagne, with the rest on the back seat, chilling in an ice bucket. The car drove off towards the sea face and, recalls Shobhaa, "We watched monster pre-monsoon waves crashing against the concrete parapet and felt perfectly in sync. This was the closest I'd got to female bonding at that point in my life."

As it happened, Zeenat had made her début as an actress the same year that *Stardust* was launched, playing the junkie in Dev Anand's *Hare Ram Hare Krishna,* depicting dope-smoking hippies. This is widely considered to be the best movie Dev Anand directed and established his reputation for finding new, nubile, young female stars. Born of a Muslim father and a Hindu mother, schooled for a time in Los Angeles and with a background in modelling, Zeenat could play the modern sort of woman, very different to the old style actresses of Bollywood. This reached its apogee in Kapoor's *Satyam Shivam Sundaram.* As Raj Kapoor himself put it, "Let people come to see Zeenat's tits; they will go out remembering the film." And he filmed her in a saree wearing nothing much underneath.

Interestingly, about this time there emerged another actress, Parveen Babi who, for a time, was known as the poor man's Zeenat Aman. Shobhaa feels that she is the most beautiful actress she met in all her time editing *Stardust.* Like Zeenat, a Muslim, but from the royal family of Junaghad, Parveen had an ethereal beauty compared to Zeenat's dusky, outdoor style, but also gave Shobhaa the impression that she was terribly vulnerable. Events would bear this out. She had shot to fame in 1976, when she made the cover of *Time* for its story on the Asian film scene, a story Parveen claimed never to have read. She was pictured dressed in bra and panties, posing in the style of a 1930s Hollywood screen goddess, displaying shapely legs and much midriff. She had quickly tasted success in *Deewar,* playing Amitabh's girl-friend, Anita (the name itself showed modernity as opposed to Radha, the name Nargis was given in *Mother India*), who becomes pregnant with his child. She featured in other Bachchan films but her life outside films was probably the most turbulent in all of Bollywood. Affairs with actor Kabir Bedi and then director Mahesh Bhatt, clearly unhinged her. In 1980, she suddenly quit films, forcing both Prakash Mehra and Raj Kapoor, who were in the middle of making movies with her, to find replacements, only to reappear while giving every impression of living in a make believe world. Shobhaa De writes, "she now existed in a delusionary world, eating up to forty egg whites and raw lettuce a day, writing reams and reams about Amitabh Bachchan's plans to eliminate her. I'd receive some of these press releases which accused the actor of conspiring with CIA/Mossad/FBI/MI5, and any other agency you can think of, to kill her. Wild theories involving radiation, poison darts, killer waves through TV transmission—Parveen covered them all. Even if the two of them had an affair and then a falling-out, her charges were those of a seriously ill person."

It was again at the Taj, in its shopping arcade, that Shobhaa De was to see Parveen Babi, her figure now bloated, her skin blotchy; De realised the waste in this once-beautiful woman.

Shobhaa De's reference to an affair between Parveen and Amitabh is interesting because that was the gossip in Bollywood and, what is more, the gossip that her own *Stardust* and *Cine Blitz* was often talking about. They also reported other alleged affairs and, in May 1982, *Cine Blitz* ran an article entitled "After four Years of Silence, Rekha's bitter outburst." Rekha, daughter of Gemini Ganesh, a famous actor of the south, had overcome the problems of a podgy, dark youth (a dark complexion in colour-conscious India can be a terrible handicap) and the problems of speaking Hindi with a very southern accent, to become a sensuous *femme fatale*. In this interview, the journalist who signed himself Swaminathan, described how he had door-stopped her at her "forbidden-to-all bungalow," being let in by a certain Jungabahadur, one of two security men, and found Rekha dying to talk about her life and loves: Amitabh and Parveen. She kept referring to Amitabh as Amitji and said ,while he had never promised marriage, he had said for "my satisfaction we could do the Gandarvavivah. We garlanded each other at Trupathi." She then spoke of Parveen and her alleged involvement with Amitabh and the interview ended with Rekha saying she would take a break from films for six months and go to the Rajneesh Ashram in America.

But ten days later the same reporter saw Rekha on the sets of *Pukar,* a film starring Amitabh; Zeenat Aman was a co-star, and Amitabh and Rekha seemed friends. The journalist wrote, "She didn't look pathetic any more and the only conclusion I could come to was that Rekha had forgiven Amitabh and Parveen." Whether this made the interview she was reported to have given another example of delusionary thinking, it is impossible to say. Years later, when Bachchan was asked about Rekha, he said, "It was pretty natural for the media to write reams about us. Stars have always been the butt of speculation and yellow journalism."

This yellow journalism, if that was what it was, was in marked contrast to the way *Filmfare* had reported the relationship between Dilip Kumar and Madhubala two decades earlier. When Bunny Reuben interviewed a desolate Madhubala, unburdening herself about her love for Dilip Kumar, he found he could not report it in full in his magazine.

India, emerging from the deep freeze of the Emergency, was finding a new voice, Bollywood in particular. It did not hide away in bungalows, far from town. This was the period when the marriage between Bollywood and cricket began to take place, quite literally. In 1979-80, when the Pakistani cricket team came on tour, their cricketers, in particular Imran Khan, were much sought-after. Their defeat at the hands of the Indians was later to be attributed to their dalliance with Bollywood starlets. One of the cricketers, Moshin Khan married an actress and, later, Vivian Richards fathered a daughter with another actress. Both Zeenat, who never recovered from the Khan assault, and Parveen, had burnt-out by the beginning of the 1980s but, while they flourished, they defined the new Bollywood film actress, the female symbols of Middle India.

It was Middle India that welcomed Mrs Gandhi's Emergency, because law and order and firm Government are favoured ideas. Mrs Gandhi's Emergency rule brought together a package that these Indians had always wanted. No sudden power-cuts, which can make life in many cities a living hell, no *bandhs* (strikes), that can immobilise cities for days, and no rioting students or workers. Although middle Indians, as a class, have benefited most from Indian democracy, they are also its greatest critics. Many of them often never vote. It is the poor in India who always vote. It is this paradox that explains the fact that Kemal Ataturk had long been every middle Indian's favourite "benevolent" dictator. Soon after Mrs Gandhi's Emergency, arguments were quickly found to support her decrees: a poor peasantry, a huge army of illiterates, and a lack of communal sense of discipline.

What was interesting was that even the rigours of the Emergency did not completely erase Mrs Gandhi's reputation as a liberal compared to the rigidity of her successor, Morarji Desai. This was not because of Mrs Gandhi's economic or political policies but because she touched those aspects of life which middle Indians hold dear. She soft-pedalled prohibition and relaxed foreign travel—things that always meant more to middle India than a free press or an independent judiciary, let alone ministerial threats to hang film editors. At the height of the Emergency rule, I complained to one of Mrs Gandhi's admirers that she had killed free speech. He laughed, "Killed free speech? Why, I have been saying what I like. People who come here can talk freely." As he did so he waved his arm round his well-manicured lawn, clearly showing the area of free speech that mattered to him. Democratic liberalism, it was felt, excited unbridled populism and Mrs Gandhi's warnings about "unlicensed freedom" (a very revealing phrase) won universal middle Indian approval. It reflected the genuine fear among many of being sucked back into the growing jungle of mass poverty from which middle Indians had just emerged.

In a sense, middle Indians were right. While in 1976, Amrit Nahata's political satire *Kissa Kursi Ka* was banned and destroyed, the same year Mrs Gandhi personally intervened to help the career of a man who can rightly claim to be the greatest director of Bollywood, the one man worthy of being spoken of as a successor to the great Ray. His greatness lies in the fact that while working with Bollywood he also demonstrated you can make movies that tell you about life, rouse you to anger or pity and have a message, but are entertaining as well. This was not just Bollywood masala, but was spiced with the sort of ingredients that great film-makers of the world use.

It was 1973 when Benegal, thirty-eight years old, after twelve years of effort, finally managed to release his first film, *Ankur*. The film, set in Hyderabad in south India, where he had grown up, dealt with rural oppression and human tragedy. The rich son of a zamindar returns home from the city and, finding that the maidservant of the house has a deaf mute husband, seduces her. The woman gets pregnant and the wife discovers the secret leading to the climax of the film. The movie, superbly filmed by Govind Nihalani, introduced a whole host of new actors and actresses: Shabana Azmi, Anant Nag and Sadhu Meher.

Various influences had been at work on Benegal before he could finally make it into films.

I admired a number of film directors but the man whose ability I've always admired was Satyajit Ray in India. In the world of cinema, Ray's coming created a revolution. What he did was nothing short of a real revolution. That affected a lot of young people. Even Mrs Gandhi was so impressed with Ray. When she was Minister of Information and Broadcasting, she started the Film Institute. The idea of what is good cinema, a benchmark of good cinema, was Satyajit Ray. You had to make good films that set the model. I also admired to some extent Ritwik Ghatak, in his time, but he was such an erratic kind of genius and he made such uneven films. I wouldn't say admired, but I did like some of the works of directors who made films for Prabhat or people like Bimal Roy, Mehboob, Guru Dutt or Raj Kapoor

And K. Asif?

Asif was theatre, rather than cinema. *Mughal-e Azam* was an attractive film, very enjoyable. *Mother India* is an archetypal Indian film. Every other film that has been made since then has taken something from *Mother India*. *Mother India* was probably the most important Indian film ever made. I don't believe any other film had that kind of impact on film-making in popular Indian cinema. The structure of the film and the story of the film. It is Nehruvian but the important thing there is that it caught the imagination of the Indian people in a fashion that you can only attribute to great epics.

Benegal, working in Bombay as a copywriter and making commercial films for companies like Hindustan Lever, struggled to make his first film:

It took me twelve years to make it. For twelve years nobody would put any money into it. I went to just about very producer I could think of. All the big ones of the time. Finally, the person who produced it was a man used to distribute advertising films, not films. A company called Blaze and the person was Mohan Bijlani

Did Benegal ever think of approaching Raj Kapoor?

Raj Kapoor? He would not have been accessible to me at that time. He would not have entertained even a conversation. Later on, he was very good. After *Ankur*, he liked *Ankur*, I got to know him.

But Ray played an important part in helping Benegal.

Satyajit Ray certainly had a tremendous impact on me because he seemed to be the kind of person who made the kind of films I wanted to make. He was a kind of guru figure. [At his university, when Benegal founded the first film club, the inaugural film was *Pather Panchali*] . He loved *Ankur*. He said very good things about it, which helped me. I invited him to see the film before I released it. It was at a little theatre called Blaze Minuet, a miniature theatre between Wodehouse Road and Colaba Causeway, near the Archbishop's house. I used to edit there. I invited Ray to see the film. He saw it and liked it very much. He insisted on writing something about it, which he did. Then it appeared in his book. He wrote a lot about it. More that that, when I showed him the film he asked, "What do you hope for this film?" I said, "I hope it will run for a week-end at Eros." He said, "It will run for many week-ends. You mark my words."

Ray was to be proved right. Benegal's film was a landmark for Bollywood: the first film to break the Bollywood format.

Some of the films went way out into what could be only connected with the kind of cinema experimentation that was going on in the West, particularly in countries like France and lots of other countries. But I was not going in that direction. I wanted to make films that would entertain people because I want to make films which I could enjoy watching. I never really moved out of making narrative films. My films always told a story. Also, when I was making these films, it wasn't as though they had had an opportunity to find their place in the world of Indian cinema. I had proper actors and actresses, people who had been trained. When I started, Shabana was a trained actress, as was Smita Patil and Sadhu Meher, the fellow who played her husband. The hero, Anant Nag, the cowardly character, was not, but he was an experienced theatre actor. Some, I went after; others, came to me. Shabana Azmi came to me.

The film came at the right time and was also important for one very significant reason. It finally broke the social barrier that had since the start of Hindi cinema kept them out of the posh cinema houses of south Bombay, where the norm was always to show Hollywood films. Benegal recalls:

That was the first time Eros had shown a Hindi film. It was easy. Because all the Fort, south Bombay cinemas, which used to show Hollywood movies had a paucity of American films. The Government of India was going to allow only a certain number of American films to be imported. The reason was at that time India had decided that they were not going to allow Hollywood films to monopolise the screens. I am talking of the early seventies. We also had foreign exchange restrictions, and these people were not allowed to take the money back. So, suddenly, all these cinemas, particularly in the metropolitan cities, where you had cinemas that traditionally showed English films, English language films, found their screen plan was absolutely free. They didn't have any films to show. So, when I started making films, these theatres were open to me. The audience that started to see my films was the same audience that would have previously seen a Western film. The clientele that missed seeing Western films, now started to see mine. So, that became a market for what today we call parallel cinema, alternate cinema, whatever. They decided to stamp that label on my kind of films. But, popular cinema itself continued in its own merry way. However, with technological advances—sounds getting better, more sophisticated surround sound, and the whole business of block-busters and television coming in—mainstream cinema had to suddenly compete with all these changes. They could no longer make the kind of films they were making. They had to approach it differently, but they didn't make the content different. Content remained the same. But many of the characters these films portrayed, changed. There are many other reasons for the changes that came. Also our cinema houses had to get better because, before that, our cinemas for years used to be dumps.

Ankur had not cost a lot of money. Even for 1973, about five and half lakhs (Rs. 550,000) was not a great deal. His next major film, *Nishant,* made in 1975, would cost more: 9 lakhs (Rs. 900,000) and also cause Benegal to come to terms with the Emergency. This meant coping with Shukla and seeing a different side of Mrs Gandhi. Here again, Ray would play a crucial part.

In this film, Benegal took a real life incident which took place in 1945 in princely India. Again, it was set in rural India and showed how the rich landowners can be tyrannical. A school teacher, played by Girish Karnad, arrives with his wife, played by Shabana Azmi. A member of the landowner's family—one of four brothers—kidnaps her and rapes her and the film, whose title means Night's End, is about the teacher seeking justice.

In the film, Benegal introduced another young actor, Naseeruddin Shah, who had always wanted to be an actor, trained at the National School of Drama and was later to become a director. Benegal had also decided to have Kulbhushan Kharbanda in the film and sent him a telegram to come from Calcutta for a two-day shoot in Bombay. He drove to Calcutta airport on his scooter and left it in the parking lot expecting to be back in a few days. Contrary to normal Bollywood practice, Benegal required all his actors to be on the set from Day One night to the end of the filming. Kulbhushan did not get on till day thirty-nine and then stayed on in Bombay for another three years, all this time his scooter was parked at Calcutta airport.

Benegal must have felt almost as neglected as the scooter as he tried to get the film past the Indian censors. Benegal has always had problems with censors. This was not the usual problems with kissing, that Bollywood films had. Benegal's problems were on an altogether different level:

> I've always suffered with the censor. Because I make a certain kind of film, and more people think that my films have this serious intent behind them, so the censors have always looked at them much more carefully. They feel my films attract greater attention and people who see them would treat them more seriously, as against films on the popular level, which the censors think that audiences don't take seriously. So it doesn't really matter what they do in those films. In contrast, in my films, when people do something in the film, it matters. So I have a constant battle, a constant tug of war.

But, with *Nishant,* it seemed he was destined to lose. It was 1976, the Emergency was at its height and Sanjay Gandhi had just launched his forcible sterilisation campaign aimed at the poor:

> This was 1976 . I had a big problem with *Nishant.* The censors banned the film. In those days it was very difficult. Meanwhile the film was being shown abroad. The film was in the Cannes Film Festival. It won the audience award. Then it was in Toronto, then in the Vancouver festival. The film had already become quite well known. Ray wrote a letter to Mrs Gandhi with signatures from Mrinal Sen (another famous Bengali film director). Mrs Gandhi had liked my first film *Ankur* which she is reputed to have shown to her diplomatic guests. She asked for the film to be sent to Delhi. She told her social secretary to get in touch with me. She saw the film and then she called the Information and Broadcasting Minister, V.C Shukla. She said to him: 'You know this will cause me and my Government a great deal of embarrassment. This is a much-lauded film. I did not see anything wrong with it. You must find a way of removing the ban.' Shukla was very angry with me.
>
> He called me to Delhi. I went to his office. He made me stand throughout. He did not ask me to sit down. He was a very arrogant man. He was having affairs with all sorts of little starlets. He said , 'I know your film. We will pass it and there will be certain conditions. I have already asked my ministry to give you a censor certificate.'

When I went to the ministry there was S.M.Murshid, Joint Secretary for the Ministry of Information and Broadcasting. This was his last day in office. He was going back to Calcutta, to the Bengal cadre of the civil service, where he came from; he would later become the Bengal Marxist chief minister, Jyoti Basu's, chief secretary. He said, 'Don't pay attention to him. We will pass it without cuts. What I will do is ask you to put a card in front of the film. The card must say: the events in the film took place before India's independence.' I said, 'I will put that; no problem.' So we put it. Whenever we had a screening there was a huge roar from the audience the moment they saw the card. The audience realised how stupid it was. That was the worst censorship problem I encountered.

Even during the Emergency, Benegal went on making films. *Manthan* made in 1976, cost 11 lakhs (Rs 1.1 million) and was financed by 500,000 farmers, each of whom contributed two rupees. It again dealt with rural India, the problems of a dairy owner, who exploits the farmers, a veterinary surgeon, who is part of a Government team, and the rise of a local untouchable leader, played by Naseeruddin Shah, who makes sure the farmers' co-operative wins.

In the decades that have followed, Benegal has tackled a number of subjects. There has been the story of Hansa Wadkar, a 1940s star of Marathi folk theatre, whose life had no shortage of men or drink in *Bhumika,* a film that Derek Malcolm thought was "a magnificent visual recreation of those extraordinary days." *Junoon* was historical, based on the Indian Revolt of 1857. A group of Indian rebel soldiers led by Naseeruddin Shah attack a British church. Grandmother, mother and daughter, Ruth, escape and take shelter with a Hindu servant. But there a man called Javed Khan, who has always fancied Ruth, finds them. When he hears Delhi has fallen to the rebels, he goes to join them, is killed, and Ruth ends her days in England, never having married. In the film, Shashi Kapoor played Javed, and his wife, Jennifer, the mother of Ruth, and they both financed the film. Made five years after *Ankur,* it cost 60 lakhs (Rs 6 million).

It proved a commercial success and the Kapoors also financed his next film, *Kalyug,* made in 1981, where Benegal borrowed from the Mahabharata to illustrate the feuding of two industrial families. That cost 85 lakhs (Rs 8.5 million) and was not well received; Garga felt that, in that movie, Benegal had "bitten off more than he could chew." But his next film, in 1983, *Mandi,* cost half as much and again showed his range, this time for comedy and wit, being based in a whore house.

By this time Benegal had, in effect, created a school of film-making with other film-makers following in his footsteps, giving greater weight to the concept of a cinema parallel to Bollywood. His cameraman, Govind Nihalani, had ventured into films in 1980, with *Aakrosh,* where a tribal, played by Om Puri, is accused of murdering his wife. He remains stubbornly silent and his lawyer, portrayed by Naseeruddin Shah, has to discover the truth. It highlighted the plight of the tribals and Nihalani showed a mastery of directorial ability. Nihalani followed this with *Ardh Satya,* which tackled the nexus between politicians and mafia and then, in 1997, came *Hazaar Chaurasi Ki Maa,* where a woman gets a call to say her son's body is in the morgue. The film marked Jaya Bachchan's return to the cinema after seventeen years, and it dealt with the problems in Bengal in the late 1960s and 1970s when, inspired by Mao's Cultural revolution in China, many middle-class young Bengalis gave up their comfortable life-styles to take to the gun and the bullet and overthrow what they considered the corrupt feudal/ capitalist system. They took their name from a place called Naxalbari in Bengal, where the revolution had started.

Three years earlier, in 1994, another film-maker, Shekhar Kapur, nephew of Vijay and Dev Anand, had emerged. Bored with accountancy, which he had studied in London, he went into films and, after a stint as actor, he got noticed in 1983 with his directorial début, the coming-of-age story, *Masoom.* He found real fame with his 1994 film, *Bandit Queen,* the story of Phoolan Devi, a real life bandit queen. Married off at an early age, she was gang-raped and then, in revenge, became a bandit before giving herself up to the authorities and eventually becoming a Member of the Indian Parliament. She would herself be gunned down, but that was some years after the film was made. The Indian censors did not like it and Devi herself protested at the film's graphic content but it was both a commercial and critical success. It was well-received at the Cannes Film festival and Philip French, in *The Observer,* would comment, "to have some notion of its moral seriousness and cinematic power you should imagine a collaboration between Satyajit Ray and Sam Peckinpah."

The success would enable Kapur to become the first Bollywood director to work in Hollywood, making the historical biography *Elizabeth*, with Cate Blanchett as Queen Elizabeth I, in 1998. After residing back in India for a few years, he returned to the US to make the 2002 film adaptation of *The Four Feathers.*

There are other film-makers, such as Aparna Sen, who also owe much to Benegal but, if he spawned his own school, then he has proved he can still be the master of the Parallel Cinema, willing to go into areas other film-makers in Bollywood dare not venture. So, he tackled Gandhi in South Africa. Then, in 2005, came his film on Subhas Bose, one of the most controversial characters in twentieth century Indian politics.

For Benegal to tackle such a controversial subject showed the man's courage. Many years ago, just as Richard Attenborough was making his Gandhi film, Satyajit Ray came to London and spoke at the National Film Theatre at London's South Bank. He was asked whether he had ever considered making a film about Gandhi. Although he neatly ducked the question, the impression created was that he did not want to handle such an explosive subject. It had always intrigued me that India's greatest film director did not want to make a film about India's greatest son. It suggested that Indian film directors, however eminent, felt such subjects were far too controversial to tackle.

This is where Shyam Benegal broke new ground but he had to tread carefully. Bose had produced a child with an Austrian woman whom he had never legally married; it was more like the sort of weddings Bollywood stars have. Many refused to accept that he had fathered a child. He had, during the Second World War, gone to join Germany and Japan to help get rid of the British from India; he had never returned from the war but his followers refused to believe that he had died in an air crash. As Benegal was making his film, a third inquiry into Bose's death was being conducted by a former judge of the Indian Supreme Court.

In the film, Benegal neatly avoided the death controversy by not telling us how Bose died. His film called *Forgotten Hero,* which dealt only with the last four years of his life, ends with the plane taking off in August 1945 from Saigon. Then Emilie, Bose's Austrian wife, is shown peeling a fruit in her flat in Vienna when she hears the news of his death through a BBC broadcast. The implication is clear but perhaps Benegal felt actually showing the crash would have been a final Bose frontier too difficult to cross.

As for Benegal's other problem (Emilie Schenkl, and Bose's relationship with his Austrian secretary), Benegal showed a marriage ceremony in Berlin some time in 1941, with a German professor acting as the Brahmin priest while the real Brahmin ACN Nambiar, who worked for Bose, looked on. No such ceremony took place; it would have been difficult in Nazi Germany. In any case, Bose and Emilie did not become man and wife in 1941, but in 1937. To be fair to Benegal, Bose has left Benegal a wretched pack of cards as regards his marriage. Not to put too fine a point on it, Subhas Bose was deceitful about his marriage both with his family and the Indian nation. He kept quiet about this relationship for eight years although towards the end of his life he appears to have suffered agonies about what he had done.

To make matters more complicated, not only was there no proper marriage ceremony, there was no marriage certificate. However, the fact remains that Subhas and Emilie were man and wife and there is overwhelming evidence to prove that, including a letter he wrote his brother Sarat; and Subhas and Emilie produced a daughter called Anita, who is still alive.

To add some masala, Benegal made the Emilie in the film more glamorous then the Emilie in real life. But, in keeping with Hindi film convention, Subhas was never seen kissing Emilie and there are no intimate scenes.

When I asked Benegal about this he said, "Amartya Sen asked me the same question. 'Why didn't you show some kissing?' I said 'Are you kidding? I have got to live in India'"

Benegal decided not to show Bose kissing because he realised that while the censor is more flexible about kissing, one of India's great icons kissing a white foreigner on the screen would have been explosive:

Our censorship is extremely crazy and whimsical and quite erratic. Western films always had kissing. Men and women kissed each other constantly in American films and in European films. The censor board in India decided that was okay for the West, but public demonstration of this kind of affection is not part of the Indian ethos, and certainly not part of everyday behaviour among Indians. So any such suggestion in films would be immediately excised. That is what happened and remained that way for a very long period of time. Kissing is now allowed. And, certainly in metropolitan cities, it is not a big deal to see young people cuddling up with each other. But I wouldn't say it's common behaviour. You don't see it happening at bus-stops and tube stations like it might happen in Britain or in America. But it certainly is a little more than it used to be in India. In the past, the censor board would automatically go for their scissors. They don't do that any more.

Benegal's Bose film is beautifully done and the portions describing Bose's escape from his home in Kolkata, via Afghanistan to Berlin, shows Benegal to be a masterful film-maker.

So, in real life when Bose was told he had left British India and was now in free tribal land bordering Afghanistan, he jumped up in the air, stamped his feet on the ground and shouted, "Here I kick George VI, here I spit in the face of the Viceroy."

In the film, Benegal makes Bose ask Bhagat Ram, his guide, for a coin which has the face of George VI. He then tosses the coin on the ground and kicks it and spits on it, with Bhagat Ram joining in. The poetic touch of the coin Benegal adds, makes this scene all the more dramatic.

Benegal dwells too long on the battle scenes in Imphal and Burma, as the British and the Japanese fought for that part of India. In his earlier historical film, *Junoon,* there had been criticism of his handling of the battle scenes of the Indian Revolt of 1857, what Subhas Bose always called the First War of Independence. The same criticism can be made of what some Indian historians call the Second War of Independence. Benegal presents the Indian National Army in a more glorious light than justified by the historical record. Their contribution to the battles was negligible and hardly very heroic. The fact is Bose's INA was in the main opposed by Indians fighting for the British. 2.8 million Indians fought for the British during the Second World War, the largest volunteer army in the world, far more than fought with Bose. Benegal does not dwell on all this and throughout the film we are presented with a Bose v. British fight when, in reality, it was a Bose v. British plus Indian collaborators.

But then Benegal had always been attracted to the INA as a subject, having as a child heard stories about Bose and his army, recruited from Indian prisoners of war the British had surrendered to the Japanese:

My father's cousin was one of Subhas Boses' Tokyo boys, the boys Subhas Bose had sent to Tokyo to be trained by the Japanese. He was with the Imperial Military Academy in Tokyo. He came back to India after the war and went through a very bad time because of his INA connections. He applied to the Indian Air Force. They would not take him because of his INA connections. They took him in 1949 or 1950 but the recruiting officer who took him was demoted. He became a brilliant fighter pilot. In 1965, he got the Mahavir Charka for the famous Sargodha attack in West Pakistan. He led the attack. Then he got the MVC over Dacca. He was taking pictures of Dacca airport. Then, later, the Indian Air Force bombed the airport in a particular way. He was a decorated officer. Eventually, he retired as Air Commodore. I heard his INA stories as a child.

And for this film, Benegal found corporate backers, illustrating the way Bollywood was becoming more like Hollywood and getting away from the cottage industry style of finance that had traditionally characterised the industry.

People from Sahara [a big Indian corporation] had contacted me. 'We want to do a series on the national heroes' they said. I said I had already made a film on Gandhi in South Africa. The only person I hadn't done anything on was Bose. That is why I choose those five years. For a lot of Indian historians that is the most controversial period and they are a little worried about dealing with that. Why should I worry about that? In making the film I had not only to get the finances but break through all sorts of barriers and look at the man from his own time.

Benegal approached the work in his methodical way in contrast to most Bollywood film-makers.

You have your project, you do your research, get your script and then get your actors and actresses. I had done auditions of all the German actresses when I was in Berlin. I had gone for a recce. It was a very Western way of making films.

But Benegal's problems were not over once the film was made. After that Benegal had to put up with legal actions by Bose's so-called followers who filed court cases, frivolous but time-consuming, to stop the film. He had a private showing for the Bengal chief minister to make sure he was happy and then found the première moved because of local difficulties. Benegal was also aware that, in tackling history, he was taking a risk.

Indians are reluctant to take to historical films. Film-makers try an estimate what would be of popular interest. In many ways that thinking is not incorrect. In India, historical films have never done well. Unless they are what we call costume dramas.

Not real history. *Mughal-e Azam* is not history. It is costume drama. Aamir Khan's *The Rising: The Ballad of Mangal Pandey*. Forget about its accuracy. Indian audiences are not concerned about that. It has been a failure because historical films do not work very well.

Benegal's film on Bose did not buck that trend. Aamir Khan's *The Rising: The Ballad of Mangal Pandey* was also not a box office success, and provoked controversy in Britain as British historians felt it did not accurately reflect the Indian Revolt of 1857. However, in 2001, Aamir Khan had shown with *Lagaan* how to spin a fairy tale as a historical drama. The history it showed was extremely debatable but the story-telling quite magical. That film would also make history as the first film that enabled Bollywood to cross the final frontier and make the biggest film-producing country in the world well-known, if not acceptable, in the West.

18

The Final Frontier

On the afternoon of August 14, 1999, a small group of people met in the sitting-room of actor Aamir Khan in south Bombay. They had gathered for the narration of a film that Khan was to act in, a fairly commonplace event in Bollywood. But what made it unusual was the care that had been taken to organise the narration and the dramatic effects the narration would have. This was a far cry from the impromptu narration that K. Asif had subjected poor Saadat Hasan Manto to back in the late 1940s for his film *Phool;* this was narration, modern Bollywood style, as the industry got ready to move into the new millennium. What is more, it would end with a film the like of which Bollywood had never seen before. The film would also enable Bollywood to cross the final frontier, get noticed in Hollywood and in the West which, for all its popularity elsewhere, it had never before reached. Not many people who came to the narration that afternoon would have predicted such an outcome. Aamir was a star actor but one of many in Bollywood then, and by no means the most important, and the narrator was regarded as a failure.

The narrator that afternoon was a director called Ashutosh Gowarikar. His two previous films, *Pehla Nasha* and *Baazi*, had fared badly and he had to work hard to even get to this point. He had had the idea for the story for three years, but the story of a group of villagers taking on the British in a game of cricket a hundred years ago was considered preposterous, and even Aamir Khan had dismissed it initially. Ashutosh had persisted, once turning up at four in the morning outside Aamir's house. Aamir had decided he would not act, but produce the film.

They were, of course, old friends, having grown up together, although their careers had taken very different paths. They had often played tennis, one of Aamir's big sporting passions, at Bombay's Khar Gymkhana, although Ashutosh was not a good player so Aamir often refused to play with him, saying it would spoil his game. If the tennis story suggests that young Aamir was something of a fussy perfectionist, then there are other stories that indicate that he could also be very stubborn. In 1970, when he was five years old, he spurned his chance to appear in the film *Pyar Ka Mausam,* which starred Shashi Kapoor, because at the shoot he refused to sit in the car chosen by the studio for the shot. His role involved being filmed in a particular car but, for the whole day, he insisted on sitting in another car which was not part of the film but was the car of his friend Reena, daughter of Raj Khosla, another film-maker. Eventually, his brother, Faisal, went and sat in the studio car. Aamir was quite happy to lose his moment of glory claiming, "I wanted to sit in Reena's car." Another Reena would became his first wife many years later and, to win her, he had to show similar determination.

After fame touched him, his nearest and dearest would tell childhood stories of his tenacity—such as when the Rubik's cube arrived in Bombay and Aamir kept attempting to solve the puzzle until he cracked it.

Perhaps it is not surprising that with a name like Aamir, which means 'the one who leads,' he displayed such a strong individualistic trait right from his childhood and insisted on doing chores by himself, getting angry if his parents tried to help. Although he could generally be quiet and reserved, certainly with his parents, with his siblings he was often domineering and even bullied them to do his bidding. And, while he was a voracious reader, and like many a young boy of his background in India, this meant from an early age reading Enid Blyton and Nancy Drew, spending all his pocket money of Rs. 20 a month on books, formal education bored him. This led to a momentous decision when he was seventeen, that he would not carry on studying beyond Standard XII but become a film director and go to Pune to study at the Film Institute there. This, given his middle-class background, where a degree is considered essential, was quite astounding but this is where his tenacity and stubborn streak was to come in useful.

His horrified parents tried to dissuade him and, in the end, it was his mother, Zeenat, who persauded her husband, Tahir, that if he was so determined, instead of the Film Institute in Pune, he could continue to live at home in Bombay and join her brother Nasir Hussain as an assistant. It also meant he could carry on his studies and go to college.

The family had long been established in films. Tahir Hussain had been a producer and, through the 1960s and 1970s, Nasir had produced memorable trend-setting musicals like *Tumsa Nahin Dekha, Yaadon Ki Baarat,* and *Hum Kisi Se Kum Nahin.* But, by the time he took Aamir on, the fortunes of the family were on the decline and initially Aamir assisted his uncle in two mega-flops of the 1980s: *Zabardast* and *Manzil.* However, he did learn about films: everything from editing to music to scripting.

It was in 1983 that he, along with Ashutosh, got his first chance to act when Ketan Mehta, looking for actors for what became a cult classic, *Holi,* held an audition for a number of students. But, with the shooting taking place in Pune, his father insisted he would only be able to shoot during vacation. He very nearly got the lead part in the film but missed out because Ketan Mehta did not like his shaven head:

My film, *Holi,* was about one day in a college campus. I was looking for totally new faces who had never acted in a film before. Both Aamir and Ashutosh Gowarikar came across as very bright and enthusiastic, energetic, focused kids. And the choice was between Aamir and Ashutosh for the lead. Unfortunately, Aamir landed up with a shaven head, so we chose Ashutosh.

Aamir followed this with *Raakh,* a film directed by Aditya Bhattacharya, where he also had to wait until the vacations before shooting his scenes.

Whether it was such acting assignments or the fact that Nasir was struggling and needed to do something different, it was at this stage that he was alerted to his nephew's talents as an actor. After three costly flops, Nasir needed to do something and, in his search for a new face, he not only turned to his nephew but tried to reinvent himself as a film-maker. This meant a new lead actress in Juhi Chawla, music direction by the new duo, Anand-Milind, and Nasir even vacating the directorial chair and giving it to his son, Mansoor Khan, although he did write the screenplay.

The result was a success. *Qayamat Se Qayamat Tak,* inspired by Romeo and Juliet, was an unabashed love story that ends in the tragic death of the lovers but which broke box-office records all over the country (the film would also make another wannabe actor think, if Aamir could do it, so could he – that actor was Shah Rukh Khan). And, just to make the story complete, during the making of it, Aamir had his own real life love drama that almost matched Romeo and Juliet, albeit with a much happier ending.

His romance with Reena Datta was what may be called a Bombay building romance. Daughter of the Bombay manager of Air India, Reena lived nearby and had been friends with Aamir and the other kids in his building, and Aamir had long been attracted to her looks. When he met her, he was taken by her strong sense of humour, which neatly complemented his own. Once, Reena was busy with a school experiment while eating something. When Aamir asked her what she was eating, she said it was éclairs and enquired whether he would like some. The moment Aamir said 'yes' and opened his palm, Reena placed a cockroach in his hand. As Aamir was to recall years later, she gave him a cockroach, and he gave her his heart.

But the couple faced a huge problem. Aamir was a Muslim and Reena a Hindu and the couple knew their families would object. Their courtship had to be discreet and their marriage a secret, with Aamir waiting until he turned twenty-one in 1986 to make Reena his wife. Nevertheless, for some time they pretended they had not married and carried on living at home as if nothing had happened. But Reena's sister, Anju, worked out the secret and threatened to tell her father when he returned from a visit to Calcutta, the ancestral home of the Dattas. Aamir pleaded with his sister-in-law but when she proved adamant he decided to make his own family aware that he was married. His parents took it well, with Tahir declaring dramatically, "We accept her as our daughter-in-law from this moment itself." It was agreed Reena would live with them and Tahir said, "We'll get clothes, etcetera, made for her."

There then followed days of high drama, Anju ringing her sister to return home, friends of Reena's father intervening and, then, father Datta returning from Calcutta and, on hearing the news, falling so ill that he had to be rushed to hospital. Aamir was persuaded by his parents to visit his father-in-law and this seemed to do the trick. Soon father Datta was so reconciled to his Muslim son-in-law that Farhat, Aamir's youngest sister, ended up marrying Reena's brother, Rajiv.

If this indicates social tensions inherent in multi-religious, multi-cultural societies like India, it also shows how far Bollywood had come from the 1940s when Yusuf Khan had to change his name to Dilip Kumar and Dev Anand could not marry Suraiya. Although, in the wider world, Hindu-Muslim tension was rising (the Bharatiya Janata Party (BJP), espousing the Hinduatva philosophy, was on the march and in Bombay Bal, Thackeray's Shiv Sena was a stridently anti-Muslim party), in Bollywood, Muslims taking to film were no longer having to change names or hide their love for Hindus.

Aamir Khan's success in *Qayamat Se Qayamat Tak* came at a crucial time for Bollywood. The film was released in 1988, when it seemed Bollywood was on its knees and would not recover. India had been late to allow television in, much later than its neighbours like Pakistan. It had only arrived countrywide in 1982, when India held the Asian Games. Through the 1980s, Indians, certainly urban Indians, took to this medium. The 1980s also brought videos to India and this meant video piracy of films and, even at times, films that had not yet been released in the cinemas. During the decade, the landscape of urban India changed as homes started getting cable connections. But this was not cabling done through digging tunnels underground but local distributors just flinging the cables over buildings and from a basement in one of the buildings screening videos. They had no compunction in showing pirated video copies of films for their captive audience.

Benegal told me:

Hindi cinema went through a bad phase in the 1980s; video was coming, television had taken away the middle-class audience, and there was not enough investment in the infrastructure for the cinema. Theatres were awful. They were flea bags. Rat infested, terrifying, nobody wanted to see a film. Projection was bad. At that time, cinema had suddenly become a staple form of entertainment for the poorest people, for people who were recent immigrants to the city. The lower half of the economic pyramid was the cinema audience. There was no way to build an image. Image building for the cinema became seriously possible when the top part of the pyramid went back to the cinema again. It happened in the 1990s. Through globalisation, freeing of economic control; all that went together. All that happened together. The multiplexes are now further changing things. The average price of a ticket in a big theatre in Bombay can vary between Rs. 20 to 200, as opposed to twelve annas, the lowest price in the 1950s.

To make matters worse, the Hindi film industry only seemed capable of producing flops. And, in 1988, it lost its greatest ever showman: Raj Kapoor. He could not have scripted a more dramatic or visual death for one of his own movies. On the evening of May 2, 1988, he was at the Siri Fort Auditorium in Delhi to receive the Dadasaheb Phalke Award from the President of India. Sixteen years earlier, in 1972, he had collected the same award on behalf of his dead father. Then, he was in his prime. He was to make another fourteen movies. But, on this occasion, he seemed to be in a different world. He did not want to go to Delhi and he kept asking friends to accompany him. The night before he left Bombay, he had a long chat with his brother Shammi, to whom he had not been close. During the conversation he unburdened himself of how he had never forgotten the death of his two younger brothers, Bindi and Devi, and the loneliness this caused, distancing him from Shammi.

In Delhi, at the Maurya Sheraton, his wife Krishna had to nag him to get dressed; he insisted on wearing his trademark white suit, but required oxygen for the ride from the hotel to Siri Fort. The May heat of Delhi can be terrible and at one stage he came out of the auditorium to have more oxygen. Then, when the time came to receive the award, he had an asthmatic attack. He got up, lurched forward, then collapsed. The event was being televised live and viewers, who were unaware of his condition, would have been forgiven for thinking he was playing the drunk. The President came off the stage towards him and, somehow, Raj Kapoor stood up, supported by his wife and friends and the award was draped round his neck. Pictures show him just about shaking hands with the President but looking as if he is half-asleep. He clearly was in a desperate state and collapsed again. The ceremony (it was the thirty-fifth National Film Festival Award), came to a halt. Raj Kapoor was rushed to hospital where he went into a coma and exactly one month later, on 2 June, died.

Nobody could replace Raj Kapoor but the 1980s did not even produce moderate film-makers. The one exception was Subhas Ghai, whose flamboyant style of film-making made some critics compare him with Raj Kapoor, and one American professor found "deep mythic resonances" in one of his hits, *Karz*. It is debatable whether he had the wider vision and the social concerns that Mehboob Khan or Raj Kapoor displayed but, nevertheless, his films, such as *Vidhata, Hero, Karma* and *Ram Lakhan*, as their titles show, proved that he knew his Hindu mythology and could use symbols very skilfully and stylishly. Other film-makers were not so successful. They tried various things to recover their markets, including cramming films with as many as three or four 'heroes' but with the quality of films at an abysmal low, both technically and aesthetically, and film music often a rehash of old classics, it did seem that India would follow the rest of the world and cinema would take a back seat to television.

Major actors and actresses would be drawn into making all sorts of films, none of which had any earthly chance of success. This was when my cousin Ashok Ghosh, who had no background in cinema, took to making films and produced *Jal Mahal*, set in Rajasthan and featuring the two leading stars of the day, Jiteendra and Rekha. Munir Vishram, who was Ashok Ghosh's lawyer, and often represented him in court cases involving his films, recalls:

> It was a big budget film of its time. A top star cast, exotic locations, action sequences and a terrible hotch-potch for a story. I remember *Mid-Day* published a review of the film titled, 'What are the good points of *Jal Mahal*' and went on to conclude that there weren't any. Ashok was so peeved at the article that he withdrew the advertisement for the film that was to appear in the *Mid-Day*. The film tanked and was pulled out from most picture houses at the end of the first week. It was dragged out for several more in a single hall in Central Mumbai, so as to not to make it lose its rural potential.

The 1980s was also to see major changes in Bollywood's one-man industry that also had a major impact on the wider industry. The decade was just a few years old when Bachchan emphasised his very special status. In 1983 Bachchan was filming in a movie called *Coolie* directed by Manmohan Desai. *Coolie* is the first shout travelers make when a train gets into a station and porters rush on to carry the luggage. From his office window near the Bombay Central railway station, Desai had often watched these workers, dressed in red shirts and dhotis and pyjamas, jump in and out of trains. He was struck by their dedication, discipline—at the end of the day they sat together and pooled all their money— and decided to make a film about them. He also turned the central character into a Muslim called Iqbal. Desai had grown up with Muslims and this was his homage to Indian secularism, a film whose central character represented the hundred million Muslims of the country. Amitabh played Iqbal and was shooting near Bangalore.

The Bangalore shoot was necessary because, while Desai had constructed the film on a railway platform, as he confessed to his biographer, "it would be absolutely impossible" to film it in Bombay. "How to control the crowds? Then we decided to go to Bangalore." The local Government there provided facilities. Desai found that "people down south are more cultured, refined" and, unlike Bombay crowds, readily acquiesced to his requests. But then, on July 25, 1982, shooting a fight scene, Amitabh took a blow in the solar plexus from his fellow actor, Puneet Issar. The blow had caught him unawares, and it did not help that he caught the edge of a sharp table as he landed and badly injured himself.

He staggered out to the lawn and lay down. The crew, not realising what had happened, thought he was faking it to get a day of. But he was in acute pain (the injury was to his abdomen), and although he walked to the car he was soon rushed to hospital where he was put on morphine. When the doctor saw him he had no doubts he must be operated on immediately if he was to survive. He was flown back to Bombay, going in and out of consciousness, unable to speak and communicating through notes on chits of paper and thirsting for water, which was being denied him. At Bombay's Santa Cruz airport, Yash Chopra had organised an ambulance to come to the tarmac to take him to Breach Candy Hospital. By this time this real life drama had united the nation in grief in a way nothing else had done before.

Mrs Gandhi, Rajiv and Sonia all visited the hospital. Trevor Fishlock, then *The Times* correspondent in India, described the real-life drama:

> His struggle for life gripped the country. Crowds kept vigil outside the Bombay hospital where he lay, pierced by tubes and fed by drips. Public prayer meetings were called and people gathered in their thousands to plead for him. Advertising hoardings were rented to carry messages urging the hero to survive. The Prime Minister and her son visited the bedside. Hospital bulletins on his condition were front-page news every day and newspapers and magazines carried large articles. In the robust way of Indian publications they spared no detail and all India knew the state of the star's lungs, stomach, intestines, throat, liver, blood, faecal material and much else. There was a happy ending to the story. The prayers were answered and the people gave their thanks to their gods. Banners were hung in the streets expressing gratitude. Advertising hoardings proclaimed with joy:

GOD IS GREAT
AMITABH LIVES

Desai made the most of the publicity and, while some accused him of cashing in, he defended himself saying he was "satisfying the public." However, when the film resumed shooting—Amitabh insisted on restarting with the interrupted fight scene—Desai changed the ending. He had originally planned for Iqbal, the Coolie, to die, but now that in real life Amitabh had escaped death, in the film he could not die, and he therefore was allowed to live. The film also reminded the audience of the moment when the incident took place. The great victim of the incident was Issar, who had inadvertently landed the punch. For a long time he was blacklisted by the industry and it was years before he got back to work, although Bachchan never blamed him.

A year after the film was released, there was another twist to Amitabh's career: he took to politics. In 1984, answering the call of his great friend Rajiv, who had succeeded his murdered mother, Indira, as Prime Minister, he decided to contest elections. He won, beating a man who was then a major political figure, H.N. Bahuguna, in his home town of Allahabad. But Bachchan was to find politics very different to films. He was linked to the Bofors arms scandal, where bribes were alleged to have been given when the Indian army bought Swedish guns. Amitabh had no connection with the scandal but was dragged into the politics of it and challenged V.P. Singh, Rajiv's successor as Prime Minister, to prove the allegations. He then launched a libel case in London against *India Abroad,* when it repeated the charges. The High Court jury found in his favour but, as it had been deliberating its verdict, Amitabh heard Rajiv Gandhi had been assassinated and flew back. Soon Amitabh gave up politics but the experience scarred him and between 1990 and 1995, he had a five-year sabbatical from films, a decision he has since bitterly regretted. When he returned he tried to bring a corporate structure to the film business in an attempt to introduce something of the Hollywood pattern into Bollywood but, with poor managers in charge, this proved such a disaster that he accumulated huge debts and had to resume his normal film-making. However, this was in the distant future. In the late 1980s, with Bollywood's greatest superstar licking his wounds, there was desperate need for something new.

But if *Qayamat Se Qayamat Tak* answered that need for a time, halting the descent of Hindi film into senseless violence, and making love stories fashionable once again, it also created a problem for Aamir Khan. His success in *Qayamat Se Qayamat Tak* had typecast him; film-makers refused to cast him in any other type of part and, as often happens, he could not replace the astounding success of *Qayamat Se Qayamat Tak*. Critics started referring to Aamir as a 'one-hit wonder'.

In the past, actors faced with such a problem in Bollywood would have signed up for as many films as possible in the hope that in numbers lay security and one of them may be a hit. Aamir went the other way and decided to do one film at a time. In the decade and a half that followed, Aamir acted in only twenty films of which twelve were big successes—a success ratio of 60%. He had succeeded in making audiences believe that his films were something special and worth waiting for, fostering a crucial sense of expectancy. It also meant that Aamir's films were not unnecessarily delayed on account of his having to juggle too many conflicting filming schedules. But this, far from being appreciated, caused problems, as did his penchant for perfection. In one film, the director was not best pleased when Aamir said the dialogue written for him was not appropriate, no Indian son, he told the director, would address his father in that fashion. Nor was he popular with Mahesh Bhatt when he asked him to give up directing *Ghulam,* since Bhatt was tied up with too many projects and had resorted to directing over the phone. In Bollywood, with stars having multiple shooting schedules every day, nobody took as much care as Aamir did, asking for retakes, and while this made the end product better, it often made the producer, who was watching the clock tick away and the costs rise, very angry.

Determined to break away from *Qayamat Se Qayamat Tak,* he played the spoiled brat with loads of attitude in Indra Kumar's 1990 film, *Dil,* which, despite its crude humour and melodrama, enhanced his reputation, giving him a new image and was an even bigger hit than *Qayamat Se Qayamat Tak.* By the time *Dil Hai Ke Manta Nahin* proved a success in 1991, Aamir was one of the bankable stars of Bollywood.

By the end of the 1990s, Aamir had done a number of films, all of them that bit different. So he had been an impish schoolboy in the 1992 *Jo Jeeta Wohi Sikandar,* again directed by his cousin Mansoor, a no-nonsense uncle with three orphaned nephews in the 1993 film, *Hum Hain Raahi Pyar Ke.* This was followed by a very Bollywood style, outrageous, over-the-top performance in the 1994 *Andaz Apna Apna,* and then came a single parent in the 1995 tear-jerker, *Akele Hum Akele Tum.*

Rangeela, the same year, was a rare film based on Bollywood itself where Jackie Shroff played the superstar, the relative newcomer, Urmila Matondkar, the wannabe star, and Aamir Khan, the street-wise hoodlum or, what Bombay calls, a tapori. What made the casting interesting was that in real life Shroff had been a hoodlum before he became a big star. Shobhaa De has described how, when she took her children down to the ice cream parlour on Napean Sea Road, a smart area of Bombay—she would see Shroff, "clad in a pair of dirty jeans, with his trademark gamcha (cloth) flung over his shoulder." There would be street fights, with chains and knuckle-dusters, and passers-by were harassed and roughed up and, if some of this was fun, there was a definite air of menace. "Jackie Shroff," writes Shobhaa De, "managed to stay on this side of the law," and then through a modelling break in a cigarette commercial made it big in Bollywood. Aamir, the well-brought-up boy, now played the hoodlum in the film. Even greater success came the following year in the 1996 film, *Raja Hindustani,* where Aamir Khan played a taxi driver with whom the visiting daughter of a multi-millionaire falls in love in a small mountain resort. Both *Rangeela* and *Raja Hindustani* were among the top ten hits of the 1990s, although *Raja Hindustani* had greater box office success, earning over Rs. 60 crore (Rs. 600 million).

In this period perhaps his most memorable performance had been in Deepa Mehta's 1999 film, *1947—Earth.* Mehta was a controversial film-maker. Three years earlier she had made *Fire,* tackling lesbianism, the love between two unhappy, lonely daughters-in-law of a Delhi family, played by Shabana Azmi and Nandita Das. The film had provoked controversy; Thackeray had condemned it, saying "Has lesbianism spread like an epidemic that it should be portrayed as a guideline to unhappy wives not to depend on their husbands?" His Shiv Sena thugs had destroyed theatres which showed the film, forcing distributors to take it off the screens. Now she tackled another taboo subject, the partition of India. Bapsi Sidhwa, the Pakistani Parsi writer, had provided the story which was a love triangle between a maid, Shanta, her masseur, Hasan, and the smooth-talking, thoroughly opportunistic, shady, suitor Dilnawaz, played by Aamir. In a cinema where heroes never really wanted to play bad characters unless they had some redeeming qualities, Aamir was happy to take on a role which had very little that was likeable, producing a finely-honed performance. The role disturbed him, and he hated the character, but relished the challenge of making him work on the screen.

By this time, Aamir was not only impressing cinema audiences but also those who moulded the opinions of the Indian chattering classes. It was soon after *Rangela* that Shobhaa De met Aamir Khan while both were at a charity do in Bangalore, and the way he handled himself, without any of the airs of Bollywood stars, won her over completely. During the show a woman rushed up to the stage and accused him of ditching her girl-friend for his wife. Aamir calmly explained that, while what she said was true, the relationship had not worked. Shobhaa writes, "I thought it was brilliantly handled, without any awkwardness and with enormous tact. I swore to myself I'd see every single film of his. I loved *Rangeela* and now, after his Bangalore performance, I'd become the complete convert."

Nevertheless, by the time Ashutosh Gowarikar, having moved from acting to directing, had persuaded his old tennis partner to look at the *Lagaan* story. Aamir Khan was by no means the biggest beast in the Bollywood jungle. Indeed, about the time Gowarikar approached him, he was fairly low down in the pecking order of the stars and not even the most important Khan in Bollywood. There were at least two other Khans who were bigger names. There was Salman Khan or, more properly, Abdul Rashid Salim Salman Khan, who had been born the same year as Aamir and had begun to specialise in softly-spoken, romantic roles, playing the comic-boy lover.

Even higher than these two Khans was Shah Rukh Khan, who was already being called "King Khan" or "Bollywood's Heart Throb." Shah Rukh (it means "Face of the King") Khan was being seen as the successor to Amitabh Bachchan as the King of Bollywood with a string of "blockbusters."

Bachchan himself, after his political traumas, was making a comeback and, this time, using television and his success as the presenter of Who Wants to be a Millionaire, proving once again the versatility of this remarkable actor.

These were not the only male beasts prowling in the Bollywood jungle. Just about the time Aamir Khan got involved in *Lagaan,* Hrithik Roshan emerged who, some would claim, had made a quicker impact than Bachchan. It had taken Bachchan five years to go from *Saat Hindustani* to *Zanjeer* before he became the one-man movie industry. Roshan had made a huge splash in his first film, albeit directed by his father Rakesh Roshan, *Kaho Na—Pyar Hai,* which was released in 2000. And then there were sons of actors like Sanjay Dutt, Anil Kapoor, and Sunny Deol, a son from Dharmendra's first wife.

In 2000, Zee Premier published a special issue called *The Journey,* a survey of Bollywood since *Sholay,* marking the quarter of a century since its release. In it, in an article entitled *Men Power,* the writer, Subhas K. Jha, after acknowledging the continuing power of Bachchan, and the rise of other stars, mentioned Aamir Khan almost in passing, saying, "Aamir Khan, the third of the trio, was never in competition with Shah Rukh Khan and Salman…he was never as huge at the box office as the other two Khan superstars." And in an industry judged by awards he had, at that stage, one *Filmfare* Award for *Raja Hindustani.*

But what he had was a niche, a steady following and he was different from the other stars. And he was, of course, an old friend of Ashutosh Gowarikar and therefore likely to listen to this idea.

It was against this background, on that August afternoon in 1999, with monsoon clouds gathering outside, that Gowarikar began to narrate his story: *Lagaan—Once Upon a Time In India.* As the invited guests arrived at Aamir's house they found the sitting-room transformed into a theatre, with a massive window-ledge of Jaisalmer stone serving as the stage from which Ashutosh would narrate the script. Facing the stage and lining the floor were huge mattresses covered with white sheets, studded with ample bolsters.

Before the narration began, the sitting-room was a hive of activity with Reena organising the sound system, food and various other things. There were several other people present whose identity became clear as Ashutosh introduced them. They included theatre actors like Raghuveer Yadav and Rajesh Vivek, Kulbhushan Kharbanda, one of Benegal's favourites and the man who had left his scooter at Calcutta airport for three years, the art director's assistants, Eknath Kadam and Sanjay Panchal. Although Aamir Khan was putting in some money, there was also a financier, Jhamu Sughand, present and, when the roll call of people was made, he put his hand up.

The narration was solely the work of Ashutosh, who played every character as if he was the sole performer on the stage.

The story he narrated was set in late nineteenth century India in the village of Champaner. Captain Andrew Russell, the vicious commanding officer of a British cantonment in India, oppresses the people of the region with high taxes (lagaan) while they are also suffering an unusually severe drought. The poor villagers wait for the monsoon to come but the ground remains dry and infertile. Fairly early on, Russell meets a villager called Bhuvan, played by Aamir Khan, who is impudent, he interferes with Russell's plans to shoot a bird, and in order to punish him, but also to display his power as the ruler of these conquered people, he offers the peasants a wager: he will cancel the taxes of the whole province for three years if a village team can beat his men at cricket. The villagers know nothing about the game and it seems a safe bet. Bhuvan takes on the challenge and, helped by the officer's good-hearted sister Elizabeth, the villagers begin to learn this English game.

Elizabeth falls in love with Bhuvan, who is himself attached to a passionate local girl, Gauri. The love story has many sub-plots. Gauri views Elizabeth as the "obstacle" predicted by the eccentric village soothsayer, Guran, until Bhuvan restores their closeness. Then there is the woodcutter Lakha, jealous of Bhuvan's relations with Gauri, he desires her himself. In revenge, he betrays the team by revealing their plans to Captain Russell. This brings in the idea of treachery prominent in Indian history, and often cited as the reason why India fell so often to foreign conquerors.

When Elizabeth tells the villagers of the treachery, they threaten to kill Lakha, but Bhuvan, finding Lakha hiding in the temple, gets him to confess. Lakha proves his loyalty the next day by outstanding work on the field of play.

In common with much of Bollywood, there is also social concern. A character called Kachra, which means dirt, and represents the village untouchable, plays a central role in the film. Bhuvan's recruitment of him in the cricket team is resented by other villagers who will not allow him near them, but they reluctantly agree, and his contribution to the Indian success in the cricket match is crucial.

The centre-piece of the story is the match, which is both a game and a battle of wits between the Indians and the English. The English bat first and make 323 runs. The villagers, despite Bhuvan's personal excellence, seem destined to lose. If the British are shown in poor light during the film and the cricket match, the ending shows that the Indians still believe there is English fair play. With one ball left in the match, Indians need a six to win. The ball is bowled, the six is not hit and the English think they have won. But then the English umpire, to the fury of Captain Russell, calls no ball; the ball is bowled again and Bhuvan hits this high and wide. Captain Russell catches the ball, but then finds out that he has stepped over the boundary rope, giving the Indians a six and victory. And, as if on cue, the long-overdue rains pour down in tremendous cascades, causing the villagers to rejoice.

Captain Russell is sent away, the British flag is hauled down, the troops depart, Elizabeth returns to England and spends the rest of her life as a spinster, mourning the love she cannot have, while Bhuvan and Gauri marry. The narrator ends the story with the words, "The name of Bhuvan vanishes from history."

The final version of the movie had some differences from the story Ashutosh narrated that afternoon but it was remarkable how during the four hours of narration he moved from the impudence of Bhuvan to the coyness of Gauri to the arrogance of Captain Russell.

By the end of the narration, the makeshift theatre echoed with cheers and applause and even Satyajit Bhatkal, a lawyer friend of Aamir who had been cajoled by Aamir to attend with his wife—it was their wedding anniversary—found himself emotionally overwhelmed. He "felt he had been privileged to preview an enormously ambitious artistic creation." "The innocence and naïveté of the story and characters—qualities long missing in modern cinema and modern life—captivated me," he would later write.

Also, in a break with Bollywood tradition, Aamir announced that any of the actors who did not like the script, or their role in the film, were free to opt out, otherwise, the members were given draft agreements to sign.

Ashutosh had brought along an eight-foot model of Champaner, the village in which *Lagaan* was set. The model, says Satyajit, took his breath away, "as even in that size, it seemed real. One could believe that the village belonged to the year 1893 and that people lived in it." Ashutosh explained to whom each house in the village belonged, the direction in which the troops would march, and where the various scenes would take place. Satyajit could see the scenes unfolding.

At the end of the evening, Satyajit "intuitively knew that *Lagaan* was something ambitious and that something important was about to happen, not just at a creative level, but at a human level as well. An attempt was being made to do things the way things should be done." Two weeks later, the phone rang and Satyajit was asked whether he would be interested in joining the production of the film. Although he was a lawyer, and knew nothing about film-making, this was an offer he could not refuse and about which he would never have any regrets. It would later result in a book about the film, *The Spirit of Lagaan—The Extraordinary Story of the Creators of a Classic.*

This would be one of two books written about *Lagaan*. The other was by an Englishman, Chris England, who, when Ashutosh was doing his narration, knew nothing about Bollywood, and was himself busy playing club cricket in England. His involvement in the film, along with other British actors and actresses, was what set *Lagaan* apart from almost every other Bollywood movie that had gone before, and helped Bollywood finally breach the Western frontier.

Had he so chosen, Aamir Khan could have worked with Western actors who had made India their home for various reasons. One of them, Tom Alter, the son of American missionaries, who has lived in India, speaks many Indian languages and likes cricket, was devastated when he was not chosen. But, from the beginning, Aamir wanted this to be different. If there were to be Englishmen and women in the film, as there had to be, then they should come from England. English actors had come before to work in Bollywood but never in such an organised way, and they had always gone back complaining about Bollywood's flaky finances and not being paid. This time it would be different.

It was shrewd of Aamir to have actors from England, as would become evident during the making of the film. England's book, *Balham to Bollywood,* has a revealing insight into how the English who had stayed behind in India, as opposed to newcomers, can behave. One of them was a man called George who was being used as an extra in the film. On this particular day he was standing in for Colonel Bowyer, Russell's superior officer.

That day's filming was to shoot the start of the match. Thousands of villagers had been bused in to be spectators, 175 buses bringing them in from all over Kutch, with special arrangements made for their water. Everything, says England "had been planned in minute detail so as to save as much faffing as possible." Except for George. As stand-in for the actor, John Row, who would play Colonel

Bowyer, he was meant to make the start of the match by leading the two teams out and tossing the coin for the match. In normal circumstances, an extra in such a position would do just that, knowing he was not going to be in the real film. But George, in his 50's, was, says England, "although born and raised in Bangalore, more British than any of us. He likes to refer to 'the Empire' as if it still exists."

He now started behaving like a major star. First, he wanted Aamir Khan to tell him what was the spirit of his character so he could perfect his walk to the wicket. He then raised a question about the tossing of the coin. If he tossed the coin, who would pick up the coin from the floor? Surely, as the senior officer, he could not do that and needed a 'coin wallah', a coin-carrier to do that. Then, what was the year of the coin? Had they made sure it was 1893? Aamir patiently explained that with the camera on top of the mountain it would not matter what the year of the coin was. Colonel Bowyer had to shake hands with Russell and Bhuvan but George objected, saying that since Bowyer was 'an old imperialist', he would surely not shake hands with a native. England writes:

> On and on he goes, raising ever more minutely detailed points, until you can almost believe the film is a movie about Colonel Bowyer's stand-in, a four-hour epic, in which critics will marvel at the precision of the lead character's stoop and the intricate snobbery of his attitudes to coinage.

Aamir entrusted the search for genuine English actors to Urvashi, who worked for a casting agency in London and, a few weeks after the narration in Aamir's sitting-room, she contacted a neighbour of hers in Camden Town, called Howard Lee, an actor who also played cricket. Known to his friends as Johnny Player, he rang his fellow-actors, who were also cricketers, and one sunny September Monday morning a group of actors, carrying their cricket gear, turned up at Paddington Recreation Ground to have an audition to be cricketers in *Lagaan*. In *Balham to Bollywood,* England describes that moment, and many others, when he and his fellow English actors and actresses encountered Bollywood for the first time. England has a particularly hilarious scene where he describes going to an Asian video shop near his home to pick up some videos and seeing a Bollywood movie for the first time. Aamir Khan's website had described him as Bollywood's naturalistic actor and, after seeing one of his films, England concluded, "if he was the naturalistic one, then the rest of Bollywood must be populated with hams that would give Messrs Sinden and Callow a run for their money."

Lee, England, and others, would later meet Aamir Khan and Reena in a London hotel where Aamir explained that the shooting would be in Gujarat which still had prohibition, a legacy of the fact that it is the home state of Mahatma Gandhi. This would mean drinkers had to apply for permits. England pretended to be very unhappy with the fact that in the film the English would lose the cricket match, and mockingly threatened to quit, which so alarmed Aamir that he promised a proper match between the English and Indian casts during the filming which, as it happened, the English won.

The English actors and actresses Aamir had chosen were unknowns, including the two lead ones, Paul Blackthorne, playing Captain Russell, and Rachel Shelley, playing his sister Elizabeth. Blackthorne, also, was not much of a cricketer and could not ride a horse but pretended he could and had to be hurriedly taught. The net cast by Aamir's recruiters was so wide that it also included a former English banker, Noel Rands who, for a time in the 1980s, had been the head of the Midland Bank in India. Although the script often took liberties with the history of the period, this was not so with the cricket.

When it came to history, the village, Champaner, was portrayed as part of a princely state ruled by a Hindu prince where the British stationed their troops and dictated internal policy, such as taxation. In reality, princely India was autonomous and did not normally have any British interference in their internal affairs. This liberty with history allowed Ashutosh to show a scene where Russell displays British arrogance when he tells the Hindu prince that he will let his people off the taxes if the prince eats beef sandwiches, beef being forbidden to Hindus. One consequence of this was it made the Prince a nationalist, who is portrayed as not liking the British when, in reality, Indian princes collaborated with the Raj and were their allies.

But, when it came to cricket, Ashutosh and Aamir kept to history scrupulously. So the two umpires for the match were both English—in 1893 an Englishman would always have umpired in a match between the English and the Indians. One of them was Noel Rands and he came away terribly impressed with the way Aamir handled the whole filming:

> I was five weeks in Bhuj, Gujarat filming the part of an umpire in *Lagaan*. Having met the producer in London (Aamir Khan's then wife Reena), and been measured for the beard that was glued on after breakfast each morning, I didn't meet Aamir until I arrived on the set. He was extremely professional. Apart from supervising the building of an excellent set (it seemed almost a crime to demolish the village, the temple, and the English cricket pavilion after filming had finished), he secured the services of the lady who worked on the costumes for *The Last Emperor* and recruited two Canadian make-up artists with experience of Hollywood. Every morning he travelled in on the cast bus, queuing for his meals with the rest of the cast. Always friendly, one was always aware that he was the 'boss'. Perhaps, even more impressive, after the earthquake a year later, which almost flattened the town, he sent his accountant on the film to Bhuj to check if the local members of the cast had survived and find out if they needed help. I'm not sure how many of the other top stars would have bothered. We all liked him.

Aamir was not afraid to take advice from his English actors; Lee says that originally Ashutosh's script called for a two-innings cricket match, but they intervened to convince Aamir and Ashutosh that this would be far too complicated and it was converted into a one-innings match.

Lagaan, bringing together two such different cultures, inevitably highlighted the differences. This is evident in the two books on the film. Bhatkal's book is a serious, earnest study of the making of the film, where he lays much stress on the spirit of *Lagaan* which meant, he says, "The tremendous commitment and teamwork of the unit members showed in each frame." England's book cleverly uses the fact that a cricket match is central to the film to narrate his own cricketing experiences and, in many ways, the climax of the book is not the film, but the real cricket match between the English and Indian cast that followed. As England put it in his introduction:

> I would dearly have loved to have been selected to represent England on an overseas cricket tour…But then, out of the blue, I was selected to go to India to play the part of 'English cricketer' in a multimillion-rupee-budget Bollywood epic film about cricket. I realised that this was as close as I was ever going to get to the dream, and promptly invested in a Biro and an exercise book.

As that introduction suggests, England saw this as a light-hearted look at film-making in India, in marked contrast to how Bhatkal saw it. Inevitably, the meetings of the two cultures produced some clashes and not just on the cricket field. At one stage, the English actors, worried that the promised Rs. 250 per diem had turned into Rs. 150 per diem, the difference between three and two English pounds, but with laundry charges deducted, talked of a strike. It came to nothing but the Englishmen and women took some time adjusting to spending weeks in Bhuj, a small town in India. To be fair, Bhuj would be somewhat alien to most urban Indian members of the cast, let alone to the Englishmen. But it was remarkable how well the cast gelled, with even some romance developing during the filming between the English and Indian members of the cast.

If having the English there in such large numbers was a new experience for the Indians, then Aamir also imposed other conditions which were quite revolutionary—and he went back to a filming practice that had not been seen since *Mother India.* In what Indians saw as his perfectionist style, he insisted that all people involved in the film engage in no other project during the making, a marked contrast to how Bollywood behaved. Incredibly for a film of this scale, certainly in Bollywood, it was shot in one start to finish schedule, lasting only six months. Twenty years earlier, Ramesh Sippy, like Aamir Khan, had built a set in a remote village but his movie had been shot over two years. *Lagaan* was on a different scale, testimony to Aamir's meticulous planning.

But, perhaps, the most dramatic innovation was that, for the first time since *Mother India,* sync sound was used. England describes how Amin, who played Bhaga, the mute, in the film, told him how this would be a first for Bollywood and it made England reflect on how dubbing has affected Bollywood acting in the past:

> The norm out here is to post-sync all the dialogue four or five months after the filming, which explains the sphagetti Western look of so much of Bollywood's output. The Indian actors are finding that using synchronised sound enables them to give slightly more subtle performances than they are usually asked for, and they are relishing the opportunity to try doing very little in front of the camera.

But sync sound also meant a big change in the way Indians behaved on sets. Because the sound would be dubbed later, Bollywood sets had always been noisy, even when the cameras were rolling, as compared to the silence that descends at Shepperton or other studios when the director shouts "action." For *Lagaan*, Aamir had to organise someone to make sure the normally noisy, loquacious Indians would shut up and this job fell mainly to Apoorva, whose name means wonderful. Known as Apu, his job as first assistant director, writes England, "was to bully, chivvy and generally order people around, and Apu seems ideally suited to the role. He is a powerfully-built chap, with a loud voice and a bit of a swagger to him." He was also a NRI (non-resident Indian), part of the Indian diaspora who were increasingly becoming important to Bollywood.

The movie showed echoes of Bollywood classics of old. So, like *Mughal-e Azam,* the movie began with a voice-over, the voice being that of Amitabh Bachchan, as if to say this was someone speaking for India.

Aamir was also very shrewd in his choice of music directors and singers. His music director was A.R. Rahman who, by this time, had not only taken over from Naushad and the Burmans, as the pre-eminent Bollywood musical director, but was a very different kind of musical director. The fact that he lived in Madras, where he had been born and where he had his studio, and had felt no need to live in Bombay, as other musicians of the past had done, was in some ways an indication of his status and his distinctive style.

But, then, everything about Rahman was different. His working methods were different. He did not start working until nightfall, as if to match a life which was a sort of Bollywood inversion. At birth, he was given a name similar to Dilip Kumar: Dilip Kumar, and was a Hindu. But, then, in 1976, at the age of nine, after the death of his father, his family fell on very hard times and being helped through this difficult period by a "Sufi" (a Muslim saint), he converted to Islam and became Allah Rakha Rahman.

What set him apart from other Bollywood musical directors was that, while he was well-versed in Indian music, from an early age he had also studied western music. At the age of eleven, he was already a skilled key-boardist and, as part of the orchestra of M.S. Vishwanathan and Ramesh Naidu, he went on world tours, accompanying well-known musicians such as Zakir Hussain and Kunnakudi

Vaidyanathan on world tours. He had also got a scholarship to Trinity College at Oxford University and was awarded a degree in western classical music, rare for an Indian musician.

By twenty-four, he had got his own studio, Panchathan Record Inn, attached to his house, where he pioneered the art of composing Indian classical and Hindustani music, using western instruments and setting a very individual style. He had started earning money by composing music for advertisements and documentaries but, in 1991, he composed the music for a Tamil Movie, *Roja,* which became a mega hit and made him a household name in Tamil Nadu. It won him the Rajat Kamal award for best music director at the Indian Film Awards, the first time ever a débutant had won. By the time he composed for *Lagaan,* he was already part of the musical crossover between India and the West, and working with Andrew Lloyd Webber on the London musical *Bombay Dreams.*

Rahman's music was complemented by Javed Akhtar's lyrics and with Asha Bhosle singing the female songs. Aamir, like everyone in Bollywood, knew how important music was, something that the English actors found impossible to comprehend. England provides a riveting scene when Aamir introduces England and Lee to Rahman. The two had been urgently summoned to Sahajanand Tower, where the entire cast was staying, to meet Rahman.

> He seems like quite a shy, sensitive man, younger than Lloyd Webber and with shoulder-length dark hair. Aamir, I notice, is being extremely deferential, and even a little star-stuck. After all, in a film industry where music is an integral part of almost every film, Rahman is absolutely the most prestigious music man around and Aamir is clearly delighted and grateful to have him on board, and is careful to treat him with the utmost respect and courtesy. The atmosphere is so heavy with awe that as I am presented to the great man I feel a strong urge to bow, as though he were royal. In a way he is—Bollywood royalty.

However, England's companion Lee, does not feel that way and he first asks Rahman what he does and then, when told, he sings "Gobbledy-gobbledy-gobbledy-gook" loudly.

England watches in horror:

> Rahman's face is a picture. A half-smile frozen in place, his eyes wide with horror, he seems unable or unwilling to withdraw his hand for fear of provoking more brutal criticism from this ebullient and overpowering Englishman.

Lee then repeats it and Aamir steps between him and Rahman while England ushers Lee away with Lee snorting, "Huh! He doesn't even recognise his own tune."

But what was gobbledygook to most English actors was wonderful music to most Indians. Rahman and his music, along with Javed Akhtar and Asha Bhosle, won many awards for *Lagaan*. By the time of Rahman's success in *Lagaan*, it was estimated that his annual income from worldwide endorsements and royalties was in the region of US$4 million. It was a prelude to further glory. He has since become so successful that he is one of the few Indian composers to have a big following in the West, as well as the sub-continent. His most recent Western musical was the Toronto/Canada production of *Lord of the Rings* in March 2006. He has attracted the attention of Hollywood, with his music being used in films such as Nicolas Cage's *Lord of War* (2005) and Spike Lee's *Inside Man* (2006). He has even composed music for a Mandarin Chinese movie, *Warriors of Heaven and Earth (Tian Di Ying Xiong,)* in 2003. And he has been awarded the Padma Shri by the Indian Government, the equivalent of a British knighthood.

On June 10, 2001, *Lagaan* was released and in order to keep his promise to the actors and villagers of Kotai (the village which was the model for Champaner), the first public screening of the film was held in Bhuj (the district headquarters of Kutch), and the film's main unit flew back to Bhuj.

Six months earlier, on January 26, 2001, a devastating earthquake had hit the epicentre in Kutch and had claimed over 13,000 lives. The drive back to the village for the screening was devastating, as masses of rubble, buildings being blasted, and villagers still living in tents were the common scenes. The earthquake had claimed many who had worked on the film. Sahajanand Tower had a single broken sink, a pipe and a tap sticking up out of the ground. Paul Blackthorne, who had flown in from England for the Indian première, was much taken by this sight and some of the cast wondered if they were doing the right thing coming back for a première in such circumstances.

But, at the Bhuj theatre, crowds started streaming in, not only from the town but from Anjar, Gandhidham, and from the far-flung villages of Kotai, Dhrang and Sumrasar. Aamir, Ashutosh, Paul Blackthorne and other Indian actors, who had come from different parts of India, stood in the foyer for over three hours to receive the people arriving. No one mentioned the earthquake.

Just before the screening, Aamir said, "We have shot in so many locations, but we have never met people as wonderful as the people of Kutch. The film we shall now see is not my film or Ashutosh's film, it is OUR film."

The theatre, with a capacity of 400, was now overflowing and, in the stalls, there was no space to stand, much less sit. Aamir and his Bollywood team left their VIP seats and went to the stalls and sat on the ground, while the villagers with weathered faces sat in their seats. Then, as if nature and the gods blessed the film, during the rain song, ghanan, the monsoon broke outside, always welcome in this desert, and led to celebrations. This disrupted the power supply to Bhuj and the screening continued with electricity from a generator.

Soon after its release in India, it was clear it would be a success both at the box office and with the critics. As we have seen, *Sholay* was one of the all-time great commercial successes but hardly won an award. That was not the case with *Lagaan,* which won eight *Filmfare* Awards and seven National Awards. Its *Filmfare* Awards included Best Film, Best Story, Best Director for Ashutosh Gowarikar, Best Actor for Aamir Khan, Best Music for A.R.Rahman and Best Playback Singer Male for Udit Narayan. Aamir Khan also won the Zee Cine Award Best Actor and Ashutosh Gowarikar the Zee Cine Award Best Director and also the Best Story. In addition, Gracy Singh won the Zee Cine Award for Best Début, Javed Akhtar the Zee Cine Award for Best Lyricist, Rahman the Zee Cine Award for Best Music Director, and Asha Bhosle the Zee Cine Award for Best Playback Female Singer.

As if to prove that *Lagaan* was no fluke, Aamir Khan followed his role in that film as the nineteenth century villager who wore dhotis, with an urban young man of the new millennium in *Dil Chanta Hai,* which went on to win seven *Filmfare* Awards, making 2001 a golden year for him.

But what would *Lagaan* do in the West? Could it finally break through the barrier which had made Bollywood so popular in the rest of the world but not the West? England and Lee and the other British actors watched it in Leicester Square in the company of a jet-lagged Aamir, Ashutosh and Blackthorne, all of whom had just flown into London. England was surprised to find that as the first song came on, the mostly Asian audience got up and left for the loo, clearly something they are used to doing, knowing how long the film will be—it was three hours twenty minutes long. By the end the audience seemed impressed and England, seeing it as a sports film, was taken by Ashutosh's camera work and felt it was much superior to *Escape to Victory*. Lee was taken with the epic sweep of the movie and both he and England complimented Aamir and Ashutosh at the party afterwards. But neither man had any great expectations of how well the film would do or any sense it would be a landmark film. Then, within days of its release, Lee was totally surprised to find it had entered the top UK charts, despite being shown only on twenty-nine screens, as opposed to the 300 to 400 of its competitors.

But there was more to come. It was nominated for the Oscars in the category of Best Feature Film in a Non-English Language. So had *Mother India* but, whereas Mehboob had to beg for money from Nehru to make the trip and not shame India's name, Aamir Khan went in style and, although *Lagaan* did not win, it had made its mark as Indian cinema's first truly crossover success.

Aamir Khan had fulfilled the dream that Mehboob Khan had dreamt all those long years ago.

In the years since then he has pursued that dream with some diligence and with both success and failure.

In November 2003, Aamir Khan even got the Prince of Wales involved to make a sort of Bollywood début. Aamir had decided that he would now tackle a genuine historical event which he felt had great crossover potential, the Indian Revolt of 1857: *The Rising: Ballad of Mangal Pandey,* with Aamir himself playing the Indian sepoy, Mangal Pandey, who led the mutiny of the Indian troops of the East India Company that escalated into a much wider revolt.

British newspapers delighted in presenting it as the Prince Charles début in Bollywood. The welcome that the Prince was given on the streets of Bombay certainly suggested that he was seen as a Bollywood superstar, with the police having to strain to keep him from being mobbed. Arti Bhargava, twenty-three, one of the thousand-strong crowd who managed to grasp his hand, said: "I wanted to welcome him to India and thank him for visiting us. He's very popular."

Not that he was acting in the film. He was visiting India and all he had to do was be present at the *Muharat* ceremony. The Prince held out a clapper board in front of Aamir Khan. Like all such *Muharat* ceremonies, it was held not on the set but in a hotel, the Regal Room of the Oberoi Towers in Bombay. As the director, Ketan Mehta, shouted "Stand by everybody," and then "Roll sound . . . roll cameras . . . and clap.," there was a brief pause, then the Prince took up his cue and, amidst loud applause, snapped the clapperboard and delivered his one line: "*The Rising. Muharat* shot. Take one."

Afterwards everybody made the right noises. "He did a good job," said Toby Stephens, the British actor who played a British officer in the film. Aamir was equally polite, "The Prince knew about Mangal Pandey but asked a few questions about him, maybe to test my knowledge," he joked.

Unlike *Lagaan, The Rising* saw well-known British actors take part. Stephens had been in a Bond movie and Kenneth Cranham was a National Theatre player. Howard Lee also returned to India to take part in the film. By now he was something of a veteran of Bollywood movies. Following *Lagaan,* he had taken part in another Bollywood movie, but more of the old type. In *Love, Love, Love,* made by Rajiv Rai and shot in Scotland, he played the butler in a Scottish castle where the laird was now an Indian. "I did not have a script for this film but was given my dialogue just before the scene was shot." *The Rising,* however, was very different and showed how Bollywood was developing since *Lagaan:*

> The first time we went, none of us knew what to expect. While we had a bound script for *Lagaan,* the whole thing was very different. For a start, the sets were much noisier than what we were used to working in. The Indians were only just getting used to sync sound. And then there was the music, which was new to us. The acting skills showed a much larger playing style then we were accustomed to. When I went back for *The Rising,* I was involved with well-known British actors, Toby Stephens and Kenneth Cranham, who has been in the last series of *The Romans.* Unlike *Lagaan,* which was shot in one place, this was shot in several. I was much taken by my experiences in Pune where, as I arrived, a crowd started following me.

I thought this was a joke by some in the cast who had put the crowd up to it for a laugh but it seems they had recognised me from *Lagaan* and this made me realise the power of Bollywood and how it can make you a star. While I was filming *Lagaan*, I was also quite taken by the fact that I would follow my team, Leeds, on television, showing how India was no longer isolated and part of worldwide television. I had not realised this before I went to India.

The Rising was one of the most expensive movies made, costing £6.5 million including £150,000 of lottery funds. This provoked much controversy as the film was criticised in Britain for allegedly distorting history and savaging British rule in India. Bobby Bedi, the film's producer, accepted that some of the scenes were conjecture but he insisted the film was against the British East India Company, not anti-Britain. He compared the British East India Company with Enron, the disgraced American energy company, and said the film had to be seen in the context of contemporary globalisation. "We live in a world where some companies try to exert as much influence over the world as possible and the film should be seen in that context."

A spokesman for the Film Council explained it supported projects on the basis of "quality, not politics."

In India, there was no controversy about whether the film was historically accurate or not. But Indians liked their history as costume drama, not as real history, and the film proved an expensive failure.

Lee says, "I did not think there was much substance to British critics who said the film distorted history. If you look back, we cannot be proud of what our ancestors did in various parts of the world. We even started the concentration camps when we fought the Boers. I suppose, what the failure of the film showed was that Indians do not much like history; that is not much in demand there. As to how filming was different in the three years since *Lagaan,* I felt there was a more international approach, sync sound had bedded in, sets were quieter. Khetan Mehta was a quiet man, a different kind of story-teller, not so caught up with glamour."

Two years later, having learnt his lesson from *The Rising,* Aamir Khan went back to the formula that had worked so well with *Lagaan* and made *Rang De Basanti,* or as it was to be known to British and American cinema-goers, *A Generation Awakens.* Made for just £2.5 million, he hoped it would succeed where *The Rising* had failed.

In the film, Sue, a struggling British film-maker, chances upon her grandfather's diary and reads about his encounters with Indian radicals and revolutionaries while serving the Raj. She travels to India, intrigued by the story of the alternative Indian struggle for freedom, distinct from the non-violent Gandhian one, featuring revolutionaries such as Chandrasekhar Azad and Bhagat Singh, who was hanged by the British. With the help of an Indian friend, Sonia, played by Soha Ali Khan, she finds actors, including Daljeet, also known as DJ, played by Aamir Khan, to make a film about them. For the young Indians, learning of what Singh and Azad did, is a new awakening and they realise they have lived selfish pleasure, seeking lives ignoring India's pressing problems.

As this new awareness dawns, tragedy strikes Sonia's fiancé, Ajay, played by Madhavan, an Indian air-force pilot, is killed during routine practice when the MiG, the Soviet supplied jets that are the staple planes of the Indian Air Force, he is flying, crashes. It turns out Ajay chose to steer the plane away from a nearby village instead of ejecting, sacrificing his life to save the villagers. The Government blame pilot error. But Sonia and her friends know Ajay was a seasoned pilot and there have been many MiG crashes of late. They discover that the crash was due to a corrupt defence minister, played by Mohan Agashe, who had signed a contract for cheap, spurious MiG spare parts in return for a large kickback.

The group decide to protest peacefully. Police forcefully break up their protest. The young men decide to emulate the exploits of their new heroes, Bhagat Singh and Chandrasekhar Azad, fighting corruption just as Singh and Azad fought the British and there is violence. Eventually (and somewhat improbably), they end up shooting the defence minister. The film upset the air force top brass, and the real life defence minister, Pranab Mukherjee, wanted the film censored. This did not happen and probably stimulated interest in the film.

The film would provoke huge debate in India. What impressed Indians was that the film did not go into the historical rights and wrongs which clearly bore many Indians and avoided clichés so common to Bollywood. Subhas K. Jha, much taken by "the delightfully unselfconscious Alice Patten," felt that here at last, "we have a film that never ceases to create a stir of echoic references and counterpoints." Before this many critics had said that Bollywood was producing consumable heroes reflecting India becoming part of the multi-national world. They were, they alleged, a world removed from the real traditional heroes of Bollywood. Now, the discussion centred on what some Indians have called Great Indian Post-Independence Depression.

Shyam Benegal told me:

> This has been the most influential mainstream movie for some years. It has had a huge influence on the students and I am certain that this has caused the movements we have seen in cases like the Jessica Lal murder case [an agitation about the killers of a Delhi woman having not been brought to justice], and also the anti-reservation agitation. The youths have been moved into action and this film has had an enormous impact.

Peter Foster, who played a part in the film as a British officer, a scene that was subsequently cut, and has spent the last two years reporting from the sub-continent for *The Daily Telegraph*, having also toured the country on a cricket tour, told me:

Rang De is definitely a big thing over here. If you check out the blog sites and internet bulletin boards—particularly with respect to the reservations issue—the younger bloggers all talk about a *Rang de*...style protest. The newspapers also talk about the "*Rang de* Basanti generation.*" The film has been a massive commercial success (exact figure disputed and hazy but about 10m dollars/45 Crore rupees), taking more than any Hindi movie for over a decade. It is definitely the 'buzz' thing at the moment. But it would be wrong to overstate this. I do think that India's rich youth are being sucked up by a television and consumer US-imported culture at a very high speed. Even in the last two years here you can visibly see things changing. Shops, restaurants, cable televison... everything is expanding so fast and the companies are being clever at making things affordable. Where these kids' rich parents lived in that very Indian compartmentalised space between rich and poor, I think the GenNext are looking outwards in a different way, leaving the old 'soul' of India a long way behind. The JNU crowd—all those lefties—sit and pontificate about the "Nehruvian legacy" but the kids know very well that Nehru and Gandhi are dead, and that raw, rampant capitalism is here and here to stay—whatever the Government tries to do with Employment Guarantee Schemes, Other Backward Castes reservations etc. This is a global world—if kids can't get seats at Indian IIMs and IITs they'll just hop offshore—hence a lot of people predicting that the latest reservations row will produce a reverse brain-drain. I think in some sense, *Rang De* is a timely reaction against some of this—it's the age old thing of young people wanting something to fight for, to campaign for. Their forefathers (as did mine) had wars to fight, ideologies to clash over...now the fight is over different things. In India it is Governmental corruption (the theme of *Rang De*...) and the impact of a globalised economy on society. In that sense *Rang De* (which I think is a pretty naff movie) tapped into the Zeitgeist. However, all that said, the younger generation of India are not exactly idealistic souls. They love everything Western consumerism has to offer—so in that sense the *Rang De* phenomenon is a paradox. It actually says more about the extent that consumerism is infiltrating society than the actual radicalisation of the youth—it's easy, clichéd 'armchair' activism. The perfect foil for all those shopping-mall going, couch potatoes. Marx couldn't start a revolution here right now. He'd just be told to sod off and go and get another ring-tone for his mobile.

The choice of the cast had all sorts of resonances. As is all too common in Bollywood, Muslims played Hindu characters and Hindus played Muslims. So Aamir played the Hindu Daljeet, while Kunal, son of Shashi and Jennifer Kapoor, played a Muslim, Aslam. But, in some ways, the most interesting choice was of the English actress, Alice Patten, to play Sue. The daughter of Chris Patten, the last British governor of Hong Kong, Alice had last featured in the British media back in 1997 when, with her eyes filled with tears, she boarded the ship that took her and her family away from Hong Kong following the British handover to China. It was a reflection of the despair many in Britain felt as this last vestige of the empire was being surrendered.

Like Rachel Shelly in *Lagaan*, Alice Patten was an unknown before she went to India, having had a few small roles in television films and a handful of plays, although one of them, *Cigarettes & Chocolate,* was directed by Anthony Minghella of *The English Patient* fame. *Rang De Basanti* was her first feature film. Patten had worried about spending five months in a country she had never been to before but her father had encouraged her to do the film, saying it would be a life-affirming experience and make her more resilient and resourceful. Patten, who had to take a quick course in Hindi—she learnt in two weeks to speak it reasonably well—gave a performance which earned her rave reviews.

Rang De Basanti was released in seventy North American cinemas and forty in the UK for the Bombay première of the film. Alice Patten, wearing ankle-length green chiffon, was quite the centre of attention, having shared a screen smooch with Aamir Khan, although the evening's compèere appeared to forget the leading lady's name, addressing her as "you with the green eyes" throughout an interview for fans outside.

Patten would later say she was never worried that making her movie début in Bollywood could make it difficult to get into mainstream films. The movie industry was becoming increasingly global, one reason why many actors from Asia were finding good roles in British and American films. She returned to the UK, from her five months in India, to play Ophelia in *Hamlet* on the West End stage which showed her Indian experience had only enhanced her profile. If she could emote using Hindi, she said she could do even better in an English-language production. "Doing the Bollywood film was a step in the right direction," according to the twenty-six year old.

The film emphasised that just as India was now part of the world economy as a valued, and at times a feared, partner, if not quite an equal one, with a growth rate of near 10%, well higher than the average Western one of 2%, Bollywood was no longer something strange immigrants watched in little known suburban movie houses in the West at ten or eleven on a week-end morning.

This was reinforced at the 2006 Cannes Film Festival when *Provoked* was released starring Aishwarya Rai, a former beauty queen turned queen of Bollywood. She had won the "Miss World" title in 1994—and in 2000 was voted the most beautiful Miss World of all time. Rai portrayed the Kiranjit Ahluwalia, a battered British Sikh housewife from West London who killed her abusive husband by pouring petrol over him and setting him alight. Her case was a landmark one, instrumental in changing English law concerning women who killed their husbands or boyfriends after suffering years of abuse.

The trigger point for Mrs Ahluwalia was reached on May 9, 1989, when her husband, Deepak, attacked her with a hot iron but neither that, nor the ten years of abuse she had previously suffered, were taken into account when she was found guilty of pre-meditated murder and sentenced to life. It took a sustained campaign by the Southall Black Sisters, a women's rights group working in the field of domestic violence, to secure a fresh trial, when the charge was reduced to manslaughter and Mrs Ahuwalia was released on grounds of diminished responsibility because she had already served three years and four months. After her case, the courts took a much more understanding view of women who had killed their husbands or partners. The title *Provoked* referred to the English "law on provocation," which was softened, as a result of "Regina *v* Ahluwalia," to take account of the abuse many women suffer prior to the act of killing.

In the footsteps of *Lagaan,* the movie had the mix of Bollywood and Hollywood stars with Miranda Richardson playing a character who befriends Mrs Ahluwalia in prison and Robbie Coltrane as the QC who takes up the legal fight on her behalf. But it was Aishwarya Rai's presence in the film which was the talking point.

Aishwarya Rai herself asked the Los Angeles-based director, Jagmohan Mundhra, to play the lead role in the film. "It was Aishwarya who asked to see me," said Mundhra, who knew he would be accused by some of turning a serious issue into "cheap entertainment." "I related the storyline to her on March 8 last year. She said she would clear her diary and we were on the set by May 6."

It was an unusual movie for this actress, who for some time has been the leading Bollywood actress. But then Aishwarya Rai ("Ash" to fans and the media) has been unusual. Indian beauty queens trying to make it in the West is an old story and a largely unsuccessful one. There have been several false dawns. Back in 1979, much was made of Persis Khambatta, a former Indian Miss World making it in Hollywood. That year she did get a part in *Star Trek* as Illia, a navigator from planet Delta, although she had to shave her head. *Now,* then a new British magazine, even put her on its cover but *Now* soon folded and Khambatta caused no waves.

Rai is different, reflecting both India's new status as a country and Bollywood's new status in the West. Another in a long line of southern belles, she was born in Mangalore, Karnataka, in November 1973, but has been one of the rare ones to make an effortless move from beauty queen to professional model to film star. Her range of films has been remarkable with over forty movies in Tamil, Bengali, Telugu and Hindi. Her first mega hit, *Devdas* in 2002, with Shah Rukh Khan and Madhuri Dixit, received a special screening at that year's Cannes Film Festival. The following year she sat on the Cannes Film Festival Jury, a rare honour for an Indian actress. *Kajra Re,* the song she performed in the film *Bunty Aur Babl.* was voted best song of 2005 and best choreographed song in a poll in *The Hindustan Times* in 2005.

Even before *Provoked,* she had proved she was one of the few Indian stars capable of making a transition to English language movies, starting in 2004 in *Bride and Prejudice.* This just about broke even in the USA but overall it produced an over 400% return on global revenue. And, while some of the movies that followed have not done well, she demonstrated her international status by appearing at the closing ceremony of the 2006 Commonwealth Games in Melbourne to promote the 2010 games which will be held in Delhi.

Aishwarya's international status can be judged by the fact that, although she has so far received two *Filmfare* Best Actress Awards, she is the one Bollywood actress the Western media can always call on, having been featured on CBS *60 minutes*. She is also the only one in *Filmfare*'s list of Top Ten Actresses to have a wax figure on display at Madame Tussaud's Wax Museum in London.

Yet, for all her success in making a name for herself in the West, and her stormy relationship with Salman Khan and well-publicised relationships with the other Bollywood actors, such as Vivek Oberoi and Abhishek Bachchan, son of Amitabh, she retains some of the traditional Indian ways. Still single, when not filming she lives with her parents.

There was much speculation before *Provoked* was released in Cannes as to why she would want to play a battered wife. One suggestion was that Aishwarya could identify with the film's theme because she had been slow to end her allegedly difficult relationship with Salman Khan.

Salman Khan shows that, while Bollywood changes to reflect the new shiny India, it also does not change. A few months Aamir Khan's junior, Salman could not be more different to the Bombay boy—Salman spent most of his childhood in Indore in Madhya Pradesh before coming to Bombay—and remains the bad boy everyone hates. A keen bodybuilder, he has always been eager to show off his physique and is famous for removing his shirt at the slightest opportunity. Having appeared in around seventy movies, he has an amazing fan following but even his official website calls him "moody and unpredictable." When he won one of his two *Filmfare* awards, Best Supporting Actor, for a small part in *Kuch Kuch Hota Hai* in 1998, he kept to his image by making an acceptance speech which was hardly gracious. He had earlier won a Best Début Award for *Maine Pyar Kiya* in 1990.

While his fans claim he has "a heart the size of the universe" and is "very sensitive," to many others he is a bit of a thug who was rumoured to have flirted with organised crime.

His life outside films seems to reinforce his image. In September 2002, he was arrested on a drink-driving charge and vehicular homicide. He lost control of his car and ran over some street sleepers; one was killed and three were injured. It was said that he was mortified and made substantial payments to the dead man's family. The case is still to go to trial. In February 2006, he was sentenced to one year in prison for shooting an endangered species, the Chinkara, but the sentence was stayed by a higher court during appeal. However, on April 10, 2006, he was handed a five-year jail term for again hunting the endangered Chinkara and spent three days in Jodhpur jail before being released on bail.

In many ways, he is an essential part of the special world of Bollywood. Handsome, charismatic and immensely popular, despite his shortcomings away from the screen, the powers-that-be will continue to gloss over his "foibles" so long as his fans love him and his films continue to make money.

If Aamir Khan is the nearest to a modern-day Raj Kapoor, then Shah Rukh Khan is a combination of Ashok Kumar and Dilip Kumar. A Muslim born in New Delhi on November 2, 1965 and, like Aamir, married to a Hindu called Gauri, Khan seems to lead what looks like a blameless private life, living mostly in his palatial mansion in Bandra playing computer games. In 2001, his son, Aryan Khan, appeared in a scene in the film *Kabhi Kushi Kabhie Gham* playing a younger version of the character played by his father, and collaborated with his father in the dubbing into Hindi of the US Animated Movie, *The Incredibles*.

His arrival in Bollywood came a year after Aamir Khan had found fame with *Qayamat Se Qayamat Tak*. It was after seeing the film that he thought he could become an actor. Shah Rukh did not think he was quite as "good-looking or as cool as they were, but somehow I felt I could do it." Having been an outstanding student (*Sword of Honour* and numerous scholastic awards), his first job was running a food restaurant in Delhi before he moved to Bombay in 1989, where he started on a television serial, before moving to movies. Since then he has never needed to look for roles and all of India raves about his extreme good looks. His success is easily gauged by the fact that he has acted in more than sixty movies and TV series, produced seven movies, received thirteen *Filmfare* Acting Awards and a string of others. Two of his movies—*Devdas* in 2002 and *Paheli* in 2006—were India's entries in the Hollywood Oscars. Much was expected of the Sanjay Leela Bhansali directed *Devdas,* which had a star cast including Aishwarya Rai and Madhuri Dixit and was then the most expensive film, costing close to Rs 600 million. But it made little stir in Bollywood and, in any case, Shah Rukh Khan, unlike Aamir Khan, professed no interest in Hollywood, despite being one of the few Indian film stars to appear on the cover of *The National Geographic Magazine* when it featured Bollywood in its February 2005 issue. Like Amitabh, he likes to do his own stunts and can do "hero" or "villain" roles but like an old-fashioned Bollywood actor, while he is the great and even convincing screen lover, he will never kiss his leading lady on the lips. He prefers to rely instead on the good chemistry he builds up with them. With one of them, Juhi Chawla, he has been friends ever since they met on the set of *Raju Ban Gaya Gentleman* and co-owns a production company, Dreamz Unlimited. Another of his production companies, Red Chillies Entertainment, has produced or co-produced at least three hits.

As opposed to Salman Khan, there is something admirable about his private life. Loyal to friends, he is still closest to the three he met at school; a chain smoker, his favourite drink is said to be Pepsi, although this may reflect his appearance in their advertisements.

As a Bollywood hero, his only conceivable rival is Hrithik Rosan but then, he has a father who can always make movies for him, indicating that Bollywood to a great extent still remains a family business.

Salman Khan, Shah Rukh Khan and Hrithik Roshan, while representatives of

Salman Khan, Shah Rukh Khan and Hrithik Roshan, while representatives of the new India, can be seen as part of the old Bollywood. They are not seen as quite as awesome as the Big Three: Dilip Kumar, Dev Anand and Raj Kapoor, but they share some characteristics.

Aamir Khan has proved to be a class apart. For a film like *Rang De Basanti* to move not only Indian audiences, but to have crossover messages for the West, is a new trend and shows the direction in which Bollywood is moving. In that sense, Aamir Khan has gone where Mehboob Khan could not. Mehboob wanted to be the Cecil DeMille of India, to make films that were not merely popular in India but also in the West. His films reached millions round the world, but not the West, and it has taken a namesake to breach the frontier of Bollywood, forty years later.

Noel Rands, who acted in *Lagaan,* has no doubt about the achievements of Aamir Khan and its wider effect on Bollywood:

> I shall always remember the occasion when, during the shooting of *Lagaan,* we had 20,000 extras one day on the set for the cricket match. Wherever you looked there were people and lunch boxes. At one stage, with the crowds getting restless, Aamir just got on his horse and sang his song and they looked at him in awe. He is by far the most professional of the Bollywood actors. Shah Rukh Khan is called the King of Bollywood but his *Devdas* did not make the same stir abroad that *Lagaan* did. Many people in Bollywood have tried to ride the success of *Lagaan*. *Lagaan* was Bollywood's *Crouching Tiger, Hidden Dragon*. It gave a different dimension to Bollywood internationally.

19

Afterword

The man sitting opposite me in a partitioned room at the far end of an office could have been any small-time, Bombay businessman. The office was certainly unprepossessing: rickety wooden tables, cane-backed chairs, dust on the floor and on the ceilings and, this being Saturday, nobody around. The tea the peon had just placed before me in a little glass, sweet tea, made with condensed milk, was the sort you get in cheap grade Bombay offices.

Except the bald man was anything but a nobody. He was used to being courted by prime ministers. Atal Behari Vajpayee, who was then India's Prime Minister, had complimented his work. The New Zealand Prime Minister, Helen Clarke, on a visit to India, had thanked him for showcasing her country and helping to increase the number of tourists who went there. What is more, four years previously, on January 21, 2000, as this man was about to get into his car to go home, two armed hit men had shot at him from close range.

The man was grievously injured but somehow managed to drive to the Santa Cruz police station to give the police a detailed description of his assailants. It was only then that he was taken to hospital where he was operated on to remove a bullet which had passed though his left arm and entered his chest. Subsequently, the then Deputy Chief Minister, Chagan Bhujbal, told the press that the police suspected the involvement of the Abu Salem faction of the Dawood Ibrahim gang in the incident. Both are fearsome mafia figures of the Bombay underworld, men the Bombay police would love to question. Dawood fled India several years ago. In the last year, Abu Salem has been extradited from Portugal after years of effort by the Indian authorities and is currently in custody.

For a year, the police had provided protection to the man, beefing up security at his Juhu residence and gun-toting policemen accompanying his son.

Yet, when I entered the office, there seemed little sign of any security and when I asked the man about the incident he said, in a tone that brooked no argument, "I don't want to talk about the underworld."

A few months after our meeting, the case finally came to court after four years (by Indian standards that is quite good going), and the man was summoned by the court to appear in the case. He made a written application for an in-camera recording of his statement of evidence. He told the Sewri Sessions Court that he had started receiving anonymous phone calls and threats to his life since it had become known the case would be heard. The accused, he said, were aware of the details of his visit to the court premises and moving around in public places had also become risky.

The Times of India, which reported this story under the headline of 'Mafia Threats' went on to say:

> Recently, the media was agog with reports that leading film-makers, Yash Chopra and Ram Gopal Varma, were receiving threatening calls from the underworld for overseas film rights. Intelligence sources had told *The Times of India* that the calls were received from the breakaway Abu Salem faction, based in Dubai. The leader of this group is referred to as 'Major'. A senior police officer had said that police protection was being given to both Chopra and Varma as a precautionary measure.

The man I had come to interview was, arguably, the most important film-maker of Bombay and the father of one of the most important stars. He was Rakesh Roshan, some time actor, director, producer but now famous for what he helped his son, Hrithik Roshan, achieve. It was under Rakesh Roshan's direction that Hirthik had notched up blockbusters like *Karan Arjun, Kaho Na... Pyaar Hai* and *Koi... Mil Gaya,* making him one of the hottest properties in Bollywood. It also emphasised how important family was.

If the mafia and the underworld were not subjects Rakesh Roshan wanted to talk about, family was a different matter. Being part of the film world was in his blood:

> I grew up in Bombay. We were quite well-to-do. My father was a music director. I grew up in a film atmosphere and then joined him as an actor at the age of seventeen. I studied at a boarding-school because I was naughty and my father wanted to discipline me. I went to movies with friends three times a week; my father found out and then sent me to boarding-school, which was really a military school. I liked sports but not studies. I did my matriculation and got first division. I did one year at college, studying commerce. I came back to Bombay and took a decision to help support my family. I joined as an assistant director. My youngest brother was twelve at the time. I was seventeen. I joined as an assistant director, making Rs. 200 a month and worked on various films.

This was Bollywood of the late 1960s when the Big Three still ruled and Rakesh interacted with them and tried to learn acting:

I was new at the time and didn't know what actors did. I had no acting experience; I learnt by just watching. I wanted to emulate Raj Kapoor more than Dilip Kumar. I liked Kapoor's outgoing, happy-go- lucky, simple guy style. I didn't get to know him much. I was impressed with Dilip Kumar's performances. Dilip Kumar was very sincere towards his work. His shooting style was very leisurely; no script; timing was everything. If he started in the morning he would take until 10:30 or 11 am for one shot and then stop for lunch. The films were narrated to the actors and their lines would come the day of the filming. There was a bound script at that time but the filming gave a lot of freedom to improvise. The theme of the film was the thing and there were different themes. The producer would come with an offer which would start with two or two and a half lakhs (Rs. 200,000 to Rs. 250,000). The actors did not have a say over which actors and actresses would star in their movies. Even today they may make suggestions but they do not have the final say.

The life of an actor that Rakesh Roshan sketched out seemed very different to the one his son enjoyed:

We would be shooting three to four films at a time and sometimes in two shifts a day. Like seven in the morning until two on one film and then 2 pm to 10 pm. It was hard work and we would go from studio to studio. Now you can't do that, just because of the traffic. You couldn't run from studio to studio, unless you had a helicopter. Actors are now just doing one or two films at a time.

So what made him give up acting for directorship?

No-one would give me a break. I had a feeling that I did not fulfill my potential and was not getting the support of the directors. Actors are just puppets in the directors' hands. So, I became a producer and produced four films. Because I joined as an assistant director, I managed to take control of the set as an actor, and that is how I kept learning. I established a banner—Filmcraft—in 1980, and produced four films under my own banner and then in 1985, I started directing. Money I had. For my first film I hired a story-writer who had an idea. Rishi Kapoor was the star in it. Eight lakhs (Rs. 800,000) was paid to him then. At that time it was a very big movie, but no one lost any money. I was now producing films and I stopped taking assignments as an actor, and just went on producing and directing. I first directed my son from 1998 to 1999 when I was thirty-five. He was disciplined and very good at studies.

Bollywood's relationship with politics has always been complex and curious. Some stars, like Sunil Dutt, Shatrughan Sinha and Rajesh Khanna, did go into politics but it isn't like the Hollywood connection with the Democratic party or the Republican connection with Arnold Schwarzenegger. Yet, in south India, some of the biggest political names are former actors and actresses who used their screen images to build their political bases. Roshan's view is:

> They have fan-clubs down there (in the south). It is not like that in Bombay. In Bombay, if they help politicians they do it as a favour. They don't get paid for it. Film stars may campaign, but are not under pressure; they just do so as a friendly gesture.

Roshan did admit that "the artists are changing, times are changing, we are following the West," particularly when it comes to film financing.

> As a result of a recent rule change, we can borrow money from banks, but you still have to put up your own assets. Banks will not give you the money if you don't have collateral. They will only lend to established film-makers. For a film of 40 crores (Rs. 400 million), for me, I don't require money because my films all make good money. I have a relationship with banks, just in case, but I haven't really used it.

But while the financing model of Bollywood may follow that of Hollywood, Bollywood, or at least Roshan, will not be showing intimate love scenes:

> I haven't shown any films with kissing and will not be doing it. It is inappropriate. My films are for the family. I am not making controversial films because people want entertainment. What kind of films do I make? I only make entertaining films. The number of songs may decrease in value. We used to have seven to eight songs in a film, but now it is coming down.

So if he does not follow the West in making intimate movies with kissing he does like going to the West to shoot his very Indian movies:

> Lots of films are made in Scotland because of the locations, not because they are cheaper. I shot in Bangkok—there is an island near Phuket—because it was beautiful. It was at vast expense; there were no special concessions given to me. I have also shot a lot in New Zealand [hence the praise of Helen Clarke]. It is like Hollywood—probably because of the coast. It is not economical. But there are beautiful locations. Christchurch and Queenstown are beautiful. We get no concession for shooting there; the locals don't really help. The film that I am making took 160 days (the longest time for any of my films) and was shot in Canada, in Banff. The travel time takes up a lot of days.

The British Tourist Authority now keeps track of the number of places in which Bollywood films are made: such diverse locations as Blenheim Palace, London tourist spots, the Scottish Highlands, and the Bluewater shopping centre in Kent. Karan Johar's *Kuch Kuch Hota Hai* was shot largely in Scotland. Working abroad has affected the working conditions under which Roshan now makes his films. Gone are the leisurely days when he saw Dilip Kumar working during the 1960s:

> When working overseas you have to have very tight schedules. The script needs to be very tight. A film length of two and a half hours or 30,000 feet of film is best, though now we are making 60,000 to 70,000 feet. In terms of business there are only one or two 'territories'—Bollywood divides India into various geographical territories—that do really well but what has changed is that 'overseas' has become a recognised territory. We are at a very crucial stage now. The trends are changing. Audiences are different. We have multiplex audiences and they are very different to single theatre audiences. Everything has changed and all because of piracy. The 1980s almost killed Indian films. Now you have to release a film in 500 or 1,000 theatres. In the old days you controlled the release in order to whet the appetite. Now you release to as many theatres as possible to beat DVD and video piracy.

The offices of Karan Johar, a short taxi drive away from Rakesh Roshan, could not have been more different. It had taken months for the researcher who was helping me in Bombay to arrange a meeting, and then a pretty little girl, who was Johar's publicist, accompanied me. The offices were in a suburb of Bombay, which had developed long after I had left the city. In the Bombay of the 1950s, when Raj Kapoor was making films, this was still a village. Now Johar's office could have been a modern advertising or marketing office anywhere in the world. The publicist, on hearing that I was writing a history of Bollywood, had asked, "What is your angle?" When I said it was just a narrative history, she looked vacant.

In terms of Bollywood names they don't come much bigger than Karan Johar. Son of Yash Johar, a noted film-maker of the 1960s and 1970s, he had first become prominent as Shah Rukh Khan's close friend in the movie *Dilwale Dulhaniya Le Jayenge,* where he also was Assistant Director and responsible for co-writing the screenplay and selecting Khan's costumes, something he did in Shah Rukh Khan's other movies such as *Dil To Pagal Hai, Duplicate, Mohabbatein, Main Hoon Na* and *Veer-Zaara.* In 1998, his directional début, *Kuch Kuch Hota Hai,* won eight *Filmfare* awards including the Best Movie, Best Director and all awards for the Best Actors in both lead and supporting roles. He was proclaimed a creative genius.

The young man sitting opposite me exuded the air of the new, confident, shiny India, which was then being advertised as an achievement of the ruling BJP Government and would soon form part of its unsuccessful re-election campaign. I had looked round the office and wondered if it was unusual to have an office like this. He had said, "No, it is quite common." He was the modern Indian who did not carry any of the old hang-ups.

> I don't try to cultivate any relationships. I talk to everyone who calls me, which is why I am talking to you. I am good with my appointments. That is my temperament.

I don't know—maybe that is unusual. My job with actors is 10% talent, 80% people handling and 10% patience.

But if all this suggested something very new, Johar's entry into films was the old Indian story: family connections. His father, Yash, was already in films having set up his own banner, Dharma Productions, back in 1976 when young Karan was just four years old:

> My father has been making films as long as I can remember. [We spoke before his father died.] So, I have been exposed to the industry from a very young age, and exposed to cinema. I think a normal upbringing back home wouldn't have included so much talk about cinema. But I think that was also a deterrent because my father's view was that I shouldn't get into the fraternity of film-making because I was not made of the stuff that the industry requires. He discouraged me but things worked out.

When Johar was growing up he often refused to say he came from a film family, or to even acknowledge he was his father's son:

> I lied to everyone that my father was making films. When my father's name would come up, I would lie and say that 'that is another Johar, I would say he was a businessman.

So, coming from a such a strong film background, did he not always want to be in films?

> No, I wanted to be but always held back. I did not think I was capable of directing. Producing was an option because my father is a producer but I found it boring. I finally met Yash Chopra's son—he was a childhood friend. We met in college, in Bombay, in HR College, and we studied commerce.

But what about the other pull on Johar, the all too common pull on middle and upper middle-class Indians for children to study and get a good degree?

> My mother comes from a very educated background, as does my father. My mother wanted me to do an MBA. My mother was very keen that I educate myself and work as a professional. She had no problem with the film profession, but she did not think I was ready for it or cut out for it, in terms of my temperament. My father thought that as well—in terms of being too timid and too weak. At that point, I didn't really know what I was doing. After I did my B Com (Bachelor of Commerce) I realised I did not want to educate myself further, and decided that films were for me.

So, how did he become a director?

As I was saying, Yash Chopra's son was the director and he came to me with the narrative. I sat with him at the writing stages. After that, he approached me to be an AV on the film, as I was involved with the writing process. I met Shah Rukh Khan for the first time professionally. We struck up a rapport and a friendship with Kajol who was the actress in *Dilwale Dulhaniya Le Jayenge* [a 1995 film starring Shah Rukh Khan]. One thing led to another and, when I made my first film, the obvious choice was to approach them. They readily agreed as we were friends, more so than anything else, and eventually I made my first film, *Kuch Kuch Hota Hai.*

For his first film he took a year and a half to write his script, and a year to shoot it. So did Johar break the established Bollywood tradition of not having a script but making up the dialogue as things went along?

Now scripts are written with screenwriter's software. It was a pre-planned production product, which was unusual. But, because I come from an educated background, I was aware…

Not that Johar showed his script to either Shah Rukh Khan or Kajol or any of the other actors or actresses in the film.

At the time they were still used to what we call narration. I had the full bound edition, but I narrated it to them because I believed I would express myself better when I spoke. It was at Shah Rukh Khan's old house. I just spoke. I read it in detail. It took me about three and a half hours. It was 8 pm in the evening, if I remember and it was the 29th of April, 1997. The air-conditioner was on. I was thirty kilos lighter then. No, I was not nervous.

As far as Johar was concerned, this was like talking to friends, except one friend was not helpful.

Kajol is quite annoying; she cackles and she screams and, if she doesn't like something, she starts fighting with you.

As Johar narrated, he thought of the man he considers his guru and how he would narrate:

I had heard how Sooraj Barjatya gave a detailed narration—he pioneered Rajshri Productions, which made *Hum Aapke Hain Kaun,* which was a super success in 1994. [It was one of the most successful, beating *Sholay's* long-held record]. He was my Guru at the time. He apparently narrated his film to every lead artist, every character artist, every cameo in the film, even the colour of the curtains. I heard in detail how he had done it. At the time I looked up to him and emulated his style.

The title of Johar's first film started with K which is also the first letter of his name. It proved significant:

I struck astrological gold with *Kuch Kuch Hota Hai*. I didn't know it then. But all the astrologers I have since met have always said K is lucky for you. Even in London I went to a mall, and an astrologer came up to me and said you have a very interesting face and you will do really well in life and by the way stick to the letter K. I attract psychics. In London, the astrologer just came up to me; she had no idea who I was. In Malaysia, someone came up to me and said let me read your hand. In Bombay, I went to a tarot card reader, and she said K is important for me. So all my films start with the letter K. I follow numerology, too. I am quite superstitious about that. No other superstitions, just numerology and astrology.

But no astrologer predicted that, as he was making his first film, he would faint:

I was in Filmistan. Yes, I was weak; I hadn't eaten in two days. I was quite stressed. The shooting was in the studio. Everyone knew everything. I was just nervous. I fell on top of my choreographer, poor thing. She obviously reacted because she thought she would nearly die with my body weight on her. Fortunately, I was not so heavy. The stars who were there all laughed. It was quite entertaining. I quite enjoyed it because after that I directed from the make-up room. They gave me a monitor and they gave me a wireless. I quite enjoyed it; really fun to lie down on a bed and tell people what to do.

Johar had grown up admiring the directors who have gone before but is not a fan of either Satyajit Ray or *Sholay*:

Shammi Kapoor was especially impressionable. Most of the films that inspired me were his. I never liked *Sholay*. *Mother India* was good. I really liked all Raj Kapoor's films. Western films—there were few at that time. My first experience of a Western film was *Roman Holiday*—my mother took me when it came to Bombay, and I went back the next day to see it again. Everyone watched cartoons. Satyajit Ray? Not really, I was always more of a Guru Dutt fan.

The older generation of film-makers lived through the horrors of partition. Johar, born long after, was unconcerned about the relationship between Hindus and Muslims, despite the political tensions in the wider world. For him the problem just does not exist.

In all of our films over the past ten years, the big stars have been born in the last twenty to thirty, so the Muslim/Hindu issue in films is not as bad. Partition was a different time.

Johar was, perhaps, most revealing when he spoke about why Bollywood film-makers do not want to make films about their great Indian leaders, leaving Attenborough to make a film on Gandhi, or indeed why historical films just do not work:

Because they become educational. No one is interested in documentaries, everyone wants entertainment, no one wants to lose money.

And it was then that Johar, the nationalist, the Indian through and through, emerged:

I want to make the films I believe in, and make good films here, and not crossover Hindi/English films. I want to stay in India. There are lots of opportunities here. Even if you call Hollywood heaven, I would rather serve in an Indian hell than a Hollywood Heaven.

In the Bombay in which I grew up, there were no auto rickshaws. In other Indian cities they are the main means of transport, but they were banned in south Bombay. I can remember Bombay trams, but they had gone by the early 1950s and, in south Bombay, neither cycle rickshaw nor autos were allowed. Now, on my way to see the granddaughter of Raj Kapoor, Kareena, who was shooting in a studio in what I still felt was jungle country on the outskirts of Bombay, I hailed my first ever auto rickshaw in Bombay. As it chugged along roads that in my childhood were paddy fields, I marvelled at the change in the landscape. I had not been here for almost forty years and gone were the fields, the pigs and hens I had seen roaming round, the huts and dirt tracks. Instead, there were now concrete buildings, paved roads, slums and the ubiquitous television aerials atop every building, even on the little tarpaulin covered shacks. Much of it was hideous but it was progress of a kind, development, but unplanned, as if a child had been let loose with a paint box.

When I got to the studio, I was told Kareena was busy so I waited outside her trailer.

Kareena was supposed to see me at 3 pm. 3 pm came and went, then 4 pm. Then a minion came and asked if I would like to sit in her make-up van parked outside the set where the shooting was taking place.

In the make-up van, I found myself in a L-shaped sitting area with a divan and three or four cushions where one could sleep. The first thing that struck me was it was air-conditioned relief from the oppressive afternoon heat. The make-up van had strip lighting, a dressing table with a box of red tissue—Jackson Murarthy tissue—a squareish mirror with a wooden frame and an arch at the top and plenty of light. In a corner stood a television set, and on a small table were piled lots of things: food, shoes, paper bags, kit bag, a mobile phone, but no books. I tried not to imagine what it would be like to be cooped up here for days on end.

The make-up van had white curtains. I parted them and could see people outside sitting on the ground. Some were eating, having brought tiffin carriers packed with food. They sat on the concrete floor and just scooped up the food with their hands and ate. There was also a concrete basketball court and it was here that I saw some European women sitting on a mat. They had emerged as if from nowhere and, intrigued by their presence, I came out of the make-up van to find out who they were.

The women were all white, none of them it seemed more than about twenty or twenty-five, and few of them appeared to be speaking English. Then, in the background, I noticed an older woman who was much darker, possibly Middle Eastern, who seemed to be someone in authority. She turned out to be a lady called Shanaz Aseedian. She was from Tehran and had come to India to study, had married an Indian and stayed. Now she was an agent whose job it was to get female extras for Bollywood films, "Girls come for a few months and then go" said Shanaz. She spots girls at all sorts of places. She spotted a girl called Agnes dancing at a wedding. She thought she was a good dancer and so approached her and now she was in a Bollywood film.

She was Agnes Johnson, a London girl on tour in India who had been approached by Shanaz on a Bombay street. She was staying in Colaba and had come to India for a wedding. She had done some acting at Shepperton Studios in London and had studied psychology in London at University College.

She didn't know much about Bollywood but she was familiar with the singing and dancing stereotype of Bollywood movies. When I spoke to her she did not know the title of the movie in which she was acting, nor the story line and gave the impression that she did not care. She was to be a dancer in the film, and perhaps act a bit. She was in it for the experience, rather than the money. She planned to stay for a month and then continue travelling. She did mention that her shoes were too small.

She then gave me a potted summary of her companions on the mat. There were about eight or nine girls, all from Europe. She was the only English girl; there was a Brazilian, a Russian, a Romanian and various other assorted nationalities whose origins she did not know and did not care.

As we spoke there was a shout and Agnes and the girls all got up and walked onto the set.

An hour later, Kareena Kapoor, the actress many in Bollywood consider the most beautiful of the Kapoors, finally emerged. People rave about her almond-shaped, light brown eyes, with a touch of green, and a voluptuous figure so similar to the heroines Raj Kapoor liked. What struck me as she sat in front of me was her serene face: a young girl of twenty-three with, at that time, no love interest and living at home. But a Kapoor.

Was it inevitable she would end up in acting?

> I did not know anything else. Initially, I wanted to be a lawyer. I studied law in Harvard in America, but ran away after six months. I always knew I wanted to act. I loved my last two years of high school (a girls' school in India) because I wasn't treated differently, I could be individualistic. My greatest satisfaction is acting. I have wanted to be an actress since I was a child. When I was about nine or ten I used to pick up the phone and say, 'I will be a movie star.'

Kareena was hoping to fulfil her grandfather's expectations but he died when she was eight. Always living with her mother and sister Karisma (her father Randhir, Raj Kapoor's eldest son separated from his wife many years ago and Kareena did not have much male influence in her life), her mother brought her and her sister up as individual people. Her father, she said, is very laid back, always looking for scripts but hasn't made a film for a while. She felt that he needed to make one soon. For a brief moment she spoke of the other Kapoors. Shashi Kapoor had retired and was putting on lots of weight. His son Karan was married in London and other son, Kunal, was producing and making commercials, not 'real' films.

The movie she was filming that day (*Fida*), had come about because a video director—Ken Ghosh—had made a previous film which was a big hit. He came to her with the script, which she liked very much as it seemed like a challenge. The film, she told me, was about a chap who goes mad. The movie was 60% complete. Kareena is the love interest who makes him worse. The film is mostly set in Bombay but there was some filming to be done in New Zealand.

Why, I wondered, unlike in her grandfather's days, was there no great leading lady like a Nargis or a Madhubala? There was no one to match the leading male actors, Shah Rukh Khan, Salman Khan, Hrithik Roshan, as Nargis had matched her grandfather?

> It is a male-dominated industry and so male actors have more prominence: To be a leading actress, beauty alone is not enough for an artist. To be a legend, one needs to be a power-packed performer, one has to have a lot of naturalness and to have ethereal beauty as well. There has to be a lot of masala—a lot of mix. Most people are lacking in something; they have one or another but not everything.

Kareena is an old-fashioned actress in the sense that she works on more than one film at a time. When I spoke to her she was working on six films at the same time. The next day she was leaving for Chennai, for another five days shooting.

Every working day was twenty to twenty-three hours, sometimes with no sleep at all. She does not find it difficult to keep all the plots and scripts in her head as she changes from movie to movie, "You have to have good memory."

In a Bollywood world where an actress tends to work for a particular director, Kareena is very proud that she works with all the directors of Bollywood. So, she has worked with Karan Johar in *Kabhi Kushi Kabhie Gham*, with Subhash Ghai in *Yaadein,* and with the Barjatiyas in *Mein Prem Ki Diwani Hoon*.

Then there was a knock on the door and she was required on the set again. As she went, I noticed Agnes Johnson looking at her, a look that suggested she thought she was a creature from another world.

During the course of researching this book, I met Shyam Benegal several times, always at his offices, Everest Building in Tardeo. The building is the sort of higgledy-piggeldy office building all too common in the Bombay I knew. Like Topsy, it had just grown up, housing a mixture of shops and offices and, on the pavements outside, several stalls selling all sorts of things from newspapers to pans, betel nuts wrapped in a leaf Indians love to chew. The taxi-drivers who took me there never seemed to know the place, and I had to direct them, following the careful instructions Benegal had given. Like all such Bombay offices, parts of it were in need of urgent repair, parts that looked like a permanent building site.

Benegal's office was the last one in a corridor which also housed a bank and stairs that had clearly seen their best days. The office itself was a long room with several tables where assistants sat. Scattered around were posters of his films. At the end was his partitioned office lined with books. This, instantly, made it different to any other Bollywood film office I had visited. Until now I had not seen a single book in these film offices. Benegal's office was like the study of a professor.

I have, in the course of my writing career, interviewed many great men of India. All of them, without exception, exuded an air of impatience, an air of contempt that they had to be subjected to an interview by a journalist, almost as if they were upper caste Brahmins and I, the untouchable. Benegal could not have been more different. For a man who is a Bollywood legend, he was totally unpretentious. I did not have to go through a publicist to arrange the interview, he had answered his own phone and did not even have any of the airs that minor Indian celebrities can display. Not for him a peon outside his office who would have demanded my business card, or even a secretary who would have told me to wait before he could say whether saab would see me.

The first time I met Benegal he had just finished his Bose film and it was not surprising that he knew a lot about Subhas Bose. But what impressed me was his detailed knowledge of Bose, including recent material based on secret files that had just been unclassified. I had just reissued my own biography of Bose; he had not only read my original book but it was marvellous to find someone in India who dealt with this controversial figure not in myths, but in historical facts. What was even more uplifting in that interview, and many others that followed, was his easy command of the history of Bollywood. In a country which prefers fiction to history, and where narrative history is the province of foreigners, he was almost a walking encyclopaedia of Indian cinematic history.

His films, as we have seen, have always been different. Observe a Raj Kapoor film and its street scenes show no dirt when, in reality, it is impossible to walk an Indian street without coming across dirt; filthy, horrible dirt. This may enhance the make-believe but it makes the streets unrecognisable. When I mentioned this to Benegal he said in his quiet, almost professorial, tone:

> Yes, the streets are very clean. Even in *Shri 420*. I would not make a film like that. That was one of the reasons I came into films. My films were a rebellion against that. But that was the set in the studios. Now they make the sets look like Bombay. I make my films outdoors.

It would have been easy for Benegal to have chips on his shoulders like banyan trees. He is not mainstream Bollywood; he has always struggled to find money for his films; the Bose film cost 25 crores (Rs. 250 million) and he has had to fight both conventional financiers and the Government. But he carries no grudges. Yes, he told me, for all the changes made, and the fact that banks can now finance films, the central concept of the financing of the industry was absurd:

> You pay an entertainment tax to the local governments. In Maharashtra, it is 55%. Not as high as Uttar Pradesh. There it is 132% of the price of the ticket. That is absurd. How can you make money in UP? Nobody minds the taxes if something comes back to the industry. It goes to the government common fund. The tax system gives the industry enormous problems. The man who has taken the least amount of risk is the person who gets the money first, the government, who have done nothing to earn it. After that the exhibitor.

But, as a film-maker, he is grateful that for all their distrust of the cinema which this taxation policy shows, it was beneficial that Indian politicians had taken so long to allow television into the country. India was one the last countries to enter the television age with the result that the impact of television on India is the reverse of most other countries:

> Had the authorities allowed television in earlier, Hindi cinema may not have had such a big impact on the Indian audience. Television has magnified the importance of cinema for Indian audiences. It has not broken away from it. Indian television has ridden piggyback on Indian cinema.

Mass television has arrived just as there has been a big change in Indian newspapers, which has also affected Bollywood:

The idea that people read newspapers to entertain themselves is an idea that has come into India only in the mid-1990s. Today you will have film stars' photographs on the front pages of the national newspapers. You are never likely to see that sort of thing in *The New York Times*.

But, perhaps the biggest change affecting Bollywood is due to India's relationship with the United States, and the profound affect this has on the cinema industry:

A film may show Indian families living in huge magnificent mansions. The mansions are not in India. The story is about India. The mansions could be in Scotland or some other place. But the film is meant to portray India. These films appeal to a certain aspirational quality in Indian audiences. Today's aspiration is be in the United States. There is the famous saying that everywhere in the world today, particularly the world outside the United States, everybody has two countries, one is their own and the other is the United States. All want to be like that, or to be there. Prannoy Roy [one of India's most famous television presenters] said the other day the great Indian ambition is to say "America keep out, but take us with you."

Yet, as we have seen, the Indian film world was much affected by film-makers who are very left-wing, if not Communist. Bachchan's first break in films came through Abbas, a Communist. What happened to that ideological basis which was for so long such an important part of Indian film-making?

Intellectually, America is doing everything that will benefit itself and nobody else. This is a common view in India but it is not necessarily a leftist vision. Large sections of the population are similarly wary of America. They feel America wants to dominate the whole world; to take over the whole world. The feeling is are they really interested in you and me? This is not just the view of the Jawaharlal Nehru University [considered India's intellectual heart and traditionally very left wing and anti-American]. JNU is no longer homogenous. It is changing and you have several points of view. There is also a lot of internal debate in JNU. But the views that are being formed have to be reconciled with the old ideological mores. It is not that easy to let go of the past, at least not let go entirely.

In the Bombay of my childhood every evening, at seven, the city came to a halt as everyone wanted to know the "*Matka*" numbers. This was Bombay's home-grown lottery run by the underworld. There was talk of underworld connections with some of them—Muslims, with Middle Eastern connections, although Benegal told me, "The matka was Hindu, not Muslim."

But now Matka has gone and the underworld is much more ferocious and into Bollywood, and much of it is Muslim, with people like Dawood and Abu

Salem prominent. One of my many meetings with Benegal came just after the publication of Suketu Mehta's book on Bombay, *Maximum City*, which details the underworld control over Bollywood. It was so pervasive that Sanjay Dutt was implicated and jailed for eighteen months In the book, Mehta narrates a story told to him by Bal Thackeray of how his father, Sunil, came to Thackeray's house in Bombay's Parsi colony. "He wept, he did aarti around my wife," going round her with a lighted lamp in homage. This was to get Thackeray, whose party was then in power at the local government, to get his son released. As Dutt senior paid homage to Thackeray, eight or nine film producers waited in an anteroom hoping this would do the trick as Sanjay Dutt was involved in many films and, if they were not completed, they would lose crores. Over the years there had been other reports of mob influence. There had been the Bharat Shah case where this Bollywood film-maker was accused of being in league with the mob. He was acquitted by the High Court but the feeling persisted that the mafia plays a part in films; a large part. Benegal took a cool, historical view:

> There was a period when they came close to doing it. It was about ten or twelve years ago. In the early 1990s. There were a few court cases. Bharat Shah, who was a very big producer at the time, was implicated. Later on he was acquitted. Gulshan Kumar (the music producer) got killed as he came out of a temple he used to go to in Juhu. The perpetrator of the killing, Abu Salem, has been extradited from Portugal. It was alleged that Abu Salem gave the gun to Sanjay Dutt. His father, Sunil Dutt, was a very fine man. But a doting father. He got compromised a great deal by his son. The growth in the Bombay underworld came about through gold-smuggling from the Middle East. Then it moved into real estate and then into films. After the expansion of Bombay, which had started in the 1970s, tapered off, there were no pickings for the mafia. That is when the underworld came into the picture. A lot of them came to the film industry, both for money laundering purposes and for extortion. Putting money into production, buying films for overseas distribution, using the laundering mechanism to get money into foreign exchange, and so on. Nothing would have seriously happened to them if it was not for their hand in the Bombay blast. Then, there were terrorist implications and the Government of India began to take it seriously.

The blasts were the culmination of the breakdown of Hindu-Muslim relations which started in December 1992 with Hindu mobs, aided by BJP leaders, demolishing a mosque known as the Babri Masjid in Ayodhya, claiming it had been built on a Ram temple and destroyed by medieval Muslim rulers. The riots that followed would convert Benegal from film-maker, who observed what others did, into a man of action who played a role in helping his fellow human beings:

The riots of the city were the worst riots to take place from January 6 to January 13, 1993. The police allowed the riots to take place. Immediately after Babri Masjid, Muslims attacked Hindus. Exactly a month later, the Hindus retaliated. In Tardeo, on this road [and he gestured at the main road past his office] all the Muslim shops were being gutted. I live on Peddar Road. I could not come in the car. I used to walk to my office. In my building are the offices of *The Midday* newspaper. *Midday* is Muslim-owned. We prevented Shiv Sena from attacking it. Narashima Rao was the Prime Minister. I had access to the Cabinet secretary in Delhi. I was on the telephone to him and told him, 'you have to get normality back in the city.' They wanted to start the buses. I said, 'please don't start the buses. It is very easy to set fire to a bus. Start the trains.' In Bombay, when trains run, everybody thinks life is normal. Then, in March 1993, came the blasts [bombs going off at various places like the stock exchange, Bombay's equivalent of 9/11]. The Government intervened and nothing happened after that blast; everything was controlled. It is healing, but slowly. It is coming together. There is no friction of that sort any more.

Yet, more than a decade later, the wounds have not healed enough for a film about that period to be passed by the censors:

A film was made called *Black Friday* by a young film-maker, Anurag Kashyap, recently released to much acclaim. Completed about two and a half years ago it had been banned. They were holding onto the censor certificate until the case had been heard. The release calls it a true story. All the characters portrayed in the film, their trials were going on now.

Benegal is sure that the most traumatic events in Bombay's life for nearly a century did not affect Bollywood? "Not seriously."

And, interestingly, when it came to Hindu-Muslim relations at a personal level there is more openness, compared to the days just before and after partition.

Both Aamir Khan's wives have been Hindus. Shah Rukh Khan has a Hindu wife and neither Aamir nor Shah Rukh nor Salman Khan have changed their names. They did not need to. When Dilip Kumar came into films, which was a little before partition, the polarisation between the communities was becoming very, very strong. Leading up to partition, those years were particularly bad. If you needed acceptance you couldn't possibly have a Muslim name. The man who played Ram, for instance, in the famous *Ram Rajya,* was a Muslim, but he had a Hindu name, Prem Adip. Similarly, the chap who played Lakshman, was a Christian. For *Ram Rajya*, probably the most popular, mythological film ever made in this country at a time when religious polarisation was at its greatest, you had a Muslim playing Ram, and a Christian playing Laksham. That was amazing. That never fails to amaze me, as an Indian. Despite Bal Thackerkay, due to Bollywood, the unique idea of a Hindu character being played by a Muslim, is not difficult. One aspect of Hindu behaviour is that it has nothing to do with belief. Hindu behaviour does not automatically contest other people's beliefs. You can't say that of other religions. Christians do, Muslims do, Jews do, everybody does, except Hindus. Which is why you can have a Hindu majority country but it is not brute majority behaviour. That is the reason. You don't contest. As long as you don't tell me what I should do. If you do not sit on my head and say my beliefs are wrong, I will never contest yours. When you look at the right-wing Hindu militancy that has developed in India, it is totally reactive. There is no ideology.

Javed Akhtar in *Talking Films*, his conversations with film historian Nasreen Munni Kabir, has said Bollywood culture "is quite different from Indian culture, but it's not alien to us, we understand it." He has suggested that for a non-Indian to understand Bollywood they should look to the Hollywood Westerns.

Never were there sheriffs and gun-slingers like the ones you see in a Western. And never was there a village with one street where a man would start walking silently and wait for the draw; this whole culture has been developed by Hollywood. And it has become a reality in itself. It's a myth that Hollywood has created. In the same way, Hindi cinema has its own myths.

In a sense, these myths are not just the ones portrayed on film. Bollywood lives are also different from most Indian lives. Here, people fall in love and marry, they marry across caste and community and religious barriers, they have affairs, divorces, and have created their own little world from which they project an India which, as Akhtar says, is different but still believable to most Indians.

The strength and power of Bollywood lies in its ability to withstand change and adapt to it. So, it has survived the arrival of television in India, and Amitabh, its greatest ever star, even used television to reinvent himself. It has also survived piracy, the Bombay mafia and the undoubted use of untaxed black money for producing films. Bollywood is always producing new myths, or so burnishing old myths that they seem new. This keeps the cinema renewing itself and drawing new adherents.

India, said the novelist R.K. Narayan, would always survive. Bollywood, we can be certain, will always be capable of reinventing itself. It remains the most wonderful example of Indian use of Western technology in a wholly Indian way.

Bibliography

This book involved massive research over four years, extracting information from many continents and countries.

Archives

British Museum, London
Collection in the India Office Library L/I Files of the Information Department
British Film Institute, National Library (London)
Collection on India, including Imagine Asia Files
National Library (Kolkata). Collection of old film magazines

Published Material

100 Films since Sholay: The Journey, (New Delhi, 2000)
Abbas, K.A., *Gods, Kings & Tramps*, (Filmfare, 1961)
Abbas, K.A., *Social Realism in Indian cinema*, (Filmfare, 1972)
Abbas, K.A., *I am not an Island*, (New Delhi, 1977)
Abbas, K.A., *Mad, Mad, Mad World of Indian Films*, (New Delhi, 1977)
Akbar, Khatija, *Madhubala—Her Life, Her Films*, (New Delhi, 1997)
Anderson, Arthur, *The Indian Entertainment Industry: Strategy & Vision*, (New Delhi, 2000)
Apte, Tejawsini, *Move Over Rangeela, Mother India is Back and Running*, (The Asian Age, 1985)
Armes, Roy, *Third World Film-Making and the West*, (London, 1987)
L'avventurose storie del cinema indiano (2 volumes), Marsilio Editori (Venice, 1985)

Baghdadi, Rafique, Rao, Rajiv, *Un Lamhon Ne Meri Taqdeer Hi Badal Di*, (1994)
Baghdadi, Rafique, Rao, Rajiv, *Talking Films*, (New Delhi, 1995)
Baghdadi, Rafique, Rao, Rajiv, *Mehboob Khan: A Director by Default, Not Choice*, (Screen, 2001)
Bahadur, Satish '*Aesthetics: From Traditional Iconography to Contemporary Kitsch*,' Indian cinema *Superbazaar*, edited by Vasudev, Aruna and Lenglet, Philippe, (New Delhi, 1983)
Baji, A.R., *50 Years of Talkie in India, 1931–1981*, (1981)
Bamzai, K., Unnithan S., *Show Business: India Today* (2003)

Bandyopadhyay, S., *Indian Cinema: Contemporary Perceptions of the Thirties,* (Jamshedpur 1993)

Banerjee, Shampa, *New Indian Cinema,* (New Delhi 1982)

Banerjee, Shampa, *Ritwik Ghatak,* (New Delhi, 1982)

Banerjee, Shampa, *Profiles: Five Film-makers from India: V. Shantaram, Raj Kapoor, Mrinal Sen, Guru Dutt, Ritwik Ghatak,* (New Delhi, 1985-1986)

Banker, Ashok, *Bollywood,* (New Delhi, 2001)

Barnouw, Erik, Krishnaswamy, S., *Indian Film* (New York, 1980)

Baskaran, Theodore S., *The Message Bearers, the Nationalist Politics and the Entertainment Media in South India 1880–1945* (Chennai 1981)

Benegal, Shyam, *The Churning,* (Kolkata, 1984)

Bhagat, O.P., *Dilip Kumar: Colossus of Indian cinema,* (Asian Voice, 2000)

Bhatkal, Satyajit, *The Spirit of Lagaan—The Extraordinary Story of the Creators of a Classic,* (Mumbai, 2002)

Bharatan, Raju, *Lata Mangeshkar: a Biography,* (New Delhi, 1985)

Bharatan, Rahy, *Jinhe Naaz Hain Hind Per Woh Kahan Hain,* (1993)

Bharati, Rahi, *The Fabulous Loves of Dilip Kumar,* (Lehren 1991)

Bhatia, Vanraj, interviewed by Ram Mohan, '*The Rise of the Indian Film Song'*, Cinema Vision India, Vol 1, No. 4 (Mumbai, 1980)

Bhattacharya, Rinki, *Bimal Roy: A Man of Silence,* (New Delhi, 1994)

Bhattacharya, Roshmila, *Mother India: Terms of Endurance,* (Screen, 2001)

Bhatt, Mahesh, *Sex in Indian Cinema: Only Bad People do It,* (New Delhi 1993)

Bhimani, Harish, *In Search of Lata Mangeshkar,* (New Delhi, 1995)

Binford, M., *India's Two Cinemas in J.D.H. Downing,* (New York, 1987)

Biswas, Moinak, *Narrating the Nation: Mother India and Roja*

Bobb, D., *Kissa Kursi Ka: the Case of the Missing Film,* (India Today, 1978)

Bollywood: Popular Indian Cinema, edited by Lalit Mohan Joshi, (London, 2001)

Booch, Harish, *Star Portraits*

Bose, Derek, *Kishore Kumar: Method in Madness,* (New Delhi, 2004)

Breckenride, Carol, *Consuming Modernity: Public Culture in the South Asian World,* (Minnesota, 1995)

Burra, R., *Looking Back,* (New Delhi, 1981)

Burra R., *Indian Cinema 1980–1985,* (New Delhi, 1985)

Chakravarty S., *National Identity in Indian Popular Cinema 1947–1987,* (Austin, 1993)

Chanana, Opender, *A Living Legend, B.R. Chopra: 50 Years of Creative Association with Cinema,* (Mumbai, 1998)

Chandra, Pradeep, *AB: The Legend. A Photographer's Tribute,* (New Delhi, 2006)

Chandran, M., *Documents,* (Mumbai, 1989)

Chatterjee, Gayatri, *Mother India,* (New Delhi, 2002)

Chatterjee, Gayatri, *Awara,* (New Delhi, 2003)

Chatterji, Shoma A., *Suchitra Sen: A Legend in her Lifetime,* (New Delhi, 2002)

Chatterji, Shoma A., *Ritwik Ghatak: The Celluloid Rebel,* (New Delhi, 2004)

Chattopadhyay, Saratchandra, *Devdas,* (New Delhi, 2002)

Chaudhuri, Shantanu Ray, *Icons from Bollywood,* (New Delhi, 2005)

Chaya, R.B., *Discordant Notes,* (Mumbai, 1996)

Chopra, Anupama, *Sholay: The Making of a Classic,* (New Delhi, 2000)

Chopra, Anupama, *Diwale Dulhania Le Jayenge,* (London, 2002)

Chowdhury, Alpana, *Madhubala: Masti & Magic,* (New Delhi, 2003)

Chowdhury, Alpana, *Dev Anand—Dashing, Debonair,* (New Delhi, 2004)

Cinema Vision India, (Mumbai 1980–3)

Cinema Year by Year: 1894–2004, (London, 2004)

Cinewave, (Kolkata, 1985)

Chughtai, Ismat, *Ab Na Pahale Walwale hain,* (Priya, 1990)

Chute, David, '*The Road to Bollywood*' Film Comment Magazine, (New York, May-June 2002)

Chute, David, '*The Family Business: No Matter Where You Look in Hindi Cinema, the Clan's the Thing*' Film Comment Magazine, (New York, May 2002)

Cinema in India (quarterly), Karanjia, B.K. and Chandran, Mangala (Mumbai, 1987)

Cinema India-International (quarterly), Ramachandran, T. M. (Mumbai, 1984–1988)

Cinema Vision Vol 1/4, Vol 2/1, (Mumbai)

Clarens, Carlos, *Crime Movies, from Griffith to the Godfather and Beyond,* (New York, 1980)

Coolie ke Dialogue, (Mumbai, 1984)

Cooper, Darius, *The Cinema of Satyajit Ray,* (Cambridge, 2000)

Cousins, Mark, *The Story of Film,* (London, 2004)

Crawford, Travis, '*Bullets Over Bombay*,' Film Comment Magazine, (New York, May 2002)

Da Cunha, *Indian Summer 78/9, 80/1, 83/84,* (New Delhi)

Da Cunha, *The New Generation,* (New Delhi, 1981)

Das Gupta, Chidananda, *Talking about Films,* (New Delhi, 1981)

Das Gupta, Chidananda, *The Painted Face, Studies in India's Popular Cinema,* (New Delhi, 1991)

Das Sharma, B., *Indian Cinema and National Leadership,* (Jamshedpur, 1993)

Das Sharma, B., *Indian Cinema: Contemporary Perceptions from the Thirties,* (Jamshedpur, 1993)

Datt, Gopal, *Indian Cinema: The Next Decade,* (Mumbai, 1984)

Datta, Sangeeta, *Shyam Benegal,* (London, 2003)

Dayal, J., *The Role of the Government: Story of an Uneasy Truce,* (New Delhi, 1983)

Dayal, J., *Indian Cinema Superbazaar,* (New Delhi, 1983)

De, Shobhaa, *Selective Memory,* (New Delhi, 1998)

De, Shobhaa, *Starry Nights,* (New Delhi, 1991)

Deep, Mohan, *Simply Scandalous: Meena Kumari,* (Mumbai, 1998)

Deep, Mohan, *EuRekha! The Intimate Life Story of Rekha,* (Mumbai, 1999)

Deleury, Guy, *Le Modèle Indou,* (Paris, 1979)

Dérne, Steve, *Movies, Masculinity, and Modernity, An Ethnography of Men's Filmgoing in India,* (Connecticut, 2000)

Desai, Meghand, *Communalism, Secularism and Dilemma of Indian Nationhood in Asian Nationalism,* (2000)

Desai, Lord Meghnad, *Nehru's Hero: Dilip Kumar,* (New Delhi, 2004)

Dev, Anand, *When Three Was Company,* (India 1991)

Dharp, B.V., *Indian Films 1977 and 1978,* (Pune, 1979)

Dickey, Sara, *Cinema and the Urban Poor in South India,* (Cambridge, 1993)

Dickey, Sara, *Opposing Faces: Film Stars, Fan Clubs and the Construction of Class Identities in South India,* (2000)

Dickey, Sara, *The Politics of Adulation: Cinema and the Production of Politicians in South India,* (Journal of Asian Studies, 1993)

Dilip, Kumar, *What I Want From Life,* (Filmfare, 1953)

Dilip, Kumar, *Brilliant Actor, Great Man,* (India, 2002)

Dissanayake W., *Cinema and Cultural Identity, Reflections on Films from Japan, India and China,* (Lanham, 1988)

Dwyer, Rachel, *All You Want Is Money, All You Need Is Love: Sex and Romance in Modern India,* (London, 2000)

Dwyer, Rachel, *The Erotics of the West Sari in Hindi Films*, (South Asia, 2000)

Dwyer, Rachel, *Mumbai ishtle in S. Bruzzi and P. Church*, (London, 2000)

Dwyer, Rachel, *Indian Values and the Diaspora: Yash Chopra's Films of the 1990's*, (London, 2000)

Dwyer, Rachel, *Angrezii Men kahte hain ke 'aay lav yuu'... The kiss in the Hindi film*, (Cambridge, 2001)

Dwyer, Rachel, *Yash Chopra*, (London, 2002)

Dwyer, Rachel, *Filming the Gods: Religion and Indian Cinema*, (London, 2006)

Dwyer, Rachel, *One Hundred Hindi Films*, (New Delhi, 2005)

Dwyer, Rachel, *Representing the Muslim: the 'Courtesan Film' in Indian Popular Cinema*, (London, 2004)

Dwyer, Rachel, Pinney, Christopher, *Pleasure and the Nation: The History of Consumption and Politics of Public Culture in India*, (Dehli, 2000)

Dwyer, Rachel, Patel, Divia, *Cinema in India: The Visual Culture of Hindi Film*, (Oxford, 2002)

Dwyer, Rachel, *Yash Chopra: Fifty Years in Indian Cinema*, (New Delhi, 2002)

Dyer, Richard, *Don't Look Now: the Male Pin-Up*, (Screen, 1982)

Dyer, Richard, *Heavenly Bodies: Film Stars and Society*, (London, 1986)

Dyer, Richard, *Stars*, (London, 1979)

Dyal, Jai, *I Go South with Prithviraj and His Prithvi Theatres*, (1950)

England, Chris, *Balham to Bollywood*, (London, 2002)

Esslin, Martin, *An Anatomy of Drama*, (London, 1976)

Filmfare, Vol 1-24, (1952–1975)

Filmindia, Vol 1-16 (1934–1950)

Ganapati, P., *Lights, Camera, War!*, (Mumbai, 2002)

Gangar, A., *Films from the City of Dreams*, (Mumbai, 1995)

Gangar, A., *Bombay: Mosaic of Modern Culture*, (Mumbai, 1995)

Ganti, T., *Casting Culture: The Social Life of Hindu Film Production in Contemporary India*, (New York, 2002)

Ganti, T., *Centenary Commemorations or Centenary Contestations?— Celebrating a Hundred Years of Cinema in Bombay*, (2002)

Ganti, T., *And Yet My Heart Is Still Indian*, (Berkeley, 2002)

Ganti, T., *Media Worlds: Anthropology on New Terrain*, (Berkeley, 2002)

Ganti, Tejaswini, *Bollywood: A Guidebook to Popular Hindi Cinema*, (New York/Abingdon, 2005)

Garga, B,D., *The Feel of the Good Earth*, (Cinema in India, 1989)

Garga, B.D., *So Many Cinemas: The Motion Picture in India*, (Mumbai, 1996)

Garga, B. D., *The Art of Cinema*, (New Delhi, 2005)

Gargi, Balwant, *Theatre in India*, (New York, 1962)

Gaur, Madan, *The Other Side of the Coin: an Intimate Study of the Indian Film Industry*, (Mumbai, 1973)

Geetha, J., *The Mutating Mother: From Mother India to Ram Lakhan*, (Deep Focus, 1990)

George, T.S., *The Life and Times of Nargis*, (New Delhi, 1994)

Ghatak, Ritwik, *Cinema India*, (New Delhi, 1982)

Ghatak, Ritwik, *Rows & Rows of Fences*, (New Delhi, 2002)

Ghosh, Nabendu, *Ashok Kumar: His Life and Times*, (New Delhi, 1995)

Ghosh, Sital Chandra, Roy Arun Kumar, *Twelve Indian Directors*, (1981)

Gonsaleves, *Stardust: the Heart knows its Own*, (1993)

Gopakumar, K.M., Unni, V.K., *Perspectives on Copyright: The 'Karishma' Controversy,* (2003)

Gopalakrishnan, Adoor, *The Rat Trap,* (Kolkata, 1985)

Gopalan, L., *Cinema of Interruptions: Action Genres in Contemporary Indian cinema,* (London, 2002)

Gopalan T.N., *Lid Off Hindustan Photo Films. Doings, Undoings, of 'Gang of Four'* (Mumbai, 1980)

Gosh, Neepabithi, *Uttam Kumar: The Ultimate Hero,* (New Delhi, 2002)

Gosh, Biswadeep & the Editors of Stardust, *Hall of Fame— Shah Rukh Khan,* (Mumbai, 2004)

Gosh, Biswadeep & the Editors of Stardust, *Hall of Fame—Aishwarya Rai,* (Mumbai, 2004)

Gosh, Biswadeep & the Editors of Stardust, *Hall of Fame—Hrithik Roshan,* (Mumbai, 2004)

Gosh, Biswadeep & the Editors of Stardust, *Hall of Fame—Salman Khan,* (Mumbai, 2004)

Government of India, *Television of India,* (New Delhi 1985)

Gulzar, Nihalani Govind, Chatterjee Sarbal, *Encyclopaedia of Hindi Cinema,* (New Delhi/Mumbai, 2003.)

Gulzar, Meghna, *Because he is.....,* (New Delhi, 2004)

Haggard, Stephen, *Mass Media and the Visual Arts in Twentieth Century South Asia: Indian Film Posters, 1947–present,* (South Asia Research, 1988)

Haham, Connie, '*Salim-Javed's Special Contribution to Cinema,*' Screen India, (6 April 1984)

Haham, Connie, '*In Quest of Heroism*', Screen India, (6 December 1986)

Haham, Connie, *Enchantment of the Mind: Manmohan Desai's Films,* (New Delhi, 2006)

Hangal, A. K., *Life and Times of A. K. Hangal,* (New Delhi, 1999)

Hariharan, K., *Revisiting Mother India,* (Sound Lights Action, 2000)

Hardy, Justine, *Bollywood Boy,* (London, 2002)

Haun, Harry, *The Movie Quote Book,* (London, 1981)

Indian cinema 1980–1985, (New Delhi, 1985)

India Today, *Momentous Years 1975–2005,* (2005)

India Today, *Films, Who's Afraid of Censorship,* (India, 1980)

Iyengar, Niranjan, *The Leader,* (New Delhi, 1991)

Jacobs, Lewis, *Movies as Medium,* (New York, 1970)

Jaffrelot, Chrisophe, *The Hindu Nationalist Movement and Indian Politics, 1925 to the 1990's,* (London, 1996)

Jafir, Ali Sarda, *The Faceless One,* (Filmfare, 1962)

Jha, Bagiswar, *Indian Motion Picture,* (Kolkata, 1987)

Jha, Subhash, K, *The Essential Guide to Bollywood,* (New Delhi, 2005)

Jain, Jasbir & Rai, Sudha, *Films and Feminism: Essays in Indian Cinema,* (New Delhi, 2002)

Jain, Madhu, *The Kapoors,* (New Delhi, 2005)

Jain, Rikhab Dass, *The Economic Aspects of the Film Industry in India,* (New Delhi, 1960)

Kabir, Nasreen Munni, *Indian Cinema on Channel Four,* (London, 1984)

Kabir, Nasreen Munni, (editor) *Les stars du cinéma indien,* (Paris, 1985)

Kabir, Nasreen Munni, *The Miracle Man: Manmohan Desai,'* one programme in Channel 4/s Movie Mahal series, (Hyphen Films, 1987)

Kabir, Nasreen Munni, Guru Dutt, *A Life in Cinema*, (New Delhi, 1996)

Kabir, Nasreen Munni, *Akhtar*, (New Delhi, 1999)

Kabir, Nasreen Munni, *Talking Films: Conversations on Hindi Cinema with Javed Akhtar*, (New Delhi, 1999)

Kabir, Nasreen Munni, *Bollywood: The Indian Cinema Story*, Channel 4, (London, 2001)

Kabir, Nasreen Munni, 'Playback Time: A Brief History of Bollywood Film Songs,' Film Comment, (New York, May 2002)

Kakar, Sudhir, *The Inner World: a Psycho-analytic Study of Childhood and Society in India*, (New Delhi, 1981)

Kakar, Sudhir, *The Cinema as Collective Fantasy'* Indian cinema Super Bazaar, edited by Vasudev, Aruna and Lenglet, Philippe, (New Delhi, 1983)

Kanekar, Shirish, *Dilip Kumar: A Photo Feature*, (Mumbai, 1978)

Kapoor, Shashi, *The Prithviwallahs*, (London, 2004)

Karanjia, B.K. *Le star-systeme*, (Les Cinémas Indien, 1984)

Karanjia, B. K., *Counting my Blessings*, (New Delhi, 2005)

Karney, Robyn (ed), *Cinema Year by Year 1894-2004*, (London, 2004)

Kaul, Gautam, *Cinema and the Indian Freedom Struggle*, (New Delhi, 1998)

Kaur, Raminder & Sinha, Ajay, J., *Bollyworld: Popular Indian Cinema through a Transnational Lens,* (New Delhi, 2005)

Kazmi, Nikhat, *Ire in the Soul: Bollywood's Angry Years*, (India, 1996)

Kazmi, Nikhat, *The Dream Merchants of Bollywood*, (1998)

Kendal, Felicity, *White Cargo*, (London, 1998)

Kendal, Geoffrey, *The Shakespearewallah*, (London, 1986)

Khosla, S.N., *Unforgettable Dilip Kumar*

Khote, Durga, I, *Durga Khote: An Autobiography,* (New Delhi, 2006)

Khubchandani, Lata, *Aamir Khan: Actor with a Difference*, (New Delhi, 2003)

Khubchandani, Lata, *Raj Kapoor: The Great Showman*, (2003)

Koch, Gerhard, *Franz Osten's Indian Silent Films*, (New Delhi, 1983)

Krishen, Pradip ed, *Indian Popular Cinema*, (1980)

Kuka, E., *Distress of Cinema Theatres*, (Mumbai, 1979)

Kulkarni V.G., *A Mixture of Brilliance and Mindlessness*, (Media 1976)

Lanba, Urmila, *The Thespian: Life and Times of Dilip Kumar,* (New Delhi, 2002)

Long, Robert Emmet, *The Films of Merchant Ivory*, (New York, 1997)

Le cinéma indien, under the direction of Jean-Loup Passek, textes de Raphaël Bassan, Nasreen Munni Kabir, Henri Micciollo, Phillippe Parain, Jean-Loup Passek, Henri Stern, et Paul Willman, (Paris, 1983)

Lent, J.A., *Heyday of the Indian Studio System: The 1930's*, (Asian Profile, 1983)

Lent, John A., *The Asian Film Industry*, (Bromley, Kent, 1990)

L'Inde, séduction et tumulte, directed by Cruse, Denys, (Paris, 1985)

Long, Robert Emmet, *James Ivory in Conversation: How Merchant Ivory Makes it Movies*, (California, 2005)

Mahmood, Hameedudin, *The Kaleidoscope of Indian Cinema*, (1974)

Manto, Saadat, Hasan, *Stars from Another Sky: The Bombay Film World of the 1940s*, (New Delhi, 1998)

Manushi, *A Journal about Women and Society*, (New Delhi, 1983-84)

Masud I and Chandran, M., *Women as Catalysts of Change*, (Mumbai 1986)

Menon, T.K.N. ed. *Indian Cinema* (Kerala, 1978)

Merchant, Ismail, *My Passage from India: A Film-maker's Journey from Bombay to Hollywood and Beyond,* (London, 2002)

Micciolo, Henri, *Guru Dutt*, (Paris, 1975)

Ministry of Information and Broadcasting, *Film Censorship in India*, (New Delhi, 1978)

Ministry of Information and Broadcasting, *The Cinematograph Act, 1952*, (New Delhi, 1992)

Mishra, Vijay, *Bollywood Cinema: Temples of Desire*, (New York, 2002)

Mitra, S., *Cinema, the Fading Glitter*, (Indian Today, 1985)

Mohamed, Khalid, *To Be or Not To Be: Amitabh Bachchan*, (Mumbai, 2002)

Mohan, Ram, *Looking for the Special Effects Man in the Small Type*, (January–March, 1989)

Mohammed, Khalid, Khan, Salim, *Dilip Kumar: The Tragedy King*, (India, 1992)

Mohammed, Khalid, *A Class Apart*, (Filmfare, 1994)

Mohammed, Khalid, *Sense and Sensibility*, (India, 1996)

Mohandeep, *The Mystery & Mystic of Madhubala*, (New Delhi, 1996)

Mujawar, Isak, *Maharashtra—Birth Place of Indian Film Industry*, (Maharashtra 1969)

Mukherjee, Ram Kamal, *Hema Malini: Diva Unveiled*, (Mumbai, 2005)

Nanda, Ritu, *Raj Kapoor: His life and films presented by his daughter*, (Mumbai 1991)

Nanda, Ritu, *Raj Kapoor Speaks*, (New Delhi, 2002)

Nandy, Ashis, *The Secret Politics of our Desires: Innocence, Culpability and Indian Popular Cinema*, (Oxford 1998)

Narwekar, Sanjit, *Eena Meena Deeka: The Story of Hindi Film Comedy*, (New Delhi, 2005)

Narwekar, Sanjit, *Dilip Kumar—The Last Emperor*, (New Delhi, 2006)

Naseeb ke Dialogue aur Geet (Mumbai)

National Film Development Corporation of Indian, NFDC News, (Mumbai 1988)

Ninan. S., *Through the Magic Window: Television and Change in India*, (New Delhi, 1995)

Nizami, (translated and edited by Dr Gekpke in collaboration with Martin, E & Hill, G), *The Story of Layla and Majnu*, (Colorado, 1978)

Ojha, Rajendra, *75 Glorious Years on Indian Cinema*, (1989)

Oommen M.A., Joseph, K.V., *Economics of Film Industry in India*, (Gurgaon, 1981)

Panjwani, Narendra, *Is This Any Way To Live?*, (India. 1995)

Parrain, P, *Regards sur Le Cinéma Indien*, (Paris, 1969)

Passek, Jean-Loup, *Le Cinéma Indien*, (Paris, 1983)

Patel, Baburao, *Mother India, Becomes the Pride of India*, (Film India, 1975)

Pendakur, M., *Dynamics of Cultural Policy-Making: The US Film Industry in India*, (Journal of Communication, 1985)

Pendakur, M., *Mass Media during the 1975 National Emergency in India*, (Canada, 1988)

Pendakur, M., *Indian Television Comes of Age. Liberalization and the Rise of Consumer Culture*, (Communication, 1988)

Poddar, Neerara, *Bismillah Khan: The Shehnai Maestro*, (New Delhi, 2004)

Prakash, S., '*Music, Dance and the Popular Films: Indian Fantasies, Indian Repressions*', (New Delhi, 1983)

Prajavani, (1986)

Prasad, M. Madhava, *Ideology of the Hindi Film*, (New Delhi, 1998)

Premchand, Manek, *Yesterday's Melodies—Today's Memories*, (Mumbai, 2003)

Raha, Kironmoy, *Indian cinema 81/82*, (New Delhi, 1982)

Raha, Kironmoy, *Bengali Cinema*, (Kolkata, 1991)

Raheja, Anita & Agarwal, Heena, *Salad Days are Here Again*, (2003)

Raheja, Dinesh and Kothari, Jitendra, *Indian cinema: The Bollywood Saga*, (London, 2004)

Rajadhyaksha, A., *Ritwik Ghatak: A Return of an Epic*, (Mumbai, 1982)

Rajadhyaksha, A., *Neo-Tradionalism: Film as Popular Art in India*, (1986)

Rajadhyahsha, Ashish & Willemen, Paul, *Encyclopaedia of Indian Cinema*, (New Delhi, 1999)

Rajendran, Girija, *Composer Steeped in Classical Idiom*

Ramachandran, T.M., *70 Years of Indian Talkie*, (Mumbai, 1981)

Rangacharya, Adya, *The Indian Theatre*, (New Delhi, 1980)

Rangoonwalla, Firoze, *Indian Filmography 1897–1969* (1970)

Rangoonwalla, Firoze, *Guru Dutt*, (Pune, 1973)

Rangoonwalla, Firoze, *75 years of Indian Cinema*, (New Delhi, 1975)

Rangoonwalla, Firoze, *A Pictorial History of Indian Cinema*, (London, 1979)

Rangoonwalla, Firoze, *Indian cinema, Past & Present*, (New Delhi, 1983)

Rangoonwalla, Firoze, *Mehboob creates Popular Hits and Films ahead of his Time*, (Screen, 1992)

Rangachariar, T., *Report of Indian Cinematography*, (1928)

Rao, Maihili, *How to Read a Hindi Film and Why*, Film Comment Magazine (New York, May 2002)

Ray, Satyajit, *An Anthology of Statements on Ray and by Ray*, (Mumbai, 1981)

Reuben, Bunny, *Raj Kapoor—the Fabulous Showman: An Intimate Biography*, (New Delhi, 1988)

Reuben, Bunny, *Follywood Flashback: A Collection of Movie Memories*, (New Delhi, 1993)

Reuben, Bunny, *Mehboob: India's DeMille: The First Biography*, (New Delhi, 1994)

Reuben, Bunny, *Dilip Kumar: Star Legend of Indian Cinema*, (New Delhi, 2004)

Reuben, Bunny, *...And Pran, A Biography*, (New Delhi, 2005)

Report of the Indian Cinematograph Committee 1927–28, (Chennai, 1928)

Report of the Film Enquiry Committee, (New Delhi, 1951)

Robinson, Andrew, *Satyajit Ray: The Inner Eye*, (New Delhi, 1992)

Robinson, David, *World Cinema: A Short History*, (London, 1973)

Roheja, D., Kathari, J., *The Hundred Luminaries of Hindi Cinema*, (Mumbai, 1996)

Sahni, Balraj, *Balraj Sahni*, (New Delhi, 1979)

Sahni, Bhisham, *Balraj, My Brother*, (New Delhi, 1979)

Saijan, Sunder, Satya, *Shri Prithvirajji Kapoor* (Abhinandan Granth 1960)

Sarkar, Kobiys, *Indian Cinema Today*, (New Delhi, 1975)

Sathe, V.P., *The Making of Mother India*, (The Movie, 1984)

Segal, Zohra (with John Erdman), *Stages: The Art and Adventures of Zohra Segal*, Kali for Women (1997)

Sen, Mrinal, *Views on Cinema*, (Kolkata, 1977)

Sen, Mrinal, *In Search of Famine*, (Kolkata, 1983)

Sen, Mrinal, *The Ruins*, (Kolkata, 1984)

Shah, Panna, *The Indian Film*, (Mumbai, 1950)

Sharma, Ashwini, *Blood, Sweat and Tears: Amitabh Bachchan, Urban Demi-god*, (London, 1993)

Shantaram, Kiran and Narwekar, Sanjit, *V. Shantaram: The Legacy of the Royal Lotus*, (New Delhi, 2003)

Shoesmith, B., *From Monopoly to Commodity: The Bombay Studios in the 1930s*, (Perth, 1987)

Shoesmith, B., *Swadeshi Cinema: Cinema, Politics and Culture: The Writing of D.G. Phalke*, (Perth, 1988)

Sivaramamurti, C., *Lakshmi in Indian Art and Thought*, (New Delhi, 1982)

Somaaya, Bhawana, *Amitabh Bachchan: The Legend*, (New Delhi, 1999)

Somaaya, Bhawana, *The Story So Far*, (Mumbai, 2003)

Somaaya, Bhawana, *Cinema: Images & Issues*, (New Delhi, 2004)

Sri Lanka, *Cinéma 76*, (1976)

Srivatsan R, *Looking at Film Hoardings, Labour, Gender, subjectively and Everyday life in India* (Public Culture, 1991)

Stardust: 100 Greatest Stars of all Time, edited by Varde, Ashwin, (India)

Suhaag Sachitr, *Geet aur Dialogue,* (Patna)

Symposium on Cinema in Developing Countries, (New Delhi, 1979)

Swaminathan, Roopa, *M. G. Ramachandran,* (New Delhi, 2002)

Swaminathan, Roopa, *Kamalahasan: The Consummate Actor,* (New Delhi, 2003)

Swaminathan, Roopa, *Star Dust—Vignettes from the Fringes of the Film Industry,* (New Delhi, 2004)

Sweet, Matthew, *Shepperton Babylon: The Lost Worlds of British Cinema,* (Chatham, Kent, 2005)

Tanwar, Sarita, *I Am An Imposter,* (Stardust, 1988)

Tanwar, Sarita, *Dilip Kumar's Most Heartrending Interview,* (Stardust, 1993)

Tendulkar, Vijay, Benegal, Shyam, *The Churning,* (Kolkata, 1984)

Tharoor, Shashi, *Show Business,* (New Delhi, 1992)

Thomas, Rosie, *'Indian cinema: Pleasures and Popularity',* Screen 26: 3-4, (Fall/Winter 1985)

Thomas, Rosie, *'Melodrama and the Negotiation of Morality in Mainstream Hindi Film'* in Consuming Modernity, edited by Carol A Breckenridge (Minneapolis, 1995)

Thomas, Rosie, *Sanctity and Scandal,* (Quarterly Review of Film and Video, 1989)

Thomson, David, *The Whole Equation: A History of Hollywood,* (New York, 2004)

Thoraval, Yves, *The Cinema of India,* (New Delhi, 2000)

Time Out Film Guide (Sixth Edition 1998), edited by Pym, John, (London, 1998)

Torgovnik, Jonathan, *Bollywood Dreams,* (London, 2003)

Tripathi, S., *Ganga Jamuna Sarswathi, Formula Failure,* (Indian Today, 1989)

Tully, Mark, *India in Slow Motion,* (London, 2002)

Vaidyanathan, T.G., *Hours in the Dark,* (New Delhi, 1996)

Valicha, Kishore, *Dadamoni: The Authorised Biography of Ashok Kumar,* (New Delhi, 1996)

Valicha, Kishore, *Kumar, Kishore—The Definite Biography,* (New Delhi, 1998)

Valicha, Kishore, *Why are Popular Films Popular? Cinema in India—* Vol. 3, No. 2, April–June 1989

Vasudev, Aruna, *Licence and Liberty in Indian Cinema,* (New Delhi, 1978)

Vasudev, Aruna, *The Role of the Cinema in Promoting Popular Participation in Cultural Life in India,* (Paris, 1981)

Vasudev, Aruna, *The Film Industry's use of the Traditional and Contemporary Arts,* (Paris, 1982)

Vasudev, Aruna, *Indian Cinema, 82.83,* (New Delhi, 1983)

Vasudev, Aruna, Lenglet, Philippe, *Indian Cinema Super Bazaar,* (New Delhi, 1983)

Vasudev, Aruna, Lenglet, Philippe, *Les Cinémas Indiens,* CinemAction 30, (Paris, 1984)

Vasudevan, Ravi, *The Melodramatic Mode and Commercial Hindi Cinema,* (Screen, 1989)

Vasudevan, Ravi, *The Politics of Cultural Address in 'transitional' cinema: a Case Study of Popular Indian Cinema,* (London, 2000)

Vasudevan, R., *Addressing the Spectator of a 'Third World' National Cinema; the Bombay 'Social' Film of the 1940s and 1950s,* (1995)

Virdi, Jyotika, *The Cinematic Image Nation—Indian Popular Films as Social History,* (New Delhi, 2003)

Wenner, Dorothee, *Fearless Nadia—The True Story of Bollywood's Original Stunt Queen,* (New Delhi, 1999)

Willemen, Paul, Behroze Gandhy, *Indian Cinema,* (London, 1980)

Zaidi, Shama, *Past By-passed,* (Mumbai, 1988)

Zaveri, Hanif, *Mehmood: A Man of Many Moods,* (Mumbai, 2005)

Newspapers and Periodicals

Asian Age (New Delhi)
Asian Journal of Communications

Blitz (Mumbai)
Bombay Chronicle
Bombay Gazette

Celluloid
Cine Blitz (Mumbai)
Cinema Vision
Cinemaya
Current (Mumbai)

Debonair (Mumbai)

Eastern Eye London

Filmfare (Mumbai)
FilmIndia (Mumbai)

Hi Blitz (Mumbai)
Hindu (Chennai)

Illustrated Weekly of India (Mumbai)
Indian Express (Mumbai)
India Today (New Delhi)

Los Angeles Times (New York)

Mother India (Mumbai)

National Geographic (Washington)
New Statesman (London)

Outlook (New Delhi)

Screen (Mumbai)
Sight and Sound
Society (Mumbai)
Stardust (Mumbai)

The Times of India (Mumbai)
The Daily Telegraph (London)
The Guardian (London)
The Hindusthan Times (New Delhi)
The New Yorker (New York)
The New York Times (New York)
The Times (London)

Reports

Indian Cinematograph Committee 1927–1928, New Delhi
Indian Motion Picture Congress 1939, Bombay
Indian Talkie 1931–1956, Silver Jubilee Souvenir Bombay
Report of the Film Enquiry Committee 1951, New Delhi

Websites

Aihara, Byron, Hindi popular 'Bollywood' cinema, http://bollywood501.com
Kingwell, Mark, http://www.artsandopinion.com/2003 v2 2/kinwell.htm
Kumar, Kanti, The Trend of Violence in the Indian Screen and Its Influence on Children'
    September 1999, http://www.bitscape.info/research/screen 3p.htm
Lutgendorf, Philip, Notes on Indian Popular Cinema' http://www.uiwa.
    edu/~incinema/
National Assocation of Theatre Owners, 'Number of US Movie Screens', http//www.
    natoonline.org/stasticssreeens.htm

List of Illustrations

All illustrations courtesy of Roli Books, unless otherwise stated

Index

Indian names can be spelt differently even by Indian sources. This is due to the transliteration into English, but in this index the most commonly accepted version has been followed.

TEMPUS – REVEALING HISTORY

Freaks
JAN BONDESON

'Reveals how these tragic individuals triumphed over their terrible adversity' *The Daily Mail*
'Well written and superbly illustrated'
The Financial Times

£9.99   0 7524 3662 7

Bollywood
MIHIR BOSE

'Pure entertainment' *The Observer*
'Insightful and often hilarious' *The Sunday Times*
'Gripping' *The Daily Telegraph*

£9.99   978 07524 4482 9

King Arthur
CHRISTOPHER HIBBERT

'A pearl of biographers' *New Statesman*

£12.99   978 07524 3933 4

Arnhem
William Buckingham

'Reveals the reason why the daring attack failed'
The Daily Express

£10.99   0 7524 3187 0

Cleopatra
PATRICIA SOUTHERN

'In the absence of Cleopatra's memoirs Patricia Southern's commendably balanced biography will do very well'
The Sunday Telegraph

£9.99   978 07524 4336 2

The Prince In The Tower
MICHAEL HICKS

'The first time in ages that a publisher has sent me a book I actually want to read' *David Starkey*

£9.99   978 07524 4386 7

The Battle of Hastings 1066
M. K. LAWSON

'A *BBC History Magazine* book of the year 2003
'The definitive book on this famous battle'
The Journal of Military History

£12.99   978 07524 4177 1

Loos 1915
NICK LLOYD

'A revealing new account based on meticulous documentary research' *Corelli Barnett*
'Should finally consign Alan Clark's Farrago, *The Donkeys*, to the waste paperbasket'
Hew Strachan
'Plugs a yawning gap in the existing literature... this book will set the agenda for debate of the battle for years to come' *Gary Sheffield*

£25   0 7524 3937 5

If you are interested in purchasing other books published by Tempus, or in case you have difficulty finding any Tempus books in your local bookshop, you can also place orders directly through our website

www.tempus-publishing.com

TEMPUS – REVEALING HISTORY

Britannia's Empire
A Short History of the British Empire
BILL NASSON
'Crisp, economical and witty' *TLS*
'An excellent introduction the subject' *THES*
£12.99   0 7524 3808 5

Madmen
A Social History of Madhouses,
Mad-Doctors & Lunatics
ROY PORTER
'Fascinating'
The Observer
£12.99   0 7524 3730 5

Born to be Gay
A History of Homosexuality
WILLIAM NAPHY
'Fascinating' *The Financial Times*
'Excellent' *Gay Times*
£9.99   0 7524 3694 5

William II
Rufus, the Red King
EMMA MASON
'A thoroughly new reappraisal of a much
maligned king. The dramatic story of his life is
told with great pace and insight'
John Gillingham
£25   0 7524 3528 0

To Kill Rasputin
The Life and Death of Grigori Rasputin
ANDREW COOK
'Andrew Cook is a brilliant investigative historian'
Andrew Roberts
'Astonishing' **The Daily Mail**
£9.99   0 7524 3906 5

The Unwritten Order
Hitler's Role in the Final Solution
PETER LONGERICH
'Compelling' **Richard Evans**
'The finest account to date of the many twists
and turns in Adolf Hitler's anti-semitic obsession'
Richard Overy
£12.99   0 7524 3328 8

Private 12768
Memoir of a Tommy
JOHN JACKSON
FOREWORD BY HEW STRACHAN
'A refreshing new perspective' **The Sunday Times**
'At last we have John Jackson's intensely
personal and heartfelt little book to remind us
there was a view of the Great War other than
Wilfred Owen's' **The Daily Mail**
£9.99   0 7524 3531 0

The Vikings
MAGNUS MAGNUSSON
'Serious, engaging history'
BBC History Magazine
£9.99   0 7524 2699 0

If you are interested in purchasing other books published by Tempus, or in case you have difficulty finding any
Tempus books in your local bookshop, you can also place orders directly through our website
www.tempus-publishing.com

TEMPUS – REVEALING HISTORY

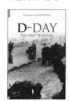

D-Day The First 72 Hours
WILLIAM F. BUCKINGHAM

'A compelling narrative' *The Observer*
A *BBC History Magazine* Book of the Year 2004
£9.99   0 7524 2842 X

The London Monster
Terror on the Streets in 1790
JAN BONDESON

'Gripping' *The Guardian*
'Excellent... monster-mania brought a reign of
terror to the ill-lit streets of the capital'
The Independent

£9.99   0 7524 3327 X

London
A Historical Companion
KENNETH PANTON

'A readable and reliable work of reference that
deserves a place on every Londoner's bookshelf'
Stephen Inwood

£20   0 7524 3434 9

M: MI5's First Spymaster
ANDREW COOK

'Serious spook history' *Andrew Roberts*
'Groundbreaking' *The Sunday Telegraph*
'Brilliantly researched' *Dame Stella Rimington*

£9.99   978 07524 3949 9

Agincourt
A New History
ANNE CURRY

'A highly distinguished and convincing account'
Christopher Hibbert
'A *tour de force*' *Alison Weir*
'*The* book on the battle' *Richard Holmes*
A *BBC History Magazine* Book of the Year 2005
£12.99   0 7524 3813 1

Battle of the Atlantic
MARC MILNER

'The most comprehensive short survey of the
U-boat battles' *Sir John Keegan*
'Some events are fortunate in their historian, none
more so than the Battle of the Atlantic. Marc
Milner is *the* historian of the Atlantic campaign... a
compelling narrative' *Andrew Lambert*

£12.99   0 7524 3332 6

The English Resistance
The Underground War Against the Normans
PETER REX

'An invaluable rehabilitation of an ignored
resistance movement' *The Sunday Times*
'Peter Rex's scholarship is remarkable'
The Sunday Express

£12.99   0 7524 3733 X

Elizabeth Wydeville: England's Slandered Queen
ARLENE OKERLUND

'A penetrating, thorough and wholly convincing
vindication of this unlucky queen'
Sarah Gristwood
'A gripping tale of lust, loss and tragedy'
Alison Weir
A *BBC History Magazine* Book of the Year 2005
£9.99   978 07524 3807 8

If you are interested in purchasing other books published by Tempus, or in case you have difficulty finding any
Tempus books in your local bookshop, you can also place orders directly through our website

www.tempus-publishing.com

TEMPUS – REVEALING HISTORY

Quacks Fakers and Charlatans in Medicine
ROY PORTER

'A delightful book' *The Daily Telegraph*
'Hugely entertaining' *BBC History Magazine*

£12.99   0 7524 2590 0

The Tudors
RICHARD REX

'Up-to-date, readable and reliable. The best
introduction to England's most important
dynasty' *David Starkey*

'Vivid, entertaining... quite simply the best short
introduction' *Eamon Duffy*

'Told with enviable narrative skill... a delight for
any reader' *THES*

£9.99   0 7524 3333 4

The Kings & Queens of England
MARK ORMROD

'Of the numerous books on the kings and
queens of England, this is the best'
Alison Weir

£9.99   0 7524 2598 6

The Covent Garden Ladies
Pimp General Jack & the Extraordinary Story of Harris's List
HALLIE RUBENHOLD

'Sex toys, porn... forget Ann Summers, Miss
Love was at it 250 years ago' *The Times*
'Compelling' *The Independent on Sunday*
'Marvellous' *Leonie Frieda*
'Filthy' *The Guardian*

£9.99   0 7524 3739 9

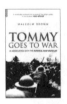

Okinawa 1945
GEORGE FEIFER

'A great book... Feifer's account of the three
sides and their experiences far surpasses most
books about war'
Stephen Ambrose

£17.99   0 7524 3324 5

Tommy Goes To War
MALCOLM BROWN

'A remarkably vivid and frank account of the
British soldier in the trenches'
Max Arthur

'The fury, fear, mud, blood, boredom and
bravery that made up life on the Western Front
are vividly presented and illustrated'
The Sunday Telegraph

£12.99   0 7524 2980 4

Ace of Spies The True Story of Sidney Reilly
ANDREW COOK

'The most definitive biography of the spying
ace yet written... both a compelling narrative
and a myth-shattering *tour de force*'
Simon Sebag Montefiore

'The absolute last word on the subject' *Nigel West*
'Makes poor 007 look like a bit of a wuss'
The Mail on Sunday

£12.99   0 7524 2959 0

Sex Crimes
From Renaissance to Enlightenment
W.M. NAPHY

'Wonderfully scandalous' *Diarmaid MacCulloch*
'A model of pin-sharp scholarship' *The Guardian*

£10.99   0 7524 2977 9